The Management of Hate

The Management of Hate

NATION, AFFECT, AND THE GOVERNANCE OF
RIGHT-WING EXTREMISM IN GERMANY

||||||||||||||||||||||||||||||||||||||||||||||||||||||||||||||||||||||||||||||||||||||

Nitzan Shoshan

PRINCETON UNIVERSITY PRESS

PRINCETON AND OXFORD

Library of Congress Cataloging-in-Publication Data
Names: Shoshan, Nitzan, author.
Title: The management of hate : nation, affect, and the governance of
right-wing extremism in Germany / Nitzan Shoshan.
Description: Princeton, New Jersey : Princeton University Press, 2016. |
Includes bibliographical references and index.
Identifiers: LCCN 2016003353| ISBN 9780691171951 (hardback : acid-free paper) |
ISBN 9780691171968 (paperback : acid-free paper)
Subjects: LCSH: Right-wing extremists—Germany. | Right-wing extremists—
Government policy—Germany. | Nationalism—Germany. | Political culture—
Germany. | Political sociology—Germany. | Germany—Politics and
government—1990- | BISAC: SOCIAL SCIENCE / Anthropology / Cultural. |
SOCIAL SCIENCE / Sociology / General. | SOCIAL SCIENCE /
Violence in Society. | SOCIAL SCIENCE / Regional Studies. | SOCIAL SCIENCE /
Ethnic Studies / General. | HISTORY / Europe / Germany.
Classification: LCC HN460.R3 S56 2016 | DDC 303.48/40943—dc23 LC record
available at https://lccn.loc.gov/2016003353

British Library Cataloging-in-Publication Data is available

This book has been composed in Minion Pro

Printed on acid-free paper. ∞

Printed in the United States of America

1 3 5 7 9 10 8 6 4 2

For Ale

Contents

IIIIIIIIIIIIIIIIIII

Part III

Illustrations

ıIIIIIIIIIIIIIIIIIIIIIIIIIIII

Preface
||||||||||||||||

WHEREAS THE AUTHOR OF THIS BOOK on the affective management of German nationalism is Nitzan Shoshan, an Israeli national, the researcher who escorted a team of street social workers, idled with their young right-wing extremist clients, and conversed with a range of other actors in Berlin's district of Treptow-Köpenick was known to most as Nate, an American anthropologist from Chicago conducting research on youth and public space. At the very inception of my research, the social workers who collaborated with me, and about whom I shall have more to say in what follows, demanded I submit to this change of identity for fear of the reactions that my true one might provoke among some of their more violent clients. They continued to refer to me by my alias always and everywhere. Yet, because German right-wing extremists often consider the United States a historical archenemy of the Reich, passing as an American could prove a mixed blessing. On one occasion, for example, late at night at a bar popular with the extreme right scene, my young informants introduced me to their acquaintances as their *Ami* (American) friend. While most people present greeted me amicably, a thin, tall skinhead reacted with plain hostility and refused to shake my hand. Visibly uncomfortable, my hosts struggled to exculpate me from his accusations—the US invasion of Iraq was heavy on his mind—and eventually succeeded in preventing the confrontation from escalating, but not before I reassured the young man that, far from financially burdening his country, my presence there, and the entire US-funded PhD research fellowship I had brought with me, represented a net benefit to Germany's economy.

Thus, in this study of the past that haunts German nationalism in the present, my double identity stood as the ghost that permanently hovered over my own position in the field. The obsessive anxiety with which I inspected myself for traces that could betray me when I prepared for my first day of work in Treptow loosened as I became progressively familiar with (and familiar as well to the people in) my field sites. But the menace of exposure continued to loom throughout my tenure in Berlin. On several occasions it came dangerously near, held at bay less by strategic prudence and more by providential fortune. I toiled, for instance, to elude police inspections and ID checks while in the company of young right-wing extremists, but the nature of my activities rendered this constant dodging precarious at best. In one instance, cordoned off by police during a demonstration with one of my informants and several dozen other people, I shuddered as the officers announced they would inspect our IDs before setting us free. I struggled to suppress a deep sigh of relief when, after a prolonged wait, they released us unconditionally.

Surprisingly for me, the young right-wing extremists I came to know not once questioned my name or origins. Suspicions about my identity abounded, but they surfaced instead among those who knew my true background, not those from whom I sought to conceal it. The social workers, for example, long wondered whether I had been serving the Mossad, and eventually Helmuth posed the question to me directly. My emphatic denials notwithstanding, the possibility continued to be raised—only half-jokingly, of course—throughout my fieldwork.

While most in Treptow knew me as Nate, many acquaintances throughout Berlin—fellow researchers, journalists, NGO staff, and so on—had met me as Nitzan. My most taxing challenge, therefore, consisted in keeping my parallel lives safely apart. Whenever they collided, my research faced a potential calamity. Since, far from an isolated island, Treptow is fully integrated into the larger metropolis, such a catastrophe seemed time and again imminent, and its effective evasion demanded intensive management. On one occasion, which I describe in detail in chapter 7, I accompanied a multiply convicted violent offender to an appointment with a counselor. Only after we set out, when my companion told me the name of his counselor, did I realize with horror that I had met the person a year earlier while conducting preliminary research, at which time I naturally introduced myself to him by my real name. There was no way back, and it was only thanks to the counselor's shaky memory that I narrowly escaped disaster.

But conducting ethnographic research with right-wing extremists confronted me with certain dilemmas that went far beyond the mere question of identity. My work demanded cultivating relationships of confidence with people from whom I was not only concealing my real name and origins but whom I would subsequently represent in ways they would likely find unfair at best, disparaging at worst. Existing anthropological literature provided me with little helpful advice on this point. Marcus Banks and André Gingrich, for example, in their introduction to an edited volume of anthropological perspectives on European neo-nationalism, insist that concerns with "moral hygiene" rather than methodological obstacles explain the dearth of ethnographic research on racist nationalism. As a remedy, they propose that scholars abandon the conventional anthropological proclivity to advocacy and relinquish sympathy in favor of empathy (Banks and Gingrich 2006). Such an approach could arguably address some of the dilemmas entailed in bringing anthropological perspectives to bear on parliamentary politics through highly mediated, "nontraditional" fieldwork—as is the case in the contributions to their volume. And yet, it hardly begins to tackle the multiple impasses of more or less traditional ethnographic research, an undertaking that requires not only the consolidation of trust with individuals but also the interactional participation in unnerving conversations and the subsequent representation of people with whom the researcher has become intimately familiar.

From another direction, Neil L. Whitehead has argued that the scarcity of anthropological literature on violence owes not only to methodological perils but, as important, to anthropologists' fear of negatively stereotyping their informants by highlighting distasteful dimensions of their culture (2004). Yet my case was different. On the one hand, having benefited from the collaboration of my informants, I struggled with how to represent their lifeworlds as complex and multidimensional, beyond their repugnant racism. On the other hand, there was the opposite concern, namely, that I may end up not representing them negatively *enough*. Put differently, my study could amount to an apologetics of their lifestyles as well as their politics. In the end, then, present throughout this book is a tension between distance and proximity that, in my opinion, exceeds the negotiation of analytical detachment and personal familiarity so common to many ethnographic studies. It is, moreover, a tension that I have increasingly come to believe cannot be resolved. If, in my research, I aimed to immerse myself in the lifeworlds of my informants, in my writing I have sought to implicate the reader, as well, in this uncomfortable proximity, while signaling at the same time unequivocal distance. To the extent that the reader may at times feel ill at ease with this proximity, I have successfully accomplished a sort of mimetic approximation of my own predicament in the field.

*　　*　　*

The first part of the book, comprising chapters 1 through 3, provides an introduction to the theoretical stakes of the study, to its empirical context, and to the research subject population at its ethnographic core. Chapter 1 reviews the relevant historical background, announces some of the crucial theoretical frameworks that guide the analysis, and offers a discussion of fieldwork and methods. Chapters 2 and 3 outline how my informants articulate their relations to cultural and ethnicized difference as they discursively constitute their own political selves by examining interview material and conversational interactions. Chapter 2 focuses in particular on their identification and self-identification as easterners, while chapter 3 turns to their construal of difference within the field of the extreme right and to their talk of immigrants and of their political adversaries on the left.

The four chapters that compose the book's second part examine in detail the governmental regimes that would safeguard Germany's nascent national project from its sinister shadow, pausing on the mechanisms through which the state administers and represses the field of the politically excluded and describing the incessant labor of carving the distinction that sets this field apart in the first place. Analyzing ethnographic materials, legal texts, and court cases, chapter 4 takes up the juridical production of what I call "political delinquency," a figure that condenses irresolvable contradictions between forceful taboos on the one hand and liberal law on the other. Its production, I show, ultimately rests on hermeneutical procedures that appeal to affective states generally, and hate in particular. In chapter 5 I shift the focus from law to its enforcement, attending to the police, its mechanisms of surveillance, and the ambiguities and excesses to which they give rise. I describe how the figure of the police informant betrays what some authors have called (dis)organized state mimesis, while haunting the most intimate relationships of my young right-wing extremist acquaintances. At the same time, I show the reciprocal nature of the sorts of contamination anxieties to which the police informant gives expression. Advancing beyond law and its enforcement to other domains of governance, chapter 6 looks closely at the vast web of governmental mechanisms through which the neoliberal state renders its targets visible and knowable, frequently with an efficacy that the police could never hope to match. I interrogate in particular how the capacity of these nonviolent forms of state mimesis to transact in knowledge rests on the tireless manufacturing of opaqueness and illegibility. Chapter 7, in turn, considers the elaboration of and experimentation with diverse therapeutic and reformative procedures on which the governance of hate relies. I argue that understandings of governance in terms of rationalist administration and bureaucratic efficacy cannot account for the irrational excesses that we find in such procedures and propose, instead, that we must approach it as heaving with affect at all levels.

The third and last part expands the purview of the study to examine how the management of hate seeks to inoculate and fortify broader affective publics against illicit forms of nationalism. In chapter 8 I look at campaigns for the production of positive affective orientations to cultural difference at the neighborhood level. I show how efforts to mobilize forces to the cause of tolerance and love of multicultural diversity testify to the capacity of affective governance to effectively recruit social actors, just as much as they betray its limits. Last, chapter 9 explores what I call the "national vision," or the political regimes that define how the nation is to be rendered in visual form. I consider the particularity of these visibility regimes in Berlin and discuss the ways in which they come to be contested, especially by extreme right-wing nationalists. I conclude by examining the national irruption of panic surrounding a right-wing extremist march on the sixtieth anniversary of the Reich's capitulation. The desperate attempt to thwart what seemed to be a national catastrophe, I show, bespeaks the degree of collective anxiety that surged around the march. I describe how the march was first neutralized and subsequently rendered invisible and how, this notwithstanding, it was crucial for the performative celebration of a tolerant, multicultural, and engaged nation.

Acknowledgments
||||||||||||||||||||||||||||||||||||||||||||

THIS BOOK IS THE RESULT of some ten years of research, reading, and writing, during which I have benefited from the insights and fellowship of many professors, colleagues, collaborators, friends, and family. I am grateful to all those who have encouraged and inspired me along the way. That this project came to fruition at all, and despite significant obstacles, owes first and foremost to the unreserved support of Helmuth, Andrea, and Daniela (their names throughout the book have been changed to maintain anonymity), the three street social workers who welcomed me into their midst and whose generosity, patience, and personal investment enriched my research in innumerable ways. I extend my gratitude as well to the young people in Treptow who openhandedly shared with me their time and their opinions and who routinely invited me to take part in their activities.

While conducting fieldwork in Berlin, many people have kindly facilitated my research, contributed intellectually to my work, and made my stay there rewarding. I owe special thanks to Uwe Neirich for long, insightful conversations and crucial practical advice; Thomas Bürk-Matsunami, Uta Döring, and Rebekka Streck for their wonderful companionship as critical interlocutors; Heide Determann and Eva Prausner for sharing their extensive knowledge and experience; Ragnar Fritz and Jan Becker for introducing me to the street social workers and continuously enriching my research subsequently; and Miriam for taking me along on her travels and providing invaluable materials from her personal archive. I thank Professor Wolfgang Kaschuba, at the time chair of the Institute of European Ethnology at Humboldt University, for welcoming me at his department.

I am enormously grateful for the support I received at the University of Chicago while working on the dissertation that would later provide the basis for this book. I am particularly indebted to my adviser, Jean Comaroff, as well as to the members of my dissertation committee—Susan Gal, Andreas Glaeser, and Michael Silverstein—who guided me with exemplary dedication, provided inexhaustible intellectual stimulation, and unfailingly offered encouragement and reassurance. While on a year of academic exchange, I was fortunate to benefit from extended conversations with Michael Taussig at Columbia University and from an enduring dialogue with Talal Asad at the CUNY Graduate Center. I am deeply thankful to Anne Ch'ien for her boundless dedication.

At the University of Chicago's Society of Fellows, I found a unique space of intellectual exchange with passionate and brilliant colleagues who engaged my work critically and generously on several occasions. Special thanks go to Greg Beckett, Andrew Dilts, Dorith Geva, Reha Kadakal, Leigh Claire La Berge, Mara Marin, and Poornima Paidipaty. I thank my research assistant, Harris Setzer, for his valuable contributions to chapter 4. I am deeply grateful to the Centro de Estudios Sociológicos at El Colegio de México in Mexico City, my academic home, for granting me the space, time, and resources to conclude this project. I am particularly thankful to Arturo Alvarado, Roberto Blancarte, Emilio Blanco, Marco Estrada, Manuel Gil, Minor Mora, David Ramírez, Patricio Solis, and Karine Tinat for welcoming me and supporting me along the way.

A great many friends and colleagues accompanied me through the process of researching and writing this book. I am eternally grateful for the friendship and intellectual camaraderie I have found in Mariana Cavalcanti, Munira Khayyat, Vyjayanthi Rao, Sandra Rozenthal, Noa Vaisman, Heiko Wimmen, Nora Rabotnikof, and Rihan Yeh, who, as interlocutors, have also brightened up my days in Berlin, Chicago, New York, Mexico City, and elsewhere. Special thanks go to Andrea Muehlebach for her careful engagement with my work, as well as to Lori Allen, Matti Bunzl, Douglas Holmes, and William Mazzarella, who have generously provided thoughtful and critical feedback on various chapters in the book. Roberto Simanowski, who introduced me to the beauty of the German language and of the city of Berlin, keenly commented upon segments of this study.

This book owes a great debt as well to critical input from colleagues at various forums where I presented portions of my study in draft form. For their attentive engagement with my work, I would like to thank participants of the Anthropology of Europe Workshop; the Politics, Communications, and Society Workshop; and the Workshop on Social Structures and Processes in Urban Space at the University of Chicago. I am grateful for the feedback I received at the Rechte Räume analysieren seminar at Humboldt University and the Entre Espacios colloquium in the Latin America Institute at the Free University of Berlin. Additional thanks for their helpful comments go to members of the Memoria y Política seminar at the National Autonomous University of Mexico and the Cultura y Poder seminar at the Colegio de México in Mexico City, as well as to members of the Urban Studies Laboratory at the Center for the Research and Documentation of the Contemporary History of Brazil at the Getulio Vargas Foundation in Rio de Janeiro.

This project would not have been possible without the financial support that it received from the University of Chicago's Social Science Division, the Leiffer Research Grant, the Social Science Research Council's International Dissertation Field Research Fellowship program, the Hannah Holborn Gray Advanced Mellon Fellowship in the Humanities and Humanistic Social Sciences, and the Josephine De Kármán Fellowship. Chapter 2 contains material that previously appeared in *Ossi/Wessi*; it is published here with the permission of Cambridge Scholars Publishing. Chapter 3 contains material previously published in the

Journal of Contemporary European Studies. Chapter 7 contains material previously published in *Cultural Anthropology.* I am grateful to Fred Appel, Juliana Fidler, and Cathy Slovensky at Princeton University Press for their sustained support and immaculate professionalism, as well as to two anonymous reviewers of the book manuscript for their insightful and helpful comments.

No words can describe my gratitude to my parents, David and Efrat, and to my siblings, Ben and Aya, who have supported me unwaveringly as I explored unfamiliar intellectual and geographical terrains. Camila and Noa, born during the process of researching and writing this book, put a smile on my face as I returned home after another day of work. Alejandra Leal contributed to this book in more ways than I could possibly mention, enduring the frustrations and exhaustions of research and writing, counseling me and supervising my progress, and making great sacrifices along the way. I have been blessed to find in her, at once, the most nourishing of companions I could wish for, my closest fellow anthropologist, and my most scrupulous critic; scarcely a page in this book does not bear her footprint.

Abbreviations

‖‖‖‖‖‖‖‖‖‖‖‖‖‖‖‖‖‖‖‖‖‖‖‖‖‖‖‖

AfD   Alternative for Germany (Alternative für Deutschland)
BPjM   Federal Department for Media Harmful to Young Persons
           (Bundesprüfstelle für jugendgefährdende Medien)
CDU   Christian Democratic Union (Christlich-Demokratische Union
           Deutschlands)
DDR   German Democratic Republic (Deutsche Demokratische
           Republik)
DVU   German People's Union (Deutsche Volksunion)
FDP   Free Democratic Party (Freie Demokratische Partei)
FRG   Federal Republic of Germany
GDR   German Democratic Republic
MAEX   Mobile Information Extremism unit (Mobile Aufklärung
           Extremismus)
MEGA   Mobile Task Force against Violence and Xenophobia (Mobile
           Einsatzeinheit gegen Gewalt und Ausländerfeindlichkeit)
NPD   National Democratic Party of Germany (Nationaldemokratische
           Partei Deutschlands)
NSDAP   National Socialist German Workers' Party (Nationalsozialistische
           Deutsche Arbeiterpartei)
NSU   National Socialist Underground (Nationalsozialistischer
           Untergrund)
OGJ   Youth Violence Operational Group (Operative Gruppe
           Jugendgewalt)
PDS   Party of Democratic Socialism (Partei des Demokratischen
           Sozialismus)
PEGIDA   Patriotic Europeans against the Islamization of the West (Patrio-
           tische Europäer gegen die Islamisierung des Abendlandes)
PMS   Politically Motivated Street Criminality unit (Politisch
           Motivierte Straßenkriminalität)
SED   Socialist Unity Party of Germany (Sozialistische Einheitspartei
           Deutschlands)
SPD   Social Democratic Party of Germany (Sozialdemokratische
           Partei Deutschlands)
VVN-BdA   Association of the Persecutees of the Nazi Regime—Federation
           of Antifascists (Vereinigung der Verfolgten des Naziregimes—
           Bund der Antifaschistinnen und Antifaschisten)

Part I

‖‖‖‖‖‖‖‖‖

A Specter of Nationalism

ON A WARM FRIDAY NIGHT in late May, I approached the dimly lit entrance to a bar in the revamped grounds of a former German Democratic Republic (GDR) factory. My ears were still ringing from the deafening heavy metal blasted on our way there by my young chaperones: Freddi, a thin and tall young man who was completing vocational training in storage logistics; Keppler, a veritable Goliath, soon to enter prison for the brutal vigilante torture of several alleged "child molesters"; and Felix, who grumbled incessantly about immigrants, their excessive numbers, their abuse of the welfare system, their delinquent proclivities, and their intolerable cultural habits.[1] For me, the anthropologist, the small courtyard in front of U-21—the bar was named after a WWII German submarine—gathered much more than merely a fair portion of the young people with whom I conducted research, some of whom we shall encounter time and again in the pages that follow.

Evident were lingering memories of the GDR and of reunification, even among those too young to have meaningfully experienced either, like Norman, a scruffy, chubby twenty-year-old, who stepped over and implored that I lend him money for beers, a "DDR" hat covering his balding top.[2] Or Sylvia, who came to remind me of our planned excursion the following morning to the season's final game of the local soccer club, a bastion of eastern pride. Unmistakable, too, were the inexorable traces of the Third Reich and the dramatic metamorphoses in recent years of how it has been remembered. A handful of people in the small crowd sported T-shirts with the inscription "May 8—Liberation Day? We're not celebrating!" (8. Mai—Befreiungstag? Wir feiern nicht!). Souvenirs from a right-wing extremist demonstration on the sixtieth anniversary of the Reich's capitulation, the shirts referenced the contemporary recasting in mainstream national discourses of Germany's defeat at the hand of the Allies as its emancipation. Lisa and Elsa, respectively, a skingirl and a neo-pagan aficionado of Nordic

---

[1] The names of informants throughout the book have been changed to maintain anonymity.
[2] Deutsche Demokratische Republik, German for GDR.

myths and Gothic fashions, joined me on the curb for a chat. Their garments and accoutrements evoked a whole universe of illicit signs associated with National Socialism. Their physical appearance at once challenged and conformed to the legal apparatuses, penal regimes, and cultural taboos that police the use of such signs in Germany. It is these mechanisms, we shall see, that are charged with quarantining the dangerous potentialities of emergent national imaginaries in the reunited Berlin Republic.

At the same time, the young people in front of the bar signaled in a number of ways the end of the postwar era. In that sense they suggested as well how the return of the national question in Germany (see Huyssen 1991; Geyer 1997; Jarausch 2006) has in fact been embedded within historical processes that have reverberated far beyond the country's borders. Later that night at U-21, eighteen-year-old Robert drew near, raving about the right-wing extremist NPD (Nationaldemokratische Partei Deutschlands [National Democratic Party of Germany]).[3] He advocated for the NPD, claiming that the party eschewed racism and objected instead only to the hordes of slothful immigrants who arrived to exploit the German state. Like his friend Felix before him, Robert also voiced anti-immigration idioms that have become prevalent throughout Europe, shaping political visions and projects not only on the far right fringes but, indeed, across the political terrain. His statements reproduced continent-wide, ethnically inflected, social Darwinist fantasies whose rhetoric—and praxis—has railed against "parasitical foreigners." He reiterated a series of xenophobic anxieties about emergent multiethnic cityscapes. His words signaled the (sometimes brutal) ways in which, from London's East End to Hungary's hinterlands and from Malmö to Athens, young European nationalists have grounded abstract global processes in the concrete physicality of foreign bodies (see Modood and Werbner 1997; Holmes 2000; Pred 2000). Listening to him, it was difficult for me not to recall certain scholarly writings on the shifting orientation of political investments in recent decades. I was particularly reminded of arguments about how social antagonisms have increasingly come to be framed as cultural differences rather than as class conflicts. One effect of these processes, in this view, has been the culturalization of racism and the ethnicization of politics in numerous world regions today (see Alonso 1994; Tambiah 1996; Žižek 1997; Pred 2000; Shoshan 2008b; Brown 2009; Markell 2009).

In turn, virtually all my acquaintances among the few dozen young people at U-21 depended in some form or another on the state for their subsistence. Few among them could harbor realistic aspirations for significant betterment to their material circumstances. As importantly, most received their remittances through various government-sponsored third-sector vocational training or mandatory welfare-for-work programs. In the words of Nikolas Rose (2000a), such strate-

---

[3] The NPD is the oldest party on the German extreme right. It has been the most prominent extreme right party in recent decades.

gies of governance seek to activate and "responsibilize" citizens through participatory schemes. In this, too, the fate of my young informants bespeaks the links between contemporary reconfigurations of political imaginaries on the one hand and, on the other hand, shifting and uneven processes of neoliberalization that have redefined modes of production and consumption, as well as the relations between states, nations, and citizens (see Soja 1989; Gupta and Ferguson 1997; Povinelli 2000; Harvey 2001; Postone 2006; Wacquant 2007).

This book takes as its point of departure the daily realities of young right-wing extremist groups in an East Berlin district in order to think through their salient place within a post-reunification project of German nationhood. The demise of the postwar order has spelled the return of the nation to the center of the political terrain in Germany as both a question and an imperative. This so-called rebirth of history provoked and still provokes severe anxieties. The traumatic legacy of the National Socialist past has loomed forebodingly over the country's imagination of its future, now compounded by what has been increasingly framed as its junior intimate, the memory of the epoch of the GDR. There is a certain disturbing irony in the fact that this historical rebirth has involved both the reemergence of a unified, democratic, liberal state and the resurgence of its doppelgänger in the figure of authoritarian, nationalist, violent currents. Young right-wing extremists have been vital for domesticating the tension between these historical horizons on the one hand and the urgencies of the historical moment on the other—albeit always nervously and tentatively.

The chapters that follow tell the story of this Sisyphean labor of domestication. They describe the immense energies expended on drawing and policing the boundaries of legitimate politics in Germany. Throughout this book we shall see how, in negotiating the project of a rehabilitated German nationhood, this labor grounds the very specters that it struggles so strenuously to exclude at its very core and betrays its own inevitable incompleteness. However, as I hinted above, the troubled enterprise of present-day Germany's national question proceeds under the sign of broader contemporary processes. Across the European continent, the policing of shifting political frontiers fuses today with the governance of emergent social peripheries. The waning of Fordist-era regimes of production, consumption, and accumulation has precipitated new configurations of social marginalization throughout the (de)industrialized world (Mingione 1996; Friedman 2003b; Hannemann 2005; Wacquant 2007). At the same time, it has also undermined certain forms of political struggle structured around nationally territorialized class antagonisms (Harvey 2001). The political ramifications of these historical shifts for the superfluous residues of an industrial European working class—with which the figures outside the bar that Friday night could certainly be counted—have been far-reaching. They have proceeded hand in hand with processes of neoliberalization that have redefined citizenship and set in motion novel modes of governing populations—especially at the bottom end of widening social polarization. The management of affect, and, in Europe in particular, what I call in this book "the management of hate," has been key to these new forms of control. This book is an ethnographic study of the sobering implications of these developments for the shape of political imaginaries today.

Understanding the political work that young right-wing extremists perform demands attention to how these seemingly disparate historical trajectories and social processes are articulated in present-day Germany. Accordingly, the purview of this study oscillates between and interweaves several scales of analysis, from the quotidian humdrum of right-wing extremist youths on the streets of East Berlin or the vernacular voices that negotiate cultural impasses in situated interactions to the hegemonic projects of a post-reunification nationalism or globally circulating idioms of politics and identity. Departing from certain scholarly approaches to the study of nationalist and ethnic conflict, my emphasis will not be on the disruptive influence of external forces on seemingly authentic local contexts, an approach that provides little insight into the contemporary extreme right in Germany. Their atavistic claims and their obsessions with purity and authenticity notwithstanding, my informants must be understood—as they too ultimately understand themselves—as internal to the historical moment and to the large-scale processes that define it. My interest is not to paint them as incommensurably other or as politically exotic species but rather as constitutively integral to the logic of the contemporary.[4]

TAMING THE DEMONS

Today, the concept of right-wing extremism (*Rechtsextremismus*) is fundamental to how most Germans imagine the political terrain. It is central, too, to how the German state sees and produces knowledge about its presumed internal adversaries. But this was not always so. In postwar Germany, the commonplace distinction between a legitimate, democratic political space and its illicit, antidemocratic margins was drawn with the concepts of center (*Mitte*) and radicalism (*Radikalismus*). Much like extremism today, radicalism used to mark political fields—whether on the right (*Rechtsradikalismus*) or on the left (*Linksradikalismus*)—as external to the spectrum of tolerated difference and as hostile to liberal democracy. Only toward the mid-1970s did the category of extremism (*Extremismus*) gradually gain currency in public and official state discourse, and especially in the terminology of the Federal Office for the Pro-

---

[4]My argument here is in agreement with Horkheimer and Adorno's classical insistence on the modernity of fascism, and their rejection of its interpretation as primordial or as oppositional to the Enlightenment. Of course, such a take on insidious and at times violent forms of nationalism rings far less comforting than their displacement to otherwheres and otherwhens (Horkheimer and Adorno 2002 [1944]).

tection of the Constitution (Bundesamt für Verfassungsschutz, henceforth BfV) (Butterwegge and Meier 2002, 18–19). Rather than simply substituting the concept of radicalism, the newly introduced category of extremism displaced it toward the political center. Radicalism gradually came to denote not the excluded extreme but rather that which, while represented as far from the mainstream, was not perceived to threaten the liberal-democratic order. The political terrain thus underwent what linguistic anthropologists would call a process of semiotic differentiation or fractal recursion.[5] Put differently, the borderland of ambiguity that separated the mainstream from the excluded—in the words of Chantal Mouffe, adversary from enemy[6]—has been baptized as a category of its own. The introduction of the category of extremism therefore sought to tame the ambiguity of the distinction between legitimate and illegitimate politics by naming it as an objective term within the universe of political possibilities. This attempt, at once hopeless and irresistible, already hinted at a nervous discomfort about the inherent tenuousness of the distinction itself.

Such a rendering of the political spectrum, to be sure, is not unique to German society. And yet its German variation is distinctive in a number of respects. Most important, it corresponds to a dominant historical narrative of the collapse of the Weimar Republic, Germany's first liberal-democratic experiment, as resulting from its helplessness against both communism and fascism. But it reflects, as well, the preeminence of the theory of totalitarianism in the Federal Republic of Germany (FRG). In insisting on the similarities between fascism and communism, the theory of totalitarianism effectively reduced so-called political extremisms to their nonidentity with a presumed mainstream. In the postwar years, this rendering answered the need to generate political and historical distance between West Germany and its two primary others: its National Socialist predecessor and its state socialist contemporary (Arendt 1973; Borneman 1993; Müller 1997; Butterwegge and Meier 2002; Hell 2006; Jarausch 2006; Rabinbach 2006).

Experts broadly agree that the category of right-wing extremism is used inconsistently to denote quite heterogeneous phenomena. Stabs at formulating precise definitions commonly outline more or less similar clusters of key attributes: nationalist sentiments, authoritarian personality structures, orientation

---

[5]The process of fractal recursion refers to the reappearance of semiotic contrasts at different scales. Thus, for example, the East/West division of Europe repeats itself within the Federal Republic of Germany, and again within the urban geography of Berlin. In the case at hand, a previous distinction between mainstream and radicalism reappears as two new distinctions, between mainstream and radicalism on the one hand and between radicalism and extremism on the other. See Irvine and Gal (2000).

[6]Chantal Mouffe has described an adversary as "a legitimate enemy, one with whom we have some common ground because we have a shared adhesion to the ethico-political principles of liberal democracy: liberty and equality." A real enemy, in contrast, is a political element with whom a democratic resolution of conflict is impossible (2000b, 102).

to violence, racism and xenophobia, misogyny and rigid conceptions of gender, attachment to National Socialist ideology, or belief in fundamental inequalities between humans (see, e.g., Heitmeyer 1992; Schubarth and Stöss 2001; Butterwegge and Meier 2002). The denotational scope of the concept is as wide and diverse as the social settings and pragmatic stakes of its deployments. One revealing instance I encountered during my fieldwork occurred in the context of the center-right Christian Democratic Union's (CDU) opposition to proposed antidiscrimination legislation required by EU directives and promoted in Germany largely by the political left. A central concern of the antidiscrimination campaign consisted in protecting women and minorities from discrimination in the job market. Mind-bogglingly, a CDU politician argued that such laws would prohibit employers from excluding right-wing extremist job applicants based on their political positions.

The ubiquity of the concept in both lay and expert discourses seems as resilient as it is oblivious to widespread dissatisfaction with it, whether on analytical or political grounds. Researchers frequently question its theoretical value, citing its agglomeration of fundamentally dissimilar phenomena, its inconsistent application, and its manipulation for electoral gains. Similarly, the concept comes under fire for its ideological entailments, for collapsing right and left, and for deflecting attention from pervasive racist, sexist, and nationalist currents that pass as innocuous, legitimate opinions.[7] Yet its force becomes all the more patent precisely in the face of the difficulty of formulating alternatives to it. To mention but one illustrative example, consider the encyclopedic volume *Rechtsextremismus in der Bundesrepublik Deutschland—Eine Bilanz* (Right Extremism in the Federal Republic of Germany—Taking Stock) (Schubarth and Stöss 2001). While the book opens with a devastating critique of the analytical merit of the concept of extremism, nearly all its chapters use the category in both their titles and their texts.[8]

The apparent tension between the analytical weakness and discursive robustness of the category of right-wing extremism makes more sense, however, if we consider the cultural stakes that converge in it. As a political category, it

[7] During my fieldwork I have repeatedly heard such reservations, for example, from antifascist activists, educators, and staff of NGOs that work to fight racism and promote democratic values.

[8] This dilemma, however, seems somewhat weaker in critiques of the concept on political grounds. Neither on the far left nor on the far right do people seem to designate themselves as extremists, instead using more nuanced differentiations: *Antifa* (antifascist), *Antideutschen* (anti-Germans), or *Autonome* (anarchists) on the left, or *Nationalisten* (nationalists), *Rechte* (rightists), or *Deutsche* (Germans) on the right. My right-wing informants often referred to their political adversaries as left-wing extremists. In contrast, those who self-identify as radical leftists in my experience preferred to call their political enemies fascists or Nazis. Some scholars have promoted the concept of radicalism as an alternative, but, in fact, the two terms are frequently used inconsistently and interchangeably, not only in lay talk but in expert discourses as well (e.g., Grumke and Wagner 2002).

marks what Allan Pred has termed "otherwheres" (1997), or a space into which a whole range of anxieties can be projected. In this sense, it indicates what one is not. Drawing on Ernesto Laclau (1996c), we may say that, because it stands beyond the frontiers of the political community, its representation involves a measure of homogenization, just as, correlatively, it allows the representation of that community itself as more or less uniform and coherent (for example, as "democratic"). But what precisely is the nature, and function, of that exclusion? Far more vital than generating difference with respect to, say, a neo-Nazi street gang or a racist political party often of trivial electoral significance, is the constitution of distance with the historical past. In Germany, today's right-wing extremists appear as concrete incarnations of more general forms that continue to haunt the present. Yet, the relation between the extreme right and the collectivity that defines itself, as it were, against it is not a simple, external dialectic between two separate terms that constitute each other through their differences. More precisely, as a political category, right-wing extremism operates in Germany as a constitutive outside. Following Jacques Derrida, Chantal Mouffe has described the constitutive outside as "present within the inside as its always real possibility" (2000a, 21). Viewed in this light, right-wing extremism is at once incommensurable with and the condition of possibility of the collectivity, at once radically external to and fundamentally constitutive of it. It reveals, then, not so much what one is not but rather the nature of deep anxieties about the potential of becoming—or, indeed, already being contaminated by—one's nightmares; hence, the profound discomfort and angst that physical proximity to right-wing extremist "things" seems to provoke among many Germans. Of course, this unbearable intimacy has everything to do as well with the fact that, far from being reified as an "object," nationalism surfaces as a "subject" within virtually every German family in the form of ancestors. The loved ones of one's bloodline thus too often slip into the material of one's nightmares.[9]

The perpetual "return of the repressed" in such encounters produces enormous strain. It calls for institutionalized mechanisms and formulaic scripts in order to tame the anxieties that it incites, to camouflage the inherent tenuousness of political distinctions, and to restore a semblance of stability. This book explores some of the many social institutions that participate in this working through of a national neurosis. Perhaps not surprisingly, a prominent place is reserved in this enterprise precisely for repressive methods. When it comes to right-wing extremism, criminalization, censorship, state persecution, or zero-tolerance approaches are often hailed by actors who would vehemently oppose them in other contexts. Throughout the chapters that follow, we shall see how the concept of right-wing extremism remains at once radically excluded and ineradicably constitutive of German nationalism today. The incessant labor of

---

[9] I thank Andrea Muehlebach for this insight.

taming the cultural anxieties that it triggers and of forever policing the exclusion of an other that obstinately contaminates the inside defines the discursive and political stakes under which this concept operates in Germany.

My decision to employ the concept of right-wing extremism in this book despite its analytical shortcomings and political baggage owes to my interest in it as an ethnographic object, for all the reasons already enumerated. Rather than attempting a more precise definition, coining some less ideologically burdened neologism, or remaining faithful to the vocabulary of my informants, my aim is to elucidate the latter's fundamental place within recent transformations of the political terrain in Germany, and precisely for that reason the notion of right-wing extremism and the immense weight attached to it appear especially appropriate. Throughout this book, accordingly, I use this notion as a pervasive local category that frames my informants—who cannot but relate and respond to it in a variety of ways—and that effectively links their activities to the ambivalences that mark Germany's emergent nationhood.

THE NATIONAL REMAINS

I have mentioned that the stakes attached to policing the frontiers of the political, and accordingly to the extreme right as a category, have dramatically escalated in recent decades. And I have suggested that this intensification has been motivated by the resurgence of the national question in the wake of the postwar era. Both claims require clarification. The Cold War division of Germany, of Europe, and of broad swaths of the world at large was a postscript of sorts to World War II that long outlived it. Its unraveling, crystallized in the events of 1989, constituted the concluding words in a saga that had shaped the globe throughout the "short twentieth century" (Hobsbawm 1994). The end of the postwar geopolitical order spelled a radical reopening of history and set in motion various efforts to recover the compasses that could reorient time in the here and now. For obvious reasons, Germans have experienced these years as particularly seismic (Geyer 1997; Huyssen 2003e). They meant at once the possibility of a certain historical closure and, inseparably, the reemergence of the long-tabooed question of nationhood. A rekindled national confidence and assertiveness has been evident, for example, in the sustained campaign for a permanent seat on the UN Security Council, a forum established by and for the victors of WWII; in the insistence on the expansion and intensification of the EU, reformed to reflect Germany's superior proportional power within it; in emergent discourses of self-victimization and suffering; in rising enthusiasm for military interventionism from the Balkans to Afghanistan, a sharp contrast with the formerly broad consensus against the positioning of German forces on foreign soil; or in the relocation of the federal government from its parochial home in Bonn to its mammoth quarters in Berlin.

But this nascent sense of normalcy spawned its own discontents. The Cold War suspension of history had meant as well the reassuring deferral of its peril—of the possibility of its return. If history turned open-ended, its outline was up for grabs. Freshly sovereign over its future, no longer hindered by division and occupation, Germany now had to assume the task of holding its own specters at bay. And it had to do so under the watchful gaze of the world at large, of Europe in particular, and of Germans themselves—some still profoundly skeptical of the success of externally coerced democracy in uprooting putatively pervasive fascist sympathies and hence supportive of intensified repression, others distrustful of the state's very commitment to the cause. The last two and a half decades have therefore witnessed a medley of power politics, nationalist reawakenings, and propitiatory gestures. The consolidation of a dominant political position within the EU has been accompanied by increased attendance of German leaders at WWII memorial anniversaries across the Continent. The public endorsement of narratives of displacement and exile has proceeded hand in hand with a foreign policy emphasis on reconciliation with Poland. The official sponsoring of commemorations of the victims of Allied carpet bombings has complemented an invigorated investment in the memory of the Holocaust. Finally, the intake at great financial cost of vast populations (East Germans, so-called German Russians) solely for their ethnic Germanness (*Volkszugehörigkeit*)—which surely highlighted an enduring ethnocultural nationalism—took place side by side with the liberalization of citizenship and naturalization laws dating to the Second and Third Reich eras, including the introduction of the long-rejected principle of jus soli.[10]

Such tensions between normal and perverse nationalism became palpably evident during the 2006 World Cup games. National and international media alike celebrated the broad, peaceful, and—perhaps for the first time since the war—unapologetic flag-waving German patriotism. Pundits praised the Germans as proud and patriotic yet hospitable and friendly. Many of my friends in Germany, however, viewed the mass spectacles of the federal flag with profound unease. Moreover, the retrospective tributes silenced the acute uncertainty that preceded the championship and that found its expression in fierce public debates over whether the country would deliver upon the motto selected for the games, "Die Welt zu Gast bei Freunden" (officially, "A Time to Make Friends" but roughly "The World Hosted by Friends"), or whether it would prove dangerously inhospitable. Against the background of several brutal racist assaults in the immediate run-up to the tournament, some insisted that officially warning visitors would prove wiser than feigning tranquillity. Beyond

---

[10] For a review of the history of German concepts of citizenship and national belonging, of their fundamental reliance on notions of culture, blood, and ethnicity, and of the long-standing resistance in Germany to considerations of territoriality and jus soli as principles of inclusion, see, for example, Preuß (2003) and Brubaker (2009).

sheer physical violence, commentators expressed concern that media images—sure to circulate the world over—would capture not only the black-yellow-red flags of the Republic, but also the black-white-red of the Reich. In a sense, the official interpellation of Germans as FRG flag-waving patriots was about the thwarting of bad nationalism through its inundation with good nationalism.

On the one hand, then, the collapse of the postwar order shook seemingly ironclad taboos to the core and released a host of demons upon the scene. The "good sides" of National Socialism or the horrors of German suffering have long found voice in the rhetoric of extreme right parties,[11] the lyrics of legally banned neo-Nazi musicians, or the chatter of intimate family conversations. Until recently, however, they rarely if ever featured in such mainstream publicity artifacts as, for example, Günter Grass's 2002 novel *Crabwalk* (*Im Krebsgang*) (2002b), a testament to the recent upheavals in taboos governing historical memory. Grass's detail-rich, harrowingly graphic narration depicts the 1945 sinking of the German ship *Wilhelm Gustloff* by a Russian submarine, in which thousands of refugees met their deaths. It amounts to a recollection of German victimhood so emphatic that, until not long ago, it would surely have placed the author himself with the radical fringes of right-wing historical revisionism. The novel reveals the multiple ways—beyond the mere loosening of taboos—in which reunification has facilitated the elaboration of such narratives. Grass's ability to preempt accusations of revisionism rests upon his skillful evocation of the uncanny landscape of the former GDR, and especially of that most clichéd chronotope of highrise communist-era residential neighborhoods (*Plattenbauten*) as the dominion of stubborn Stalinists, nostalgic nationalists, and violent skinheads.[12]

But, on the other hand, the historical rupture demanded a revision of the national question, and of its place in history. Historians have shown that the ideological foundations of fascism had been consolidated and had become prevalent throughout Europe decades before fascist movements seized political power (Nolte 1969; Sternhell 1995 and 1996). The wedding of an organic nationalism with a revised, anti-Marxist version of socialism at the dawn of the twentieth century spawned antidemocratic, antiliberal, and anti-Enlightenment currents throughout the Continent.[13] In Germany, however, 1945 was expected (and was

---

[11] Embodied, for example, in the figure of Georg Strasser and the socialist wing of the National Socialist German Workers' Party (Nationalsozialistische Deutsche Arbeiterpartei [NSDAP]).

[12] For an excellent history of *Plattenbauten* neighborhoods in the GDR and a discussion of their post-reunification resignification as underclass urban peripheries and their emergence as a social problem in a changing historical context, see Hannemann (2005). For a more extended discussion of Günter Grass's novel *Crabwalk*, see Shoshan (2016).

[13] Ernst Nolte (1969), in a seminal study of France, Italy, and Germany, identified a spiritual turn at the end of the nineteenth century that provided the roots for a particular form of anti-Marxism in which socialism and nationalism coexisted. At its basis, according to Nolte, the fascism that developed subsequently opposed the philosophical transcendence of both Marxist socialism and European liberalism. Despite important disagreements with Nolte (e.g., about the significance of racism or the purely negative character of fascist ideology), Zeev Sternhell has also argued that

sometimes assumed) to mark the definitive end to such ideological traditions. The events of 1989 therefore posed difficult questions. Has the postwar order truly eliminated the roots of the malaise or has it merely alleviated its symptoms? Many Germans I met during my research still struggled to find answers to such questions. People who on one occasion would assess the threat from the extreme right as negligible, on another would proclaim that, in fact, little has changed and that the enduring fascist inclinations of their countrymen could boil over at any moment, especially in the grip of economic stagnation. As I prepared to leave, acquaintances who earlier professed their patriotic pride would beseech me, jokingly, "Please don't leave us alone with the Germans" (as the familiar saying goes, every joke also has a funny side to it). How Germans respond to and manage such uncertainties has carried—and will continue to carry—far-reaching implications for the country's political ambitions, especially on the European scene.

Hand in hand with transformations in discursive forms and with the historical exigency of revising nationhood, since the late 1980s the country has witnessed a surge in public preoccupation with purification from the traces of National Socialism. In the context of a state project to recover the national and render it normal once again, the rigid, compulsive hold over its perverse flights has come to define its embryonic form. In other words, the crusade against insidious, illicit nationalism, as an obscene potential that lurks within the most ordinary forms of life, has ingrained itself as the constitutive kernel of a post-reunification national project. The groups that stand at the center of this book have been vital for this enterprise. Throughout the following chapters, and in diverse sites and moments, we shall encounter the paradoxes to which it has given life.

It would be erroneous, however, to assume that a narrative of national identity had been previously absent in Germany. Numerous scholars (e.g., Habermas 1991; Borneman 1997; Huyssen 2000) have rightly insisted that, for the better part of the postwar period, the notion of a West German nationhood successfully structured itself around the tropes of material prosperity and economic competitiveness (Wohlstand Deutschland and Standort Deutschland). Skyrocketing productivity and purchasing power defined the parameters for officially endorsed expressions of patriotic pride and for the German state's own

---

fascism appeared first as a cultural phenomenon. For Sternhell, the fascist synthesis of an anti-materialist revision of Marxism with what he terms "tribal nationalism" was a general European phenomenon and an integral part of the Continent's cultural history that appealed to innumerable intellectuals from across the political spectrum (1995). For a study that examines contemporary European far right nationalism within this broader history of fascism, see Holmes (2000). While my understanding of fascism is informed by this literature, in this book I place emphasis on right-wing extremism as a particular contemporary convergence of a number of historical processes that largely unfolded after the periods of the cultural consolidation of fascist ideology and of its emergence as a political force.

modes of self-legitimation and of managing the problem of its past. As late as 1979, Michel Foucault, reflecting on the postwar history of German neoliberalism, could still write:

> History had said no to the German state, but now the economy will allow it to assert itself. Continuous economic growth will take over from a malfunctioning history. It will thus be possible to live and accept the breach of history as a breach in memory, inasmuch as a new dimension of temporality will be established in Germany that will no longer be a temporality of history, but one of economic growth . . . In contemporary Germany we have what we can say is a radically economic state . . . that is to say, its root is precisely economic. (2008, 86)

Scholars have also shown how, a full decade later, Wohlstand nationalism played a key part in precipitating the swift and unconditional dissolution of the GDR. At the time, Habermas sarcastically baptized this dynamic as "a unified nation of angry DM [deutsche mark] citizens" (1991). In fact, many political dissenters in the East dreamed of a genuinely reformed and democratic socialism. But the elections that sealed the fate of the GDR were marked by fanciful promises that employed the national narrative of universal material affluence. This, even as that same narrative had already become all but obsolete, a nostalgic fantasy more than a viable futurity. Just how sour such promises—and the expectations to which they had given rise—have since turned was painfully evident in the acerbic tone with which Helmuth, one of the social workers whom I accompanied in my research, once recounted to me how a thick layer of advertising posters that a billboard in his neighborhood had accumulated over the years was scrubbed down to reveal a 1990 CDU election campaign ad that vowed, "Prosperity for all!" (Wohlstand für alle!); he shook his head disdainfully.

The end of the Cold War and its bringing of the national question into focus, then, arrived at a historical moment in which, for well over a decade, the dominant rendering of patriotic pride along economic lines had slowly been crumbling. The defunct promise of universal prosperity, tarnished since the mid-1970s by rising long-term unemployment and receding rates of economic growth, set into motion quests for other horizons of national identification.[14]

[14] Starting in the late 1970s, scholars have documented a steady decline of employment, growing wage differences, increase in working hours, weakened labor unions, rise in temporary and part-time jobs, progressive dismantling of labor protections, and a segmentation of welfare recipients. While a number of these processes were already well under way before 1989, reunification exercised a clear catalyzing impact on them. Current unemployment rates in Germany, while low compared with certain years over the past two decades and lower than many other European countries, are still very high relative to their pre-1980s levels. Income inequality, as measured by the Gini index, has been on the rise since the mid-1980s, as have relative poverty rates. Their negative consequences have disproportionately affected older cohorts, younger cohorts, women, immigrants, and residents of the former GDR territories (Knecht 1999; Mayer, Diewald, and Solga 1999; Pohl 2000; Kapphan 2002; Ludwig and Dietz 2008; Hassel 2010; Silvia 2010; OECD 2014; Statistisches

Concomitantly, in the throes of an economic slowdown, a large population of foreign residents could no longer be imagined as temporary workers. Indeed, many increasingly came to perceive their continued presence as a burden on the national economy. The troubled encounter with this reality of permanent immigration, rather than temporary solutions for labor shortages, brought to the surface as never before the latent, lingering notions of ethnocultural nationhood and placed them front and center in public debates. Thus the fall of the Berlin Wall found the questioning of seemingly durable historical taboos and the revisiting of national narratives already well under way,[15] even as it drastically redefined both the stakes and the terms of these processes. The ideological repercussions of reunification and the fall of communism became inscribed within an already disrupted and fragmented national project that had seen its key bearings melt into air and that had been desperately hunting for new ones. Significantly, the confrontation with new forms of social marginalization implied the vanishing viability not only of a national temporality of material prosperity but inseparably too of biographical expectations and aspirations.[16]

NEW POOR, OLD GHOSTS

The interpellation of a nascent national imaginary into being has called forth apprehensions about the latent, sinister potentialities that it may awaken, resulting in a compulsive preoccupation with maintaining a tight grip on the frontiers of the "legitimate" political spectrum. These processes have been inseparably imbricated with public fears about those burgeoning marginalized populations, from the older generations of laid-off workers to younger cohorts facing diminishing prospects of entering the workforce. The question of how to govern their hopes and expectations, their affective attachments and aversions,

---

Bundesamt 2014). In recent years, to be sure, Germany has become Europe's economic "powerhouse," rather than the "sick man" of Europe that it was during my fieldwork. Still, the processes outlined above have continued unabated, and universal prosperity has remained a defunct promise for many.

[15] Among the most prominent and controversial expressions of these processes, scholars often list the 1979 screening of the unprecedentedly successful fictional television series *Holocaust*, which many take to herald a new epoch in German remembrance of the crimes of National Socialism; Kanzler Kohl and former president Reagan's visit in 1985, on the anniversary of V-Day, to the Bitburg military cemetery, where Waffen-SS soldiers had been buried, despite a broad public outcry in both Germany and the United States; the Historikerstreit of the late 1980s, which pitted intellectuals who argued for the comparability of Nazi and Soviet atrocities against those who insisted on the uniqueness of National Socialism and the Holocaust; and ongoing political exchanges that emerged in the 1970s but picked up pace in the 1980s about whether Germany is, or is not, a land of immigration (*Einwanderungsland*) (see Habermas 1988; Torpey 1988; Olick 1998; Huyssen 2000; Eidson 2005; Brubaker 2009).

[16] For a discussion of poverty trends in contemporary Germany, see Ludwig and Dietz (2008).

has therefore become vital. After all, at least as dominant historical narratives would have it, the unemployed masses occupied a leading role within the cast of characters that catapulted the Nazis into power. In a broader perspective, the concern with social unrest has left an indelible mark on the notably long and innovative history of the welfare state in Germany, beginning already with nineteenth-century experimentations in the national collectivization of risk through social insurance and the provision of certain welfare benefits. Even the German neoliberals of the Freiburg school, whose ordoliberal doctrine revered competitive markets and dominated postwar economic policy in the FRG, insisted on the indispensability of a strong state that would continually intervene in the social sphere to assuage the destructive potential of "massification" and "proletarianization." The shift toward Keynesianism of the late 1960s that followed the rise of the Social Democrats to power after the first postwar recession entailed an expansion and intensification of state concern with social discontent.[17]

Public fears about the dangerous potentialities that today's new poor spell, expectations from and attachments to the figure of a strong, paternalistic state, as well as the very governmental mechanisms already available for social intervention and welfare provisioning, all share these historical genealogies. But the nature of the anxieties that emergent forms of social marginalization call into being and the challenges they pose to German nationhood are very much grounded in the present, as are, too, the contemporary responses they would seem to incite. The management of this threat forms a hesitant, nervous, hardly coherent yet momentous endeavor of affective governance. Its elaboration, experimentation, and performance fall under the dominion of the state, if we understand the latter—as I do in this book—as extending far beyond its formal frontiers to include a host of institutional sites, discursive genres, and political technologies that propagate its ideological effects throughout the social

[17] The Freiburg school economists, while emphatically committed to the sanctity of competitive markets, rejected laissez-faire free-regulation assumptions as superstitious. Instead, they emphasized the social preconditions for the existence of free competition, which included the curbing of economic pressures toward massification, impoverishment, and proletarianization. They viewed the irrational social consequences of capitalism as a threat to the sustainability of liberal markets. Thus, a resilient economic order must be both free and humanly acceptable. For them, guaranteeing the social preconditions for economic freedom and competitive markets formed a continuous political task that required the constant intervention of a strong state. Such a state would function as the organizational center for mediating the interdependence of the economic sphere with the political, social, and other spheres. In the ordoliberal view, then, the free economy is nothing less than a practice of governance (Rieter and Schmolz 1993; Biebricher 2011; Bonefeld 2012). Officially committed to ordoliberal social market economy, postwar West German policy in fact always included a measure of Keynesian instruments and welfare provisions. The scales shifted drastically toward Keynesian policy principles starting in 1967, in response to the recession and with the formation of a grand coalition that included the Social Democrats. This included the expansion of redistributive measures and of automatic stabilization instruments such as unemployment benefits and deficit spending. The redistributive effects of the period were immense, as was the rise in social spending (Schnitzer 1972; Nachtwey 2013).

(Gramsci 1997 [1971]; Althusser 2001; Trouillot 2001). It is a project of governance that targets broad national publics and seeks to orchestrate, induce, and defuse a set of indispensable yet potentially inflammable affective dispositions. It addresses, of course, affective attachments to those no-longer-viable, Fordist-era futurities of job security, material prosperity, and consumer patriotism. But it also targets affinities to the figure of a state whose sovereignty and legitimacy increasingly come under attack. This figure today confronts challenges both from below, through forms of unruliness and disorder at the social and political margins, and from above, through transnational institutions of governance—most important, the EU—with questionable or entirely lacking democratic credentials. At the same time, this project of affective governance must attend to the appeal of competing national imaginaries with their divergent figurations of historical narratives. Finally, and perhaps most important, it seeks to mold affective relations to distinct forms of otherness that are variously construed as cultural, religious, or ethnic in their essence.

In this book, I understand affective relations as at once objects and effects of governance. But I also consider the very mechanisms of governance themselves as laden with affective stakes. Such a view requires that we set aside analytical distinctions between, on the one hand, affects as putatively autonomous, pre-social intensities, and, on the other, their subsequent mediated qualifications as articulable emotions (see Massumi 1995). Much less does it subscribe to a notion of affects as unlimited, emergent potentialities that herald the possibility of freedom from social regimes of linguistic and institutional mediation. Instead, in conversation with recent literature in the humanities and the social sciences, my emphasis here will be on social and political projects of regulating, generating, and neutralizing affective publics. I am interested, moreover, in thinking about these very projects as haunted by affects that are, if often not entirely articulable, then nevertheless always already historically qualified. Yael Navaro-Yashin (2012), for example, describes how in postwar Cyprus affects are politically induced by administrative and legal orders. She explores how, in turn, such affects are sedimented in and mediated by the materialities of a scarred landscape. From quite a different direction, Andrea Muehlebach (2012) has documented how in neoliberal Italy past attachments to Fordist forms of work have been incorporated into regimes of unremunerated, affective labor and "ethical citizenship." In these and other cases, affective publics emerge as always already marked by "the competing ways in which they get partially harnessed to social and political projects of value" (Mazzarella 2013, 40). Their outlines and their governance in this perspective index certain shared historical sensitivities and are consequently ideological and political from the start (Berlant 2011, 14–16, 158–59), even if they may exceed any particular framing. Both producers and loci of affects, the institutions of affective governance are never fully reducible to the putative rationality of bureaucratic governmentality (Navaro-Yashin 2012, 31–33). They always exude, as it were, a certain excess to rational calculation. It is at the burgeoning bottom of an increasingly uneven social topography and at the simmering margins of the political terrain that they operate with special zeal and give rise to particularly palpable excesses, which is only a different way of saying that the social and political margins are precisely those spaces where these excesses become especially visible.

The young people who gathered outside the U-21 bar on that late May night with which I opened this chapter, and the sorts of projects of affective governance that gravitate around them, crystallize this contemporary encounter in Germany between new poor and old ghosts. Consider Rene, a burly skinhead whom I had only vaguely known until then, but who came up to me and enthusiastically laid out his plan to establish a youth club for him and his peers. No doubt he assumed I could help him sell the idea to the social workers with whom I collaborated. His appeal to me referenced a common trope with which far right-wing groups have sought to win support among young people. According to this refrain, the state has abandoned its "German" youths. In Berlin's Treptow-Köpenick, where I conducted my fieldwork, organized extraparliamentary groups and the federal NPD headquarters, which sits in the district, have diligently and efficaciously deployed such rhetoric. The resonance it has found among local youths set into motion a sustained campaign for a "German youth club," which included regular demonstrations, marches, and a petition to the mayor. The campaigners demanded a venue that would cater specifically to young right-wing extremists. Many of them had been barred from attending already existing establishments, and for good reason, since their presence there was not unwarrantedly perceived as threatening by many other visitors. Backed by experts, NGOs, and youth workers, the municipality flatly rejected their demands.

The refusal to funnel public resources to sponsor the leisure activities of Rene and his friends rests on impeccable reasons, which it is not my aim to question here.[18] However, what such dismissals fail to recognize are the reasons why the campaign for a German youth club found such broad resonance across the district. Its success registered the social realities that my informants faced daily: uninhabitable, at times dangerous domestic settings, in part the effect of long-term unemployment and alcoholism; a diminishing capacity to access other spaces and activities, admission to which usually requires payment, and the prospects of a future in which such capacity continues to decrease; and, not least, a historical moment in which austerity cutbacks and schemes of budgetary and administrative restructuring result in ever scarcer public resources,[19]

---

[18] In the past, the sponsoring of public establishments for right-wing extremist youths has not only meant the public funding of intolerant, exclusionary venues but has also turned out to strengthen local nationalist groups by providing them with space and infrastructure for their activities, even when, as had often been the case, such establishments were designed to assist in the "normalization" of their visitors.

[19] During my fieldwork, the Berlin government pushed forward with such reforms throughout the city under a general restructuring plan described as *Sozialraumorientierung* (social space orientation) (Bezirksamt Treptow-Köpenick 2005).

particularly compromising the ability to address social needs in marginalized urban peripheries. The story of Sylvia, the die-hard soccer fan, is exemplary in that regard. After the youth club in her neighborhood where she passed most of her afternoons shut down, an acquaintance invited her to join him and his friends, a clique of right-wing extremist soccer ultras. She gradually came to surpass many of her peers there, not only in her soccer fanaticism but also in her enthusiasm with the NPD. Notwithstanding their clear merits, then, zero-tolerance policies overlook the fact that political identifications are less a given state of things and more a dynamic process of consolidation. They therefore too often fail to address the forces that pull some far into the right-wing fringes.

In present-day Germany, the figures of Sylvia, Rene, and their friends stand simultaneously for the supernumerary masses and for intimations of genocidal nationalism. Throughout this book, we shall see how their story unfolds at the intersection of monumental efforts to govern and domesticate both threats, and we shall witness the sorts of excesses that this fusion calls into being. What I call the management of hate in this book consists in the strenuous labor of orchestrating the encounter between the two, the compulsive spawning of public imaginaries about them, and the unrelenting investment in their cultural repression and political excommunication. The management of hate, to be sure, is in this sense a particular instance of what I have already described as affective governance. It betrays in particularly patent ways, however, how the putatively rational and economistic paradigms of governance in fact answer to quite other scenes of political conflict and cultural contestation. As chapters 4 and 5 show, the management of hate holds a particular interest in governing right-wing extremist delinquency. But, as I argue particularly in chapters 8 and 9, it also encompasses a range of practices and institutions bent on fomenting certain affective dispositions and curbing others in so-called mainstream publics. And while specific political constellations and electoral results may push and pull it in more or less distinct directions, the management of hate in general forms an endeavor that transcends shifts in parliamentary power and perseveres through the rise and fall of governments and coalitions.[20]

In Germany, the management of hate, thus understood, forms an actually existing regime of neoliberal governance that clusters distinct discourses and practices and that seeks to orchestrate public affects. The concerns to which it responds reveal themselves as saturated with class anxieties, and chapter 5 especially pauses on the post-Fordist affects with which it overflows. The management of hate accordingly orients itself with special vigor toward the emergent peripheries of present-day capitalism. In the German context, however, it can

---

[20] In chapter 8, I describe some of the programs established during the Social Democratic Party of Germany (Sozialdemokratische Partei Deutschlands, or SPD) and Greens coalition rule under the leadership of Chancellor Gerhard Schröder and explain how they have persisted, even if under different names, throughout the rule of the conservative union under the chancellorship of Angela Merkel.

only be understood in relation to the country's very particular twentieth-century history, as a collective mode of "learning to live with ghosts" (Derrida 1994, xviii). Put differently, it appears as a reflexive process of national becoming that stands between life and death, between past and present, and between spectral presences and post–Cold War geopolitical and cultural projects, which include the rebranding of the Federal Republic as a cosmopolitan country of immigrants. If it now bears the shadows of both the National Socialist and communist pasts, it is especially the former that has generated heightened angsts and that has served for mobilizing people into action. It is largely the weight of that past, too, that has shaped the management of hate as a field of governance traversed by an excitement with the obscene, a voyeuristic desire to see precisely that which is so strongly tabooed, a series of fantasies about the occult world of right-wing extremists in which the fetish of the state links up with the fetish of the nation.

The uneasy encounter in Germany between new poor and old ghosts at the same time is embedded within processes that have transformed the possibilities of formulating and performing political projects at a global scale, and this in at least two important ways. First, a number of authors have documented how the commodification of increasingly expansive spheres of life in the post-Fordist era, evident in the proliferation of consumer identifications and diversification of niche markets, has meant a rising colonization and fragmentation of the social.[21] I will describe some of the effects that such processes have exercised on the extreme right in Germany in chapter 2. For now, let us note that ever more fragmented consumption habits have increasingly come to define the terrain for fabricating not only cultural but also, and inseparably, political difference. In other words, under late capitalism the proliferating consumption cultures of the market have frequently become the defining modalities for articulating political identifications (Holmes 2000; Comaroff and Comaroff 2001).[22] The irony

---

[21] Thus, looking at the shift from urban politics to commercialization, David Harvey has discussed the postmodern relation between market power, product differentiation, and the increasing fragmentation of urban space (1989). Ana Maria Alonso has described the aestheticization and commodification of ethnicity and its effects on the national space (1994). Elizabeth Povinelli has examined the interrelations between economic slowdown, commodification, and the marketing of indigenous culture in Australia, as well as the threat spelled by multiculturalism to the Australian state and nation (1998). Fredric Jameson, from a different direction, has argued that late capitalist commodification has led to a postmodern fragmentation of the subject, of social life, and of the city (1984). Andreas Huyssen, meanwhile, has attributed the increasing fragmentation of national politics of memory, both in Germany in particular and around the globe more generally, to its growing commercialization and "musealization" under recent processes of economic globalization (2000). Jean Comaroff and John Comaroff have argued that the dominance of consumption at the cost of the erasure of production under "millennial capitalism" has meant the fragmentation of class culture and politics and the turn from homogeneity to difference in the nation-state space (2001). Slavoj Žižek too has identified an increasing commodification of politics in today's Europe (2006).

[22] Thus, in post-Soviet Lithuania the negotiation of contemporary public identities and their relation to the political present has proceeded hand in hand with, for example, the renaissance of "Soviet" sausages, which, although produced in the "West," have become the embodiment of a

here, of course, is that such processes have accelerated precisely at a historical moment in which, across much of the (de)industrialized world, the burgeoning ranks of the new precariat see both their capacity to engage in consumer identifications and their ability to wage class-based political struggles waning (Steinmetz 1994; Harvey 2001; cf. Balibar 2004b; Banks and Gingrich 2006). At this juncture, the nation surfaces as an alternative to globalist consumerism and commodified subjectivity but at once, too, as itself a niche market and a consumer identity for the economically excluded.

But, second, the figure of the nation itself has become progressively fractured, a distant cry from the homogenizing project that—if not always in practice, then commonly enough as an imagined horizon—stood as the hallmark of the modern nation-state. The shift from "homogeneism" (Blommaert and Verschueren 1998) to the officially endorsed celebration of diversity (whether linguistic, ethnic, religious, culinary, or other) within the national space bespeaks certain reconfigurations in the nation-state relation under what some have described as neoliberal multiculturalism (Taylor and Gutmann 1994; Žižek 1997; Povinelli 1998; Holmes 2000; Hale 2005; Jackson and Warren 2005). Thus, even as some may brandish it as a cure-all for the fragmentation of the social, the nation itself already appears as a particular term in a heterogeneous political landscape. As claims upon the state, far from disappearing, realign themselves into nascent collectivities, the nation becomes, for example, the structuring principle for new particularistic idioms of entitlement and discrimination— recall the demand that the municipality establish a "German youth club." Inseparably, and as we shall see particularly in chapter 8, civil society emerges in this context as the panacea for suturing the splinters of the social (Comaroff and Comaroff 2001). And hand in hand with the rise of civil society, forms of incivility and disorder have emerged as privileged sites for visibilizing the state and as yardsticks for assessing the state of the nation (Comaroff and Comaroff 2006). The repercussions of such shifts are evident in the compulsive redrawing of the political distinction that marks and excludes the extreme right in Germany. They come into focus, as well, in how my informants articulate and perform their political selves.

ON THE STREETS OF TREPTOW-KÖPENICK

While throughout this book I analyze a variety of different sources, the groups with whom I lingered at parks, train stations, and soccer stadiums at the southeastern edges of Berlin stand at its ethnographic core. Diffuse and unorganized

vanished mass utopia that now returns in the form of consumer choice (Klumbyte 2007). In postreunification Germany, as many observers have noted, the bifurcation of national identity into East and West has relied upon—or better yet, has been interpellated by—the creation of a nostalgic market for GDR-era commodities and material artifacts (see, e.g., Berdahl 1999; Bach 2005).

groups, such as those of my informants, have played a key role in the surge of right-wing extremism after reunification, and especially in the rise in racist and political violence. Their nature has frustrated conventional methods of social science research on the extreme right, which tend to focus analytically on political parties, organizational structures, ideological discourses, electoral behavior, and charismatic leaders. But, for a number of reasons, it has also impeded their ethnographic study. Perhaps most crucially, the criminalization and tabooing of these groups has meant that their members often view strangers with (not entirely unjustified) suspicion, rendering access to them difficult. Nevertheless, given ample anthropological research in challenging and sometimes dangerous settings, the fact that, to the best of my knowledge, no similar ethnographic fieldwork has been conducted to date no doubt owes as well to the moral aversion that the groups with which I worked provoke.[23] Be that as it may, as I embarked upon this project, I could find little guidance in existing literature on how to overcome the methodological and ethical conundrums that it entailed, most urgent of which was the question of access.

Preliminary research in the summer of 2003 suggested that street social workers who serviced the groups in which I was interested could perhaps assist me. But it was not until I returned to Berlin in August 2004 and met with Andrea, Daniela, and Helmuth that I began to sense how rewarding this path could prove. During the sixteen months that followed, I accompanied them regularly on their daily rounds in Berlin's southeast, where they introduced me to their young, right-wing extremist clients. Helmuth, the eldest of the three, was thirty-six years old when I met him, a large man whose autodidactic intellect, local erudition, and creative imagination made for innumerable fascinating and informative conversations. The son to a family closely allied with the ruling Socialist Unity Party of Germany (Sozialistische Einheitspartei Deutschlands, or SED),[24] he was about to graduate from the border troops' officer course in 1989 when, as he put it, "everything that had constituted my life until then became absolutely worthless." Yet he associates the events of that year with an intoxicating sense of emancipation, mostly from his own ideological fetters. Unemployed, his academic diploma void,[25] he worked at odd jobs until becoming a street social worker in 1994. Thirty-three-year-old Andrea, who was tall and had long brown hair, spent much of her childhood abroad with her parents, who served in the GDR's diplomatic corps. An extraordinary sense of compassion, unwavering personal integrity, and an intimate tenderness won her great affection among the young people she served. After reunification, with her business management diploma unrecognized and the firm where she

---

[23] The relatively rare ethnographic studies in this field, while excellent in their own right, tend to rely on highly mediated sources such as media representations, discourse analysis, Internet websites, or, at best, structured interviews (Holmes 2000; Gingrich and Banks 2006).

[24] The SED was the ruling party in the GDR.

[25] Academic credentials gained under the GDR were often not recognized after reunification.

worked out of business, she took up various low-rank jobs. She eventually concluded that her talents and ambitions would remain frustrated lest she improved her academic standing. She graduated from a social work program in 2000, became a street social worker immediately thereafter, and was pursuing a second degree in criminology at the time of my research. From a small town in Brandenburg northwest of Berlin, twenty-six-year-old Daniela wore her blond hair in a ponytail, and her fair skin featured colorful tattoos that testified to her love of music. Time and again, her shrewd judgment of character and ability to divine the full picture from the sometimes scanty intimations that her clients and my informants often provided left me speechless. Daniela entered high school already after reunification. Her educational and professional trajectory was therefore not truncated by the fall of the GDR in the same way as her older colleagues'. Following high school, she came to Berlin to study for a degree in social education. She had met Helmuth and Andrea while she was still a student, and they recruited her to their team in 2001.

The three of them worked for the independent street social work provider Gangway. The organization was founded in 1990 and, at the time of my research, employed some fifty social workers in teams of three or four across most of Berlin's districts. Gangway received its financing partly from the city government and partly from district municipalities. Helmuth, Andrea, and Daniela worked under semiannual contracts with the district of Treptow-Köpenick. They targeted young, socially marginalized, and predominantly right-wing extremist groups that congregated routinely in several outdoor locations. When I presented my project to them and inquired whether they would allow me to accompany their team in order to gain access to the groups of their clients, they welcomed the idea. In fact, throughout my fieldwork, they went out of their way to help me with my research in innumerable other ways as well. With time, our arrangement grew more flexible: they would charge me with performing various errands with their clients on my own, and I would progressively arrive at Treptow-Köpenick independently to spend time with my informants.

Treptow-Köpenick is Berlin's largest district, extending over almost 20 percent of the city's landmass. Scenic water expanses and forests comprise about a third of its surface, and its landscape teems with the dissonant contrasts of Germany's reunited capital: from Köpenick's quaint old town on Youth Island or the bucolic sandy beaches and wide waterways of the Spree and Dahme Rivers to the bright contemporary architecture of the recently established "Science City" at Adlershof, the sprawling residential neighborhoods of communist-era high-rises in Altglienicke, the vast and daunting span of the Soviet War Memorial, or the long stretches of dilapidated industrial ruins. Settlement in the area surged dramatically with the rapid industrialization of the late nineteenth century, and since then it has juxtaposed some of the city's social elites and better-off families with broad working-class populations, the latter largely concentrated in its southern half, Treptow, where I conducted my fieldwork.

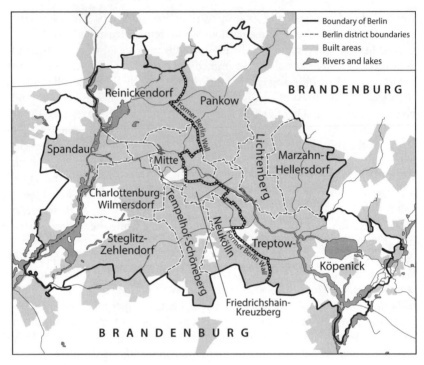

Map 1. Berlin.

The Social Democrats (SPD) and the Party of Democratic Socialism (PDS) have solidly dominated local politics in the district. For well over a decade, however, Treptow-Köpenick has also gained a certain disrepute for the presence of extreme right currents. It hosts the federal headquarters of the NPD, which has won some of its best electoral results in the district, and especially in those same areas on which the social workers focused their efforts. Militant extra-parliamentary organized groups (henceforth *Kameradschaften* [pl.]; *Kamerad-schaft* [sing.]) have also been active in the district. The social workers were inti-mately familiar with some of their members, who persevered in their activities despite the official banning of their groups as anticonstitutional organizations by Berlin's Ministry of the Interior in 2005. Additionally, the district has wit-nessed regular right-wing extremist demonstrations and a significantly higher than average incidence of violent, sometimes grotesquely brutal assaults. My research led me to make the acquaintance of several among their perpetrators. Not least, extreme right sympathizers in Treptow-Köpenick benefited from the hospitality of various establishments—bars, restaurants, shops—that catered to them, relied on their patronage, and provided them with infrastructure for lei-sure, consumption, and, at times, clandestine meetings. With Helmuth, with my young informants, and at times on my own, I made it a point to frequent most of these locations during my research.

My fieldwork, however, focused neither on political parties nor on clandestine cells but on the relatively diffuse and dynamic groups that gathered in a number of outdoor sites and whose members the social workers serviced. Because of their fairly heterogeneous compositions, I can only provide here a rough description of their general outlines. Gender mixed, their ages varied from the midteens to the midtwenties. Their socioeconomic backgrounds by and large ranged from underclass destitution to solid working-class households and their educational records from dismal to low. Many suffered from precarious domestic settings, with violent, abusive, alcoholic, or neglectful parents. In turn, violence, alcoholism, and delinquency were widely prevalent within their ranks, and a significant proportion, especially among the men, boasted criminal records for both petty and serious offenses: theft and shoplifting, physical assault and damage to property, arson and trespassing, possession of illegal weapons and debt evasion, or a range of criminal transgressions against laws governing right-wing extremist "things," which I lay out in detail in chapter 4. Few were gainfully employed and most depended on state disbursements. The more fortunate made their way into government-funded vocational training programs, but their prospects of subsequently securing salaried positions seemed slim. Virtually all came from East German households whose adult members have often been unemployed for the better part of the past two decades. Racism and xenophobic nationalism were deep and widespread, yet awareness of formal politics was, for lack of a better word, astoundingly rudimentary— several of my informants, for example, could not correctly name Germany's chancellor at the time. Only a handful had participated in organized political groups or attended demonstrations.

Question 3

The social workers appealed to these groups with various subsidized leisure offerings—movie outings, bowling alley and billiard hall visits, excursions to the country, graffiti workshops, and so on—in order to break their dull routine but, first and foremost, as a cornerstone for winning their trust and for consolidating relationships that would enable long-term individual counseling. In such counseling they addressed a wide spectrum of needs: vocational training and job applications, health care, securing apartments, legal services, accompanying people through penal procedures, maneuvering labyrinthine state bureaucracies, or obtaining welfare and other benefits. Beyond the long hours at their clients' outdoor hangout spots, then, they shuttled almost daily between welfare, employment, and youth offices; courts and hospitals; and prisons and attorneys—all of which at best made for a very weak notion of a work routine. Speaking again in general terms, however, we would typically gather in the early afternoon at their office, located in the basement of a community center, to coordinate and plan the workday's schedule and complete various administrative tasks. From there, we would deploy to various outdoor locations, occasionally for prearranged meetings with individuals but more often to linger about, make new acquaintances, catch up with older ones, plan group activities, collect information, or thrash out their clients' personal problems. The open-ended nature of our visits, their irregular itineraries, and the protracted hours of random chitchat offered excellent opportunities for extensive observation and spontaneous conversations with the groups I set out to study. But the social workers, themselves increasingly an object of my research, also constituted a superb source of information on the youths they served in their own right, commanding detailed knowledge of their biographical backgrounds, their social networks, criminal records, or political orientations.

Much like the groups we found there, the locations we visited presented a shifting and diffuse geography. Nevertheless, we especially attended to three areas with a high incidence of young, socially marginalized, right-wing extremist groups. All three were located in Treptow, the district's southern part, which was particularly hard-hit by the virtually total deindustrialization that followed reunification and where several sites emerged as regular meeting spots for such people. The first, a *Plattenbauten* residential area colloquially known as the "Ghetto," exhibited most glaringly the devastating impact of economic stagnation and rampant unemployment. Once within convenient proximity to labor sites, its location on the city's frontier has since rendered it an isolated enclave severed from today's urban geography of production and consumption. Under the countless windows of gray high-rises, benches and public squares have become the territory of long-term unemployed adults and abject youths. The latter presented more acute destitution and lower educational levels than elsewhere in the district, and many cast their votes for the NPD. A second area included the neighborhoods of Johannisthal and Schöneweide, at the heart of Treptow, which fared somewhat less badly than the Ghetto owing to their central location and superior integration into the urban infrastructure. Favorite outdoor hangouts in Johannisthal and Schöneweide included a park, a number of playgrounds, and an abandoned industrial zone. But these two neighborhoods also offered a relatively abundant selection of consumption, entertainment, and leisure establishments that young right-wing extremists routinely frequented. And they served as home turf for some of the city's most militant groups and activists. Finally, the last area consisted of the environs of the Grünau train station, on the city's southeast, which functioned as a peripheral transportation hub linking highway, train, trams, and numerous bus lines. In sharp contrast with the first two areas I described, few among the young people who gathered in Grünau daily also resided in the neighborhood. Instead, their groups assembled loose social circles from across the district. A hard core of fanatical fans of the local soccer club Union, however, provided a fairly stable social nucleus.

My entrance to the field alongside the social workers shaped my research in a number of important ways. At some level, to be sure, their young clients perceived me as different from the social workers. As time progressed, I estab-

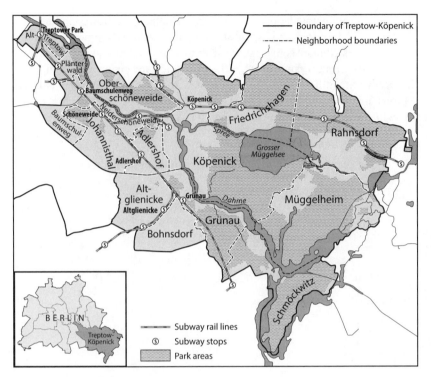

Map 2. Treptow-Köpenick.

lished personal relationships with my informants, spent more and more time with them independently, and participated in activities that clearly transgressed the boundaries of social work: accompanying them to soccer matches, joining them on weekend outings, or spending a night over beers at their apartments or hangout spots. My foreignness, too, stood in sharp contrast with the sophisticated local erudition of the social workers. Despite the initial suspicion that it provoked, my foreign identity slowly gained positive value, as my informants would test their English proficiency, take pride in my support for their local soccer club, or inquire about life in the United States. More significantly, perhaps, as the stranger "who comes today and stays tomorrow," I often sensed I benefited, as Georg Simmel (1971, 145) once put it, from "the most surprising revelations and confidences . . . about matters which are kept carefully hidden from everybody with whom one is close." In the German context, this meant that my informants would express opinions that, because so strongly tabooed, I felt they would less likely confide to, say, a German researcher.

The crucial place of street social work in mediating my research, at the same time, has meant an empirical focus on public outdoor spaces, disadvantaged groups, and young populations.[26] At a more profound level, however, the many hours the social workers and I spent strolling the streets of Treptow or shuttling between sites facilitated conversations with them not only about my informants but also concerning a range of other themes critical for my investigation, from the legacy of reunification to the present state of German nationalism at large. As constant interlocutors, their words offered me fresh perspectives that themselves begged for analysis. The more their own crucial place in the management of hate revealed itself to me, the more they became key informants in my study. For reasons of expository clarity, and in order to distinguish between them and their young clients (my "informants"), I refer to them throughout this book as "the social workers."

[26] None of this implied absolute exclusion of other perspectives. The primacy of public space in street social work, for example, did not preclude insight into private places, whether during home visits for individual appointments, delivering or collecting documents, assisting with setting up apartments, or spending an evening chatting and listening to music. Similarly, while largely underclass, group compositions were heterogeneous and also included better-off individuals. Still, to the extent that interior private spaces came under my scrutiny, they were predominantly the apartments of individuals who spent much of their leisure time outside. Similarly, the focus on socially marginalized groups brought me into contact with social circles in which they made up a considerable portion. And the older informants whom I came to know were often adults who sustained significant relations with younger people.

IIIIIIIIIIIIIIIIIII 2 IIIIIIIIIIIIIIIIIII

East and West, Right and Left

THE LATE-CAPITALIST PROLIFERATION of consumer identities, the post-Fordist rise of new forms of precarious labor and social marginalization, recent shifts in national imaginaries and historical narratives, and, perhaps most significant, the seismic impact of reunification have all left their palpable marks on the German extreme right in a number of ways. In this chapter, I review some of these latest developments that have reshaped the extreme right in Germany over the past couple of decades, pausing in particular on the contemporary legacy of the East/West divide in the post-reunification era and on its political significance both nationally and, more specifically, for the young people with whom I worked. However, right-wing extremism in today's Germany must also be understood in relation to a broader, Continental, and shifting landscape of nationalist and far-right currents and the ongoing processes from which it has emerged. Accordingly, and while I do not aspire to offer a broad and comprehensive assessment of European right-wing extremism,[1] I open the chapter with a brief discussion of important trends that have reconfigured far right nationalism across the Continent in recent decades, and whose impact the German context has not escaped.

To be sure, if, as we saw in chapter 1, the category of right-wing extremism suffers from an acute lack of precision in Germany alone, any discussion of a European far right nationalism inevitably clusters a seemingly overwhelming heterogeneity of forms and processes. After all, one could reasonably question the analytical viability and advisability of collapsing together the early triumphs of the Front National in the south of France, marked as they were by the legacy of decolonization and an orientalist nostalgia for empire (Veugelers 2012), with the regionalist localism and secessionist project of the Lega Nord in Northern Italy (Stacul 2006; Bulli and Tronconi 2012) or Pim Fortuyn's chauvinistic

---

[1]For comparative studies of recent developments in far-right, nationalist politics across Europe, see Holmes (2000); Gingrich and Banks (2006); Kalb and Halmai (2011); Mammone, Godin, and Jenkins (2012b and 2013b).

crusade in defense of Dutch values of democracy, tolerance, and liberty (Sunier and Ginkel 2006) with the political polarization in Belgium between a French-inspired Front National, especially present in the economically depressed, French-speaking Wallonia, and the Flemish Vlaams Belang of the relatively prosperous north, with its strong emphasis on a nationalism defined by ethnic descent and biological consanguinity (Jamin 2012).

Nevertheless, right-wing nationalism across Europe bears the stamp of certain similar, recent processes, if not always in the same manner, to the same extent, or with the same effects. Numerous scholars, for example, have linked the upsurge in far right movements in places as distinct as England, Hungary, Sweden, Romania, or the Netherlands with shifting configurations of class belonging and with increasing socioeconomic insecurities and inequalities (Pred 2000; Gingrich 2006; Sunier and Ginkel 2006; Goodwin 2008; Shoshan 2008b; Kalb 2011; Petrocivi 2011; Jaschke 2013). The situation I described for post-prosperity Germany is in this sense not entirely unique. As Don Kalb (2011) has noted, in both Eastern and Western Europe, nostalgic narratives have come to reference traumatic experiences of dispossession that have accompanied processes of neoliberalization. Sometimes such narratives express the loss of actual conditions of job security and well-being. Often, they capture the vanishing of imagined futurities, whether of socialist utopias or of capitalist comfort and opulence. Throughout the Continent, they have frequently become politically signified in nationalist terms (Kalb and Halmai 2011). Against the background of widespread deindustrialization and the progressive unraveling of the European working class, and abetted by the apparent incapacity of the political left to articulate alternative responses to these processes, nationalism has emerged as an increasingly appealing horizon with which to render them legible (Holmes 2000, 103–62). In some cases, as, for example, Britain or Germany, a strong emphasis on welfarism has anchored itself at the center of contemporary nationalist politics. More commonly (and often in parallel), new European nationalisms have provided the idioms with which such socioeconomic anxieties could be formulated as cultural preoccupations (Banks and Gingrich 2006).

The increasing culturalization of politics, in Europe as elsewhere, and the progressive evacuation of class idioms from mainstream political discourses have complemented a paradoxical process: on the one hand, and not only in Germany, a general shift toward jus soli principles of citizenship is presently observable (Miller-Idriss 2006), while on the other hand, across the European far right, ethnocultural notions of nationhood seemed to have gradually marginalized other national imaginaries (e.g., imperial, territorial, multicultural). Both of these seemingly contradictory developments have proceeded under the sign of several distinct processes of transnationalization, of which Europeanization has exercised an especially salient influence on nationalist politics in recent decades (Banks and Gingrich 2006). Today, to be sure, indignant opposition to ongoing EU integration on the European far right has become commonplace.

But earlier European nationalisms, including National Socialism and Italian fascism, incorporated strong pan-European strands (Mammone, Godin, and Jenkins 2013a). More recently, far right movements have in some cases entertained ambivalent and shifting relations to the EU project, especially in its earlier phases. The Austrian Freedom Party, for example, enthusiastically supported Europeanization as recently as the late 1980s, when, in a sharp makeover that also included the shift from Pan-Germanism to a distinctly Austrian nationalism, it rebranded itself as a vociferous critic of the EU (Fillitz 2006). Northern Italy's regionalist, secessionist right-wing has maintained an equivocal orientation to European integration, in which its members have seen the potential for partially carving up nation-state sovereignty and redistributing it to subnational regions (Bulli and Tronconi 2012). In a related manner, the overwhelming predominance in today's European far right of ethnocultural nationalisms (Banks and Gingrich 2006; Gingrich 2006) has eclipsed other notions of national belonging, from secular republicanism to multiracial imperialism. While right-wing nationalists have by and large sustained a concentrated attack on the EU's encroachment upon national sovereignty (e.g., Sunier and Ginkel 2006), Europeanization has also shored up an emergent far right European nationalism in the figure of a pan-European integralism (Holmes 2000) or an ethnopluralist Europe of Fatherlands (Mammone, Godin, and Jenkins 2012a and 2013a; Von Mering and McCarty 2013). Not least because they are relatively well represented in its elected political organs (and especially in the European Parliament), the EU itself has become a significant source of funding for such movements. The ways in which Europeanization has thereby contributed to a regime of racial exclusion have not been lost on its critics from the left (see, e.g., ENAR 2005).

At the same time, while Europeanization has entailed new regimes of exclusion, pervasive hostility on the European far right to EU integration and expansion has been inseparable from the single issue that today most categorically cuts across and brings together the Continent's varied nationalists: the politics of immigration. Given the freedom of movement and residence within the EU and the absence of any consistent European immigration policy (Jaschke 2013), integration has been perceived—correctly—to critically compromise the ability of member countries to effectively set the terms of their own immigration policies as sovereign nation-states. Meanwhile, Europe's eastward and southward territorial push, and especially the question of Turkey's bid for full EU membership, have served as a rallying cry for right-wing extremists of all colors and have been profitably deployed to fuel a range of xenophobic anxieties. As the virtually uncontested top priority of far-right nationalists in nearly every European country today (see, e.g., Fillitz 2006; Gingrich 2006; Hervik 2006; Sunier and Ginkel 2006; Bulli and Tronconi 2012; Jamin 2012), the politics of immigration has also become strongly dominated by Islamophobic discourses. As chapter 3 will make clear for the German case, Islamophobia has not only become a political banner uniting the voices of different right-wing extremists but also runs like a thread across the political imaginaries of so-called mainstream publics, where Muslim immigrants have been increasingly construed as a civilizational threat to a series of putatively shared, Western, European values (Asad 2003b; Bunzl 2005; Mammone, Godin, and Jenkins 2012a; Von Mering and McCarty 2013). Often such civilizational doomsday scenarios bind culturally framed anxieties about Muslim immigrants together with socioeconomic fears of rising unemployment and dwindling welfare provision, as well as tropes of criminality and public (in)security (Holmes 2000; Pred 2000; Banks 2006). They thus render (particularly Muslim) immigrants as not only culturally incommensurable but also socially parasitical and incorrigibly delinquent. In chapter 3, we will explore in detail how this triple signification of the menacing immigrant as threatening cultural otherness, as essentialized criminal predispositions, and as welfare parasitism dominates the xenophobic discourse of the young right-wing extremists with whom I worked in Treptow-Köpenick.

YOUNG, NATIONAL, SOCIAL

In Germany, however, reunification and the shadow of National Socialism have inflected the extreme right in certain specific directions. In East Germany, and notwithstanding official denials, neo-Nazi groups had been active already in the early 1980s (Wagner 2001; Bugiel 2002). They emerged at the fringes of already marginalized subcultural scenes (punks, hooligans, skinheads) and, compared with their western brethren, they were poorly organized and of trifling numbers. The state classified and treated them—as it also did the punks, hooligans, and skinheads—simply as *Asoziale* (asocial), a default category for social misfits against which repressive measures included, for example, prohibitions on residence in or entry to Berlin, incarceration, and occasionally so-called *freigekauft* (literally, bought into freedom) exchanges in which the FRG paid the GDR western currency for handing over (political) prisoners.[2] Following an assault by a neo-Nazi skinhead mob on a punk concert in 1987, the government was forced to finally acknowledge the presence of "fascist" elements in its territory. And yet, while the GDR lacked neither institutionalized discrimination nor everyday racism, it was only after 1989 that verbal harassment and physical violence against immigrants surfaced as a significant problem. As a man of

---

[2] Starting in the late 1960s and until 1989, West Germany "bought" some 34,000 prisoners from the GDR for a total estimated at between 3.5 and 8 billion DM. The category of "political prisoners," however, did not exist in the GDR (which classified them simply as criminals) and was, rather, an imputation by the FRG. Among the prisoners were also neo-Nazis, some of whom—like the brothers Peter and Frank Hübner or the neo-Nazi rocker Arnulf-Winfried Priem—returned to live or engage in political activism in the East following reunification (Hasselbach and Bonengel 2001, 110; Jaschke, Rätsch, and Winterberg 2001, 125–29).

Ethiopian origin who arrived to the GDR as a student in 1980 and today heads a local intercultural center in East Berlin recalled:

> and then came the transition [*Wende*, i.e., 1989]. Really, that is. And then in the transition, it was difficult for us, because these people, who never had any contact with foreigners, when they received their freedom, they openly harassed people on the street. Then they really started to harass and to assault, and naturally I was afraid then . . . I bought an old car, a small one, for my family, so that we won't use public transportation.[3]

As movement, political organization, commercial activities, and cultural practices underwent significant liberalization, right-wing extremist currents seem to have turned more widespread, visible, and aggressive, culminating in fatally brutal pogroms against asylum seeker shelters in the years 1991–92.[4]

In turn, these developments impacted the extreme right throughout the Federal Republic in at least four important ways. First, unlike its predominantly conservative, economically right-wing forms in the preunification West, right-wing extremists today have swung decisively toward the reassertion of the socialist strands of National Socialism.[5] Established Western political parties have perhaps most visibly appealed to GDR-style rhetoric of social solidarity. The traditionally West German and socioeconomically conservative NPD and DVU (German People's Union), for example, have placed the "Wir sind das Volk!" (We are the people!) slogan of the so-called Monday demonstrations (*Montagsdemos*) at the heart of their election campaigns.[6] More radical extraparliamentary groups have similarly deployed socialist tropes in their propaganda, where the interests of the working class and their oppression by the rich frequently take central stage. Popular slogans in nationalist Internet portals and on banners,

---

[3] This periodization accords with similar findings in other studies (see, for example, Partridge 2012).

[4] Several complex processes fueled the growth of nationalist identifications, and violence, in the post-reunification East. One factor seems to have been the massive efforts of various western groups, often with the help of returnees who, already well before official reunification was concluded, brought with them financial resources, organizational skills, institutional networks, propaganda materials, and a wide array of commodities (Stöss 2000; Hasselbach and Bonengel 2001; for a more detailed analysis, see Jaschke, Rätsch, and Winterberg 2001).

[5] Interestingly, the marked shift in emphasis appears as the obverse of shifts in the political alignments of British working-class-cum-underclass ultranationalists in London. In London's East End, a socialist working-class consciousness had always been inflected by racist nationalism, traceable to its historical embeddedness in British colonialism. As class idioms all but evaporated in the postindustrial, Thatcherist era, such political consciousness has turned into a blatantly bigoted nationalism with a residual socialist flavor (Holmes 2000).

[6] The German word *Volk* carries special associations with National Socialist vocabulary, signifying at once the socialist concept of the working people or the masses and the nationalist notion of a pure ethnic nation. The popular weekly Monday demonstrations demanded political reforms and liberalization, and played an important role in bringing down the GDR, even while, for many of their participants, this was not their intended consequence.

stickers, flyers, or graffiti include, for instance, "Kapitalismus zerschlagen!" (Smash capitalism!), "Sozialismus ist braun" (Socialism is brown [in reference to the color associated with National Socialism]), or "Echter Sozialismus ist national" (Real socialism is national[ist]). In right-wing extremist demonstrations, orators declare, "the struggle is not about left and right, but about top and bottom." Both political parties and extraparliamentary groups enthusiastically supported the broad protests against the so-called Hartz IV reforms in the fall of 2004,[7] often joining mass demonstrations led by labor unions and left-wing organizations, for whom the uninvited guests generated tremendous embarrassment and triggered panicked debates about how to keep them away.

Critics from the left have—to be sure, with some degree of justification—condemned this apparent socialist turn as cynical electoral strategy (e.g., Pätzold 2005). But such assessments overlook the fact that the marriage of nationalism and socialism has long defined the margins of the political right in Europe; indeed, historically, it was fundamental for the emergence of fascist ideologies in the late nineteenth and early twentieth centuries (Sternhell 1995). No doubt, throughout the last century distinct far-right nationalist movements in Europe have unevenly incorporated socialist tropes into their rhetoric, at times foregrounding working-class anticapitalist commitments and at other times embracing free market nationalism. The economic conservatism of the extreme right in postwar West Germany owes something to the legacy of the annihilation of the socialist wing of the National Socialist Party under Hitler, as well as to the political polarization of Cold War Europe. The significance of reunification to the recent resurgence of a strongly socialist nationalism in Germany—and, arguably, to the surfacing of similar currents elsewhere in Europe—can therefore not be overstated.

Even more important, however, dismissals of socialist talk on the nationalist fringes as inauthentic, manipulative strategy fail to address the extent to which the right-wing socialist tide reveals itself far beyond the rhetoric of political campaigns and the pronouncements of public leaders. It is equally evident, for example, in park-bench conversations (frequently between the chronically unemployed) or in lay political analysis among friends and family. In such informal settings, recollections of full employment and generous welfare often blend with ethnic imaginations of the nation, admiration for National Socialist labor policies, racist scapegoating of immigrants, and, in the East, nostalgic remembrances of the GDR era. In such nostalgic fantasies, which operate as critical

---

[7] Consisting of a major reshuffle of unemployment and welfare policies aggressively promoted by then chancellor Gerhard Schröder, this restructuring constituted the fourth and last phase of Germany's "Agenda 2010," a series of labor market reforms named after Peter Hartz, who headed the commission mandated with formulating recommendations on the reforms. The approaching advent of Hartz IV witnessed massive mobilizations and regularly recurrent protests throughout Germany, many of which employed the loaded label *Montagsdemos* (see above) with reference to the GDR and 1989.

incisions into the here and now (see also Holmes 2000), socialism runs like a thread that weaves together the Third Reich, the GDR, and the present, over which its spectral absence hovers in the form of resentment and discontent.

A second major transformation in the nature of today's extreme right in Germany has consisted in its demographic makeover. In the West, more or less well-organized political parties, civil associations, or publishing houses on the fringes of the political right with continuous genealogies stretching back to the war era or before it have traditionally been dominated by culturally conservative older elites. In the East, where such foundations were absent, new recruits came largely from younger generations. The subcultural scenes and political idioms that ensued there have preserved the youth flavor with which they emerged (again, recall the campaign for a nationalist youth club in Treptow) even as the first cohorts have already reached middle age. That most of my informants considered increased government concern with youths as a pressing political priority, of course, had everything to do with their own age. However, especially hard-hit by high and lingering unemployment, they and others in the biographical phases of high school termination, professional training programs, or recent entry into the narrow labor market with slim prospects of obtaining work demonstrate particular receptivity to this youth-oriented rhetoric.

Third, younger and more socialist, the German extreme right since reunification has also witnessed a great diversification of cultural forms beyond the skinhead and hooligan aesthetics in vogue since the seventies. Especially among its more militant sympathizers, many have adopted the look of the antifascist and anarchist black block. At demonstrations, alongside garments featuring Gothic letterhead inscriptions or neo-Nazi rock bands' insignia, marchers sport T-shirts with the familiar iconic portrait of Che Guevara, whom they view as a fighter for national independence and emancipation from the yoke of American imperialism (and whose black, red, and white color combination conveniently matches that of the Reich). Even more ubiquitous are Palestinian headscarves, which, beyond their political anti-Zionist significance, and much like on the political left, have become trendy fashion items. The designs of clothes as well as banners have incorporated more diverse color palettes and textual elements that emulate the aesthetic conventions of comic books, digital media, or graffiti, all of which, until not long ago, had been strongly associated with the political left and spurned as "cultural pollution." An ever-increasing use of English, previously censured as linguistic contamination and similarly identified with the radical left, is everywhere evident.[8] Music, which fulfills a number of critical and interrelated functions (recruitment, financing, community building), has

[8] For example, demonstration banners, clothing items, or graffiti feature such English slogans as "Fight Jews," "Reds better run," "Smash the reds," "Fight terror, defend Europe!," "C4 [an explosive] for reds," or the skinhead rhyme "I've been pushed too far, now it's time to fight; I will never stop, until the wrongs are made right."

likewise undergone extensive diversification, incorporating such genres as hip-hop and techno, which until recently had been tabooed as un-German.[9]

This proliferation of styles, commodities, and cultural forms, and the novel interpretations and appropriations of existing fashions and consumer iden-tifications among largely working-class youths, in certain respects echo the themes that, during the seventies, captured the attention of a number of British scholars affiliated with the then emergent field of cultural studies. Authors such as Paul Willis (1977), Stuart Hall (1976), and Dick Hebdige (1979) documented the dynamic mix of subcultural groups that emerged among British working-class urban youths in the postwar decades. Looking at nonconformist coun-terschool cultures, skinheads, punks, and other countercultural phenomena, these authors argued against the prevalent reading of the provocative, at times shocking stylistic and cultural innovations of these groups as mere superficial chaos. Instead, they insisted that such novel countercultural phenomena in fact gave expression to complex articulations of both critical perspectives and less critical emulations of the capitalist system and of working-class values and ex-periences. The apparent rejection of conventional aesthetics just as much as of mainstream normative values constituted a certain interpretation of and re-sponse to the structural location of working-class youths in society. The moral panic with which the dominant culture reacted to some of these countercul-tural currents and subcultural practices reflected its refusal to acknowledge and to question its own ideological mystifications about the social order.

No doubt, the diversification of cultural forms, the revaluation of social-ist idioms, and the articulation of provocative political postures among young right-wing extremists in Germany suggest certain correspondences with the logic of countercultural subcultures. But the approach I develop in this book is different in several important respects. To begin, in contrast with the au-thors mentioned above, my interest is not in exploring subcultural practices as sites of working-class resistance and ideological critique but rather to consider young right-wing extremists as at once fundamental to and the effects of a cer-tain project of affective governance. To the extent that my young informants articulated critical perspectives on their society—and they did so in fact quite frequently—they generally expressed their discontents quite explicitly as so-cial and political critique, and far less so through their cultural practices and aesthetic preferences. Insofar as there was anything truly shocking or innova-tive about the cultural forms they incorporated and appropriated, this was so rather for the more traditional and orthodox-minded among their nationalist peers than for mainstream society at large, which reacted with panic not to the clothes they carried but, precisely, to the politics for which they stood. For the groups I studied, tellingly, cultural identifications played a minor—often

[9] For an extensive survey of musical developments and analyses of music's role in the extreme right scene in Germany, see Dornbusch and Raabe (2002).

insignificant—role in defining belonging and in shaping social relationships when compared with allegiance to xenophobic, far-right nationalism. As important, the semiotic perspective that informs my analysis throughout the study contrasts sharply with the approaches to discourse that cultural studies scholars both criticized (e.g., Willis and Corrigan 1983) and employed (e.g., Hebdige 1979).[10] Rather than positing the reality of a social structure that enters into complex articulations with a more or less autonomous symbolic system in the cultural sphere, I understand signs as inextricably embedded in social and political processes, with all their ambiguities and incoherencies, and as always operative in a range of relations that are not symbolic in their nature.[11]

Finally, a fourth dimension in which the impact of reunification and the end of the Cold War on right-wing extremism throughout Germany has been evident over the last couple of decades consists in a number of shifts in ideological emphases beyond the socialist turn. As elsewhere in Europe, immigration tops the list of political discontents and fuses seamlessly with preoccupations about unemployment, criminality, or EU expansion. More particular to Germany, however, are conflicts over the commemoration and memorialization of World War II. The number of participants in marches honoring Rudolf Hess, the "German" victims of Allied carpet bombings (which right-wing extremists refer to as the bombing Holocaust, or *Bombenholocaust*), or German military casualties has swelled. Right-wing extremists have also protested against changes in dominant memory cultures, and especially the accelerating erection of memorials to the victims of the Nazi regime, from the Holocaust Memorial in Berlin to a range of smaller monuments and synagogues-cum-memorials elsewhere. Furthermore, antiglobalization idioms have become integral to the political lexicon of the extreme right in Germany, where—much like on the left—they often appear synonymous with opposition to "American imperialism." Antiglobalization rhetoric lends itself well to incorporation into the extreme right's political idioms not only because of the latter's recent socialist turn but also because it offers an up-to-date and more widely tolerated substitute for the traditional figure of Jewish capital. Its sweeping appropriation by the NPD, for example, has marked a clear turn away from the party's traditional middle-class bourgeois values (Botsch and Kopke 2013). The interweaving of

[10]Especially in their heyday at the end of the seventies and the start of the eighties, cultural studies authors engaged—sometimes admiringly, sometimes critically—with strongly structuralist semiotic approaches to culture whose most paradigmatic expression arguably consisted in Roland Barthes's classical *Mythologies* (1972), in which Barthes identifies an underlying dominant ideological system that defines the logic behind a broad range of seemingly disparate cultural objects and phenomena.

[11]In particular, and as I explain in more detail in chapter 4, my understanding and foregrounding of signs and signification processes owe to the semiotic philosophy of Charles Peirce, according to which symbolic (that is, purely conventional) sign relations are but one of three possible forms of signification that include as well relations of iconicity (i.e., similarity) and indexicality (i.e., physical co-occurrence).

antiglobalization and anti-American rhetoric, of up-to-date aesthetic forms and subcultural identifications, and of traditional themes such as immigration or the memory of World War II allowed the young people with whom I worked to articulate contemporary mass-marketed images and consumer desires with time-honored legacies of German nationalism. Thus, at the hangout spots where they passed their time, at the soccer matches to which I accompanied them, or among the marchers at political rallies that regularly rumbled through the district, I encountered a broad spectrum of garments, slogans, hairdos, and opinions on matters of the day.

IMAGINING *OSSIS*

Xenophobic nationalisms throughout Europe, as we have seen, have been fairly consistent in targeting the figure of the (Muslim) immigrant, if in little else besides. This singular importance of anti-Islamic xenophobia across otherwise often quite varied movements corresponds quite closely to the commonsensical rendering of the political spectrum among the young people with whom I worked: left and right are really the same, except on immigration. But the story I tell in this book, if it belongs with a larger narrative about European right-wing extremism at the dawn of the twenty-first century, at another level is keenly interested in understanding the peculiarities of the national question and the management of hate in Germany. In chapter 3, I explore in detail how young right-wing extremists in Berlin articulate their relations to immigrants and ethnic alterity and how they negotiate layers of otherness in order to trace, in their own voices, their rendering of dominant imaginations of the social and political landscape. In the remainder of this chapter, however, I extend my reflections on the lingering impact of reunification into the quotidian discourses and practices of the people with whom I worked. My aim is to interrogate the persevering salience of the legacy of the East/West division of Germany, and how it continues to shape the ways in which these groups understand themselves and articulate their political orientations.

The merging of the memory of the GDR with that of the Third Reich and the concomitant imagination of the East as a neo-Nazi space have outlined a position for the right-wing extremist easterner, or *Ossi*. As we will see presently, the call to occupy that position has been answered. But before I turn to examine the quotidian effects of these discursive interpellations, a consideration of how the trope of the extreme right has operated in public imaginations of the East so as to fuse these two pasts is in order. If the spectral presence of National Socialism calls forth pervasive anxieties, strict taboos, and an enormous labor of repression that come to bear on the figure of the right-wing extremist, then that figure must also be understood against the historical horizon of 1989 and its aftermath. In the mass media, in parliamentary debates, in scholarly literature, and in a range of other discursive contexts, the trope of "Nazis in the East" has been pivotal in representations of the new federal states—so pivotal, in fact, that the phrase "right-wing extremism is not only an eastern phenomenon" ordinarily frames, apologetically as it were, discussions that turn out to revolve entirely about the East. A variety of terms—"nationally liberated zones" (*National befreite Zonen*), "fear zones" (*Angstzonen*), "no-go areas"[12]—have been coined or adopted to describe eastern landscapes under the allegedly de facto domination of neo-Nazi skinhead gangs.

The extent to which the East serves as the marked category in discussions of right-wing extremism is everywhere evident, whether it appears as an explicitly named location or as a conspicuous absence. Consider the following illustrative example. The documentary film *Dead in Lübeck* (*Tot in Lübeck*) investigates a 1996 arson attack on an asylum seekers' shelter in which ten inhabitants were killed and many more injured. The case remains unresolved. The documentary paints a picture of obstinate denials and suspiciously incompetent investigation efforts. It portrays a collective repression of the idea that the attack could have transpired "here" and a resilient denial that the perpetrators could have come from among "us." But nowhere do the "here" and "us" appear to reference anything beyond Lübeck and its residents; nowhere do they render the town, for example, as in any way representative—as a synecdoche, in other words—of West Germany, where it is located. In analogous cases in eastern towns, this would have been unimaginable, indeed impossible. In such cases, speakers would be compelled to employ shifters like "here" and "us" also in reference to the easternness of places and of people. Their refusal to frame racist violence in terms of the East would be broadly interpreted as complicity. Indeed, the corpus dedicated to considering the extreme right—and particularly racist violence—as both *in* the East and *of* the East is enormous, and includes journalistic reportage, academic literature, documentary films, novels, and television shows.[13]

Once the supposed link between the East and the right had been effectively established, theoretical explanations quickly followed.[14] Authoritarianism

---

[12] Each of these evocations of lawless lands in representations of the former GDR territories, of course, comes with its own political genealogy and ideological commitments: "nationally liberated zone," a paraphrase of a radical anti-imperialist Latin American phrase, is a term associated with the discourse of right-wing extremists, but in fact has been propagated by the media well before its popularization among nationalists (Döring 2008); the concept of "fear zones" has been adopted from feminist discourses about urban space; and "no-go areas" have generally been associated with civil war situations or with contexts of acute gang violence. For some examples of use, see Schröder (1997); ZDK (1998); Verfassungsschutz Brandenburg (2001a); Kleffner (2002); Weiss (2003); Staud (2005a).

[13] For a few illustrative examples, see Schröder (1997); Mentzel (1998); Wagner (1998); Zentrum demokratische Kultur (1998); Rau (2001); Bugiel (2002); Grass (2002a).

[14] I provide a more detailed review of theoretical explanations of right-wing extremism in chapter 7.

theory, for example, was classically elaborated to comprehend the vulnerability (or predisposition) of Germans to National Socialism.[15] It linked deep-seated Kaiser-era cultural norms and family structures with Hitler's rise to power. In post-reunification Germany, the same theoretical model has been transposed to trace an ostensibly special Ossi vulnerability to right-wing extremism back to GDR traditions of order and discipline, lingering relics of a backward past (Butterwegge and Meier 2002; cf. Boyer 2006a and 2006b).[16] The implication, of course, is that the West, by contrast, has already conquered its fascist-authoritarian heritage. The construal of the easterner as deterministically bound by a collective consciousness, her behavior and thought prescribed by cultural injunctions, is redolent of colonial discourses. Like figurations of the colonial subject, the Ossi is depicted as not quite yet the autonomous agent of Western liberalism, not quite yet free of tradition. For this reason a violent racist assault *in* the East will appear both as a synecdoche, as representative *of* the East, and as a metonym, as comprehensible *through* the East.

Theoretical frameworks, in turn, have both informed and drawn upon therapeutic interventions in which the East and easterners appear as the authoritarian other of a democratic West.[17] In such interventions, which always straddle (or better, perform) the distinction between state and civil society,[18] the image of a tolerant and democratic political culture appears as the symbolic representation of a lack. The East appears deficient, incomplete, in need of education, therapeutic rehabilitation, and, at times, even emergency procedures, to safeguard it from the two historical traumas that it has yet to surpass.[19] As scholars

[15] Developed by Theodor W. Adorno and others (1950), the theory employed a psychoanalytic approach to account for the rise of fascism as a mass phenomenon and provided a conceptual basis for the development of the F-scale, a quantitative instrument for measuring fascist orientations. The theory relates the emergence and consolidation of fascist orientations to a particular personality type, itself the consequence of distinct, intimate relations and early childhood experiences, and of culturally pervasive family structures that cultivate traditionalism, submission to authority, antidemocratic attitudes, and hatred of marginalized social groups.

[16] In one particularly scandalous case, in August 2005 the CDU's Jörg Schönbohm explained a multiple infanticide case in Brandenburg by reference to the mother's GDR past and by implication, as critics were quick to point out, to the shared biography of all easterners (*Berliner Zeitung* 2005d).

[17] In chapter 7 I consider a number of therapeutic methods that aim to reform right-wing extremist individuals. In chapter 8 I examine at length the program Civitas, which, during my time in the field, dominated the spectrum of interventionist efforts against xenophobia and right-wing extremism in the East as a region.

[18] I describe the ways in which such interventions mark and resolve that distinction concretely in the situated practices of local organizations in chapter 8. My view here is in-line with a number of authors who have noted how strategies of governance have shifted under the neoliberal state, while expressing skepticism with regard to claims that state power has been declining (Mitchell 1991; Comaroff and Comaroff 2001; Trouillot 2001; Aretxaga 2003; Sassen 2003; Comaroff and Comaroff 2006; Sharma 2006).

[19] Not surprisingly, in colloquial parlance such interventions are often described as arrogant *Besserwessis* (a pun on *Besserwisser*, meaning know-it-all) telling "us" (easterners) what's good.

have noted, it is difficult not to notice how these interventionist discourses perform a close narrative variation on the aftermath of the war. The narrative structure of the Allies—particularly of the United States—as the good protagonist defeating a barbarian totalitarian regime and subsequently reconstructing the economy, setting up democratic institutions, and instilling liberal values has changed only slightly. In a sort of iconic transposition, the Federal Republic here appears as the strong, liberal, capitalist state fixing up a post-totalitarian territory: providing aid for economic reconstruction, reeducating the masses in democracy, introducing new consumption habits, and, not least, administering the purges of perpetrators (cf. Borneman 1993; Glaeser 2000). During the Cold War, the figure of the GDR enabled the FRG to open up a distance not only with its contemporary state-socialist rival but also, by implication, with its National Socialist past. The contrast with East Germany allowed the West to corroborate and reaffirm its liberal democratic credentials and hence to fortify its claim to a radical difference with the Third Reich.[20] After 1989, however, the East has continued to serve the same purpose, casting Germany's liberal-democratic society as mature enough to crusade for what it once had to be taught.

The analogy between the two narratives of 1945 and 1989, and the consequent fusion of the historical horizons for which they stand, take many forms, some quite extreme. The wholesale purges that followed reunification—in government branches, academia, juridical professions, media establishments, law enforcement, and leading positions in education or health (see, e.g., Borneman 1992; Glaeser 2000; Boyer 2001)—far exceeded the halfhearted denazification procedures in the immediate postwar West.[21] GDR archival material, and especially Stasi (Ministry for State Security) files, have been made accessible to the wide public to an extent that Third Reich and Gestapo documents had not been even decades after the war, and even for scholars and experts.[22] In chapter 9, I will discuss in greater detail the campaign to erase physical traces of the GDR past from public space. For the time being, let us note that, for many easterners, one of the particularly disturbing dimensions of this campaign consisted in the renaming of streets that commemorated antifascist resistance fighters who after the war had supported communism. The erasure of their memory from public

[20] Of course, the GDR for its part used the FRG for precisely the same purpose, identifying fascism with capitalism and presenting socialism as the surest defense against it (see, e.g., Borneman 1993).

[21] The purges reached far beyond Stasi employees or SED loyalists; beyond, too, the broad files of party members and the tens of thousands listed in Stasi files as informers. They also included the relatives of such people and, in academic institutions, their students.

[22] It is important to recall that, far from an arbitrary decision by the federal government imposed upon a passive population, the opening to the public of classified GDR archival materials was performed (also) in response to wide demands by many East Germans. However, the fact that here, in contrast to elsewhere, the voices of former GDR citizens were heard and their demands so duly and promptly granted exposes the political will on the side of the federal government to conduct this chirurgical intervention.

space de facto placed them on equal ground with their Nazi enemies, whose names were similarly removed following the war (Verheyen 1997). In the domain of political discourse, meanwhile, the concept of extremism has effectively linked fascism and communism, the PDS (Party of Democratic Socialism, the electorally successful offspring of the GDR's ruling party, the SED) and the NPD.

A dialectic of proximity and distance with the easterner as a subaltern national figure has been evident in fields as disparate as discourses about child-rearing practices, variations in linguistic forms, confrontations of divergent professional cultures, or contrasts in spatial orientations (Boyer 2000; Glaeser 2000; Stevenson and Theobald 2000). It has left its indelible mark on budget worksheets, Bundestag deliberations, policy papers, mass publicity, and scientific discourse just as much as on spontaneous interactions, at soccer games, at the pub, or at the workplace, through jokes and side comments, or in the negotiation of personal and professional relationships. The figure of the right-wing extremist has been key to this dialectical constitution of a liberal Germany against its own internal negativity, its own limit; its own specters. The immense social resources spent in this labor of othering and the wide array of invested forces betray deep anxieties about the lack of difference, about proximity and contamination, about being and becoming.

GRANDPA WAS SS, DAD WAS STASI

For me, the anthropologist, the incessant and sometimes counterintuitive articulation between these two horizons—the GDR and the Third Reich, being an easterner and being a right-winger—first emerged in the field in myriad quotidian moments and situated voices. Far outside the institutional walls of government agencies or the academic community, far, too, from the artifacts of knowledge that they produce and propagate, on the shabby benches of run-down playgrounds, amid the ecstatic multitudes at the local soccer stadium, or underneath the dull gaze of countless windows of communist-era high-rises, similar images and imaginations come to light in a variety of everyday situations and narrations of self. In certain settings, their proximity, and the ways in which, in their proximity, they reciprocally index each other, become taken for granted, almost banal. Let me illustrate, by way of two examples, how this happens.

Consider the scenery at local third-league soccer matches of the hugely popular club Union. For the die-hard fans I accompanied, as for many soccer enthusiasts around the world, their club stood for a vast range of meanings and functions.[23] The team's actual performance was, if not entirely, then almost be-

---

[23] Union constitutes a site, a discourse, and a ritual for the creation and maintenance of social relations. Counting among the clubs' fans shapes consumption habits, defines adversaries, and ar-

side the point, and it has performed badly pretty much since its foundation in 1906.[24] During my fieldwork, for example, when Union slipped from the third North-East German regional league to the fourth local (Berlin-Brandenburg-Mecklenburg-Vorpommern) league, those whom I accompanied to its games hardly complained.[25] Instead, they appreciated lower entrance fees, shorter travel to matches, and cheaper beer. Older fans describe the club as an under-dog, working-class team fettered by lack of political sponsorship in the GDR. Following reunification it has maintained a strong eastern flavor in dichotomy with the western Hertha, Berlin's flagship club. It has also won bad publicity as home to violent, racist, right-wing extremist hooligans. Many of my friends in Berlin expressed sincere concern for my personal safety, as well as for the sound-ness of my judgment, upon learning of my visits to Union matches. I found the crowds at the stadium at once far more diverse and much more ordinary than what their reputation had led me to expect. Yet it was also easy enough to spot ultranationalist fashion items, right-wing extremist rough prison tattoos, racist harassment of "non-German" players, or how all these merged with the club's Ossi signature. Black leather jackets would display the GDR flag, the emblem of the Young Pioneers, or the logos of socialist commodities next to the Iron Cross, the digits 88, or the black sun.[26] GDR hats would shade pendants with miniature representations of Thor's hammer.[27] Coats decorated with "Ostber-lin" (East Berlin) in Gothic script would half cover banned right-wing extremist shirts. I found similar semiotic convergences at matches of another East Berlin club, BFC Dynamo, once associated with the Stasi and nowadays with neo-Nazi hooligans. As if to drive the point home, some BFC Dynamo fans would wear T-shirts with the print "Grandpa was with the SS, dad was with the Stasi, I'm with BFC Dynamo."

Or consider an August evening on which I found Danny and Norman at Khan's, a favorite hangout, leaning over the table between them, their hands busy. Nineteen-year-old Danny cultivated a trendy, contemporary, rightist skin-head appearance: his dark hair meticulously clipped, three silver hoop earrings

---

ticulates sentiments of nationalism and political identity. It also produces a temporality organized around repetitive events and projected schedules and prescribes what leisure is about. It no doubt enriches language with a range of lexical terms and metaphors. Not least, Union fandom generates a plethora of narratives (comic, heroic, tragic) and chronotopes (the train ride, the line outside the stadium, the match) that serve diverse purposes.

[24] Since my fieldwork, however, a determined management seems to have turned the club's for-tune around.

[25] This refers to the numbering of German leagues at the time of my research. The numbering changed in 2008 following a restructuring of the league system.

[26] The Iron Cross was the Reich's badge of honor; the number 88 stands as an encrypted acro-nym for the illegal "Heil Hitler," H being the eighth letter in the alphabet; and the black sun was an SS symbol.

[27] A much-loved jewelry piece in extreme right-wing social milieus.

Figure 1. Fans at a Union match. The woman wears necklaces with the Iron Cross and Thor's hammer pendants; a rendering of the triskelion, a three-pronged symbol also known as the Celtic swastika, is visible behind the Union scarf of the man behind her.

with Gothic-style designs dangling from his left ear, two silver rings with a skull and an Iron Cross on his left hand, almost invariably a blue jacket with red lining left open just enough to expose a legally banned shirt beneath it, light-colored pants, and New Balance sneakers.[28] In the early nineties his family moved from West Berlin to the Ghetto (see chapter 1) where they could afford a bigger apartment. His mother, a butcher, for many years now has not worked due to a health disability and has lived off a modest pension. His father, a construction worker, left home when Danny was young and returned a few years later. He died in 1998. "It is much better without him," Danny dismissed my expression of sympathy, describing his father as "a real asshole" who violently abused him and his siblings. He lived with his mother, her new boyfriend (who also did not work for health reasons and received welfare), and his two younger siblings. His two older siblings had already moved out. Danny graduated from secondary school (*Gesamtschule*) with an extended general school certificate (*erweiterter Hauptschulabschluss*). While this placed him at the bottom of the German hierarchy of school diplomas, it nevertheless represented an educational achievement few among his peers could boast, allowing him to enter a relatively competitive carpentry vocational training program. With two years of training still ahead of him, he was pessimistic about his prospects of securing employment in his profession and intended to enlist in the military, in which he saw the promise of high earnings and world travels.

Norman was a twenty-year-old whose starkly disheveled appearance stood in sharp contrast with Danny's. A fanatical fan of Union, he lived with his parents in a quiet neighborhood near the Grünau train station. He graduated from secondary school without qualifying for any diploma but, with the help of the social workers, succeeded in securing a place in a mason training program, at the very bottom of the vocational hierarchy. He failed all three opportunities for which he was eligible to pass the final exam. Time and again he stumbled into and out of various welfare-to-work positions and low-skill vocational training programs where he was invariably and summarily dismissed for tardiness, nonattendance, or unsatisfactory performance. When I met him, he had been working part-time at IKEA in a welfare program that complemented his state remittances, but he was soon fired on suspicion of stealing. He later illegally sold newspapers door-to-door in a fishy scheme that required him to commit for two years, but he left, under threats of violence from his employers, after only a month due to police harassment. Subsequently, he cleaned himself up and entered a course that would have qualified him as a guard for a private security company, only to fail the final exam. Norman had a marked proclivity for alcohol, brawls, and misdemeanors. A black hat with the acronym DDR (German for GDR) inscribed in white at its front covered his receding hairline.

---

[28] The popularity of New Balance sneakers among German right-wing extremists is broadly understood to owe to the brand's N logo.

Seated across from each other at the outdoor beer garden at Khan's, a Bangladeshi eatery adjacent to the Grünau train station about which I will have more to say in chapter 6, Danny and Norman held their cell phones in their hands and snickered intermittently. Norman had been copying ring-tones from Danny's cell phone to his own. Once they were done with the exchange, they let me transfer the audio files they had shared to my own phone. The assortment included an unidentifiable sound-clip of a childlike female voice that talked about killing all the blacks and Jews; some virulent lines, dubbed into German, by the character Derek from the film *American History X*, a cult movie among German right-wing extremists that tells the story of a militant neo-Nazi skinhead; a techno mix, also of unidentified authorship, that included rhythmically repetitive shouts of "Deutschland, Sieg Heil" (Germany, hail victory!), the National Socialist chant that, during the Third Reich, accompanied the Hitler salute; and an orchestral performance of the melody of the national anthem of the GDR.

Such momentary flashes of visual and auditory convergences appear as well in nostalgic narratives, voiced in distinct social contexts. The right-wing extremists with whom I worked, too young to have retained any meaningful memories of life in the GDR, frequently spoke affirmatively about it, just as they did about the Third Reich. "Before almost everything was better," as one of them put it, "if everybody says so, there must be truth to it." Many shared similar opinions. In my research, the circulation of such narratives appeared in places like the Kugel, a small square at an entrance to the Ghetto, where almost daily young people gathered from the rows of colorless buildings and overheard older unemployed men wax nostalgic about cheap beer, low expenses, strong solidarity, and full employment.[29] GDR hats were plentiful, as were neo-Nazi fashion items: earrings or pendants with Gothic designs, T-shirts featuring Nordic mythological symbols, or black, white, and red jackets with the inscription "Berlin—the Reich's capital" (Berlin—Reichshauptstadt).

The young people at the Kugel found themselves in a dialectical suspension between two nostalgic horizons. The first came to life in the figure of the men seated across from them, whose daily recitations of longing invoked a GDR past that captured the imagination of the young audience. The elderly home behind the Kugel embodied the second nostalgic horizon. Gino, a slim twenty-year-old whom I first met at the Kugel, and about whom I will have more to say in the chapters that follow, was born in a small town near Dresden. His family moved to the Ghetto in 1990, when he was six, after his stepfather at the time found work in coal delivery in Berlin. He had no contact with his biological father, who left home a few years earlier. His mother, a housewife and the daughter of leather factory workers, became a supporter of the right-wing extremist Repub-

---

[29] Elsewhere, I discuss in detail the circulation of narratives at the Kugel and the nostalgic modes in which both the GDR and the National Socialist pasts come to be remembered there (Shoshan 2012).

Figure 2. The Kugel. A residential building and the elderly home are visible in the background.

likaner Party after reunification. In Berlin, Gino was kicked out of one school after another for misbehavior and alcohol abuse before dropping out entirely without earning any academic diploma or vocational certificate. His mother had had several different partners since they arrived at the Ghetto, all of whom lived in their apartment, and most of whom Gino remembered as violent and abusive. He left home to settle in a friend's apartment when he was nineteen years old following a violent confrontation with her. Gino was no stranger to the elderly home adjacent to the Kugel, his favorite hangout spot. As he once recounted to me, "There were also some [at the elderly home] that . . . you could see it in their eyes, all the things they've done . . . I went in there on my own, because I wanted to simply ask them . . . I did not become a nationalist for nothing . . . that's why I had to listen to what they said." Often, the circulation of similar memories of WWII and the Third Reich proceeds in family and other intimate contexts. Gino's own grandfather, who still lives in Saxony, taught him about weapons and told him stories of manly brotherhood and courage during the war. A faded black-and-white photograph of the grandfather in a Waffen-SS uniform stood on the dresser in his apartment.

As they travel across generations, dinner tables, and benches at the Kugel, certain temporal shifters like "then" (*damals*) or "before" (*früher*) come to in-dicate a distance between the present and an amorphous past in which red and brown blend indistinguishably. When I asked my young informants to clarify what they meant by "then" or "before," I encountered a nonspecifiable referent: "earlier," "just before," or "the way things once were." Andreas Glaeser, in his superb ethnography of the Berlin police, argues that for officers from the East, the shifter "today" shatters time into incongruous fragments (2000, 182). In the case at hand, by contrast, temporal shifters perform a feat of historical fusion. More than a few of my young right-wing extremist informants proclaimed to me their desire to see the Berlin Wall rebuilt—a statement that should be understood, of course, as metonymic of fantasies of full employment, no immigrants, and authentic solidarity. The wall, as a cipher for reunification, appears in the image of a temporal partition between now and then whose reversal holds the promise of return.

These temporal convergences between the two pasts of the GDR and the Third Reich—at times lasting, at others quite momentary; some seemingly fortuitous, others less so—reverberate in the ways in which young right-wing extremists align Ossi and rightist selves (and, respectively, *Wessi* and leftist others). In other words, the same semiotic contrasts that take part in the fabrication of one set of differences (Ossi versus Wessi, rightist versus leftist) reappear in virtually identical form in the production of the other set, so that the two constantly slip into each other. Below, I describe four different domains in which these two sets of contrasts seem to align themselves with each other in the speech of young right-wing extremists: an ethics of personal solidarity, a moral economy of violence, an uneven access to the state, and a regime of cultural authenticity.[30]

Gino, Norman, and their friends outlined an ethic of friendship and solidarity structured by steadfast reciprocity and informal intimacy that they understood as distinctly Ossi, and to which they opposed Wessis as materialist and conceited. Consider twenty-one-year-old Uta, for whom living with her Wessi boyfriend only reaffirmed her convictions about the differences between them. Short and plump, her shoulder-length blond hair pulled backward, Uta came of age at the Kugel and its environs. Her father, with whom she had barely any contact since her parents separated when she was twelve, used to work for the Stasi. Like him, her mother's next long-term partner also suffered from alcohol abuse. Her mother had earlier switched between many jobs and training programs and at the time was struggling to establish herself as an in-home day care provider. Uta dropped out of school and left home to live with her boyfriend when she was sixteen. She later returned to vocational school but the grades with which she graduated only barely sufficed for a subsequent low-skill service professions training program, which she never completed. She then picked up her secondary education once more and had been studying at the time toward a technical school certificate (*Realschulabschluss*) that, so she hoped, would

---

[30] For a more extended discussion of these differentiation strategies and of the interpellation of Ossi/rightist subjectivities, see Shoshan (2008a).

offer her access to more competitive vocational training programs. Like many among her friends, Uta defied neat distinctions: she voted SPD and PDS, kept her appearance clean of political implications, favored hip-hop and techno over "nationalist" music, and even smoked marijuana occasionally.[31] But, as we will see in chapter 3, one would look in vain for meaningful differences between her political worldview and that of her more conspicuously and self-consciously right-wing friends. Uta described her boyfriend, who had been completing a metalworker vocational training program, as follows:

> We [Ossis] are certainly not so materialist. Like, we share more, and we're really not as materialist and so directly focused on money, you know. And with him you notice, for example, that he's very materialist, I mean, it's quite extreme.

Romantic relationships with Wessis, however, presented a rare exception for those with whom I worked in Treptow. Even friendships were scarce, and where they did evolve, my informants would attribute them to the disposition of their Wessi friends to assimilate socially by emulating Ossis and taking on their ethical standards. Consider seventeen-year-old Freddi, born and raised in Treptow. His mother, a store clerk by training, had worked as a cook in a local amusement park. His father, trained as a car mechanic in the GDR, had found a well-paying job with the Berlin Water Company. He left his parents' spacious house at sixteen after a particularly brutal incident with his father, who often used violence to discipline him, and since then had lived in no less than six different apartments. He graduated from secondary school with a mediocre general diploma (*Hauptschulabschluss*) and spent a year working informal manual jobs and applying for vocational programs before he was admitted to storage logistics training. Freddi accounted for the handful of friendships he had consolidated with Wessis who had moved to his neighborhood in the following manner:

> They prefer it; many Wessis say, "Ossis are cooler" ... they say they get along better with Ossis than with their fellow countrymen, with their own people, with Wessis.

Such Wessis, a select few, may accordingly become baptized as honorary Ossis:

> I told [my Wessi friend], "You're an Ossi right?" "What? No, I'm a Wessi!" [he replied]. And I'm like, "Well then, you can consider that as a compliment." Just because he was totally okay, I don't know, I found it right.

Similar differentiation strategies appear to operate for the pair rightist/leftist. Freddi recalled how his nationalist friends came to his aid when, particularly penniless, he could not afford basic necessities like toilet paper, cigarettes,

---

[31] Young nationalists often talk of hip-hop, techno, and smoking marijuana (in contradistinction to heavy metal music or alcohol consumption) as the habits of leftists and foreigners. In fact, however, more than a few young right-wing extremists in Berlin listen to techno and hip-hop and consume marijuana.

or food. He was proud of how they rushed to his side when he found himself outnumbered and under the threat of violence. Most of all, he glorified how they once covered up for his complicity in a certain criminal incident for which they were found guilty on charges of burglary, theft, physical injury, and damage to property:

> That's what a real friend is, and something like that I see among the Deutsche [lit., Germans, i.e., rightists], among the neo-Nazis, that's sticking together. Most of those I know would take a knife in for you, they would get beaten up for you. Something like that doesn't happen often among leftists.

Much like this ethics of solidarity and the similar contrasts it draws between easterners and westerners on the one hand and leftists and rightists on the other, young right-wing extremists elaborate a set of differences and convergences within the domain of a particular moral economy of violence. Here, leftists and Wessis appear as immoderately brutal at best, fanatically sadistic at worse. By contrast, my informants would explain, rightists and Ossis do indeed occasionally act violently, but they do so either for "fun"—that is, as play among friends—or in response to unwarranted provocations. Even then, the young rightists I knew would add, they always kept within certain reasonable boundaries. Gino, whom I mentioned above, had already been convicted of several violent offenses, including serious physical injury. Here is how he distinguished between his social cliques and western ones:

> I mean in the West in general they're just somehow, well, how should I say it, keen on beating [schlagfreudig]. All the Ossis, here, it's never like that. I don't know why it's so or where it comes from. They're just, they take more drugs maybe or something like that, I don't know, they're just like that. Or they just start hitting faster than Ossis and just don't talk.

Compare Gino's formulation of a moral economy of violence through the contrasts he outlines between Ossis and Wessis with his assessment of differences between nationalist and antifascist violence:

> The Antifa is just really shameless, so to speak. They only stop when you really can't move yourself. The rightists don't do it like that. I'm not trying to do propaganda for rightists, but it's just like that. I know very well, I was also in fights. But the rightists just stopped quickly, so to speak when he screamed or when his nose started bleeding, just so they know, "Okay, he can't defend himself anymore, he's down on the floor," so to speak. But those who go on kicking those who lie on the floor, that's also quite a thing. It's a shameless thing to do. That's just the way it is with the Antifa.

Wessis, it is often said, just like leftists, are even known to assault women. The implication here, of course, is that nationalists and Ossis know better. Needless to say, the extent to which these fantasies held water was both negligible and largely irrelevant. We shall have occasion to encounter Freddi again in chapter 3 bragging about kicking a Turkish man on the floor, and violence against women was pervasive. Nevertheless, in these fantasies, westerners and leftists alike are conjured as sharing a moral deficit. Bloodthirsty and ruthless, they flout the norms of civility by which easterners and rightists abide, even, and especially, in violence.

A third domain in which these two sets of contrasts collapse into each other has to do with how, for right-wing extremists in East Berlin, Ossis and rightists alike suffer from institutional discrimination, if in different ways. Both mark positions from which to voice resentment against unequal proximity with and access to power—usually conceived in the figure of the state. As right-wingers, the people with whom I worked complained of unfair treatment. Legal repression and political persecution (which stand at the center of chapters 4 and 5), they insisted, singled them out while turning a blind eye to their leftist adversaries. If concerns about anticonstitutional and antidemocratic politics are really at issue in their criminalization, they asked, why should a similar penal regime not apply to openly communist parties and organizations, or to symbols associated not only with National Socialism but also with the GDR or the Soviet Union? Why should Stalin not suffer the same fate as Hitler? And why so many memorials for the communist resistance but none for the fallen German soldiers? Young right-wing extremists on various occasions voiced their frustrations in the form of these and similar questions. Frequently, too, they would accuse not only the state but also mass media representations of intentional and unfair bias, that is, of scandalizing the extreme right while ignoring (some would say, silencing) the violence of leftists and immigrants.

Speaking now as Ossis, my informants would list a range of other grievances against institutional discrimination. Provisions for reckoning the quantities of various state remittances, for example, distinguish between beneficiaries who reside in the new federal states and those in the old ones. Freddi again:

> People say, "There is no East and West anymore." Wouldn't that be nice? I see that in my [vocational training] class. I'm the worst paid one in my class, because I'm the only one who gets paid by the East rate. There's still a West rate and an East rate . . . [so I'm] an East-rate-loser [*Osttarifverlierer*].

Expressing his resentment against what he perceived as unwarranted discrimination against easterners, Freddi coins a pun on the phrase *Wendeverlierer* (transition loser), a term used derogatively to refer to former GDR citizens whom reunification impacted negatively. Presumably reflecting uneven costs of living, differential pay scales for the former GDR states apply not only for welfare and state allowances, but also for salaries in the public sector or in temp-job agencies, and for a range of other employers. But differential rates of welfare and other state allowances are perhaps especially glaring in the case of Berlin, where West and East come together.

As easterners, my informants complained as well of discrimination at the workplace by scornful Wessi superiors and of frequent bantering from colleagues. Take Ole, a tall and large-bodied nineteen-year-old who was born in a small nearby town in Brandenburg. His mother, a store clerk at a supermarket, moved to Berlin with his younger brother after separating from his father when he was thirteen. Ole joined her in Treptow two years later, after his father, a machine fitter by training who had worked in landscaping, became unemployed and alcoholic. He continued his secondary education in Berlin and graduated with a technical school diploma. Ole, who at the time was completing his third and final year of vocational training as an electrician, protested:

> When I started at work, for example . . . Well, my company is after all in Spandau; that's West, and since that's where we are, there were also many people from the West. And then there was this sort of, let's say, teasing. One guy there ate a banana and said to me, "Hey, look here, do you know this thing here? Do you know it?"[32]

We have seen how Wessis who assimilate and who acknowledge the moral superiority of easterners may become baptized as honorary Ossis. But the reverse process of metamorphosis also holds true: Ossis at the winning end of discrimination, who fail tests of material inferiority on the one hand and moral superiority on the other, can come to appear too Wessi. Freddi, for example, positioned himself as a discriminated Ossi with respect to his good friend Karsten, who was also an easterner:

> If I now got to know [Karsten] for the first time, I would say he is a Wessi. It's just like that; don't ask me why, but I would immediately say he is a Wessi. Because I know that he is an Ossi but I just say so that he's a Wessi. Because he's also, like totally arrogant and . . . he gets everything handed to him on a fucking silver platter [er kriegt alles in den Arsch geschoben], more or less, from his parents, [who are] lawyers. He really gets fucking everything on a silver platter. He got an apartment. He got one thousand euro starting capital. I didn't. I didn't get anything, more or less, you know. I got everything here [in my apartment] completely on my own.

In other words, Ossis who are perceived as having benefited from unfair privileges are not allowed to complicate the plot—they are simply reclassified as Wessis.

A fourth and last domain in which, for Freddi and his peers, the rightist and the easterner inhabit a similar spot is a regime of cultural authenticity. As rightists, they simply took it for granted that their lifestyles and political visions followed authentic German traditions—at least far more so than those of leftists. Tellingly, right-wing extremists refer to themselves as "Germans" (Deutsche), a term they employ interchangeably with *Rechte* (rightists) or *Nationale* (na-

---

[32] West Germans have ridiculed East Germans for allegedly rushing across the border as soon as the wall fell and gobbling unfamiliar fruits such as kiwis and bananas.

tionalists). Notwithstanding the cultural shifts I have described earlier in this chapter, which have transformed the German far right in recent decades, many young nationalists continue to emphasize linguistic and aesthetic forms they view as authentically German and to associate those they view as foreign imports with the political left. For example, young right-wing extremists generally consider drug use as alien pollution and typically leftist, while thinking of alcohol as indigenously German and characteristically rightist.

In turn, as scholars have shown, from the western point of view East Germans have been absorbed into the reunified nation as past sedimentations of more authentic—if not necessarily laudable—German traditions, including, but not limited to, their alleged authoritarian tendencies (Boyer 2001 and 2006b). According to West German acquaintances of mine in Berlin, easterners greeted even close friends with handshakes, a habit they found odd and that they associated with older generations and culturally "traditional" people. They, by contrast, preferred the hug as a form of greeting among friends. East German acquaintances of mine, meanwhile, generally viewed the hug as a western importation of foreign mannerisms and, by implication, as culturally alien. Most of the easterners I knew also followed what they described as the "correct" German way of telling the time, while most westerners used a "hybrid" form.[33] In dominant representations, just as much as in the linguistic and corporeal performance of self, easterners have been cast as authentically grounded in ethnotypically German traditions. In contrast, and depending on the speaker, Wessis have been construed either as emancipated from such traditional bonds or as corrupted by Americanization.

In these and other ways, for young right-wing extremists in Berlin (and, I would argue, for many others in Germany), a certain indexical association between the Ossi and the right-wing extremist has come to appear almost intuitive. Of course, the fabrication of an Ossi/right-wing extremist alterity, if it serves to exorcize the nation of some of its demons by projecting them onto an internal other, also charts paths of inclusion. The very blending of the GDR and the Third Reich grounds the East's history in familiar terrain, in "our" history, even if in an allochronic (that is, as belonging to a different time) manner. The Ossi as right-wing extremist gestures toward a shared past, a common identity, and an essential likeness, blemished only by a certain historical tardiness, by uneven progress through history. The very form of exclusion here provides the means for eventual reintegration as an earlier, obsolete version of the national we. In some sense, then, all these apparent contrasts in fact turn out to draw

[33] According to the "German" convention, parts of an hour are indicated always by the round hour to come, rather than by that which has passed. Thus, in German "quarter nine," "half nine," and "three quarter nine" (*Viertel-*, *halb-*, and *drei viertel neun*) correspond respectively to the English "quarter past eight," "half past eight," and "quarter to nine." Many westerners I knew seemed to maintain the German convention for "half nine" but reverted to the English-style "quarter past eight" and "quarter to nine" (*Viertel nach/vor*).

the boundaries not of exclusion from but rather of inclusion in the national collective. In chapter 3, I shift my attention to the absent third in this inclusive exclusion: the essentially alien figure of the immigrant who must either be tolerated as different (multiculturalism) or conform to a presumed dominant culture (*Leitkultur*), despite her fundamental otherness (integrationism). More precisely, I turn to look both at the relations that young right-wing extremists in Berlin elaborate to that figure and the ways in which, against that figure, they construe and imagine a range of other social relations.

The Kebab and the *Wurst*

IF, FOR THE YOUNG PEOPLE WITH WHOM I WORKED, the distinctions that carve the German nation into East and West divide it as well into right and left, then the East/West dichotomy marks for them also, at another level, the difference between those who belong to that nation and those who do not. Almost furtively, the old political division of the Cold War shifts in their discourse to designate an urban landscape of ethnic difference whose uneven spatial distribution becomes part of their geographical imagination. Their predicament as they navigate a heterogeneous cityscape in which they cannot but routinely live out a proximity with those others whom they perceive as threatening is, of course, in some sense the predicament of every city dweller, the very material from which urban sociability emerges[1]—even if those others and the dangers they signal have historically taken very different and context-specific forms. The city has always gathered diverse populations, ethnically and otherwise; it has always involved encounters with the foreign, the strange, and the menacing; and it has always hosted places that marked danger for some, home for others.

Nevertheless, the position of right-wing extremists in East Berlin also reflects recent global processes that have reconfigured relations of alterity in urban contexts, redrawing both political agendas and quotidian habits. The ways in which, for example, shifting patterns of immigration have changed configurations of alterity in European cities (in some, no doubt, far more so than in Berlin[2]) is evident enough if we pause to think of Franz Fanon's reflections on walking the streets of Paris in the early 1950s as a black man (1967), which today would no doubt

---

[1] Georg Simmel, for example, describes urban sociability as inherently antagonistic, entailing an intensification of violent stimuli that results in a blasé attitude and productive of negative forms of social relations, of mutual aversion and repulsion, as strategies of self-preservation. Often, Simmel argues, the freedom of the metropolis is not a pleasant experience (1964).

[2] Douglas Holmes, for example, identifies a sense of "exile at home" among BNP (British National Party) supporters in London as a way of making sense of the ethnic heterogeneity of their working-class neighborhoods (2000, 124).

require revision.[3] But beyond long-term demographic changes in the composition of urban Europe, shifts in the visibility of certain forms of difference owe also to more recent transformations in political cultures. A number of authors have linked contemporary reconfigurations in the terms under which identities become essentialized and embodied with the emergence of late capitalist forms of social differentiation, evident in broad processes of ethnicization—of politics, of violent conflict, of identity construction, or of the nation-state (Alonso 1994; Tambiah 1996; Žižek 1997; Brubaker and Laitin 1998).[4] The increasing centrality of ethnicized alterity to the formulation of political subjectivities and to the elaboration of political projects and imaginaries has been accompanied by a rise in certain forms of conflict often glossed as "ethnic" (Tambiah 1996; Brubaker and Laitin 1998; Friedman 2003a). But of course, the rise of ethnicity and of a corresponding notion of culture as standard markers of difference has also gone hand in hand with the public celebration of diversity, its active interpellation, and new modes of visualization that it has acquired in the city.[5]

THE BEER AT LITTLE ISTANBUL TASTES BETTER

Its regime of authenticity—the mechanisms by which it claims for itself ahistorical validity—notwithstanding, our contemporary notion of ethnicity is very much a product and construct of our time, the result of a contested and unstable process of constitution upon which a variety of investments converge, and not some primordial identity.[6] The label "ethnic," whatever its particular referent, is always a political claim with certain stakes attached, never purely descrip-

---

[3] This, of course, implies neither that Fanon's arguments about race and colonialism have ceased to be relevant nor that ethnically or racially marked others in today's Europe no longer experience racism and discrimination. For two excellent studies of the lingering and robust significance of race in today's Germany and Europe, see Chin et al. (2009) and Partridge (2012).

[4] The rise of ethnicity to the foreground of differentiation strategies in the time of globalization— with its concomitant transformations in market structures and nation-state power—has, according to several of these writers, dovetailed the commodification and fragmentation of the social landscape. Commodification and ethnicization have in this view reinforced each other. The constitution of ethnic identities has increasingly become linked with their commodification, at times even with their incorporation and trademarking, so that commodities themselves have become segregated according to their "ethnicity" (Alonso 1994; Comaroff 2005).

[5] Scholars have described the culturalization and ethnicization of politics, not only in Europe, as reflecting realignments in the strategies and structures of the multicultural ethnicized state (Povinelli 1998 and 2001; Jackson and Warren 2005).

[6] The emergence of our contemporary notion of ethnicity has been traced, on the one hand, to recent ideological and institutional shifts in nation-state forms, which have increasingly abandoned grand homogenization and standardization projects in favor of policies and discourses of plurality, heterogeneity, and segmentation of the national space, and, on the other hand, to the rising concentration of global diasporas in urban metropolitan settings (Tambiah 1996; Povinelli 1998; Comaroff and Comaroff 2001; Calhoun 2007).

tive (Brubaker and Laitin 1998). As notions of ethnicity have in many contexts increasingly encroached upon categories of race or nationality as markers of authentic difference, racism and nationalism have been repackaged in cultural terms.[7] In today's Europe, both institutionalized discrimination and spontaneous bigotry often take the form of cultural racism (Holmes 2000; Pred 2000).

Consider Danny and Sebastian. Danny is the fashionably dressed collector of neo-Nazi cell phone ring-tones whom we met in chapter 2. His friend Sebastian is a bony nineteen-year-old with light-colored short hair and a brash attitude whom I routinely found at the Kugel. His family moved from another neighborhood in Treptow to the Ghetto soon after its construction was completed in the early nineties. His parents separated a few years later, and he had been living near the Kugel with his mother, who worked in a local housing company. Sebastian finished general secondary school without qualifying for any diploma or certificate and, barring brief and intermittent periods in welfare-for-work jobs, had been mostly unemployed until he finally secured an apprenticeship in industrial cleaning.

One August afternoon Sebastian, Danny, and I sat to talk at Little Istanbul, a local Turkish restaurant-bar, where they and their friend Klaus took turns at the slot machines. Flipping through his wallet, Sebastian exposed an NPD election sticker attached to its inner lining. His brief pause seemed calculated to ascertain that I perceive the careful provocation. Some three months earlier he and a friend had been chased "with carving knives" (in his words) and banned from Little Istanbul after rioting and threatening its owners. Sebastian clearly felt it important to reassure me that such incidents, while recurrent, always end with reconciliation. As if to prove his point, he exchanged jokes with the waiters who served beer to our table. They returned a polite smile.

Shortly after the waiters left, our conversation turned to politics. "I would start by prohibiting and shutting down all their businesses," Sebastian declared, "but sooner or later all foreigners living here should leave the country." Given his determination, I inquired why he and his friends patronize Little Istanbul and not one of the typically "German" establishments nearby. "One simply gets used to it," he replied, "and besides, the beer here tastes better." Danny sipped his beer as he grumbled about the penetration of foreign cultures into his homeland. He had yet to decide, he said, whether to follow his heart and vote for the NPD or to adopt instead a more pragmatic approach and support the CDU in the

---

[7] Douglas Holmes understands the emergence of culturally framed political discourses of bigotry in today's Europe as part of an integralist project concerned with cultural tropes and pluralist notions of incommensurability. This project represents a fresh resurgence of long-standing counter-Enlightenment European traditions, now mobilized in the confrontation with "fast capitalism" and a growing sense of alienation. I add to his argument by highlighting the ways in which the discourse of cultural/ethnic incommensurability and the interpellation of cultural/ethnic collectivities surface also from the very logic of the multicultural, neoliberal state of the present (cf. Holmes 2000).

upcoming elections.[8] I asked him what being a rightist meant for him. "Standing up for one's country," he answered. Giving jobs to "Germans" first and fighting against the "deteriorating situation" in Germany, he added: the flooding of the landscape with foreign businesses, the proliferation of immigrant ghettos, and the abuse—by foreigners—of the welfare system. Danny and Sebastian articulated a discourse of resentment and self-victimization in cultural rather than racial terms; they talked of the threat of foreign *cultures*. Meanwhile, their bodily gestures—how they would nod their head and roll their eyes in the direction of the Turkish staff of the restaurant—signaled plainly enough the ethnic collectivity that they construed as the agent of cultural pollution.[9]

Cultural and ethnic alterity, distilled in the image of certain immigrant agglomerations, defines, for the groups I studied, the central political issue of the day, far more so than, say, the memory of the war, the restructuring of the welfare state, or anti-Semitic Jewish conspiracy theories. The ethnically marked immigrant stands for them in this sense not only as an object of deep hatred but also as a prism through which to fabricate (and as a yardstick by which to measure) political contrasts. A common and oft-repeated rendering of the political spectrum among my informants—and one that unmistakably reiterates the contrasts between easterners and westerners that I described in chapter 2— holds that "leftists are for foreigners and rightists are for Germans." Karl, an eighteen-year-old activist in a politically organized circle of right-wing extremists, pronounced that

> [l]eft and right don't mean much . . . the left is against the state and the right is against the state, but, the left is against the right because the right is against foreigners but the right at the same time is against the left . . . actually they're both the same, only, out of ten opinions both sides have only one [i.e., immigration] that diverges, but otherwise they're the same.

Karl held a general secondary school diploma (*Hauptschulabschluss*) and was completing vocational training as a mechanic. He lived in Johannisthal with his mother, a shop clerk at a discount chain store, and had no contact with his father, who left home when he was a young child. Stylish and trendy, a Slipknot tattoo on his arm,[10] Karl drew on contemporary, globally circulating fashions

---

[8] In Germany's federal parliamentary system, political parties must win at least 5 percent of the proportional party vote or three directly elected delegates to enter Parliament, an unrealistic expectation for the NPD, which recorded its best result of 3.6 percent in 1969 and has never reached even 2 percent since. Votes for parties that do not qualify for parliamentary representation, like the NPD, are therefore in a sense wasted.

[9] This ethnicization and culturalization of racism on the German extreme right echoes broader shifts in the political terrain in Europe, and particularly its realignment regarding the issue of immigration and, specifically, concerning a cluster of stereotypifications of ethnicized Muslim minorities (Asad 2003b; Bunzl 2005).

[10] Slipknot is a popular American heavy metal band.

in performing his political identity. An avid consumer of popular American television and cinema, Japanese comic books, and the music of international heavy metal bands, he would fantasize about driving expensive cars under palm trees in the wide avenues of warm American cities, not about regenerating a pure Aryan nation. However, his political activism and his consumption of a range of illicit nationalist commodities made him, no doubt, a political deviant. And as such, his entire cosmos seemed to revolve around the gravitational force of immigration. In-line with the nationalist turn to socialism that I described earlier, he flatly opposed cuts to welfare but advocated compulsory labor for the unemployed in order to combat, in his words, the laziness of "foreigners": "Out of 100 percent of foreigners, one can really throw out 95 percent because [only] the other 5 percent want to work and accomplish something here." Even more promiscuous than Germany's welfare system, Karl insisted, were its asylum policies, which allowed virtually unrestricted access into the country and in turn the abuse of state resources. He would talk affirmatively about the EU but express concern about its expansionary plans—in other words, about Turkey's bid for full EU membership, which was pending and hotly debated at the time. Educated and articulate, Karl advanced economic ("only countries that would be useful" should be included), geographical ("Turkey is mostly not directly in Europe"), and human rights ("they still practice stoning there and all that, and capital punishment and that's not allowed in EU countries") arguments to support his case. When pressed, however, his concerns revealed themselves to revolve less around economic analysis, geographical frontiers, or abstract notions of human rights and more about fears rooted in his xenophobic (or, more precisely, Islamophobic) perception of the here and now: "If Turkey became part of the EU then anyone could travel as they wished, and then, of course, they would all come to Germany . . . and already more and more people are always coming here; mainly it's Turks and Arabs from down south."

Karl's seemingly homogenizing talk of "foreigners" and "immigrants" in fact turned out to distinguish carefully between several ethnic stereotypes. "Chinese" are "quiet" (*ruhig*),[11] not visible in public after the workday is over, steer clear of trouble (*Stress*), and "always work hard": selling cigarettes on the black market or running flower shops, grocery stores, kiosks, produce stands, and restaurants. Russians, like Africans, are also "quiet" and hardworking, "usually at construction sites, because they are naturally stronger . . . they usually do manual labor." At the end of the day, according to Karl, "it's really just these Turks and Arabs who don't work." "[They] are outside all day," he said with indignation, "one always sees them . . . they're always making trouble, like robbing people or threatening or stabbing people." His rage focused on these "strange

---

[11] With this label Karl (like many of his peers) designated an East Asian and Southeast Asian population, largely consisting of immigrants of Vietnamese background who arrived in East Germany as workers and remained following reunification.

people" (*komische Leute*) who made "strange sounds" with their tongues and used a strange Turkish-German dialect and whose neighborhoods—Kreuzberg, Neukölln, and Wedding—he avoided:

> There are many [Germans] who already start to talk like they always do, weird sounds like *ts ts* [tongue clicks] I'm sure you know it, or, it's always these strange . . . *ts ts*, they always do that, always after every word, very strange, or they make their own dialect, this Turkish-German (*Türk-Deutsch*), that's quite terrible.

Karl's words delineated a population of Middle Eastern immigrants as at once different from others and itself undifferentiated, as ethnically marked and somatically identifiable not only through vision (as embodied alterity) but also through hearing (as linguistic strangeness) or taste and smell (as ethnic food). As classificatory schemata, the distinctions he outlined between different ethnic groups, but particularly between East Asians, Africans, and Russians on the one hand and Turks and Arabs on the other, reproduce the Ossi/Wessi dichotomy by contrasting immigrants associated with the East with those associated with the West.[12] They reveal the multiple resonances between different layers of otherness—East and West, right and left, German and foreign, hardworking and lazy immigrants—and how such layers come together and reinforce each other in everyday imaginations of alterity.

Karl's indignation points at some of the ways in which the ethnicization and culturalization of social difference have been reflected in contemporary urban landscapes.[13] Of course, the ethnic organization of urban space is not in itself a new phenomenon. Historically, it has often given territorial expression to an ethnic division of labor while at the same time reproducing that same division.[14] In late capitalism, however, while the spatial configuration of ethnicity in urban space has remained inseparable from hierarchical social orderings, it has also seemed to increasingly exhibit a certain autonomy. The boundaries that

[12] Immigrants of Turkish and Arab backgrounds arrived in West Germany, and in Berlin their largest concentrations are in the western districts of Kreuzberg, Neukölln, and Wedding. At the time the wall fell, East Germany hosted a significant population of temporary workers from Vietnam, as well as apprentices and students from Ethiopia, Angola, Mozambique, and a number of other African countries. Most of the Vietnamese who remained in Germany maintained their residence in the city's east, particularly in Lichtenberg. Meanwhile, of the massive numbers of Russian immigrants who arrived in Berlin following reunification, the better part has settled in the eastern neighborhoods of Treptow, Marzahn-Hellersdorf, and Hohenschönhausen. In contrast, the presence of African residents in today's Berlin is largely the result of post-reunification immigration, and stronger in the city's west.

[13] In the social sciences, the paradigm of the "ethnic city"—of residential neighborhoods, community affiliations, spatial strategies, and municipal politics understandable from the viewpoint of ethnic groups—has become one of the leading approaches to the study of urban structures and processes in metropolitan settings (Low 1996).

[14] Allen Feldman, for example, describes the long history of segregation and of processes of mixing and unmixing along ethnic/religious/class lines that have given rise to the ethnically divided landscape of today's Belfast (1997).

mark cultural and ethnic differences in contemporary metropolitan landscapes frequently appear difficult to classify according to strictly structural criteria, corresponding less to territorial units and more to social relations negotiated in everyday situations of mixing and proximity.

The tenuous and continuous constitution and contestation of such boundaries relies on somatic sensibilities that take embodied alterities as their object. In the geographical imagination of right-wing extremists, different bodies give rise to certain spatial orderings of difference through sensual apparatuses. In the visual field, the constitution of an ethnic cityscape depends on an embodied semantics of identification that, beyond skin color, include an entire range of aesthetic registers and visual markers: from the architectonics of bodily demeanors or the stylistics of fashion to stereotypified perceptual hygienics that distinguish clean from dirty, normal from deviant, or healthy from sick. Such visual matrices of identification inform spatial strategies of avoidance—for example, Karl's aversion to places with too many "strange people." Food, to which I shall return in detail below, organizes somatic differences within the domains of taste and smell as indexical of particular ethnicities and of their emplacements in specific sites. Auditory sensibilities also contribute to the constitution of ethnicized spatialities as they capture foreign languages, unfamiliar music, or peculiar sounds.

Douglas Holmes has noted how the constant encounter with "foreign bodies" triggers a sense of collective humiliation for far right residents of multiracial underclass neighborhoods in London (Holmes 2000). Notwithstanding that Treptow-Köpenick's immigrant ratio is low, even for Berlin, and falls far short of mixed neighborhoods in London, here, too, tangible, quotidian encounters with embodied otherness redefine the urban landscape: Muslim women strolling in the park and past the benches on which my informants congregate, bus and tram stops where the shifting gazes of commuters betray a sense of discomfort at the presence of people of Middle Eastern appearance, or a range of ethnically marked and immigrant-owned businesses—restaurants, Internet cafés, kiosks, flower shops, grocery stores—that dot central avenues with a variety of ethnic indexes (Greek, Indian, Vietnamese, Turkish). Boundaries materialize fleetingly in the arbitrary encounters of an urban everyday, then dissipate.

Like Karl, Uta (whom we met in chapter 2, complaining about the materialism of her West German boyfriend) also complained of excessive immigration, wide-open borders, and foreigners' abuse of the welfare system as the country's top problems, followed closely by rising criminality, the result of juridical leniency and luxurious prisons. Conveniently, both merged for her in the figure of the "criminal foreigner" who took advantage not only of the welfare system but also of the criminal system and whom she, like Karl, linked with a specific ethnic profile:

> [The rest of the immigrant groups] are not so many, that is still manageable, it's still agreeable . . . it's not oversettled (*übersiedelt*) or too bad but especially those Turks and Arabs and all of that, everything that's this one type (*Sorte*), that's too oversettled, it's just too much.

Uta narrated a quotidian friction with this "one type" of immigrants through stories of a brawl at the shopping mall, threats at a court-mandated antiviolence seminar, or a series of incidents at the vocational school: a stabbing of a class-mate, harassment by other students, or noisy Turkish music and loud Turkish conversations that obstructed her studies. Her narratives were at the same time discursive renderings or "spatial syntaxes" (de Certeau 1984) that constituted and authorized a certain geography of alterity. The schools she attended, her antiviolence seminar, or the shopping mall marked certain areas as ethnically different and dangerously violent. Like Karl, she, too, did her best to avoid these areas, her imagination of which articulated visual perception, auditory sensi-bilities, and somatic modalities of taste and smell:

> That's why I avoid the areas where I don't necessarily want to be provoked. A friend of mine lives also in Neukölln, and I'm happy that I have to walk only five minutes [from the train station] to her place and the same going back, and that's okay. But I would never settle there. Never. It stinks there so badly for me. When you enter the hallway of her building, sometimes it smells like garlic, sometimes it smells stale, and here it doesn't stink so bad. Perhaps we cook with different spices. That's possible. But the Turks, oh no, even when you walk down the street, every kebab place smells different.

Uta's geographical imagination and spatial strategies rest on a web of so-matic modalities that incorporate otherness into material things: bodies, foods, smells, sounds, buildings, and so on. In a similar way, Freddi explained what defines someone as politically rightist as follows:

> Well, [you are a] rightist after all if you have something against Turks. I mean, only because they are after all dirty . . . I have absolutely no patience for Turks because, I don't know, I can't stand them, they smell, they stink.[15]

Uta complained of systematic discrimination in favor of immigrants in state institutions. In her view, "they" acquired inordinate amounts of welfare money without working, while she and her boyfriend, both in vocational training pro-grams and struggling to pay their debts, had to navigate bureaucratic labyrinths in order to afford basic necessities. The courts, she said, disbursed inexcusably light sentences to multiply convicted, violent Turkish drug traffickers,[16] while she considered her punishment for a minor brawl disproportionally high. In her vo-cational training program, she added, she constantly witnessed pro-immigrant

---

[15] In their investigation of anti-Semitism, Horkheimer and Adorno pause on the role of such somatic markers in the mimetic desire of the fascists toward the object of their hatred. Particularly the sense of smell, they argue, embodies "the archetypal longing for the lower forms of existence, for direct unification with circumbient nature, with the earth and mud. Of all the senses, that of smell—which is attracted without objectifying—bears clearest witness to the urge to lose oneself in and become the other" (2002 [1944], 184).

[16] Like others in her circles, Uta thought German courts refrained from issuing harsh sentences to foreigners so they wouldn't be deported.

discrimination. She resented the public funding of mosques. And she was furious at immigrants who, by failing to master German, extended discrimination into the labor market, where employers increasingly valued bilingual workers. The real culprit, she reflected, was ultimately the state:

> Sometimes you get treated like you're the last piece of crap . . . too many foreigners is not good . . . you see it nowhere else . . . but here they want to hand everything to the Turks on a fucking silver platter and everything must be provided for them . . . and that's why you can't really lay the blame with the foreigners, because it's not their fault really, they get a license to do it, and they simply take advantage of it for the most part. But the state is really itself responsible for this when it creates such a mess.[17]

For members of the groups with which I worked, the state often appeared as a site of experiences of discrimination. Consider Ole, whom I mentioned in chapter 2, a clownish hooligan who at once invited and subverted generic classifications. Neither the political left nor the political right seemed to interpellate him entirely; or, rather, both interpellated him at once. An SPD and PDS voter, he considered himself a rightist because of his stance on immigration. He took precautions to deny any racism on his part, making sure to mention, for example, his personal relations with "foreign" colleagues at his vocational program and with his local kebab vendor or his support for foreigners who work, pay taxes, and speak German.[18] Almost in the same breath, he would complain of "asylum shelter Germany" (*Asylheim Deutschland*): unduly lenient laws and unconditionally open borders, all due to the lingering historical shame of World War II. In his narratives, the institutional settings of state bureaucracy—the employment or welfare offices—elicited discrimination. People "should be able to talk German and not with their hands and feet," he said, "because many [immigrants] go there and [with] 'I no understand,' they already win [what they want]." Linguistic otherness—foreign words, broken speech, bodily gestures, and the incapacity to speak German in institutions governing the dispensation of public resources—appeared to Ole not as an exclusionary drawback but rather as an unfair advantage. In the end, however, his worries concerned less legal codes, government policies, or state institutions, and more how immigration appeared to the "ordinary person":

> It's fine if people come, but it can be pushed too far . . . it shouldn't stand open for everyone, which is somehow the way it appears to us right now, even if the law

---

[17] In this her grievances echoed similar perceptions of pro-immigrant discrimination by the state among supporters of the British National Party in London (Holmes 2000).

[18] In doing so, Ole performed common strategies for the negotiation of racist nationalism and a heterogeneous everyday: equating foreigners with an ethnicized "Middle Eastern" collectivity, postulating a moral distinction between useful and parasitical immigrants, suspending political convictions for individual relations in his immediate environment, and, all the while, evoking figures of criminality, violence, idleness, and abuse of the welfare system.

prescribes something else or says something else or equally with the statistics. But for people on the street, it looks nevertheless different.

Ole's xenophobia was rooted in his quotidian experience, not in legal frameworks or statistical quantifications but in how immigration "appears to us," to "people on the street"—not what "people on the street" think about it, but literally how it becomes sensually perceptible to them. Foreign sounds and visual markers of otherness structured his perception of the urban landscape: "[I dislike Neukölln] first because of the high ratio of foreigners, many youth gangs that are not of German origin . . . and also because a lot [there] is dilapidated, I also see a lot of poverty, and that's not pretty." These visual markers informed an aesthetic judgment of the urban landscape that tied together immigration, criminality, poverty, unsightliness, and threat. At stake, importantly, were not concrete experiences but a perceptual-aesthetic ordering of immaterial, yet for Ole, clearly evident boundaries: "[It's not that] I was assaulted or harassed there, which is something that of course could happen anywhere; it's just that there's a border for me there that I don't like to cross."

DISTINCTIONS IN THE LANDSCAPE OF OTHERNESS

The right-wing extremists with whom I worked articulated the configuration of difference in the cityscape through sights, sounds, and smells attached not only to human bodies but equally to tangible sites—streets, neighborhoods, offices of state bureaucracy, vocational schools, restaurants, shopping malls— that became metonymic of ethnic otherness and generative of spatial orderings. Their visual perception of "strange" people, the olfactory sensation of "strange" odors, or the auditory encounter with "strange" languages outlined regions, sites, boundaries, and circulations of strangeness in the city. It should come as no surprise that Kreuzberg, Neukölln, and Wedding repeatedly appeared in their discourse as figures of spatial negativity par excellence,[19] of otherness in pure form. As pure negativities, they operated as opposites not of real places but rather of fantasies. To Ole and his friends, they reflected the negative form not of their real home district (which, as they noted, itself overflowed with foreignness, perils, and uncertainties) but of their fantasy of it. As otherwheres into which social maladies become projected (Pred 2000), they marked the opposite not of actually existing Treptow but rather of what, for them, it could become, should become, and once was.

But boundaries are shifting and porous entities (Balibar 2002; Casey 2007), and Treptow—which shares a long frontier with Kreuzberg and Neukölln—also

[19]The three neighborhoods with the highest ratio of Turkish and Arab residents (see footnote 12 above).

stood for them in constant danger of pollution. Karl shunned Treptowerpark, a recreational area on the district's west, "because it is a little, it's on the edge of Kreuzberg, it already starts there that different-looking, strange people come . . . brutes [*prols*] and people who make trouble, just people who get on my nerves." The spatialization of strangeness in the city thus becomes a matter of flows and intensities, of the circulation and percolation of semiotic values through spatial interfaces in the landscape.

This geographical imaginary aligns itself along an East/West ordering of the city, no less important than proper place-names like Kreuzberg or Neukölln, that draws a continuum of familiarity and strangeness. In this rendering, Kreuzberg and Neukölln become synecdoches for the West at large as a region preferably to be avoided.[20] With the historical frontier evaporated into a misty, ethereal geography, an absent border whose precise course none of my young informants could quite trace, the distinction between East and West has taken on a range of specifications and significations beyond its Cold War coordinates.[21] It generated various binary territorializations of safety and danger, familiarity and strangeness, or comfort and uneasiness. For some, certain "eastern" districts (Mitte, Prenzlauer-Berg, or Friedrichshain) have been so contaminated by the West that they have become de facto indistinguishable from it.[22] Indeed, as we have seen with Karl, my informants' home district itself, broad swaths of it already too polluted by strangeness, appeared as a fractal recursion (the reiteration of the same contrast at a different scale; see Irvine and Gal 2000) that mimicked their geographical imagination of the wider urban landscape. The three cases that I describe in what follows illustrate distinct renditions of the East/West spatialization of the city and of the district, all of which, however, also significantly inform the geographical imagination of ethnic difference.

Axel was a short, thin, and pale sixteen-year-old with long black hair. His father, who had done prison time in the GDR for attempting to escape over the wall, had been suffering from depression and alcoholism and, like his older brother, worked as a supermarket cashier. His mother, trained as a hairdresser, had been working odd jobs, most recently at newspaper stands and bakeries. When I met him, he pursued a high school diploma (*Abitur*) at a gymnasium (the highest level of German secondary education), played guitar and dreamed of becoming a music star, and fought for more visiting rights with his one-year-old son from an estranged ex-girlfriend. Until shortly before our acquaintance, however, he was a key figure in the local right-wing extremist scene of

---

[20] A synecdoche describes the representation of the whole by one of its particular parts.

[21] As a rule, the East-West boundaries that right-wing extremists in Berlin narrate trace a line always at or to the "east" of where the wall once stood, never to its "west." But just how far into the historical east of the city the ephemeral boundary that dichotomizes its landscape in the present runs varies greatly.

[22] Many foreigners and westerners have settled in these districts since reunification, partly owing to pervasive underoccupancy and to processes of gentrification.

Johannisthal and Schöneweide, an organized group of committed nationalists that developed from a circle of junior high school friends. Axel became the right hand of Becker, the thirty-something chairperson of the local NPD chapter who recruited disgruntled young followers from throughout the district. Involvement in organized political activities ensued. He has gradually drifted away from this crowd over the past year or two.[23] This notwithstanding, and while he now identified himself as neither rightist nor leftist but as "alternative,"[24] his rendering of the cityscape scarcely differed from that of his past friends. Neukölln was for him the heart of darkness, while he described Baumschulenweg, a residential neighborhood bordering Neukölln, as a nest of armed "Ghetto people" and violent foreigners unsafe for people like him, and even Johannisthal, at the district's center, according to him, has not escaped the impact of adjacent districts:

> Lately I see in Johannisthal too many people running around who make trouble . . . who provoke and harass people on the street . . . [they are] young bullies who think they're some young gangsters, like, for example, they think they come from the Bronx in America; they think they have to create a ghetto here in Johannisthal.

Axel's East/West geography, in which boundaries—for example, between Neukölln and Baumschulenweg or Baumschulenweg and Johannisthal—serve as interfaces for diverse flows, resembles that of Elsa, a seventeen-year-old native of Baumschulenweg. The daughter of a baker and a housewife, Elsa failed to qualify for any school diploma and no vocational program would admit her. She was completing a yearlong government-sponsored prevocational professional training program in low-skill service jobs that interspersed classroom periods with brief apprenticeships: at a shopping mall shoe store, at a restaurant kitchen, and as a hotel maid. A Germanic mythology enthusiast, she wore her ultranationalist neo-paganism on her sleeve with innumerable earrings, thick silver bracelets, heavy silver rings, and Pitbull or Lonsdale fashion brands.[25] She was intimately linked both with the cliques of hard-core Union fans that gathered in Grünau and with the militant nationalist groups of Karl and Axel, whose gatherings she occasionally attended. In the past, Becker attempted to recruit her as his deputy in Grünau; she declined. Under pressure from her parents to move into a place of her own, her daunting search for an apartment

---

[23] A surprise call by Antifa activists may have contributed to his abandonment of political activism, which, however, was a protracted process of disengagement at least equally motivated by his incorporation into different social circles at his new school and by the progressive contraction of his quotidian life into private spaces that came to eclipse the earlier significance of the youth club and the public park.

[24] The category of "alternative" for young people throughout Germany designates certain musical tastes and dress codes rather than political belonging; hence, Axel's use of it underlined his desire to appear apolitical.

[25] The two brands are popular among skinheads and hooligans.

was burdened not only by meager financial resources but also by a geographical imaginary of otherness that outlined a progressive East-West gradation of strangeness and familiarity, danger and safety, or pollution and purity that run through her district. Under the influence of Neukölln, immediately to its west, according to Elsa, her once peaceful and quiet neighborhood had become the dominion of violence, crime, and "bad people" (read, people of Middle Eastern appearance). Under the creeping encroachment of the West, strangeness spread eastward, unabated, into the remotest corners of her district, pushing her into ever scarcer and more distant refuges. Despite their remoteness, their inferior transportation infrastructure, and their poorer consumption and leisure offerings, Elsa would only consider the district's easternmost neighborhoods, on the Brandenburgian frontier, where she eventually settled.

A final East/West rendering comes from these very borderlands, where, on one unusually simmering morning in May, we idled in front of the Bretterbude kiosk outside the Grünau train station: Sylvia, Robert, and Meier, all approximately twenty years old, NPD supporters, and zealous Union fans; Norman, whose face showed the bloody traces of a late-night brawl; twenty-year-old Martina, upbeat about her previous night's sexual conquest; Michael, in his late twenties; Kurt, in his midthirties; and me. The train station area serves as a local hub for transportation, consumption, and leisure, with bus, tram, and train stops, a highway exit, and a shopping mall. Below the tracks and facing the mall, the Bretterbude's wooden hut offers a range of snacks, beverages, and magazines. Its shanty-like appearance exudes an air of desolation. Outside, three standing tables under a small roofed patio face a busy sidewalk and constitute a local institution for at least three different groups of regular clients: long-unemployed men begin to trickle in by late morning, chasing bottles of beer with shots of schnapps; commuters, mostly manual laborers, stop by a few slow hours later to mark the transition from labor to leisure, from production to consumption; and in the late afternoon young crowds arrive. The last group had evolved from a small core of Union enthusiasts to a multitude of youths, as the kiosk's not entirely gratuitous reputation as a neo-Nazi den grew. Transformed from a charmless wooden shack of older alcoholics into a magnet for abject youths, the Bretterbude stood for many of its younger customers as the site where they had become properly nationalist.

On that morning Michael, divorced and a father of three children, saw his cheerful temper dissipate when Martina disclosed that his current girlfriend had been cheating on him. He ranted about his romantic misfortunes and exposed self-inflicted scars on his arms as evidence of his suffering. He then praised himself as a responsible father and warned of the perils of child raising in today's degenerated society. He found the pervasiveness of drug dealing particularly worrisome. Of course, he confessed, he too consumed marijuana occasionally. But he would promptly kill anyone he caught dealing drugs to his children, he declared. Toothless, emaciated, and starkly unkempt Kurt, a Bretterbude regular

Figure 3. The Bretterbude. A hangout for Union fans and, at the time of my research, a favorite meeting spot for young nationalists.

who had relocated from Treptow to a satellite town a few train stops into Brandenburg, intervened. He abandoned the city, he explained, not for love of countryside, nor for a lower cost of living, but rather to flee the western afflictions that have steadily metamorphosed a once-familiar landscape into a place of danger and strangeness. He was, in Holmes's phrase, "an exile in his own homeland" (2000, 130). Grünau, on Berlin's southeastern edge, marked for him a last frontier, a borderline he would not cross—"at least under the present state of things." What lay to its west he judged as irredeemable and overpopulated with immigrants. Nods of agreement welcomed his appraisal, which triggered an exchange on the idleness, criminality, and welfare-dependency of immigrant groups. In the chronotope (Bakhtin 1998b) that emerged from this interactionally elaborated narrative, space (East/West), time (creeping decline), and social difference (women, immigrants) bound together figures of social maladies: criminality, idleness, narcotics, violence, dependency, and infidelity.

For my young informants, then, ethnic otherness always appeared emplaced within a spatial ordering of difference in the cityscape, even if the precise contours of their geographical imaginations varied. As Franz Fanon classically noted (1967), the corporeality of embodied otherness grants it an insuppressible facticity and reifies it as material presence in a way that may appear to precede any contextual—including spatial—determination. Yet, its somatic compulsion notwithstanding, embodied alterity remains, of course, through and through a socially constructed form of difference, with respect both to the sorts of markers that come to stand for otherness and to the processes of stereotypification that grant these markers meanings.[26] Such semiotic processes vary not only across distinct cultural contexts or historical periods but also across interactional settings, where situated interpretations reflect particular articulations of time, place, and notions of social difference. In describing his amicable relationship with his kebab vendor as an alibi for racism, for example, Ole voiced notions of time (working hours), place (the Turkish train station eatery), and social roles (an ethnic division of labor) that converged to define "Middle Easterners" as tolerable, even welcome, behind the counter of a kebab stand, where, as it were, they blend unthreateningly, nay harmoniously, into the scenery. For Karl, too, ethnic otherness in Kreuzberg or Neukölln stood for danger, but "any Turk who lives here in Schöneweide works. One has a kiosk, the other has his Internet café, a restaurant, a produce shop. Each of them works. There are no Turks here who don't work."

Signs of otherness that bind foreignness and social ills (criminality, idleness) stood for Karl and his friends in other places and times for industriousness and normativity.[27] Recognition entailed for them, then, an engagement with a range of contextual cues that defined the terms of particular encounters, a broad interpretative sweep in which sign and scenery informed each other in a reciprocal dialectic.[28] Anthropologists have argued that emergent regimes of legibility, especially in metropolitan settings, have generated novel forms of uncertainty and modes of telling, at times with brutal repercussions. The delimitation of context and its naming appear indispensable for stabilizing ethnic identities as well as for practices of recognition—the ethnic other subsumes, and rests on, contextual determinations.[29] For my informants, ethnic otherness seemed to solicit

[26] Before particular corporeal markers become understood, and mobilized, as signifiers of otherness, they must be posited to perception as signaling difference (ethnic, gendered, political, and so on). The tongue clicks of Middle Easterners about which Karl complains or the odors of foreign foods that upset Uta present themselves to them as incommensurable alterity, thanks to the socially mediated processes from which they emerge as such. As a sign, embodied alterity presents a paradigmatic instance of an indexically iconic semiotic relationship; signifier and referent merge in it, and appearance is collapsed onto a presumed essence (Peirce 1960; Parmentier 1994; Irvine and Gal 2000).

[27] This is in-line with Mike Davis's observation that, in gated communities in the Los Angeles area, the sight of ethnically marked pedestrians may provoke the security apparatus that monitors the neighborhoods or appear as innocuous depending on the time of day and the routes they take, which define them as either domestic workers or potential burglars (1992).

[28] I agree here with Andreas Glaeser, who insists that "the consideration of context is ... extremely important in analyzing how a particular tropic identification"—whether, in his case, of eastern and western police officers, or, as is the case at hand, of an ethnic otherness—"functions within social interaction" (2000, 51).

[29] Thomas Hansen has described naming in Bombay/Mumbai as a spatiotemporal fixating act generative of identity and contingent upon a certain indeterminacy for its efficacy (2002). What the act of naming fixates is the setting within which the indeterminacies of Hindu and Muslim identities become resolved. Allen Feldman has developed an analogous argument about the ethnic segregation of Belfast, where a history of mixing and unmixing, of a spatially configured ethnic division

various context-dependent interpretative procedures. In the encounter with otherness, an inherent ambiguity could only be tentatively domesticated through
a situated dialectic of constitution between bodies and scenery.[30] If Turks
and Arabs in Neukölln appeared to them both plainly identifiable and singularly emblematic of an entire range of social discontents, in other places (e.g.,
Schöneweide) they stood for a morally normative notion of respectable citizenship (i.e., economic independence, industriousness, tax contributions). When
Karl contrasted the hardworking and upright Vietnamese ("one sees them everywhere during daytime but one doesn't see them outside in the evenings anymore") with the Turks and Arabs who "are outside the whole day," he carved
also a temporal boundary that rendered alterity as either virtuous or criminal.
The criminal immigrant and the upright immigrant are in that sense also temporal and spatial stabilizations of meaning. In Andreas Glaeser's words, "the
reading of space identifies spatial features with something beyond space itself"
(2000, 48).[31]

At times, the contingency of markers of difference upon context means that
they may appear, for my informants, as simply illegible; or, to paraphrase Mary
Douglas's (2002) felicitous phrase, as alterity out of place. Outside the soccer
stadium of Union, for example, with its reputation of an ultranationalist, "German" fan base, where Elsa, Sylvia, Meier, I, and a few others lingered before a
match, I became fixated by Elsa's silent stare at a group of five men standing
nearby and chatting in Turkish, by her wide-open eyes and look of disbelief.
"What was that?" (Was war das?), she asked loudly and with an air of flab-
bergasted distress, after the five men walked away. Elsa was up front about her
dislike of "foreigners"—at her vocational training, at the mall, on public trans-

---

of labor, of an interface of physical barriers, and of the territorialization of violence and death offers
an interpretative framework for concrete practices of "telling" (1991). Arjun Appadurai, in turn,
has argued that globalization has set into motion new orders of indeterminacy, spawning "vivisec-
tionist" techniques that posit the ethnic body itself as the site for eliminating uncertainty (1998).
Such "investigative" violence, Appadurai has argued, produces concrete, graspable bodies out of the
large-scale abstractions and diffuse labels of a rapidly globalizing present. Jonathan Friedman has
criticized these views on various counts, tracing violent ethnic conflict not to globalization but to
shifts in capitalism, in nation-state hegemony, and in the commodification of difference (2003a).
For Friedman, uncertainty is mounting about increasingly elusive boundaries and not about identities, which he considers well known and plainly recognizable. Ethnic violence, then, would in his
view be concerned with eradication, not identification.

[30] Étienne Balibar has argued that identities are defined by their boundaries (2002; 2004a). In
the words of Edward Casey, "we are boundaries" (2007). Both Balibar and Casey underline at the
same time the inherently equivocal character of boundaries. Thus, precisely that which is supposed
to define identity remains itself always indeterminate.

[31] "Space," Merleau-Ponty reminds us, "is not the setting (real or logical) in which things are arranged, but the means whereby the position of things becomes possible" (1962, 243). Thus, perception, always already emplaced, enfolds not only spatial boundaries or visual horizons but the entire
gamut of implicit motivations that render it meaningful.

portation. Ordinarily, there was nothing outrageous about their presence; they were simply there for her as objects of aversion. Yet outside the stadium of her favorite soccer club, in this eastern part of the city, surrounded by crowds of skinheads, the five Turks struck her not as signals of social decay but quite plainly as out of place, as shockingly illegible.

TALKING IMMIGRANTS

In chapter 2, we saw how young nationalists' performances and enunciations of Ossi identifications intertwined with and drew on those figures of East Germanness that emerged within the dominant discourses of national publicity. The ways in which they imagined and mobilized immigration and ethnic otherness similarly mimicked the outlines of far more general forms of encountering difference in today's Germany and Europe. Elsa's jolt at the fleeting freeze of shattered frontiers among the throngs of soccer devotees reiterated, at the margins of the political terrain, a variety of tropes that pervade the so-called mainstream, licit political discourse. Far right modes of engaging with ethnic alterity turn out to share a disturbing discursive intimacy with allegedly legitimate political postures.

Consider how Elsa's distressed astonishment echoes other modes of encountering ethnic, religious, or cultural difference as "out of place," for example, how broad populations in Europe perceive mosques as material signs of something alien in (and to) the urban landscape. In Berlin, all of the city's roughly 120 mosques—serving more than 200,000 Muslim residents—were located in the city's historical West (Rohde 2006). In 2006 the construction of the first mosque in the East, in the district of Pankow, commenced. The plan ignited broad protests in which right-wing extremists mingled with so-called mainstream conservatives, the former advocating the immediate deportation of all "foreigners," the latter struggling for a measure of political respectability. The two groups converged not only on the streets but also in other sites. The chair of the Pankow CDU, a key activist in the protest, sparked a political scandal when he granted an interview about the mosque to a journal officially classified as right-wing extremist (Strauss 2006). The leader of the movement against the mosque defended himself in the press as a lover of tolerance, citing both his lesbian daughter and his Nigerian neighbors as proof, but "thought it must have been a joke when he read . . . in the newspaper that a mosque would be built in his neighborhood" because "no Muslim has ever lived in 'his part of the city'" (Peter 2007). He and other residents who fought to thwart the mosque's construction framed their struggle not around immigration or religious difference in the city of Berlin, much less in the Federal Republic of Germany, but around their perception of it as out of place in their own neighborhood (recall Ole's talk of how immigration looks to "us on the street"). As a sign allegedly illegible within the local scenery, the mosque triggered not only incredulous disbelief (much like Elsa's) but also deep anxieties about what it could, in fact, signify.[32] The protests, in turn, were perfectly in-line with pervasive discourses across Europe in which mosques appear as out of place.[33] They echoed, as well, debates about where Muslim women's head coverings and other supposedly religious symbols belong, and where they do not.[34]

The significance of ethnic alterity, and of its emplacement in the cityscape, for the articulation of political visions and commitments among young right-wing extremists in Berlin ultimately reflected the place that immigration occupies today as a singular obsession of European political discourse at large,[35] even if their language was often more explicitly racist. In recent decades, preoccupations about immigration have shaped debates about unemployment and welfare, demographic projections, criminality and law enforcement, labor laws, educational reforms, and budget allocations or the expansion of the EU, debates in which distinctions between left and right have often been blurred.[36] In German political discourse, anti-immigration rhetoric has been abundant (Karapin 1998). My informants' condemnations of "asylum shelter Germany," their complaints about excessive immigration, and their alarm about allegedly wide-open borders cite voices that have gained wide publicity during 1990s debates on immigration and asylum policies (Halfman 1997). The "asylum compromise" of 1993 constituted an official endorsement of the narrative of undue leniency toward refugees, while the remainder of the decade witnessed political clashes over proposed reforms to Kaiser-era citizenship laws and Third Reich residency laws.[37] While the reforms, when they finally passed, challenged to some

[32] Protesters mentioned, for example, shari'a law, arranged marriages, and women coerced into burkas as possible scenarios for the imminent future of the neighborhood.

[33] Consider the case of Switzerland, which has prohibited the construction of minarets altogether following a national plebiscite. In various other European countries, such blanket prohibitions or, in lieu of them, drastic restrictions, have been proposed, debated, and at times approved. See, for example, Foulkes (2007) and Traynor (2007).

[34] At some level, at least, at stake in such debates is often precisely defining the places in which embodied expressions of otherness would be "out of place," for instance, in schools, public offices, on the streets, and so on. See, for example, Walzer (1997) and Scott (2010).

[35] To be sure, immigrants in Europe have long stood as external to the nation and as paradigmatic deviants of modern state power, repeatedly emerging as a "social problem" in need of intervention (Sassen 1999). Recent discourses about otherness in Europe, however, have come to focus virtually exclusively on Islam and Muslim communities while domesticating a range of alterities formerly considered foreign (Bunzl 2005).

[36] For example, the heated debate about the headscarf in France pitted against each other the idioms of individual liberty and that of collective entitlements for religious freedom, while in the Netherlands Pim Fortuyn's inflammatory (and, for a while, widely popular) anti-immigrant rhetoric purported to defend the Dutch values of tolerance against intolerant Muslims (Walzer 1997; Van der Veer 2006).

[37] The *Asylkompromiss* put into place various measures to obstruct both the application for and granting of asylum status.

extent the seemingly ironclad link between citizenship (*Staatsangehörigkeit*) and ethnic belonging (*Volkszugehörigkeit*), they have also fortified ethnic stratification through the differential juridical construction and incorporation of distinct groups (Senders 1996).

But beyond any direct statutory or policy outcomes, these political contestations propagated a vocabulary ("asylum shelter Germany," open borders, deportations) that seeped into the utterances of the right-wing extremists with whom I worked as citations and that invested immigration with sinister meanings. The very terms of this vocabulary betrayed the difficulty of incorporating the immigrant other, who, even as a naturalized citizen, persisted as lexical difference: as immigrants (*Migranten*), foreigners with a German passport (*Ausländer mit deutschem Pass*), or, most collegially, co-citizens (*Mitbürger*) (Pred 2000; Schröder 2001). Thus, Karl's objections to Turkey's EU membership bid referenced political discourses of far wider publicity and articulateness than the rhetoric on the extreme right fringes of the political spectrum. The CDU and the Christian Social Union (Christlich-Soziale Union; CSU) especially have strategically positioned the question of Turkey at the heart of their political campaigns. As leader of the opposition at the time, Angela Merkel proposed a nationwide petition against Turkey's accession to the EU.[38] Her idea was warmly embraced by the DVU and the NPD, which proceeded to carry it into practice, leaving the CDU little choice but to swiftly and unceremoniously scrap it. For Karl and his peers, however, geopolitical, economic, and human rights debates about Turkey's EU membership fed into everyday experiences and imaginations of contamination and decline, which, so they believed, threatened to accelerate tenfold.

Beyond the topics of Turkey and refugees, talk of "foreigners' criminality" (*Ausländerkriminalität*), so central to the political imaginary of young right-wing extremists and to the rhetoric of the parties they support, also appear relentlessly in mass publicity and broadly circulating political idioms throughout Germany and Europe more broadly (Jäger, Cleve, and Ruth 1998; Gingrich and Banks 2006). Consider, as one notable example, the 2008 reelection campaign of Roland Koch (CDU), at the time a close ally and protégé of Merkel, to governor of the state of Hessen. Koch called for drastic tightening of legal and penal frameworks in the face of what he described as unbearable levels of immigrant youth violence. Experts were quick to dismantle both his diagnosis and his proposed remedies.[39] But for many, the storm that Koch's campaign incited already bolstered perceptions of foreigners' criminality as a national threat and

---

[38] Merkel's proposal was particularly notable because German conservative politicians have long resisted the introduction of the instrument of plebiscite into the country's constitution.

[39] Crime rates among immigrants, commentators observed, have in fact steadily declined. The heavy-handed penal measures Koch proposed, it was noted, have long been discarded as ineffective. Experts also argued that ineffective treatment of juvenile offenders in Hessen resulted not from legal deficiencies but rather from the incompetence of Koch's own administration.

authorized narratives of a helpless state (Sievert and Bittner 2008; Thorer, Rickmann, and Sievert 2008). Similar discursive reverberations appear concerning anxieties about employment or about demographic speculations. Both themes converged marvelously in Jürgen Rüttgers's (CDU) 2000 "Kinder statt Inder" (Children instead of Indians) campaign slogan in the North Rhein-Westphalia governorship elections. The catchphrase targeted the SPD-led federal government's plan to issue thousands of permanent residency permits for high-tech workers. Again, to the CDU's embarrassment, the right-wing extremist Republikaner Party immediately borrowed the slogan for its own campaign. On the other side of the political spectrum, party leader for the socialist WASG (Arbeit und soziale Gerechtigkeit—Die Wahlalternative [Labour and Social Justice— The Electoral Alternative]) and former SPD chairperson Oskar Lafontaine triggered a scandal when he warned, also during an election campaign, of "foreign workers" (Fremdarbeiter, a phrase carrying strong National Socialist associations) who would steal jobs from Germans.

In matter of fact, the electoral efficacy of such rhetorical strategies for hailing political constituencies remains questionable.[40] But their outlines resurfaced in the discourse of my informants time and again. They provided them at once with monolithic stereotypifications of immigrants and with a series of criteria for their differentiation. Recall Karl's distinction between the upstanding Vietnamese and the lazy Turks, or between the industrious kebab-stand vendors of Johannisthal and Schöneweide and their indolent brethren of Kreuzberg and Neukölln. In his speech, a certain chronotopic configuration of otherness in the cityscape articulated with the logic of social utility to generate distinctions between usefulness and dependency, diligence and idleness. This social Darwinist yardstick with which Karl and his peers traced boundaries across the city, and within their neighborhood, received official authorization from Schröder's immigration policies, which glorified the importation of high-tech labor while pressing forward with the exportation of refugees and with the vilification and responsibilization of the socially marginalized. In turn, my informants' culturalization of racism sat well with the threat that Muslims have been perceived to pose to civilizational notions of Europeanness within wide discursive fields across the Continent.[41] Their words cite, in mediated form, the fierce debates about the nation's cultural future that accompanied Germany's long-overdue coming to terms with the permanent presence of immigrants, and particularly

[40] Merkel's proposal flopped, Koch and the Hessen CDU suffered a humiliating loss of support (their worst result in four decades, though the deadlock following the election eventually resulted in new elections, which they carried, in large part thanks to a spectacular debacle by the SPD), and Rüttgers similarly failed the race for governorship, although, of course, many other factors besides their anti-immigration campaigns played a role in determining the outcomes.

[41] Talal Asad has observed that Islam in today's Europe is encountered as a civilizational alterity (2003b; see also Bunzl 2005). Similar patterns are evident in the United States, for example, in the writings of Samuel Huntington (1997).

of those with a Turkish background.[42] Their preoccupation over linguistic difference also emulates political discourse. When Ole complains of foreign languages at state offices or when Uta grumbles about linguistic discrimination in job ads that ask "for a Turkish[-speaking] medical assistant," they reiterate concerns that Bundestag legislators often enough express in parliamentary committees.[43]

Public debates in *die Mitte der Gesellschaft* (the mainstream, literally the middle of society) seep into the discourse of right-wing extremists and provide perceptual schemata for making sense of encounters with alterity and for imagining urban landscapes. They authorize enunciations about the excess, criminality, violence, or social dependency of immigrants, about their civilizational otherness and special privileges, and about the typologies (useful versus useless, normal versus deviant) that govern interactions with them (at the Bangladeshi train station eatery, the Turkish kebab restaurant, the Vietnamese grocery store, etc.). But beyond stereotypifications of and distinctions between and within different ethnic groups, these broad discursive fields allow interlocutors to differentiate between themselves against the third-person figure of the immigrant. If immigration today appears as a central obsession of European politics, this is at least in part because it presently serves as a fundamental prism for formulating and performing political differences at large.

We have seen how, for my informants, talk of immigration refracted right and left: leftists are pro-immigrants, rightists are "for Germans." But right-wing extremist immigration discourse also structured a fractal recursion (Irvine and Gal 2000) of the political spectrum at large within the borderlands of that very spectrum. Consider Uta's painstaking—if clumsy—effort to appear tolerant of Muslim religious practice:

> This thing with the mosque, okay, I can understand it. Hmmm . . . somehow but
> not quite really because if I go to Turkey . . . I can't just arrive there and say . . .
> "Can you build me a church because I think it would be pretty?" No one would

---

[42] In these debates, the recognition of difference often remained subservient to a notion of "dominant culture" (*Leitkultur*): a fundamental set of German values, norms, and behaviors that would define the infrastructure, so to speak, upon which cultural ornamentations could be tolerated.

[43] I had the opportunity to witness such Bundestag discussions on multilingualism in Germany on several occasions during a brief internship with an SPD representative. Here, too, we find parallels with debates in the United States, where not only political conservatives but also academics such as Samuel Huntington express fears about the multicultural threat to the cultural identity of the nation. Huntington identifies a grave danger in linguistic diversification, and particularly in Hispanic bilingualism, not because the alleged cultural and linguistic isolation of Hispanics may obstruct their successful integration and could thus contribute to the development of a marginalized ethnicity, but precisely because in his view it grants bilingual Hispanics an unfair and privileged access to resources, for example, through discriminatory job hiring (2004). For an in-depth exploration of the anxieties that have surfaced around the issue of linguistic alterity in the age of ethnic identities, see Silverstein (2003). For more on the relation between language and nationalism in Germany and elsewhere in Europe, see Blommaert and Verschueren (1998).

ever do that for me. They would just all show me the finger. But here they want to hand everything to the Turks on a fucking silver platter and everything should be done for them, more or less.[44]

With her judgment, Uta positioned herself in relation to the range of pronouncements on mosques across the political spectrum, some of which I have already reviewed. But she also sought to situate herself in relation to her peers, as more moderate and reasonable than most. She and her friends regularly drew on widely circulating discourses about immigrants, asylum policies, or Germany's historical responsibility to fabricate such contrasts between themselves. In doing so, they copied the contrasts that configure the broader political spectrum—tolerance and intolerance, moderation and extremism—and that relegated them to its fringes in the first place. Within the presumed frontier of the political field, these differences are reiterated.[45]

Consider two further examples. I met eighteen-year-old Robert at Grünau, where he and his friend Rene operated the kitchen at Khan's, the newly opened eatery where, in chapter 2, we met Danny and Norman exchanging ring-tones (I return in detail to Khan's in chapter 6). They took charge over the business whenever its owner, Mr. Khan, was away—that is, most of the time. A Union soccer fan and an NPD enthusiast of modest height, with short brown hair and a trimmed goatee, he proudly wore banned fashion labels and frequented nationalist establishments. One night, outside the doors of a bar popular with the extreme right scene, he described the NPD to me as an authentic alternative to the dullness and incompetence of established politics, superior to the rest in its ideas and its commitment for change. He objected to any comparison between the NPD and the NSDAP (Nationalsozialistische Deutsche Arbeiterpartei [National Socialist German Workers' Party]).[46] The media, he said, misrepresented the party as extremist, violent, and racist toward immigrants, whereas in fact they were not after good immigrants who worked and paid their taxes, like Khan. They only wanted a stop to the flood of immigrants who arrived in Germany intent on funding their parasitical laziness through the country's generous welfare system, he continued. Robert's monologue invoked immigration to

[44]The mosque in Pankow—which featured extensively in the news at the time and clearly inspired Uta's comments—in fact relied exclusively on private donations for its construction.

[45]The question, of course, is not whether my informants do, in fact, actually replicate any particular contrast, nor even whether some ostensible original exists. What counts is the successful and, as it were, retroactive construal of their sameness, the felicitous fabrication of the "copy" as a copy of something (Gal 2007).

[46]Interestingly, few right-wing extremists I knew romanticized Hitler himself, though many worshipped other prominent Nazis, like Rudolf Hess. Like Robert, they seemed to accept the account of the Third Reich as catastrophe, albeit with a nationalist twist: Hitler was a disaster because he ran the war incompetently, opening a second front and granting the Allies victory instead of reaching an agreement with the United Kingdom after occupying most of Continental Europe, and leaving Germany's national territory smaller than it had been before the war.

anchor the NPD (and by implication, himself) somewhere between mainstream and extreme—reiterating the contrasts that govern the political terrain at large squarely within its frontier—by mimicking the sorts of gradations of tolerance of immigrants operative more broadly. Recall Sebastian, also an NPD supporter, who, sitting in Little Istanbul, disagreed with Robert: eventually they all have to leave, he said.[47] But many of Robert's peers carved a moderate and reasonable space for themselves within the so-called extreme, positing always the next one over as the real, mean, violent, racist, and extremist Nazi. The fans of Union, notwithstanding their club's fame as home to neo-Nazi hooligans, insisted that "here it is just about fun," and pointed instead at their principal rival at the time, BFC Dynamo, as the club whose fans "are all Nazis."[48] Moderation and extremism can be projected onto soccer clubs just as well as political parties. The real witch is always one soccer club over.

Freddi, for example, disagreed with Robert's characterization of the NPD as moderate and tolerant. Freddi described his social circles as almost exclusively composed of neo-Nazis, while excluding himself from that category. In his life, he told me, he sought to emulate the "virtues" of his (authoritarian and violent) father: moral integrity, hard work, discipline, firmness, and nationalism. Freddi liked to savor the tunes and lyrics of banned music, in which he saw a manifesto of his moral values and an anthology of historical role models: heavy metal songs and "folk" ballads about cultural degeneration, political corruption, "German" WWII victims, Rudolf Hess, or the SA leader Horst Wessel. One night I found him at his apartment with a younger girl, a gymnasium student. He played two newly acquired CDs for us: soft rock ballads and loud heavy metal pieces that lamented the corrosion of pride, extolled the camaraderie of troops, eulogized the sacrifice of unnamed heroes, and vowed to follow in their footsteps. The girl seemed ill at ease. She didn't like "this music, nationalist music," she replied, when Freddi asked for her opinion. She found the music poor and the lyrics "problematic." There was nothing "Nazi" about the music, Freddi quickly retorted. The songs did not incite hatred or violence, he claimed, and besides, even his "nigger" cousin—Freddi's uncle was Cuban—enjoyed them. Why should such music be banned, he asked us? The girl seemed unconvinced, and Freddi carried on. People of other countries that have perpetrated injustice nevertheless take pride in their culture, without the dilemmas that cause so many legal prohibitions in Germany. Think of Stalin, who was even

[47] Robert's dependence upon a Bangladeshi immigrant probably had some impact upon the way he positioned himself as an NPD supporter. Most NPD supporters that I knew personally seemed to locate themselves closer to Sebastian—all immigrants would eventually have to go.

[48] Elsa's bewildered reaction to the Turkish-speaking men betrays something about what she had been accustomed to take for granted, and hence about the dominant structure of the club's fan base. The group I accompanied there no doubt included a majority of NPD supporters and more than a few characters who answered quite closely the stereotypical figure of the neo-Nazi in the eyes of most Germans.

more of a dictator than Hitler, he proclaimed. Why must only Germans suffer this way? Why should his generation pay for Hitler's sins?

For Freddi and his friends, *Nationale* (nationalist, right-wing extremist) music formed a domain against which to fabricate not only a subcultural identification but also a moral economy, historical consciousness, and political action.[49] Freddi's advocacy sidestepped the girl's critique, instead reframing the argument around legal bans and construing his musical consumption as a quotidian politics of resistance. *Nationale* music offered Freddi a position he viewed as moderate, as located somewhere between dominant, liberal, democratic narratives and neo-Nazi historical revisionism and rejecting both the unconditional condemnation of the Third Reich as pure evil and the unreserved neo-Nazi veneration of Hitler as dogmatic and untenable extremities. His comparison between Hitler and Stalin echoed the voices of conservative parties to the Historikerstreit.[50] But Freddi credited instead his father and grandfather, who in his eyes acknowledged the bad aspects of both the Third Reich and the GDR while recognizing their memorable ones—exemplary leaders, heroic sacrifice, solidarity and camaraderie—for his "balanced" view. Like him, they also enjoyed "foreign food" (read, Turkish kebab) occasionally while objecting to its excessive preponderance. Like him, they would also gladly accommodate the occasional kebab stand or immigrant in their neighborhood but were opposed to what they perceived as their immoderate presence.

Much the same as Robert, Freddi also projected gradations of moderation and extremism across the political spectrum, but one that identified the NPD with "hobby fascists" (*Hobbyfaschos*) and the DVU with "serious nationalists":

FREDDI: I find it totally depressing, the whole system. They say "freedom," "freedom of expression." Well, I, it's not like I say we should shave the Jews' hair or anything like that, that they should be hanged or anything like that.

NATE: But why don't you?

FREDDI: Well, that's because of [what happened] before, the Holocaust and all that, that was awful. It was [awful], that's true. But something like this [music], a commemoration only of the soldiers or those in the present . . . [It's] also not against the reds here or something like that, you know. [These bands] are here today and not in those days . . . and that's what they're singing about. It's like you're not allowed to say that the system is shit and all that . . . I don't understand really, why they're so heavy-handed with it. The leftists here are allowed to [act] against Nazis and [say] "Nazis out!" By this they mean us, of course, they mean nowadays, that is, more or less us, my people more or less . . . I have so many friends who really know something. They're like thirty-three [years

---

[49] For a well-rounded collection of essays on nationalist music and its social significance for right-wing extremists, see Dornbusch and Raabe (2002).

[50] See footnote 15 in chapter 1 about the so-called Historikerstreit.

old] . . . they're not this kind of "hobby fascists" who walk down the street and only because a Turk happens to be standing there they beat him up. [They] really think for themselves . . . [about] politics of course, DVU. NPD I find also terrible.

NATE: Why?

FREDDI: "Foreigners out!," this whole thing, I find it totally terrible. This sentence for example, "foreigners out," that simply doesn't work . . . I can't accept it. And then there are people who sit inside the DVU who really think for themselves.

NATE: DVU more than NPD?

FREDDI: Yeah, for sure, if you ask me. They say . . . just the way I also see it, the kebab place can stand there. It can stand there, but not in such excess. They also say then that there shouldn't be such places like Kreuzberg and Neukölln, but rather that it should all be distributed everywhere, because this way it [the immigrants] would . . . in the first place they more or less become dangerous because they all sit on top of each other. If it were distributed everywhere, let's say two Germans to one foreigner or something like that, then we do away with it, you know what I mean? Then it just wouldn't be a problem. Then it would always be the case that Germans won't have to feel fear on the street.

NATE: But tell me, I always thought that the DVU also say "foreigners out," don't they?

FREDDI: But not this way, no, not so blatantly, not so blatantly as the NPD, it's the NPD after all among all those bully-Nazis everywhere.

Freddi found the NPD far too extreme, far too blatant in their hateful rhetoric, a home for shallow "hobby fascists" and "bully-Nazis." "Serious nationalists" supported the more moderate DVU, which opposed unrestrained flows of immigration and particularly those who abused the country's welfare system. The similarity with Robert's discourse, and the modes in which both borrow on dominant political contrasts in order to position themselves discursively, is striking, even as their electoral conclusions are at odds. The differences that carve up the political field at large resurface within their fringe milieus. In much the same way as the category of (right-wing) extremism grants dominant voices a horizon against which to appear as moderate and tolerant, analogous narrative strategies of displacement govern the performance of moderation and the generation of positions from which to enunciate a bigoted politics within the allegedly excluded political extreme.

EVERYTHING IN MODERATION

The resonances between ethnic otherness, urban landscape, and political contrasts come into sharp focus around food. To be sure, the consumption of any ethnicized commodity entails proximity with the ethnicized other.[51] Eating, however, implies quite literally the material incorporation of the other's reified—cooked—essence into one's own body, the physical absorption of its culinary expression, its flavors, odors, foreign-ringing names, and the values attached to the collectivity to which it "belongs." A constant tension results between consumer desire and anxieties about pollution and bodily well-being—tangible bearers of a "metaphysical peril" (Holmes 2000, 87). How the physical self navigates the space between antiseptic avoidance and careless indulgence, how it engages contaminating otherness, says something as well about the political self and provides a discursive domain within which to situate it. Political subjectivity unfolds between the *Wurst* (sausage) as proper German nutrition and the *Döner* (kebab) as the seductive sensuality of otherness. Talk about ethnic food always operates, too, as the authorization of certain spatial imaginations of otherness in the urban landscape, of its emplacement in specific sites and regions. The spatial distribution of culinary diversity is understood as iconic of the spatial distribution of embodied otherness. Both the body and the city appear in such renderings as German spaces under threat of alien penetration. The extent of their degeneration becomes evident in the incidence of kebab locales and in the consumption of their products.

Sitting at Little Istanbul, Sebastian pronounced uncompromising views on immigrants, calling for the banning of their businesses and for their blanket deportation. His routine patronage of a Turkish-owned and managed restaurant clearly presented for him not the least of tensions with the views he expressed. Rather, he sought to perform himself, against the background of immigration, as provocatively extremist, a rebel, in relation to his peers. His friend Danny, for example, an equally enthusiastic lover of the NPD and of banned right-wing extremist apparel, who talked to me of the degenerative impact of foreign cultures in Little Istanbul, struggled to appear moderate in relation to Sebastian: "I am not an extremist," he said, disagreeing with Sebastian's call for blanket deportations. The problem for him was the excess of immigrants and their restaurants, he said. Both Danny the sensible patriot and Sebastian the unyielding neo-Nazi were outflanked by Lukas, their chubby, baby-faced friend whose well-to-do parents and high school diploma placed him a notch above the rest of them. Also an NPD supporter, Lukas attended demonstrations sporadically and agreed with Sebastian that all immigrants should be deported. Immigrants, he explained, were responsible for all of Germany's problems, from unemployment to criminality. In contrast to his friend, he said, he remained true to his word by eating only "German food" and never at Turkish or Asian restaurants.[52]

---

[51] More precisely, ethnic consumption creates a proximity with stereotypifications of the collectivity for which the commodity stands as an indexically iconic incarnation.

[52] These two cuisines occupied most forcefully the slot of the other in his—and others of my informants'—culinary landscape. On several opportunities he happily ate at Italian restaurants and at McDonalds, which apparently for him belonged with "German food." Whereas he too spent

In the company of Lukas, Sebastian, or even Danny, it becomes easier to understand, perhaps, how Freddi distinguished himself as a moderate—a distinction that he too draws on a restaurant menu. Even his father, he noted to me, once brought Chinese food for lunch when he came to visit.

> It's like this, I have nothing [against foreigners]. I go to the kebab stand . . . to eat kebab, I go to eat Greek. The only thing I'm against is that they're all too many there, too many. A kebab stand on every corner is too many. [There are] three stands around here now. One kebab stand in front of the train station here, that would have been enough for Adlershof [his neighborhood]. Or a Greek [food stand]. And it's just too many.

The putative distribution of ethnic food in urban space indexes for Freddi the prevalence of ethnic bodies. Both are harmless in moderation. A few immigrants or a kebab stand will do no harm, nor would the moderate physical consumption of gastronomical otherness. It is as if the same toxic substance—safe only in small quantities—that threatens the cityscape penetrates the body too through ethnic cuisine. Food and eating served Freddi as a domain within which he could situate himself politically as moderate and reasonable through quotidian performances. The dangers spelled by the proliferation of ethnic food venues to the physical self generates as well a geography of violence. If too much kebab appears to threaten the physical well-being of German diners, kebab stands emerge as uncanny locations, sites of unknown and unpredictable dangers to German bodies:

> FREDDI: It was [outside] Morgensonne, a favorite bar of ours. Me [and three friends] were only walking around and then in our drunkenness we sang a couple of chants, just for fun and not to bother anyone. We [wished] a wonderful good evening to everyone. We sang there.
>
> NATE: But what sort of [songs]?
>
> FREDDI: Well, "Germany Awake" [*Deutschland erwache*] or something like that, you know, some sort of . . . it was out of drunkenness. And in any case then two [men] come from the kebab stand there. A teeny-weeny man comes out . . . a Turk, and a rather large [man] . . . like a pasha . . . and the small one says suddenly, "What is 'Germany'? 'Germany,' ha ha ha!" [in a mocking voice]. And the other comes along and smacks [my friend]. Well [my friend] didn't like that naturally and hit back, right? And the large man, I was standing in front of him with [my friend]. I was lucky that [my friend] was standing next to me. I would have been done with in no time [otherwise]. Well [my friend] punched his head once and he fell over. He probably stumbled or something like that. Yeah, and then, well, it was wimpy after all, it was the first time that I

---

many an afternoon at Little Istanbul, he felt that by limiting his purchases there to alcohol, he remained true to his principles.

kicked people [lying] on the floor, because I was really scared. Had they stood up we would have been done with at once, we would not have been able to do anything. I had then that day Docs [Doc Marten boots] on, well, strong boots. I doled out such blows. I mean, he didn't bleed or anything like that, but he certainly didn't get up.

In Freddi's story the kebab stand appears as a dangerous, foreign site in the national and urban geography. It harbors unforeseen risks to the German body just as it scars German landscapes. As a dramatic disruption, it interferes with Freddi's notion of fun: four friends, heavily intoxicated, strolling about on a pleasant night and politely greeting passersby as they howl neo-Nazi chants, not looking for trouble, mind you, not trying to provoke or harass anyone, until the kebab stand violently cuts short their ostensibly harmless, leisurely pastime. His narrative charts a trajectory between familiarity and strangeness, safety and danger, between Morgensonne as a German place and the kebab stand as an anti-German place from which sinister forces that would menace the nation surge. Of course, this perilous journey also opens, at the same time, a narrative space within which Freddi and his friends play the part of national heroes, an opportunity for the performance of personal sacrifice, and the itinerary of vigilantes out on patrol, intent on literally beating national threats (such as mockery of Germany by "foreigners") to the ground.

As a spatialized condensation of otherness, the kebab becomes the concrete symbol of embodied alterity within the geographical imaginaries of my informants. Narratives like Freddi's, which link ethnic otherness with violence and danger, circulate as hearsay and weave into the broader discursive fields of mass publicity, where immigrant violence and criminality are scandalized, gaining the status of social facts. With Lukas on its "extremist" flank and Freddi at its "moderate" limit, a spectrum of political positionings rests on these "facts." If for many readers—as indeed sometimes to me—the distinctions they performed often appear shallow, for them they signal glaring differences. Uta summed up her typology of possible positions on immigration and food as follows:

Well, there aren't really any real rightists. For me real rightists are those who follow through with their opinions, who really say "bloody foreigners" [scheiße Ausländer] and then really don't eat kebab, don't ever go to the pizzeria, [who] follow through with this thing. And these others, who really don't have a clue . . . the others who . . . stand there and then yell "Sieg Heil" but then don't give me an answer why they yell that or what they find so great about it . . . The people who look up to Hitler, who say, "Okay, that is a role-model, that is for me the best man," they have a crack in their head in my opinion. They're not quite normal. Those who just say "bloody foreigners out!" and then also keep to their own rules and don't have anything to do with [foreigners] and so on, about them I say, "Okay, they act upon their opinions." And the others are in my opinion all hangers-on. I can't say "bloody foreigners out!" but the next minute stand at the stall and get a kebab for myself. That doesn't make sense, right? [In that case] I would not be allowed to ever eat their junk. It's that simple. But those others who really [say,] "Sieg Heil" and "Heil Hitler" and "Hitler is mine" and all that, well they, I find them not quite normal. They need to let [their] grandma and grandpa explain it to them a little bit and then maybe they would understand me.

Uta invoked immigrants and foreign food in order to describe four different types of nationalists. First, those who swear allegiance to Hitler and the Third Reich appeared to her "not quite normal," as if they "have a crack in their head," as beyond the pale of legitimate political positions. These were, in her view, extremist neo-Nazis.[53] Next came those who, like Lukas, distanced themselves from National Socialism but remained true to their nationalist principles in their gastronomical praxis. Uta described this second group as too extremist for her, yet legitimate and coherent. Third, we find those who—like Sebastian—howled chants and talked tough but whose eating habits betrayed their hypocrisy and superficiality, revealing them as fakes and flakes. Finally, Danny, Freddi, and Uta herself emerge in this classification as moderately and reasonably positioned on ethnic alterity, sporadically savoring a kebab yet wary of unwholesome overindulgence, tolerant of the occasional immigrant yet opposed to the excessive presence of "foreigners." In sum, Uta's rendering of her social milieu left place for lunatic fanatics, authentic extremists, fickle phonies, and reasonable moderates.

At the same time, Uta's discourse too appeared redolent of the very same contradictions that, according to her, the kebab signified for some of her friends:

NATE: Do you ever eat kebab?
UTA: Yes, well, once in a while I do, I eat it gladly but I don't have to live [in Neukölln].
NATE: Well, there is enough around here.
UTA: Well, not really. I mean, here it's not that hugely represented. I mean, here in Köpenick there is one [stand] . . . but it doesn't taste good at all. I mean, I at least don't eat kebab there. Many [people] eat there but I don't like it. It has to be tasty for me or otherwise I don't get it.
NATE: There by the [train station] on the main street there are . . .
UTA: Yeah, there are quite a lot there, but when you sit here in the evening you don't really feel like going all the way there to get yourself a kebab. It would be nicer after all if we had one of those here.

The problem with the kebab, plainly put, is that it is both too much and not enough. As indexical of embodied otherness, it serves as a prism of sorts that allows the refraction of political hues and the positioning of selves within

---

[53] Notably, it is only this group that she describes not through the tropes of immigration and foreign food in the present but rather through its relation to the National Socialist past. This corresponds to her perception of it as incomprehensibly fanatical.

vernacular social contexts. But it remains always a slippery sign, a tentative, interactional gesture always on the verge of being undone. It pits conviction and temptation, nutrition and contamination, desire and danger, honor and hunger against each other. It ensnares all but the fittest and betrays those whose palates do not match their words. It embodies at once a threatening otherness and the possibility of its tenuous domestication through personalized relations with vendors. It simultaneously exudes corporeal danger and offers physical gratification.

Part II

Penal Regimes of Political Delinquency

IT MUST HAVE BEEN AROUND 6:30 IN THE MORNING, Freddi recalled, when police troops in riot gear kicked open the door to his apartment. They would have hardly needed to rake through the place in order to net a handsome booty of illicit paraphernalia. Freddi had been sharing his small apartment with his friend Gino, widely known throughout the district as SS-Gino for the tattoo that decorated the fingers of his right hand. At the time, Gino was serving one of his numerous incarceration terms, but his abundant assortment of right-wing extremist odds and ends remained, compounding Freddi's own rich collection of banned music CDs.

And yet, the cache of dubious articles failed to distract the cops from their mission. They had raided the apartment to hunt for a particular pendant of the Odal rune, following a tip from an unnamed informant who claimed he had seen Freddi strolling the streets with the chevron-like symbol dangling from a chain around his neck. Like other runic characters (*Runen*), the Odal rune is popular among German right-wing extremists, gesturing at once to the mythical horizon of a pagan Arian past and to the historical horizon of National Socialism, which has employed these symbols extensively. Borrowed from ancient Germanic script,[1] the Odal symbol served also as the emblem of an SS unit and, more recently, of the banned postwar organization Viking Youth (Wiking Jugend), among others. Having located the item, the police confiscated it, and the state attorney later laid charges against Freddi—not for the possession of the jewelry piece per se, but rather on the suspicion that he had paraded it outdoors.[2]

---

[1] Runic script dates back to an early Germanic alphabet used throughout Northern Europe in the first millennium BC.

[2] The parallels here with the recently much-discussed case of the Muslim veil and French *laïcité* are palpable. As the discussion below will make clear, these parallels ultimately refer to certain shared secularist assumptions about the distinction between public and private, and they extend to other prohibitions on public behaviors and displays (e.g., sexual acts, nudity, alcohol, and so on).

The sudden eruption of the force of law onto the snoozing daybreak of what, for Freddi, would have otherwise been another unremarkable morning hints at how the young people at the center of this study encounter the opaque, intricate mechanisms for the governance of hate in their daily lives. It is these mechanisms that, in today's Germany, produce the figure that I have called the political delinquent (Shoshan 2011). The once-provocative notion that the category of delinquency, rather than descriptively referencing an objective social reality instead constitutes a "political operation" (Foucault 1995, 277), hardly requires mention in our post-Foucauldian age. Mindful of the distinct historical cofigurations of crime and politics,[3] my use of the concept of political delinquency is accordingly not meant to disavow the political nature of the category of delinquency as such but rather to specify a particular articulation of the two. Specifically, in the case of political delinquency, a relatively explicit political project (unlike, e.g., the crude resistance of social banditry) comes together with a strong sense of delinquency in its conventional meaning (unlike, e.g., in the case of political prisoners). In contemporary Germany, Freddi, Gino, and their friends stand at once for a political agenda deemed sufficiently menacing to warrant intensive state persecution (a racially pure nation, Third Reich antidemocratic authoritarianism) and for the sorts of criminal forms that commonly characterize the figure of the delinquent.

Freddi's story raises a number of important questions that will guide our exploration of these mechanisms and of their impact on young right-wing extremists in this chapter. How, for example, does the legal banning of right-wing extremist things tally with the constitutional prohibition of censorship? What assumptions about symbols, their users, and the context of their deployments— what semiotic ideologies—underpin the interpretative frameworks under which law regulates nationalism and xenophobia in Germany? In what ways do liberal, secularist distinctions between private and public and presuppositions about intentions and motivations define and enable the drawing of the political distinction? And how do legal regimes and mechanisms of surveillance appear in the quotidian everyday of those whom they target?

In pursuing these lines of inquiry, we shall see how the traces of denazification, of that originary exclusion upon which the Federal Republic of Germany was constituted as a "militant democracy" (Weiss 1994), have been profoundly inscribed at its very heart. From its inception, the FRG walked a tightrope in

---

[3] Foucault notes the central importance for the emergence of the category of delinquency of the need to graft criminality onto popular leaders and social struggles (1995, 273–75). In turn, Eric Hobsbawm (1969) famously coined the phrase "social bandits" to capture the slippage between a certain figure of rural criminality and a crude mode of political resistance. The category of political prisoners has likewise indicated a certain (uncomfortable) articulation of criminality and politics (see, e.g., Feldman 1991). From a different perspective, Jean Comaroff and John Comaroff (2006, 223) have insisted on the fundamentally political stakes of "crime talk."

its attempt to settle the paradox inherent in its precarious relation to its past.[4] The urgency of signaling a total break, a radical and irreversible discontinuity between the nascent liberal democratic order and its totalitarian National Socialist predecessor, entailed two contradictory impositions. On the one hand, it implied the absolute necessity of fortifying the Federal Republic against the return of the repressed by implementing constraints that would ensure beyond doubt the suppression of the demon of National Socialism in particular and of German "militarism" more generally. It required, therefore, repressive mechanisms for constraining political liberty and the freedoms of expression and association. On the other hand, it spelled an imperative need to codify and institute a political order that would drastically contrast with this haunting past precisely through its commitment to liberal-democratic rights and freedoms.[5]

Thus, totalitarianism was cast as an absolute other through the strict emphasis on and guarantee of all that which it violated, namely, liberal freedoms, human rights, democratic citizenship, the equality of men, and so forth. "Human dignity shall be inviolable," so opens the German constitution (Grundgesetz; henceforth, Basic Law). The allegedly successful transformation of West Germany's institutional frameworks and political culture along these lines allowed it to conceive of itself—and to present itself—as the authentic departure from National Socialism and from what were perceived as longer-lasting German traditions of militarism and authoritarianism. The absence of censorship and the constitutional guarantees on liberal freedoms served not only to mark a drastic break with National Socialism but also, and as importantly, to signal a fundamental contrast between the FRG and its contemporary state-socialist rival, the GDR.

Both the democratic and the repressive impositions permeate the legal codes of the Federal Republic in a variety of texts and subtexts. The tension between them appears, for example, in Article 139 of the Basic Law, concerned with assuring the continuing validity of denazification policies enacted by the occupying Allies. Article 139 pronounces that legal procedures "for the 'Liberation of the German People from National Socialism and Militarism' shall not be affected by the provisions of this Basic Law," including when they collide with fundamental liberal rights.[6] In other words, West Germany's constitutional code excludes from both its jurisdiction and its guarantees of rights and freedoms the regulations established by the occupying Allies in order to sanitize the German nation from its maladies, a project that, perhaps against the hopes and

[4] In fact, the raison d'être of both German states comprised the generation of a radical distance with respect to National Socialism, albeit in very different ways (Weiss 1994).

[5] This paradoxical relation to the National Socialist past was reiterated in debates about the deployment of German troops in Kosovo, where "never again war" was pitted against "never again Auschwitz" (see Huyssen 2003a, 73).

[6] All translations of the German Basic Law included here are taken from the official English edition published by the press office of the German Bundestag (German Bundestag 2001).

visions of some in the immediate aftermath of the war (Weiss 1994), has since turned into a permanent feature of the political culture of the Federal Republic.

Such tensions are by no means merely latent. Far from disavowing them, legal application often places them at the center of juridical deliberation. Consider, for example, the following statement by a court in Lower Saxony, cited here in a ruling of the Constitutional Court of Berlin in which it upholds a disciplinary procedure against a police officer reported to have expressed National Socialist ideas:

> The liberal democratic constitutional order stands in the sharpest possible contrast to the National Socialist system of injustice (*Unrechtssystem*). The recent formation of our democracy is thoroughly shaped by our experiences with the totalitarian system that preceded it. The establishment of effective legal guarantees that would ensure that such political trends never again gain influence over the state dominated the thoughts of the authors of the constitution.[7] (Verfassungsgericht Berlin 2007)

In the same breath, the court insists on the dominant place that National Socialism, as a sort of radical other, played in the formation of the postwar German democratic order, and proclaims both the democratic and the repressive imperatives as the evident results of this absolute exclusion. Not infrequently, different courts seek an equilibrium between these two imperatives, weighing the relative potential harm that could be caused to the democratic system on the one hand and to individual rights and freedoms on the other by either conviction or acquittal. In 2010, for instance, the Federal Constitutional Court overturned a decision by the Munich Higher Court that placed a five-year publication ban on a convicted right-wing extremist, citing the constitutional principle of proportionality and the need to strike a balance between the possible damage to society on the one hand and the harm that would be caused by the infringement on the person's freedom of expression on the other (Bundesverfassungsgericht 2010). On another occasion, a person who distributed an open letter to members of the Bundestag (Federal Parliament), in which he compared the Federal Republic unfavorably with the Third Reich, was found guilty of severe denigration of the state by a court in Frankfurt am Main. The Federal Court of Justice rejected his appeal against the ruling, arguing that the constitutional guarantee of the freedom of expression could not justify such excessive disparagement of the state (Bundesgerichtshof 2002a).[8]

---

[7] All translations of court rulings are mine.

[8] Curiously, while the Federal Court upheld the lower court's conviction, it did overturn the prison sentence, arguing that the constitutional right of freedom of expression, while not sufficient to acquit the defendant, nevertheless must be taken into account in deciding upon the appropriate punishment.

To be sure, the tension inherent in the ultimately irreconcilable entailments of these legal codes and of their conventional juridical applications replicates in some ways the conundrum of the limits of liberalism more generally. And yet the incessantly shifting contours of this tension, the authorizing idioms and historical imaginaries that it invokes, the unparalleled political stakes invested in it, and the fierce struggles over it all become meaningful against the collective memory of a very uniquely German horizon, firmly locatable in the years 1919–45 (Weiss 1994). Shades of this tension resurface across the penal process, from the legal code itself to its juridical interpretation and application, from the language of verdicts to deliberations about appropriate punishments. The immoderate excesses to which it occasionally gives rise are sure to strike many an outside observer as plainly absurd. From calls to ban the swastika across the EU (politely declined by countries with significant Hindu populations such as the UK) to the criminalization of WWII model airplanes faithfully decorated with their Luftwaffe symbols or school bans on New Balance sneakers, which some administrators have evidently come to associate with neo-Nazi fashion, they betray the lingering salience not only of the memory of the Third Reich but also, and as importantly, of a hegemonic narrative about the fall of the Weimar Republic. It is with these traces, with these excesses, and with the manners in which they reveal themselves to young right-wing extremists that this chapter is concerned.

In order to pursue these questions, some elucidation of the institutional architecture that governs right-wing extremist discourses and practices is indispensable. It will serve as a basis for interrogating the ideologies upon which these penal frameworks and their concrete applications hinge, and for discussions of law enforcement in subsequent chapters. As we shall see, the convoluted governance—and production—of political delinquency creates a wide space of ambiguity necessary for its operation. How should the juridical process incorporate and approximate notions of intentions and motivations? When is an association between a sign and an organization strong enough to justify the sort of infringement upon the freedom of expression that its banning would entail, and how to estimate the strength of the association? What uses of prohibited symbols clearly signal disapproval and may therefore be condoned? At stake in these ambiguities is precisely the possibility of negotiating the contradictory impositions of denazification and militant democracy.

"THERE SHALL BE NO CENSORSHIP"

The place to start our exploration of how this tension between the democratic and the repressive impositions manifests itself in the legal code, in juridical practice and law enforcement, and in the daily lives of young right-wing extremists is no doubt the Basic Law. Articles 5 and 9 of the German constitution respectively guarantee the freedom of expression and the freedom of association, and bear direct impact on the penal governance of political deviance.[9] Both reflect at once the fundaments and limits of a liberal order: the constitutional promise of an absolute guarantee of individual liberties, including the right to form collectivities, and at the same time the inevitable constraints upon these liberties, formulated in general terms and relegated to the authority of subsidiary legal codes (e.g., the criminal law). The unique tensions of the German case unfold within these subsidiary codes, and through several mechanisms of legal regulation that include, most prominently, laws for the protection of young people, laws against defamation and incitement to hatred or violence, and laws governing the legality of organizations. Bestowing flesh and blood upon abstract constitutional constraints, these legal mechanisms detail an arsenal of criteria, procedures, and punitive measures for the liberal-democratic state's struggle against those who, by broad publics in Germany, are viewed as its enemies. They rely on a sequence of distinctions that render their application a precarious act of situated interpretation.

Let me pause briefly on the nature of these mechanisms, which will be important for understanding the penal governance of right-wing extremism in Germany. First, the Protection of Young Persons Act has as its central concern the curbing of whatever may adversely impact the moral development of children and adolescents, and it outlines the legal and administrative framework for criminalizing or otherwise constraining such risk factors.[10] As the Federal Constitutional Court put it on one occasion:

> The significant constitutional interest in the undisturbed development of youth has as its aim, among other things, to prevent the rise of racial hatred, belligerence, and anti-democratic tendencies. The ideology of National Socialism is intrinsically

[9] The first two paragraphs of Articles 5 and 9 read as follows:

Art. 5(1): Every person shall have the right freely to express and disseminate his opinions in speech, writing, and pictures and to inform himself without hindrance from generally accessible sources. Freedom of the press and freedom of reporting by means of broadcasts and films shall be guaranteed. There shall be no censorship.

Art. 5(2): These rights shall find their limits in the provisions of general laws, in provisions for the protection of young persons, and in the right to personal honor.

And:

Art. 9(1): All Germans shall have the right to form corporations and other associations.

Art. 9(2): Associations whose aims or activities contravene the criminal laws, or that are directed against the constitutional order or the concept of international understanding, shall be prohibited.

[10] Translations of the Protection of Young Persons Act are taken from the official English version published by the Federal Ministry for Family, Senior Citizens, Women, and Children (BMFSFJ 2002).

shaped by such ideological elements. Its glorification, rehabilitation, or playing down in the media can lead youths to "socio-ethical confusion," which could justify the limitation of its dissemination so as to protect youth. (Bundesverfassungsgericht 2007a)

The law details both specific limitations (e.g., on smoking, drinking alcohol, gambling, etc.) and general frameworks for formulating—whether by statutory legislation or by administrative decree—and implementing legally binding decisions in particular cases. Most important for our purposes, it regulates the periodic generation by a committee of experts of a "List of Media Harmful to Young Persons," and specifies the institutions authorized with the implementation of the bans indicated in the blacklist. The committee, which goes by the name of the Federal Department for Media Harmful to Young Persons (Bundesprüfstelle für jugendgefährdende Medien, or BPjM),[11] is a rather peculiar forum. It assembles a sundry assortment of cultural "characters" (MacIntyre 1984) who must together assess the moral repercussions of specific media on young people: representatives of the federal government, each of the federal states, public institutions responsible for the welfare of Germany's youth, educational institutions, youth NGOs, officially recognized religious groups, and the domains of art, literature, publishing, and media providers. It is up to these experts, as delegates of society, to delineate the outline of a morally upright upbringing.

Alongside items judged to plainly transgress against the criminal code, and that are therefore banned altogether, the blacklist that the BPjM publishes enumerates those items that are deemed morally or spiritually harmful to the proper *Bildung* of responsible members of German society, and that fall under strict regulations aimed to thwart the exposure of young people to them. Constraining the dissemination of such articles to young people thus forms a key concern of the Young Persons Act. Of most importance to young right-wing extremists are the verdicts that the BPjM passes on music and films. Frequently, my informants seemed to understand quite well the grounds for particular decisions, say, on their beloved musicians. That the lyrics of songs by such neo-Nazi groups as Landser—which hailed the "race war," called for the mass poisoning of Berlin's Turkish neighborhoods, or described refugee shelters in flames—prompted a ban from the BPjM they took as self-evident. As often, however, they appeared puzzled by the experts' decision, for example, in the case of the so-called folk singer Frank Rennicke, whose acoustic ballads have been significantly more subtle in their nationalist and xenophobic tenor.

To my knowledge, none of the young people with whom I worked has ever glimpsed the blacklist of banned media, though most knew of its existence and

---

[11] This is the official English translation. However, "review board" would be a more faithful rendering of *Prüfstelle* into English than "department." The BPjM operates under the Federal Ministry for Family, Senior Citizens, Women, and Children (BMFSFJ).

seemed relatively well informed about the legal status of particular items. Gino, for instance, once provided me with a detailed rundown of all the violent skin-head movies he had seen. From *American History X*, which, despite its explicit violence, has not come under any ban, to the Australian cult film *Romper Stomper*, which the BPjM has included in its list, he demonstrated a firm grasp of their legal status. His friend Freddi, one of my principle suppliers of extreme right music, showed a similarly refined knowledge of the legality of the different CDs that he would lend me. He would classify them as either neutral (or, at least as he saw it, bereft of political valence), *Rechte* (that is, politically far right, yet legal), or, finally, banned.

Freddi, Gino, and their friends encounter the Protection of Young Persons Act and its consequences not through officially released documents, such as the List of Media Harmful to Young Persons, but rather in its concrete penal effects. The legality of their belongings comes into focus whenever, guided by the decisions of the BPjM, police search their apartments or their bodies, confiscate items, and at times raise criminal charges and instigate judicial processes against them. Body searches in particular have been a routine practice in the train stations, kiosks, and bars where I worked. And playing blacklisted music too loud can result in legal charges due to complaints from annoyed neighbors (Amtsgericht Rathenow 2006). But as important, young right-wing extremists are made aware of these bans by the ways in which their favorite music CDs or film DVDs circulate and in their manner of acquiring such illicit media. Gino described trips across the Polish border, where such banned neo-Nazi CDs were readily available in outdoor market stands. Others among his peers traded CDs among themselves or copied individual tracks from one cell phone to another. It is the very acquisition of such media through clandestine networks—whether through under-the-table commercial exchange or through circles of like-minded friends and acquaintances—that, for them, marked their legal status.

A second set of legal mechanisms for regulating the freedom of expression runs through several clauses of the German Criminal Code that target assaults on the honor of individuals and groups. Incitement to hate or violence, denigration of collectivities, libel, slander, positive representations of violence, agitation, insult, defamation, injury to official symbols, and abuse of the memory of the deceased all fall under this quite heterogeneous rubric.[12] It is under these laws, for example, that a denial of the Holocaust, a glorification of the Third

---

[12] Sections in the criminal code that fall under this category include §90 (Denigration of the Federal President), §90a (Denigration of the State and Its Symbols), §90b (Anti-Constitutional Denigration of Constitutional Organs), §103 (Insult to Organs and Representatives of Foreign States), §104 (Injury to Flags or National Emblems of Foreign States), §130 (Agitation of the People), §131 (Representation of Violence), §140 (Rewarding and Approving Crimes), §166 (Insulting of Faiths, Religious Societies and Organizations Dedicated to a Philosophy of Life), §185 (Insult), §186 (Malicious Gossip), §187 (Defamation), §188 (Malicious Gossip and Defamation Against Persons in Political Life), and §189 (Disparagement of the Memory of Deceased Persons). All transla-

Reich, or a racist statement would fall. The ruling, mentioned earlier, against the author of an open letter to the federal representatives of Germany on charges of the disparagement of the state, was based on these laws. The excerpt of the letter cited as the root of the problem reads as follows:

> You have all made of the Federal Republic a dirty-money republic (*Bimbes-Republik*), a pigsty for sale, above which your creed stands tall: never again should there be a self-confident, actually sovereign German state. You subdue yourself to French, American, but above all Jewish desires and commands all too willingly and all too zealously . . . The Federal Republic is not a state! . . . The Basic Law is not a constitution and was not agreed upon freely by the German people. It therefore could never serve as the constitution or even as the basis of a sovereign state . . . The Basic Law is the justice of occupation . . . Hence, it would have been the duty of the federal government to dissolve the makeshift entity established by the occupation that is the Federal Republic . . . Instead it has elevated the Basic Law, which is the arbitrary creation of enemy forces, into a quasi-constitution . . . The Reich must return! The Federal Republic belongs to the saddest and most undignified chapter of our German history and must end and be replaced by the Reich as soon as possible. (Bundesgerichtshof 2002a)

The author of the letter appealed to the Federal Court of Justice against his conviction by the regional court at Frankfurt, arguing that the ruling violated the constitutional guarantee of the freedom of expression. The Federal Court rejected his appeal on the grounds that his statements constituted the sort of malicious talk that the criminal law was designed to prohibit.

Of this second set of legal mechanisms, some paragraphs in the criminal law are particularly relevant for the sorts of transgressions for which my informants were likely to face criminal charges: "Agitation of the People" (*Volksverhetzung*, section 130), which criminalizes in general the public incitement of hatred or violence against groups and, in particular, the public approval, denial, or playing down of National Socialist crimes and the public approval, glorification, or justification of National Socialism at large, which the law defines as an injury against the dignity of its victims; "Representation of Violence" (*Gewaltdarstellung*, section 131), which defines as criminal the public dissemination of representations of inhumane violence that glorify it or play it down or that injure human dignity; the insult of individuals or groups, which includes Holocaust denial (section 185); and the disparagement of the memory of the deceased (section 189).[13]

---

tions from the German Criminal Code are taken from the English version published by the Federal Ministry of Justice (BMJ) and reproduced online by the German Law Archive (1998).

[13] There are a number of other sections that regularly come to bear on right-wing extremists, including prohibitions, for example, on the disparagement of the state and its symbols. Rainer Hoffman provides a relatively comprehensive review of these sections (as they relate to hate speech) and assesses their relative efficiency in courts (1992). For additional discussion of the legal mechanisms

These sections of the criminal law hence encompass a broad range of pronouncements on history and contemporary politics that would likely appeal to certain right-wing extremists, from anti-Semitic jokes to stances on racist violence or on its victims in the past or in the present. Their wording—"incitement," "dignity," "insult," "disparagement," "maliciously," and so on—opens up an ambiguous legal space and authorizes widely varying interpretative assessments on the nature of particular pronouncements or actions. Specific verdicts therefore frequently become overturned as cases meander their way through the hierarchy of juridical authorities. Whereas lower courts often show a more pronounced deference to the criminal code and, accordingly, a greater predilection for convictions, higher courts, and especially the Constitutional Court, appear to demonstrate a greater concern with protecting constitutionally guaranteed liberties, and hence a more skeptical attitude to previous guilty verdicts. Thus, in February 2002 the Federal Court of Justice overturned the conviction of an NPD activist by a Rostock state court according to sections 130 (agitation of the people) and 90 (denigration of the state) of the criminal law. Addressing a crowd at a national NPD meeting, the defendant called for radical change in Germany: "We need a coup [*Umsturz*] . . . We need to take to the barricades, we need to take to the streets . . . without sacrifices [*Opfer*] and without blood there will be no new Germany!" He further accused the police of doing nothing to stop antifascist activists from beating him at an earlier demonstration and implied that their failure to act resulted from an intentional policy "from above." The state court at Rostock judged his statements at the party rally to constitute both an incitement to violence and a denigration of the state. The Federal Court, in contrast, emphasized the priority of the constitutional guarantee of the freedom of expression and argued that the relevant sections from the criminal code must be interpreted and applied narrowly, so as not to violate this freedom (Bundesgerichtshof 2002b).[14]

---

used to limit the freedom of speech in Germany, and specifically in relation to the memory of National Socialism and the Holocaust, see also Stein (1986) and Weiss (1994).

[14] For additional examples, see Bundesverfassungsgericht (2010), mentioned above, where the Constitutional Court rejected a publication ban placed by a lower court, and Bundesverfassungsgericht (2007b), where the Constitutional Court overturned a lower court's decision against a government employee who published in a journal officially classified as right-wing extremist. Nevertheless, the tendency for higher courts to overturn convictions and to prioritize constitutional principles over criminal law is by no means universal. In one case, for example, the Federal Court of Justice accepted an appeal by the state attorney against an acquittal by a lower court of a lawyer accused of incitement, and in particular of denying the Holocaust. The state court at Hamburg considered that his pronouncements, while they would usually fall under section 130 of the criminal code, in this particular case should be excepted because they were protected from such limits to the freedom of expression by their status as defense in a court of justice. The Federal Court argued that, since the lawyers' incendiary statements carried absolutely no value as legal defense, they did not fall under this exception and he could be prosecuted according to section 130 (Bundesgerichtshof 2002d).

While my informants felt the penal effects of these two legal mechanisms—the Protection of Young Persons Act and the sections in the criminal code that limit the constitutional right to free expression—often enough, a third legal mechanism weighed most heavily on them. It comprises sections 86 and 86a of the criminal code, which prohibit the dissemination and public use of symbols and means of propaganda of unconstitutional organizations and political parties, such as "flags, insignia, uniforms, slogans, and forms of greeting." The law makes specific reference to former National Socialist organizations and in effect bans such high-profile symbols as the swastika or the SS emblem together with a host of less familiar ones, as well as phrases such as "mit deutschem Gruß" (with a German greeting) or "Heil Hitler," gestures such as the Hitler salute, and other illicit semiotic entities. Because of the constitutional clause against censorship, in themselves such signs cannot be placed under legal prohibition. Instead, their outlawing appears in the criminal code almost as a derivative function—as if it were a mere by-product—of a different set of legal restrictions whose concern is rather with placing limits on the constitutional freedom of association, and that regulates the criminalization of counterconstitutional organizations. What comes under their jurisdiction, then, are not particular symbols but rather more generally the dissemination or use of any sign associated with a banned organization in a way that could promote the organization or its goals.

In sections 86 and 86a the criminal code simultaneously includes two opposite movements of inclusion and exclusion. On the one hand, it extends its applicability by means of a principle of similarity, stating that "symbols which are so similar as to be mistaken for those named [as banned] shall be deemed to be equivalent thereto." With this, the code precludes the possibility that minor changes to a prohibited sign would place it outside of the law's reach. But the principle of similarity also introduces a critical dimension of ambiguity into the process of adjudication. On the other hand, the criminal code constrains itself by a principle of exception, declaring itself suspended "if the means of propaganda or the act serve to further civil enlightenment, to avert unconstitutional aims, to promote art or science, research or teaching, reporting about current historical events or similar purposes." Note that in elaborating these exceptions, the law does not simply tolerate any use of the symbols of banned organizations, as long as such use performs no propaganda, but places a blanket prohibition on the use of such symbols and specifies a number of exceptions that come into effect only in particular cases. In doing so, it places the burden of proof on users, who often appear before it as defendants and who must corroborate their innocence by successfully appealing to one of its exceptions.

As if to preempt likely confusion, Germany's federal and state-level "Authorities for the Protection of the Constitution" (Verfassungsschutzbehörden) regularly issue informational booklets that aim to educate the public on banned organizations and that provide carefully captioned, crossed-over illustrations of their symbols (see, for example, Verfassungsschutz Berlin 2001; Verfassungsschutz Brandenburg 2001b; Verfassungsschutz Sachsen 2001; Bundesamt für Verfassungsschutz 2004). Nevertheless, time and again German courts are called upon to resolve the ambiguities that inevitably arise. Is the association between a given symbol and a banned organization strong enough to predominate over other historical or contemporaneous uses of the same symbol? Is the similarity between one symbol and another close enough to consider the two identical? Is a particular use of a symbol that has not been banned in general but that carries some association with National Socialism illicit enough to justify a conviction? Conversely, does a specific use of a symbol that has been banned come under one of the exceptions to the law, and hence remain permitted?

Such questions have brought forth a series of legal cases and appeals, for example, in the case of the clothing brand Thor Steinar, which specializes in the manufacturing of garments and accessories for the extreme right market. I will discuss this interesting instance in more detail below, but for now let me point out that verdicts on the similarity of the brand's logo to the symbols of prohibited National Socialist organizations varied greatly not only between different legal instances but also across the different states of the Federal Republic and in relation to different events and settings in which the brand's items appeared. As a result, my informants time and again pondered the legal status of their clothing. Similar confusion was triggered by a verdict against the use of Nazi symbols on antifascist items.

The legal frameworks for regulating and constraining the constitutional guarantees of liberal freedoms, then, operate in Germany according to three rationales: first, the safeguarding of the proper moral *Bildung* of as yet not fully mature and hence precariously positioned young people; second, prohibitions on the disparagement of people and the assault on their dignity, particularly as this pertains to victims of violent acts, and especially with regard to the history of National Socialism; and third, the banning of anticonstitutional organizations and of the entire symbolic repertoire associated with them. Needless to say, right-wing extremists often face various other charges for transgressing criminal laws, for example, for physical assault or vandalism, yet it is through these legal rationales that their possibilities of expression, performance, and political practice become targets of the repressive apparatuses of the state in particularly vigorous ways.[15]

---

[15] Germany, to be sure, is not alone in regulating the freedom of expression and the freedom of association. It does, however, present an approach that, while it may seem to resemble the legal governance of hate and extremism elsewhere, in fact entails quite a distinct rationale. As a result, its reach and ambition are far broader in scope than, say, that of hate speech laws in the United States or of the banning of the Fascist Party in Italy, to name but two prominent examples (Stein 1986; Coliver, D'Souza, Boyle 1992; Niesen 2002; Stradella 2008).

LEGAL (IN)DISTINCTIONS

The language of these legal codes demands a great deal of interpretative labor for the adjudication of particular cases, whether in its reference to principles of similitude or to assumptions about intentions and motivations. Possible transgressions must be entextualized, or rendered into a meaningful, coherent text, and this in turn demands the invocation of various cues that indicate their relevant frame of reference. As we shall see, it is only within this interpretative terrain that we can make sense of the raid on Freddi's apartment and of his subsequent indictment. To be sure, and notwithstanding what literalist ideologies may claim (Crapanzano 2000), no legal code can operate without the deployment of interpretative frameworks and contextual presuppositions. Law seems always to entail a degree of ambiguity, a fact that has been documented and analyzed in a variety of geographical and social contexts.[16] Legal ambiguities vary, of course, as much in their nature as they do in their effects and in their functions. From the perspective of jurisprudence, a conventional distinction is often made between patent and latent ambiguities, the first describing the sorts of juridical difficulties that may arise out of blatant contradictions in a legal text, and the second designating potential ambivalences in reference and interpretation. In some cases, the question of whether such ambiguities are framed as accidental results or as intentional formulations may come to bear upon their resolution. And yet, whether patent or latent, ambiguities generally appear from this perspective as heterogeneous to the legal code itself, as an obstacle to be avoided in its elaboration rather than as constitutive of it and as fundamental to its application in the sense upon which I insist here. What also escapes this classification is the way in which legal ambiguities seem everywhere to perform a certain useful labor, to generate certain productive effects, to allow certain strategic maneuverings, rather than simply to obstruct or confound the operation of the juridical apparatus (Edelman 1992; Harris 1996; Bybee 2000; Grattet and Jenness 2005).

In the German case, the legal regimes that govern political extremism in general and right-wing extremism in particular incorporate certain indeterminacies into their formulations in several interesting ways. Most prominent among these are certain notions of publicness, exegetical understandings of intentions

---

[16] For a comparative anthropological consideration of the ambiguity of law and of the ambivalent relation to it that different groups develop, see Harris (1996), and particularly Sue Fleming's discussion in the same volume of how legal ambiguity enables land grab in Mozambique. Lauren Edelman has shown how the very ambiguity of labor law in the United States renders compliance with it an act of symbolic performance that leaves a great deal of latitude for organizations to apply it according to their interests (1992). Grattet and Jenness have shown how police agencies in California mediate between the legal code and its actual enforcement in ways that resolve the ambiguities of hate crime laws according to a variety of distinct logics (2005).

and motivations, and presumed commonsensical distinctions in the slippery slope between difference, similarity, and sameness. All three of these spaces of ambiguity, on which more shortly, are drawn upon and mobilized in the juridical process. Furthermore, the ambiguities that surface from these legal principles are frequently resolved retroactively at the court. Thus, often the use or dissemination of a specific symbol cannot be known to constitute an offense until it has been defined as such by juridical authorities in the course of adjudication. Only subsequently does the decision circulate through various channels—mainstream media, right-wing extremist Internet forums, word of mouth—and defines the legal status of future acts of a similar nature.

In one exemplary case, a manufacturer of fashion items designed for the extreme right niche market set out to test the legality of a new design, a stylized Celtic cross, by placing it on a shirt and displaying it publicly, then proceeding to place a charge against himself at the police station. The Federal Court was called upon to decide whether the use of the symbol, even when divorced from any markers that would indicate its historical association with a banned organization, and despite its multiple other historical and contemporary usages, would constitute an offense. The court ruled positively and emphasized that, from a juridical perspective, the crucial criterion remains whether the symbol had been employed by a banned organization (Bundesgerichtshof 2008). In another case, a Dresden court convicted the manufacturer of merchandise destined for the antifascist and punk scene, which featured crossed-over swastikas and other similar oppositional representations of National Socialist emblems, for distributing the symbols of banned organizations. In considering an appeal against the Dresden decision, the Federal Court argued that clear, visible distancing from the symbols—for example, by portraying them crossed over or hurled into trash bins—was sufficient to provide a legal exception to the items in question. It overturned the lower court's decision on all but one item, a CD that, according to the ruling, exhibited its opposition to the banned symbols in a manner that would be intelligible only for members of the punk scene, and that hence would not be sufficiently clear for the general public (Bundesgerichtshof 2007). Moreover, quite different criteria seem to be employed by different courts and in different cases for deciding on the legal status of particular symbols (see, e.g., Bundesgerichtshof 2002c; Brandenburgisches Oberlandesgericht 2005; Bundesgerichtshof 2009). And when local rather than federal courts are at issue, such ambiguities can be resolved quite differently in different states within the Federal Republic. For young right-wing extremists setting out to follow their soccer club for a game away from home, dressing up for a night out, or deciding which music to blast from their sound systems, all of this may generate an acute sense of confusion.

The first level of ambiguity, as I mentioned, concerns the publicness of potentially criminal acts. Legal prohibitions, I have already noted, generally apply to acts performed in public settings or in ways that render banned items publicly visible, accessible, or obtainable. Rather than being banned per se, then, many illicit nationalist symbols are instead banished across the divide that separates what are taken to be fundamentally different domains of life in secular modernity: the public and the private. In this sense, they present an interesting analogy with religious symbols and practices, which have similarly become confined to a presumed private sphere and excluded from a purportedly separable public domain under modern secularism. More tellingly, perhaps, we find here an even closer intimacy between criminalized right-wing extremist practices and a whole set of behaviors considered morally reprehensible or obscene (sexual practices, nudity, the consumption of certain substances) that while not in themselves banned have likewise been heavily regulated and limited, if not always strictly to what is ordinarily viewed as the private domain, at least to settings that are perceived as not entirely public. As Talal Asad has insisted, the distinctions between private and public serve to regulate practice and thus enable modern modes of power (2003a). These distinctions—and others of vital importance to modernity—are not simply "there" but rather must constantly be regenerated in the very operations of modern power. As codified in legal registers, they partake in the "enchanted displacement"—to borrow from Jean Comaroff and John Comaroff (2001)—through which law becomes fetishized and conceals itself as a product of and an enabling framework for power (see also Mitchell 1990).

For young right-wing extremists, in turn, the private/public distinction appears as spatially congruous with certain boundary notions of "inside" and "outside." Recall that the charges brought against Freddi did not cite his possession of the Odal rune pendant but the allegation that he had paraded it on the street. In Freddi's social milieu we find a range of similar items ubiquitously and plainly displayed in private spaces—apartments or rooms—but kept at a safe distance from the doorstep, from the threshold that separates a (private) interiority and a (public) exteriority. Arguably the most prevalent among these items is the imperial war flag (*Reichskriegsflagge*),[17] which, while historically associated with Prussia and with the Second Reich rather than with National Socialism, has become a favorite emblem among right-wing extremists. While not banned per se throughout the Federal Republic, because of its evocation of monarchist militancy, the public display of the flag can lead to confiscations and to penal consequences in particular cases. A number of my informants, however, nevertheless hung versions of the flag over their beds or in the more

[17] In its original version of 1871, the imperial war flag featured a black cross with an imperial eagle in its center and a black Iron Cross over black, white, and red stripes in its upper-left corner. In the legally banned National Socialist versions of the flag, a swastika replaces the eagle, but these are rarer than the imperial versions, and sure to lead to harsher punitive consequences. Different versions of the flag (and there are quite a number of them, including some that were in official use during the Weimar Republic) can become legal liabilities if displayed in public and judged to pose a risk to the public order.

intimate corners of their living spaces. Their refrain: "What you do in your apartment is your own business."

Susan Gal (2002) has argued that the public and the private cannot be understood as two separate spheres held apart by spatiotemporal boundaries, no matter how ambiguous or porous such boundaries are imagined to be. While people's explicitly articulated notions of the public/private distinction generally describe it in terms of such frontiers, Gal has shown that, in actual semiotic practice, we often find the public and the private recursively embedded within each other, inseparably, the one emerging, sometimes fleetingly, within the other. And indeed, from a purely juridical standpoint, and notwithstanding the folk conceptualizations that right-wing extremists hold, the distinction between private and public is less about different types of places, such as indoors versus outdoors, and more about different types of interactional settings ("participation frameworks," in Erving Goffman's [1981] terms). The "publicness" of an act is understood in German jurisprudence to consist in its "perceptibility to a major number of people who are not linked with each other by personal relations" (Stegbauer 2007). From this perspective, an act can take place "publicly" in someone's private apartment or conversely "privately" on a park bench. Thus, the problem with Freddi's Odal rune was not that he carried it outside his apartment but rather that it was so placed as to be visible to a passerby who then reported its public appearance to the police. While it seems likely that the passerby in question in fact knew Freddi (otherwise it would be difficult to imagine how Freddi was identified and subsequently located), presumably the pendant would have been visible as well to any stranger walking past him on the street. During the raid on his apartment, the police, in turn, ignored a wealth of illicit items that were scattered about, not because these were any less suspect than the Odal rune but rather because they were not reported to have been seen "in public."

While my informants, then, commonly understood the publicness of an act in terms of its location, law enforcement and juridical authorities are called upon to attend at least as much to the social setting in which it occurred. In practice, however, courts interpret and apply the law in a less consistent manner. For example, a lower court in Brandenburg rejected a complaint filed against a neighbor who allegedly blasted banned music from his apartment window, the lyrics of which included such unsavory phrases as "Germany to the Germans, foreigners out!" (Deutschland den Deutschen, Ausländer raus!). One of the reasons cited for this decision was that the music was playing inside the person's apartment, and hence in his private space (Amtsgericht Rathenow 2006).

The interpretation of the publicness of an act therefore requires further distinctions between "personal" and "impersonal" relations, as well as between "small" and "large" social circles, according to which the nature of the interactional setting of the act can be assessed. Depending on such assessments, the display of a symbol associated with an illegal organization in a person's bedroom can become a public act in the context of an event—say, a party—with a large number and not well-controlled composition of participants; just as, conversely, the carrying of such a symbol on the streets can remain legal as long as it is imperceptible to passersby. The difficulties that result from such already-ambiguous distinctions become all the more acute when they are brought to bear on digital media, where traditional notions of publicity and privacy are often critically destabilized. Thus, for example, Andreas Stegbauer (2007, 181–82) notes that the supreme court of the state of Hesse "ruled that showing a swastika in a computer mailbox [*sic*] which could be accessed by anyone with its number has to be subsumed under the term 'publicly,' regardless of the number initially being restricted to a small circle." Stegbauer explains that profound conundrums arise with regard to the jurisdiction of German laws governing the dissemination of right-wing extremist symbols on international media: "German spectators of a football match in Poland being broadcasted on television in Germany were punished for showing the Hitler salute in the stadium because, by transmission, the symbol was perceived here. In a sense, part of the action took place in Germany." But the possibility of extending the jurisdiction of these laws to foreign Internet servers appears far more problematic.

We might suppose, then, that a public/private distinction, notwithstanding its vagueness, nevertheless underpinned the prosecution of Freddi for displaying his rune outdoors. But here we encounter yet another level of ambiguity. For what confounded Freddi most was that, in fact, the Odal rune had not been banned at all, not even in public. Its association with the banned organization that employed it as its logo was never deemed sufficiently formidable to prohibit its use. As a matter of fact, the very same symbol appears today on certain ranks of the Bundeswehr (the German Federal Defense Force). The raid, the confiscation of the pendant, and the trial that followed only make sense if we consider a second dimension of the legal mechanisms we have been examining: their reliance upon notions of motivations and intentions. Beyond assumptions about the social setting of an act, they also incorporate interpretations about the type of person who committed it and the sorts of intentions and motivations that were likely to stand behind it.

The legal code itself introduces such notions, for example, in specifying as punishable the dissemination of propaganda intended "to further the aims of a former National Socialist organization," in limiting its scope to propaganda "directed against the free, democratic constitutional order or the idea of international understanding," or in excluding from its purview acts that serve "to further civil enlightenment, to avert unconstitutional aims, to promote art or science, research or teaching, reporting about current historical events or similar purposes." From a juridical perspective, the official guiding norm for determining the culpability of users concerns their knowledge of the link between a specific symbol and a banned organization. Note that establishing an explicit intention to employ the symbol for promoting the aims of an illegal organization is unnecessary—once awareness of the link can be assumed, it is the symbols themselves, so to speak, that intend. Put in semiotic terms, such norms recognize in the prohibited sign the metapragmatic function of a second-order indexicality. In other words, the sign says something about its user and, in so doing, it sets up the presumed contextual framework that governs its own signification and interpretation.

Runic characters especially fall under this ambiguous legal limbo. On the one hand, their use not only far predates the National Socialist era but also appears prevalent in a variety of other, unrelated contemporary contexts.[18] They are thus generally not uniquely or even primarily linked with National Socialist or other banned political groups. On the other hand, National Socialism drew upon them extensively, and they played a prominent role in its symbolic lexicon. Their actual deployments on the far right therefore often do appear to reference the National Socialist past. But other symbols also pose similar problems. For example, the ubiquity in popular culture of depictions of skulls, which decorated SS uniforms and helmets, renders their blanket prohibition both impractical and indefensible. Yet such depictions may nevertheless trigger law enforcement measures when appearing in conjunction with particular people, in particular settings, or in proximity to certain other suspect signs. We find in juridical discourse a good measure of interpretative labor that seeks to unearth and substantiate such indexical links between signs, people, and their putative intentions. In one illustrative instance, a Berlin-Brandenburg appeals court ruled that certain symbols (for example, the imperial eagle), which in and of themselves were not illegal, could under certain circumstances and in conjunction with illicit indicators justify the persecution of a person whose home and car were raided and searched (Oberverwaltungsgericht Berlin-Brandenburg 2010). That Freddi indeed had his Odal rune confiscated and faced legal charges for its display owed, then, neither to the rune in itself nor quite to Freddi himself but rather to how first the police and later the courts interpreted the union of the two.

The widespread deployment of National Socialist symbols in protests against right-wing extremism presents a particular challenge for determining the motivation of users. The banners, publications, or clothing of innumerable leftist groups portray caricatures of Hitler or swastikas crossed over, tossed into trash bins, crushed under boots, or smashed with hammers. Surely, one might suppose, such degrading representations of the symbol could not be taken as propaganda for National Socialism. And yet, as I mentioned above, two state courts upheld a conviction against the manufacturer of punk and antifascist merchandise for distributing precisely such portrayals of swastikas. The judges

---

[18] The Y-shaped Lebensrune, for instance, frequently decorates tombstones across Northern Europe, while the Odal rune, as already noted, marks certain German military ranks.

presiding in the case considered that a swastika remained a swastika even when employed against neo-Nazis, and hence independently of any presumed motivation of usage. Their decision triggered panic in leftist political milieus about the criminalization of antifascist activism (and, lest we forget, of significant portions of their wardrobe). And not without reason: the ruling gave rise to arrest warrants against activists, confiscations of countless items, raids of private apartments and of the offices of firms that produced and sold antifascist and punk paraphernalia and fashion, fines, and even legal charges against several prominent public personalities, including the chairperson of the Green Party (Seils 2007). Bringing some two years of heated legal debates and activist angst to a close, the Federal Court of Justice ultimately overturned the rulings and in so doing lifted the ban. Its rationale referred to the unambiguous marking of opposition to National Socialism, and thus to intentionality not in the sense of the putative motivation of individual users (what antifascist activists sought to communicate with the symbols) but rather in the sense of a clear indication of intent contained within the sign itself (Bundesgerichtshof 2007).

These legal regimes that reconcile the constitutional ban on censorship with the juridical banning of signs thus open up a whole field of semiotic ideology: a shared set of specific notions about how the relations between signs, meanings, texts, contexts, referents, and interpretations operate and are to be understood. Let us take a closer look at the logic of this ideology using Charles Peirce's (1960) classical distinction between iconic, indexical, and symbolic semiotic relations. For Peirce, all relations of signification (which for our purposes we may think of as relations between signs and their referents, or what Peirce calls the "base" of the semiotic process) can be reduced to three general classes. First, an icon is a relation in which a sign references something by similitude, and for which a map as a representation of a geographical area would be a paradigmatic example. Second, an index describes a relation of proximity or coexistence between the sign and its referent; a weathervane may serve as a good illustration of this class. Finally, a symbol is a relation between a sign and an object of reference that is purely conventional, and in which we find neither resemblance (iconicity) nor co-occurrence (indexicality). Language is the paradigmatic domain of symbolic signification: the relations between most words and referents are strongly symbolic. Peirce emphasizes that we should think of these relations of signification not as mutually exclusive types but rather as dimensions of the semiotic process of signification that, in particular cases, may become more or less dominant.

When we look at the legal governance of hate, at first glance law generally appears to construe the signifying relations between signs and the organizations for which they come to stand as symbolic, that is, as nothing more than conventional. Put differently, the law acknowledges that the association of the swastika, the Odal rune, or the skull with National Socialist organizations is in a sense arbitrary.[19] It grants that the relation between such symbols and banned organizations has been no more than a historical accident, and accepts that they have carried a range of other meanings in different contexts and for different publics. The only relevant question from this perspective remains whether, in the supposedly shared symbolic vocabulary of today's Germany, they have gained a more or less strong association with the banned organizations that once deployed them. The law is concerned, then, with whether people have come to ordinarily identify them with these organizations.

But at the same time, and precisely because of this association, the conventional symbolic relation often slips into an indexical one of proximity. The presence of these forbidden signs is never only a semiotic representation in the sense that, for example, the word Jupiter in this sentence might represent the largest planet in our solar system. It is always also the tangible presencing of that which they represent. As signs and insignia of banned organizations, they are in a sense at once these very same organizations. Their appearance seems to effectively perform the work of the organizations for which they stand (the disturbance of the constitutional order, the disruption of international peace, and so on). Finally, they also emerge as iconic relations of similarity. The symbols themselves become depositories for the qualities of that for which they stand. The Hitler salute or the SS symbol already contain within them, as it were, the traits of authoritarianism, fascism, racism, violence, and so on for a broad public in Germany. They thus come to be perceived and treated as iconic signs, as forbidden things that mimic other forbidden things, in the same sense that racist neo-Nazi violence today is viewed as replicating National Socialist violence in its very form.

Note that, as I already mentioned, the symbolic, iconic, and indexical types of signification are not mutually exclusive. Quite the contrary, they are very much reciprocally reinforcing dimensions of the relations between signs and their referents, and they slide into one another often. The presumed strength of the purely conventional, arbitrary association (i.e., of the symbolic dimension) between a particular item and a banned organization informs the legal engagement with that item. It is central for assessing whether this specific illicit association (say, between the swastika and the National Socialist Party) overshadows other plausible—and permissible—conventional ones (say, the swastika as a Hindu or Buddhist symbol). In one instance that I already cited above, the Federal Court of Justice ruled that the so-called stylized Celtic cross, which had been used by a banned right-wing extremist organization in the postwar era, remained prohibited regardless of its context and mode of presentation and whether it included any additional references to the banned group

[19] Though this is certainly not always the case. For example, representations of Hitler and certain National Socialist hymns fall under these laws as well, and clearly cannot be described as only symbolically—in Peirce's sense—related to National Socialism.

(Bundesgerichtshof 2008). For their part, my informants complained bitterly about the criminalization of certain runic characters, which, they insisted, historically preceded National Socialism and therefore carried no intrinsic (in other words, only a symbolic) link to it.

At the same time, in proportion to its strength, the arbitrary, symbolic relation between such symbols and banned organizations reinforces and articulates with a variety of iconic relations of similitude and indexical relations of proximity. Thus, courts repeatedly voice concern about the possibility that extreme right signs could be interpreted by different publics, both at home and abroad, as implying similarities between the Federal Republic and the Third Reich (see, e.g., Bundesgerichtshof 2000a and 2000b). Such signs then appear as indexical with the *Unrechtsstaat* and as inflicting intolerable harm to the image of the democratic, constitutional state by rendering it as iconically similar to the former.[20] The symbolic dimension reciprocally strengthens the indexical dimension of co-occurrence, the degree to which the item appears to concretely presence the forbidden, to effectively advance the latter's illicit schemes in the here and now of its instantiation. It is precisely this last dimension, the way in which prohibited signs not only represent but serve as propaganda of prohibited organizations, that provides the legal justification for their banning. No doubt, the interdiction on the use of these signs betrays something about the actual fragility of that image, about its anxious management.

So far I have been considering the relation between signs and organizations. In fact, signs and organizations always stand in a triadic configuration that includes a third figure, which we may for convenience call "users." All three—signs, organizations, and users—come into play in concrete acts of legal interpretation. Assumptions about whether the "average German" knows of the link between a particular sign and a banned organization determine the legal status of that sign. The following line of reasoning is taken from the final verdict in the case of a police officer who was dismissed for carrying an oversized tattoo of a Wehrmacht infantry soldier (*Landser*) on his back and who appealed against his dismissal. It is typical of many other cases. According to police regulations, the court states,

> tattoos and similar skin paintings are in principle allowed; however, they cannot be visible while on duty, with the exception of sports. The tattooing of the body of a police officer in itself presents no breach of duty. The case is different if the appearance (form and size) and the content of the tattoo in particular cases gives rise to an impression that is harmful to respect and trust . . . The tattoo of a "Landser" is sufficient to give a neutral observer the bad impression that the appellant glorifies soldiery and war. With this message, the tattoo in question clearly

[20] The term *Unrechtsstaat* is usually translated as "tyranny." In Germany, the term bears strong associations with National Socialism. It designates the opposite of the *Rechtsstaat*, which, in turn, is associated with the Prussian monarchy and describes the constitutional state and the rule of law.

violates [the law]; because the reference to a "Landser," which in everyday linguistic usage and in the jargon of the Defense Forces means a soldier of the infantry (compare, e.g., wikipedia.de), in many cases today serves to glorify the
Wehrmacht together with its soldiers and to symbolize war and violence. (Oberverwaltungsgericht Berlin-Brandenburg 2009)

The orientation of the user to the relation between a specific sign and a
banned organization also becomes a matter of interest for legal interpretation.
Is the user ignorant of the illicit association between the sign in question and an
illegal organization? Indifferent to it? Averse to it? Or perhaps sympathetic to
it? In the case of the dismissed officer, the court moves subsequently to consider
and reject the argument that the Landser tattoo unequivocally discloses right-
wing extremist sympathies. The verdict recounts in some detail the National
Socialist origins of the emblematic image.[21] But it determines that the officer
would not have been aware of the historical link and accepts the plausibility of
alternative narratives. The court concludes:

> Other behaviors that hint [at a right-wing extremist orientation] or statements
> that suggest it by the appellant are not known until now; quite the contrary, the
> appellant has repeatedly made statements distancing him from such a worldview.
> (Oberverwaltungsgericht Berlin-Brandenburg 2009)

In turn, the perceived strength of the association between a sign and an
organization—the link between the swastika and the NSDAP stands out as particularly strong, for example—informs the interpretation of the user's actions.
A strongly associated sign such as the swastika (but equally the SS symbol or
the Hitler salute) marks the user as neo-Nazi, as having an illicit orientation
to the sign/organization. A weaker one, such as a Thor's hammer jewelry piece
or the wearing of certain brands, may merely cast suspicion on the user. Put differently, the link between signs and organizations projects itself upon the users
(see, e.g., Brandenburgisches Oberlandesgericht 2005; Bundesgerichtshof 2008;
Oberverwaltungsgericht Berlin-Brandenburg 2010).

Viewed from a different perspective, we could think of the law here as at once
invested in and frustrated by the triadic classification proposed by the language
philosopher J. L. Austin (1975). In his exploration of the ways in which words
can do things (rather than only communicate meaning, as the philosophical
canon of his day could lead one to believe), Austin famously distinguishes between three different dimensions of every speech act. The first of these is the act
of saying something in its denotative, referential sense, which Austin calls the
locutionary act. For example, the locutionary act of the phrase "the matches are
all gone" consists in a descriptive statement about the lack of matches,[22] a ref-

---

[21] The original drawing is by Wolfgang Willrich, a strong enthusiast of National Socialist art.
[22] I borrow this phrase from an article by Susan Ervin-Tripp (1976), where she uses it to illustrate the structure of directives in English.

erential predicative declaration that, furthermore, can be tested for its validity and judged as true or false. A second dimension of the speech act, which Austin calls its illocutionary force, concerns not its denotative meaning but rather what it aims to achieve—that which is intended in saying something. In our example above, the illocutionary force of the statement will conventionally not consist in providing information about the absence of matches. Instead, more often a polite request is implied. From the perspective of illocutionary force, we are dealing here with a directive that aims to guide the listener into the appropriate action. Finally, Austin calls the actual consequence of the speech act, that which is in effect performed or achieved by saying it, its perlocutionary effect. Returning to our example, the perlocutionary effect may or may not be similar to the illocutionary force: the listener could, for example, fetch more matches, ignore the statement, roll over the directive to yet another person, or recast, perhaps with some irony, its illocutionary force (for example, by responding "yes, indeed, they *are* all gone").

It is easy to see how Austin's triadic distinction corresponds, respectively, (1) to the locutionary act of fixing an imperial war flag on one's bedroom wall or of hanging a miniature Thor's hammer pendant on a necklace (the conventional meaning of these symbols as referencing historical events or mythological traditions); (2) to the illocutionary force of displaying these objects in this manner, the act performed in hanging the flag or displaying the pendant (expressing a nationalist spirit, solidarity with other users of these symbols, toughness, personal interest in German history or Nordic mythology, a camouflaged sympathy to National Socialism); and (3) to the perlocutionary effect that is in fact achieved (the impression they make upon different observers, the reactions they draw from peers or strangers, the fear they may provoke). In a sense, the legal discourse that I have been examining here struggles to draw precisely these distinctions as it elaborates reciprocal relations between the three dimensions, attends to each, and considers their relative importance.

It should be clear, then, even from this cursory discussion of Austin's speech act theory, that we must add context to the three elements—sign (illicit item or symbol), referent (banned organization), and user—which we have already discussed as crucial for legal interpretation. Whether a given symbol appears in a pedagogical panel about ultranationalist phenomena, on the jewelry piece of an individual strolling down the street, or in the context of a right-wing extremist demonstration or concert often defines the nature of the legal response to its display. Is the audience composed of concerned citizens who have gathered to learn about right-wing extremism or of neo-Nazis commemorating the Allied bombing of German citizens? Are its members personally related to the user, mere acquaintances, or complete strangers? All these questions introduce considerations about the concrete interactional setting of the act into its legal exegesis.

Consider, for example, the case of Miriam, a self-professed "antihate" activist who has made it her life's calling to locate, photograph, and obliterate signs of racism and right-wing extremism in her hometown, Berlin, and throughout Germany. As I witnessed on several occasions on which I accompanied her, Miriam departs for her expeditions equipped with a camera and an elaborate toolkit that allows her to first document, then remove, erase, paint over, or scrape off virtually any material that stands in her way. Over the years, she has put together some of her countless photographs, accumulated during more than two decades of relentless activism, into a traveling exhibit titled *Hate Eliminated* (*Hass vernichtet*), which has been shown in numerous locations. Her personal collection amounts to a comprehensive compendium of right-wing extremist and racist slogans, symbols, and codes. She also visits schools, where she takes students on "antihate" excursions and seeks to mobilize them for the cause.

Miriam rarely misses an opportunity to protest against right-wing extremists, and such are aplenty in Germany. I had run into her at a number of demonstrations against right-wing extremist marches. She arrived—as she always does, she said—with a piece of cardboard hanging from her neck on which she mounted a selection from her collection of photographs: images of swastikas, SS symbols, NSDAP inscriptions, anti-Semitic phrases, and other spoils of her crusades. She carefully captioned the photographs with clearly antifascist slogans, for example "He who remains silent, agrees" (Wer schweigt, stimmt zu). Yet how police officers, who are massively present in such events, responded to her visual protest was entirely unforeseeable, she said, and ranged from indifference to confiscation or even threats of legal charges.

To be sure, Miriam's baffled indignation at what she perceived as attempts to criminalize her antihate protest exposes how she (much like many right-wing extremists, if for different reasons) encounters law as arbitrary violence. And yet, no doubt, the fact that she has nevertheless been able to march in public with photographs of banned symbols on display reflects the significance of context—here, demonstrations against racism and right-wing extremism— within the calculus that determines how law interprets and treats such images and their users. The meanings of such images (the locutionary act), their aims (the illocutionary force), and their consequences (the perlocutionary effect) are assessed in relation to their concrete instantiations. Given the constitutive ambiguity of context, its inexhaustible openness and depth, and the plurality of positions from which it can be assessed, it is difficult not to see how inconsistencies, contradictions, and ambivalences appear in its interpretation and hence, too, in the interpretation of the act of displaying illicit signs.

Yet while looking to ground the act so firmly within its situated particularity, these legal frameworks at once revoke its concreteness and specificity by embedding it within a decontextualized universe of communicative uniformity, a homogeneous symbolic order. This, too, appears as the effect of a constitutive contradiction: the dependence of any code, of any script on reiteration, implies an ultimate autonomy from context (Derrida 1982). In practice, the tension between contextualization and decontextualization expresses itself perhaps most palpably in the inevitable reliance of law on the legal fiction of an impartial observer (*unbefangener Beobachter*), the radical other, we might say, of a situated audience. For example, the identification of a symbol as the reiteration of another, as the semiotic replication of an emblem once associated with a banned organization, demands a notion of similarity and familiarity. Such a notion, in turn, presumes the viewpoint of an average, neutral member of a uniform speech community as arbiter. This principle of similarity and the notion of an impartial observer that complements it are indispensable. Without them, the slightest modification to banned symbols would suffice to evade their prohibition. It is only from a putative commonsensical perspective that concrete appearances of symbols, their precise renderings, their relation to other signs, or their embeddedness in social contexts may be judged to invoke a banned organization.

The ambiguities that emerge from such norms reveal themselves plainly in the case of the clothing brand Thor Steinar. Its products were hugely popular among my informants, who often paraded them at the Kugel and elsewhere. Their pricing rendered especially their higher-end items—jackets, shirts, and trousers—an accessible luxury for only a handful of the young people with whom I worked. But some of them succeeded in accumulating sufficient funds to purchase a single exemplar, while many others settled for the brand's more affordable accessories—caps, beanies, key chains, or belts. The popularity of many prized brands on the right-wing extremist scene—such skinhead fashion items as Alpha jackets, Doc Martens boots, Fred Perry or Lonsdale shirts—extended into various other subcultural milieus and therefore only ambiguously indexed the political sympathies of their wearers. The Thor Steinar insignia, in sharp contrast, seemed to indicate unequivocally a far right self-identification.

According to reliable Antifa sources,[23] the Brandenburg-based firm that owns the brand belongs to two men intimately involved in right-wing extremist circles. Its line of products is comprised of trendy, contemporary fashion items of relatively fine quality. The design of items in its collection seamlessly fuses modern military themes with Nordic motifs—names of ancient Norwegian towns, runic characters, references to Vikings and mythological figures, renderings of certain animals, and so forth. Indeed, the label's name already gestures toward the Nordic god and his legendary hammer, iconic representations of which are ubiquitous among neo-pagans and right-wing extremists alike.

But both the Nordic and the military designs can also be seen as gesturing—though always obliquely, as it were—toward the symbolic vocabulary of National Socialism, and particularly of military SS units (Waffen-SS). The brand's original logo, an upward-pointing arrow crossed by an N-shaped zigzagging streak, invited precisely such interpretations. The firm insisted that it combined

---

[23] A general term for antifascist organizations and groups.

the two innocuous runic characters that stand for "T" and "S," corresponding to the brand's acronym. But according to at least two other possible readings of the logo, it consists of legally banned runic characters that have served as symbols for National Socialist, SS, and postwar banned organizations.

Emphasizing the latter interpretations, Antifa groups have waged a relentless public campaign against the brand. In 2004, a provincial court in Brandenburg ruled in favor of a plaintiff who had noticed the logo on the shirt of a passerby and claimed it resembled banned symbols. Beyond convicting the defendant, the verdict in effect criminalized the brand throughout its home state of Brandenburg. Shops and company offices were subsequently raided and innumerable items confiscated. Several other states promptly followed suit, their courts handing fines to wearers of Thor Steinar products. The case swiftly turned into an international affair, illustrating the extent to which German nationalism always stands under the watchful eye of the world at large, a fact that German courts often take into account in formulating their decisions (see, e.g., Bundesgerichtshof 2002d). Czech courts, also struggling with right-wing extremist groups, quickly emulated the German precedent and declared the logo illegal. Meanwhile, the Norwegian media created a scandal over the use of the country's flag and of the names of its ancient towns on "Nazi garments." The Norwegian government eventually filed legal charges against the firm for the unauthorized use of its official symbols. Appeals against the ban were repeatedly rejected.

The firm recalled its banned merchandise and discontinued the use of the original logo, replacing it with a new symbol that consisted of a tilted cross with two dots at its sides. But a year later the Brandenburg Court of Appeals overturned the initial verdict. Discussing the case of a Thor Steinar key chain, the court ruled that identifying the similarity between the symbols represented on the brand's logo and the symbols of banned organizations would require not only the sort of expertise that the average observer would not possess but also the careful examination and mental manipulation of visual elements that the casual, distracted passerby would be unlikely to perform (Brandenburgisches Oberlandesgericht 2005). It thus rejected the applicability of the similarity clause to the Thor Steinar case, declaring that no danger existed for the confusion of the original logo with unconstitutional symbols by ordinary people under ordinary circumstances. The decision brought some two hundred pending legal cases to a close. But the ban still holds in other states, including Berlin, and is also strictly enforced by soccer clubs, schools, and other organizations (RBB 2004a; Märkische Allgemeine Zeitung 2008; Recherchegruppe "Investigate Thor Steinar" 2008). Interestingly, the court noted in its justification of the decision that continued media coverage of the controversy over the label could eventually shift the tide and bring about a situation in which the average, casual observer would immediately recognize its similarity to the banned symbols, thus justifying a reconsideration of the case.

Viewed from this impersonal, impartial perspective, then, some signs may contain illicit elements yet go unheeded. Other signs, however, appear to wield a force that defies any attempt at their contextualization. Indeed, such precisely was the tenor of the Federal Court of Justice in its ruling on the case of the stylized Celtic cross, mentioned earlier. An even more telling case is the story of the Nigerian soccer player Adebowale Ogungbure, who spent a substantial portion of his career as midfielder in a number of different German clubs. In 2006, during a match between his team at the time, FC Sachsen Leipzig, and the club Hallescher FC, Ogungbure became the target of a rain of venomous racist chants hurled at him incessantly from fans of the opposing team. Ogungbure expressed his indignation at the spectators by performing a Hitler salute and placing two fingers above his mouth to emulate the Führer's singular moustache. With this gesture he evidently sought to communicate to the audience his opinion of it. He immediately became the target not only of an angry mob but also of a criminal investigation against him for performing the illegal gesture (charges were quickly dropped, however, following a public outcry). A similar incident transpired when a group of young right-wing extremists with whom I worked seized a "leftist" graffiti sprayer red-handed and, law-and-order loyalists that they were, turned him in to a police patrol. As they transferred him to the custody of the police officers, the sprayer waved the Hitler salute at his "neo-Nazi" capturers. There seemed to be a consensus among my informants that his gesture was meant not as identification with Nazism but rather as a condemnation of those who turned him in as "Nazis." Still, the policemen informed him that the performance of the Hitler salute would be added to the other charges against him.[24]

The concrete ways in which such penal mechanisms came to bear upon my informants, then, corresponded to an intricate interplay between contextualizations and decontextualizations, assumptions and distinctions, motivations and publics, mores and codes, and users and signs. This is why Freddi's Odal rune, despite its wide prevalence as a licit symbol (e.g., on military ranks), could nevertheless become a legal liability for him under particular circumstances. And it is the ambiguities of all this interplay that explain why, in certain cases, signs that would ordinarily be prohibited or that may clearly communicate illicit meanings remain legally tolerated.

While no doubt constrained by these legal impositions, right-wing extremist activists have also become adept at evading and manipulating them. For example, activists have used the slogan "Glory and honor to the Waffen-SS" (Ruhm und Ehre der Waffen-SS) in propaganda materials and on banners in rallies and demonstrations. In 2005, the Federal Court of Justice considered a case that has

---

[24] It appears, however, that in practice courts tend to be forgiving of similar misbehaviors, such as, for example, the performance of the Hitler salute in protest against police brutality during a demonstration (Bundesgerichtshof 2007).

been meandering its way through lower legal instances for several years against three members of an extreme right fraternity (Kameradschaft) for their use of this slogan. The Federal Court overturned an earlier conviction, arguing that the phrase corresponds to no slogan known to have been employed either by the SS or by any other banned organization (Bundesgerichtshof 2005). A revision to the criminal code, however, has since then allowed courts to convict right-wing extremists for employing the slogan, not for its resemblance to the symbols of banned organizations but rather for honoring National Socialism.

Similarly, my informants found creative ways to legally display prohibited symbols. One popular practice consisted in donning a shirt with the worldwide popular skinhead insignia LONSDALE, topped by a jacket placed just so as to let the first four letters of the legally banned acronym of the National Socialist Party (NSDAP) remain visible. CONSDAPLE, a German spinoff imitation of the original British brand, targets specifically the right-wing extremist niche market and allows its members to expose the acronym in its entirety. At the same time, the use of National Socialist symbols for purposes other than the advancement of illicit aims sometimes does suffer from legal curtailment. For example, the humorous portrayal of an image of Hitler on a postcard or the historically faithful decoration of a WWII model airplane with a swastika were deemed illegal by German courts (Stegbauer 2007). The young people with whom I worked frequently expressed their confusion about these mechanisms of censorship without censorship, which they described as inconsistent and perceived as impenetrable.

INDETERMINATE INJUNCTIONS

Thor Steinar's ordeals, just as much as those of Miriam, tell us something about the wide field of indeterminacy that the legal governance of the political margins in Germany generates, and upon which it relies. To be sure, in their rulings courts rarely acknowledge ambiguity as such. Instead, they make reference to the need for "balance": between clashing legal norms, in assessing and interpreting the relevance and nature of contextual factors, or in elaborating understandings of the relations at work between signs, users, and referents, all while presenting the results of their deliberations as conclusive and unequivocal. And yet, the gamut of their rulings reveals how this very indeterminacy allows legal and penal practice to pragmatically, if always tentatively and partially, reconcile the basic contradictions between the sweeping criminalization of a whole range of symbolic practices on the one hand and the principles of liberal democratic freedoms enshrined in the constitution on the other. In this sense, these legal regimes supply the technical instruments (interpretative norms, contextualization procedures, semiotic ideologies) for negotiating the paradoxical entailments of German postwar politics.

For my informants, two forms of illegibility shrouded this legal machinery with a veil of opacity. We could describe the first as the "why" behind the bans, or the rationale that presumably underpins and justifies their intricate legal architecture. Young right-wing extremists would express no bafflement about bans on, say, marching under the banner of the swastika, performing the Hitler salute, chanting "Sieg Heil," or advocating the extermination of Jews and immigrants. Whatever their opinion about such prohibitions, they considered the reasons behind them clear enough. What mystified them was that space of ambiguity with which we have been concerned here. Thus Elsa, for example, her extreme right sympathies notwithstanding, expressed a broad consensus in her social milieu when she conceded that the freedom of expression should have its limits. And yet she and many others complained bitterly about the legal banning of Thor Steinar, which, in her view, invoked nothing but the Germanic mythology of Thor, Odin's son, and his legendary hammer. Such myths, Elsa insisted, had their origins long before the Third Reich and bore no relation to National Socialism. For her, legal bans in Germany have spiraled out of control to the point where everything has come under prohibition: German mythology as much as images, symbols, or CDs. In chapter 3, we saw a similar logic with Freddi, the aficionado of nationalist music, in his conversation with the girl from the gymnasium for whom he played his CDs. Recall his animated response to the girl's unfavorable opinion on the music he played for her, and his diatribe about the senselessness of the bans on it.

Freddi and Elsa expressed the views of many among their peers: understanding why one would want to ban the swastika, or songs calling for brutality against immigrants, yet incapable of grasping the logic behind the prohibitions placed on other, in their opinion harmless, symbols and cultural products. But another, second level of illegibility revolves around not the rationale that legitimizes these legal constraints but rather the technicalities of the constraints themselves, their specifications and operations, their "what" and their "how." In the case of Thor Steinar, for example, the ban was initially strictly applied in Brandenburg and only later implemented in Berlin. It remained in effect in the capital even after its subsequent annulment in Brandenburg. For some of the young people with whom I worked, passing from Berlin to Brandenburg required no more than crossing the street on their way to school or to visit friends, or following Union to a league match. Thus, as the legal battles over the brand's logo were being fought, my informants debated confusedly the legal status of their garments. Their deliberations were informed—and confounded—by newspaper articles, television news headlines, postings on Internet forums, divergent rumors, and, indeed, the hardly consistent rulings of different legal instances. They seemed equally perplexed when attempting to account for why their homes were searched and their possessions confiscated, all of which fit uneasily with the mantra "what you do in your apartment is your own business," to which they nevertheless continued to cling. At the same time, as I have already noted, in their daily life the murkiness of statutory law merged indistinguishably with diverse administrative directives issued by various authorities and institutions: schools, soccer clubs, malls, and so forth. In a way, their bafflement was different perhaps in degree but not in substance from the confusion shown by judges as they sought to interpret and implement the legal code. But understanding the murkiness of law requires that we attend not only to legal stipulations and interpretative conventions, but also to its enforcement and, particularly, to how the state scrutinizes its political margins. I turn to this task in chapter 5.

The State Inside

LAW APPEARED FOR MY INFORMANTS as a sequence of ambiguities and illegibilities, as a force that intermittently (and, in their eyes, with seeming arbi-
trariness) intruded into and upset their day-to-day lives. At first view, there is
a certain despotism, a certain violence, a certain opaqueness to Law that these
legal ambiguities would seem to produce. But perhaps, instead, this despotic
violence has always already been there and has merely announced its presence
in this form. On the one hand, Law proclaims its presence while keeping its figure carefully hidden. In much the same way, in Kafka's story "Before the Law"
(1953), the gatekeeper at once suggests that the Law resides somewhere behind
the open gate and announces its inaccessibility to the man from the country.
In Kafka's story, the man from the country asks the gatekeeper who sits before
the Law to enter the Law. Although the gate is open, the man passes the rest of
his life seeking in vain to gain entry. As he is dying, the gatekeeper proceeds to
shut the gate. The man never sees the Law, never knows it, never knows what
it is, never knows whether it is in fact there, where he assumes it to be. And yet
he feels its presence through the authority of the gatekeeper, an authority from
which the threat of violence is never too far.

On the other hand, precisely these legal ambiguities bring to the fore the
sovereign, violent, and self-authorizing nature of Law. As Walter Benjamin in
his essay "Critique of Violence" (1986a) highlighted, this is indeed the nature of
every contract. The lawmaking, executive force of Law, as Derrida (1992) would
later point out, bespeaks the slippage between the meaning of the German word
Gewalt as legitimate authority and its meaning as arbitrary violence. It is this
slippage between legitimate authority and sovereign violence that, according to
Derrida (1992), forms the paradox inherent to Law always and everywhere—not
only in its most patently ambiguous moments. The paradox of Law, in Derrida's
view, is the effect of its constitutive reliance on a violence that must orient itself
toward a *certain* specific, determinate order while at the same time, in its founding role, always remains prior to and incommensurable with (because impossible to measure against) *any* particular order. Everywhere and always Law seems

to follow—while everywhere and always at once disavowing—its kernel of truth (Žižek 1989): a retroactive, reiterative, and self-authorizing logic in which no reference is made to reason (see also Laclau 1996a; Agamben 1998; Aretxaga 2003).

And yet, something in the encounter between the right-wing extremist and the penal regime of political delinquency nevertheless disturbs the ordinary disavowal of the violence of Law. For those who enter such encounters, playing along with the "as if" game that sustains the legal edifice appears difficult. On many occasions, I witnessed the young people with whom I worked struggle to articulate their experience of this conundrum. In chapters 3 and 4, we saw something of this mystified puzzlement in how Freddi pondered the bans that have been placed on his favorite music while playing illegal tracks for me and a young girl at his apartment one night over beers. But, whether with regards to Thor Steinar garments, runic characters, or the public/private distinction, bewilderment seems often to be the rule, not the exception. Government-generated blacklists, administrative injunctions, interdictions in the legal code and those resulting from juridical verdicts weave themselves into the lives of Freddi and his friends through various forms of mediation. They appear as prescriptions and proscriptions that are at once quotidian and mysterious, ordinary and enigmatic. They oscillate undecidedly somewhere in the space between those two meanings of the word *Gewalt*: between the legitimate exercise of authority on the one hand and discretional, arbitrary violence on the other. This promiscuous slippage between legitimate force and arbitrary violence, between Law and exception, pollutes the seemingly humdrum everyday with traces of something other, of the repressed, occluded power of the sovereign. It is therefore at once a slippage between the familiar and the uncanny that disrupts their lives. Somewhere between the *Heimlich* and the *Unheimlich*, these sovereign acts of prohibition stand as constant reminders of Law's articulated reasoning as an ex post facto discourse of justification that would conceal how, in the end, it is force without signification.

This fundamental paradox of Law, as Benjamin insisted, is distilled in the figure of the police, where the distinction between lawmaking and law-conserving violence collapses.[1] In the modern state, Benjamin tells us, the police constantly resolve in practice the constitutive undecidability of Law, and in their situated decisions the making and the enforcement of Law blend indistinguishably:

> [I]n a kind of spectral mixture, [lawmaking and law-preserving violence] are present in another institution of the modern state, the police. True, this is violence for legal ends (in the right of disposition), but with the simultaneous authority to decide these ends itself within wide limits (in the right of decree). The ignominy of such an authority . . . lies in the fact that in this authority the sepa-

---

[1] For a similar interpretation of Benjamin's argument in the context of South African apartheid policing, see Hansen (2006).

ration of lawmaking and law-preserving violence is suspended. Police violence is . . . lawmaking, for its characteristic function is not the promulgation of laws but the assertion of legal claims for any decree, and law-preserving, because it is at the disposal of these ends . . . [T]he "law" of the police really marks the point at which the state . . . can no longer guarantee through the legal system the empirical ends that it desires at any price to attain . . . Its power is formless, like its nowhere tangible, all-pervasive, ghostly presence in the life of civilized states. (1986a, 286–87)

In collapsing the modern institutional distinction between lawmaking and law-preserving violence, according to Benjamin, the figure of the police at once precedes Law and follows it. It crystallizes in a particularly telling way the constitutive contradiction of Law, the result of its undecidability. It is crucial to note that for Benjamin, this suspension of the distinction between lawmaking and law-preserving violence goes hand in hand with a certain spectral quality of the police in the modern state. It is a "spectral mixture," an "all-pervasive," intangible presence, which in this sense extends both the making of Law and its enforcement throughout the (civilized) social world.

This spectrality of the police, then, means not immateriality per se, but rather that it lacks any *specific* substance, essence, or location. Its place in Benjamin's thought was not lost on Derrida, who interpreted it to imply that the police is present wherever there is force of Law, that is, wherever a social order is enforced and regardless of how this enforcement comes about or who guarantees it concretely (1992, 1009–11). Indeed, as Derrida might say (cf. 1994, xviii), as a specter the police is never really present as such precisely because its ghostly nature goes far beyond its flesh-and-blood, uniformed representatives. Where the police is in actual fact present in the conventional sense of the word—that is, where policemen are afoot—it is animated by the spirit of Law, which, as spirit, incarnates itself in it but is never really limited to its physical location (cf. Derrida 1994, 3–6).

For Derrida, however, the suspension of the distinction between the founding and the preserving of Law takes place already prior to its enforcement. Following Montaigne, he argues that Law, if it means anything at all, always already implies its own enforceability. Justice, then, already implies violence, without which it would be impotent, while, conversely, violence itself would be arbitrary without a concept of justice. Thus, in Law the two meanings of *Gewalt*, legitimate authority and arbitrary violence, are inextricably fused from the start. Their constitutive mixture, for Derrida, follows from the logic of iterability, which inscribes not only the possibility but indeed the promise of repetition already at the heart of the originary instance. Put differently, the very act of founding Law already entails future acts of its conservation, while every such act of conservation at once refounds the Law. What we find, then, is not a clear distinction between lawmaking and law-preserving violence that can be suspended at particular moments but rather a constitutive and differential contamination of the two (1992, 997).

According to this reading of Montaigne and Benjamin, the police indeed announces the suspension of any neat distinction between the founding and the conservation of Law. However, it does so not as the institutional site or moment of this suspension but rather as its spectral incarnation, for the suspension itself belongs already at the heart and origin of Law; hence, precisely, the spectrality of the police. For it need not necessarily appear in the form of uniformed—or, for that matter, plainclothes—officials at all in order to be present. In fact, the police, as the force of Law, seems more commonly to remain invisible yet for that no less efficacious, a spirit without physical incarnation or, in Montaigne's words, a "mystical foundation of authority" (Derrida 1992, 937) that defines the terrain of Law.

I shall pause presently on how the distinction between the making and the conservation of Law is collapsed in the very tangible presence of law enforcement officials of all shades and colors, both insofar as these varied agents of the Law themselves transgress their legally prescribed mandates and insofar as they decide on how, when, where, and against whom to enforce legal and administrative regulations. But perhaps the less obvious point on which I insist here (after all, are we not all too familiar with stories of police officers transgressing their legal authority or differentially imposing the law?) concerns the all-pervasive, ghostly presence of the police, even in the absence of its tangible representatives. Surely we can sense this ghostly presence whenever SS-Gino, the multiply convicted, self-proclaimed "nationalist antichrist," slips a ring or two over his fingers to mask (though only partially) his legally banned SS symbol tattoo, at once acknowledging the spectral presence of the police and unequivocally announcing the existence of an illegal tattoo. It would seem to hover nearby, too, en route to a soccer match, as Danny and his friends mulled over the current status of his Thor Steinar shirt. They deliberated whether he should zip up his jacket or even wear the shirt inside-out to hide its logo, in order to avoid any complications. As we neared the stadium, they pondered whether, once past the ticket booths and well amid the thick multitudes of fans, he could perhaps reveal it with safety.

In the field, I could discern it on many similar occasions. Consider a visit I paid to Freddi's apartment in the aftermath of a party and shortly before he vacated it. Freddi left his parents' house following a particularly gruesome assault by his father. Stipulations placed upon his state remittances and a tight budget repeatedly cornered him into dubious subletting arrangements that sooner or later resulted in forced evictions. Meanwhile, the various apartments he inhabited while I conducted fieldwork served routinely for raucous parties where public taboos could be transgressed. Entering his apartment, I stumbled upon a floor cluttered with beer bottles, cigarette butts, food scraps, and viscous stains that for some time distracted my attention from the walls, where chaotically and hastily smeared black paint only partially obscured the outcome of a night of vandalistic mayhem. Fearing that the police might soon pay them a visit to enforce their pending eviction order, Freddi and his friends sought to cover, with whatever paint they could obtain, the glaringly incriminating residues of their feast. Much, however, remained visible: a Star of David scribbled above a doorway, a rhyme that read "You are the greatest swine around, because you sleep with Jews" (du bist am Ort das größte Schwein, weil du mit Juden lässt dich ein), drawings of the Iron Cross and of the flag of the Third Reich, an inscription of the popular right-wing extremist slogan "At the end [there] is victory" (Am Ende ist der Sieg), and more.[2] "We didn't have enough paint," Freddi explained. How he and his friends hastily and clumsily covered as best they could the incriminating symbols and phrases they had scribbled on the walls of his apartment, leaving enough scattered remnants to conjure a gruesome image of what surely laid beneath the messy smudges of black paint, testified to the extent to which the force of Law haunted even their most intimate activities and spaces.

For are such tactical maneuvers, fundamental to the quotidian praxis of my informants, not at the same time intimations of the force of Law, of the ghost of the police? In fact, I would suggest that in them we find more than one ghost at play, or better yet, in conflict. To explain what I mean by this, let us recall how, in his majestic *Witchcraft, Oracles and Magic among the Azande*, Evans-Pritchard suggests that in Zande society the menace of witchcraft is all-pervasive and haunts every member of the community. This menace is countered with frequent recourse to magic and oracles, often provided by the witch doctor (1976, 65–66). Thus magic and witchcraft, *ngua* and *mangu*, appear as two spectral forces that are constantly at odds. Evans-Pritchard describes a battle between these two occult forces, the one good and the other evil:

> Having on many occasions observed the behaviours of people at séances, I am sure that they are to some extent thrilled by the display. Witchcraft is hovering near them, for it is seen by the witch-doctors who attack it with their medicines; magic is operative all round them, and magical shafts are flying from point to point; . . . a battle of two spiritual powers is enacted before their eyes, magic versus witchcraft. (1976, 111)

It is a battle between two spiritual powers. This spiritual battle, to be sure, is linked with particular physical actors (the witch, the witch doctor, or the oracle) and expresses itself in certain tangible effects (illnesses, disasters, deaths). And yet, it proceeds at an immaterial dimension and hence is not limited to the

---

[2] The phrase "du bist am Ort das größte Schwein, weil du mit Juden lässt dich ein" dates back to National Socialism, when it was used to mark German non-Jewish women accused of having sexual relations with Jews. The phrase "Am Ende steht der Sieg" was a National Socialist war propaganda slogan.

sum of its concrete appearances. It haunts Zande society in general. In a similar vein, Peter Geschiere (2008) has insisted on how both witch and witch doctor represent equally occult forces in contemporary Cameroon. For Geschiere, the institutional meddling of the state in the business of witchcraft via the mediation of the witch doctor as a legally authorized figure implies a certain uncomfortable tension between sorcery and the state. While both enter into a certain occult strife in the campaign against witchcraft, the force that each of them commands nevertheless refers to a different source of authority.

Taking our cues from Evans-Pritchard and Geschiere, I want to suggest that we could usefully describe the sort of troubled terrain with which we are dealing here as the arena of an occult battle between the ghost of the police and the ghost of National Socialism, both at once always present (inasmuch as they appear as all-pervasive haunting figures) and at the same time never quite present (insofar as they always exceed the concrete forms in which they incarnate themselves and which they animate). If this is so, it seems to me that what we encounter in this spectral clash could also be understood as a certain constitutive contradiction between the fetish of the state and its ominous shadow, the fetish of the nation. Of course, that would place an ironic spin on Aretxaga's argument that, as she puts it,

> [i]t is in the studies of violence that the state—what we imagine as the state, what we call the state, that ensemble of discourses and practices of power, that elusive subject that can so much affect the life of citizens—appears most clearly as working against the nation. The very concept at the heart of the nation, "the people," becomes an object of fear and violence by a state that wants to have absolute control of a nation it is at once dividing and destroying. "The people" is invoked and torn apart through the creation of ever-present enemies: criminals, communists, subversives, guerrillas, terrorists. (2003, 397)

Aretxaga is discussing here how the surveillance and security apparatuses of pathologically violent states turn against a certain construal of the nation. As we have already seen, the penal regimes of political delinquency in Germany render blatantly clear the anxiety of a state we would not ordinarily consider as excessively brutal, as well as the repressive violence to which it resorts in the face of the menacing figure of the nation. Aretxaga is concerned with a state in search of absolute control on a campaign to destroy "the people." Our case appears somewhat less clear-cut: first, because it is precisely against the shadow of such absolutist violence, incarnated in the memory of National Socialism, that the contemporary German state battles as it persecutes young right-wing extremists; and second, because the relation in Aretxaga's passage between the nation and the people hardly captures the way in which the German state, far from attempting to dominate the former by targeting the latter, instead seeks to banish the nation from the demos altogether. "The state," Aretxaga cautions, should then be thought of in ways that are not necessarily totally dislodged from the nation but neither attached to it. Rather one should consider a variety of relations that are ambivalent, ambiguous, hostile, violent, porous . . . in which the nature of the hyphen is more a cipher than a self-evident reality. (2003, 398)

In Germany, this hyphenated, antagonistic relation pits against each other the force of the Rechtsstaat and another, occult force that would spell the threat of its annihilation. It is, thus, a struggle that rages far beyond the legal mechanisms of censorship without censorship that we examined in chapter 4. The all-pervasive spectrality of the police demands of us to pay heed to how the sensory apparatuses of the state operate in a diffuse and inconspicuous manner, and how they encounter—and in turn are encountered by—right-wing extremists in a variety of intimate situations. My informants did not experience this force of Law as some indivisible sovereignty, as an authority that either reigned over or was absent from a certain territorial dominion (as terms like "nationally liberated zones" might suggest). Such a concept of the sovereign as an absolute force seems to follow from the imagination of sovereignty as the power to decide on the exception, as proposed by Carl Schmitt (1996). In this view, the sovereign is only sovereign to the extent that it attains this power of decision, and remains a mere political contestant so long as it has not. But such an either/or conception of sovereignty, while it may work well for political theory, becomes muddled in the lived realities of actually existing sovereignties, which always remain both partial and contextually achieved. Young right-wing extremists in Germany, as we will see, experience sovereignty not in absolute terms but rather as a porous and uneven topography in which state and nation contest and interlace with each other.

In this chapter, I examine the ways in which the state observes the political delinquent and look at how the figure of the police haunts the quotidian spaces of sociability and friendship of right-wing extremists in Germany. Beginning with the concrete presence of different law enforcement agents in spaces of sociability, our discussion will lead us to the far more ambiguous and equivocal figure of the police informant, which, as a spectral potentiality, contaminates the most intimate of interactions and situations. The police informant shows the organized mimesis through which the state seeks to trace its illicit underside. The notion of the organization of mimesis (Taussig 1993, 68; Horkheimer and Adorno 2002 [1944]) describes the way in which civilization more broadly and the fascist or violent state more particularly, while repressing the primitive mimetic faculty, at the same time also orchestrates it and places it in the service of domination. As we shall see, however, the police informant turns out to illustrate not only organized mimesis but also what others have called disorganized mimesis. The latter concept refers to "an excess . . . that reveals the state more as parody than as mimicking agent" (Aretxaga 2000, 49), to the instrumentally irrational performance of mimetic state practices, and to the fantasies that these practices play out. At the same time, as will become clear, the spectrality of the police informant intervenes in and subverts a certain politics of friendship that is central to how young right-wing extremists conceive of themselves. In so doing, it haunts and ultimately shatters their utopian desires for an authentic, true nation.

POLICE OVERKILL

There appeared to be hardly anything immaterial, however, about the various teams of law enforcement officers that regularly converged upon the young crowds outside the Bretterbude kiosk at the Grünau train station. As I described it in chapter 3, the Grünau train station area stands on the district's southeast and forms a local transportation hub. The Bretterbude's small roofed patio constituted a local institution and a place for sociability for several groups of regular clients whose comings and goings dictate its daily rhythms, including the groups of adolescents and young adults with whom I worked. Some of them still attended school, while others struggled through vocational training programs, welfare-for-work positions, temporary and informal jobs, or extended periods of unemployment. More than a few of them sought refuge at the environs of the train station from difficult domestic circumstances.

The latter group made the Bretterbude its hangout not long before my arrival to the field, and had meanwhile evolved rapidly from the small core of dedicated Union soccer fans to a large crowd as the reputation of the kiosk snowballed through the district. Not entirely gratuitously, during the same years the Bretterbude had quickly gained fame as a neo-Nazi den, attracting the attention of multiple and at times antagonistic forces: numerous police units, far right activists who sought to recruit both cadres and rank-and-file, militant antifascists who sent out masked, camouflaged agents for photographic missions, and the street social workers whom I accompanied. The Bretterbude in turn has constituted those that it gathered under its roof. For many—recall Sylvia, who arrived there after her youth club shut down due to budget cuts—it was precisely where they became properly nationalist, a place politically formative in its quotidian rhythms, which mediated the exchange and circulation of phrases and narratives, the consolidation of solidarity, and the inculcation of particular habits.

The Grünau train station area in general and the Bretterbude kiosk in particular drew the attention of a variety of agents of law and order. Some of them uniformed, others plainclothes, some representing the civil police while others the criminal police and others still municipal units of public order, some belonging to teams specializing in youth-violence or right-wing extremism, yet others to preventive police forces, they maintained a constant watchful eye and a heavy hand over the groups around the kiosk. Andrea, who side by side with her full-time occupation as a street social worker had been completing a degree in criminology, took an interest in their activities that had less to do with her professional responsibilities and more with the thesis project on which she was embarking at the time. Repeatedly, she would note with furious indignation how particular police units transgressed the specific limits of their distinct legal mandates. In this constant, street-level mixture between law-conserving and lawmaking violence, the preventive police would engage in investigative practices, private security guards would harass teenagers who congregated near but outside the mall, and uniformed municipal police officers would come to their aid by imposing the mall's regulations outdoors and hassling youths with body searches. Bereft of the erudition in the knotty lore of laws and regulations governing police work that Andrea commanded, the young people at the Bretterbude could hardly weed out those instances in which one law enforcement unit breached protocol and strayed into the jurisdiction of another. Yet it took no specialized knowledge to figure out that the police cars that sometimes parked across the street, the patrols that occasionally walked past or stopped by, and every so often the body searches and identification checks signaled a heightened interest on the side of repressive state apparatuses in registering and curbing their actions that surpassed the attention ordinarily bestowed upon the average citizen.

But beyond its power to transgress the legal boundaries of its own mandate, that is, beyond the power of the police to at once enforce the law and remain external or prior to it, law enforcement collapses the distinction between law-preserving and lawmaking violence, perhaps even more significantly in its discretionality, in its unique prerogative of deciding where, when, and upon whom to impose the law. In other words, granted that the police never enforces the entire corpus of the law universally, evenly, and absolutely, the very decision to impose any law already contains within it a founding violence. This, in my reading, is what Derrida means when he states that every act of conservation of the Law is at the same time a refounding of the Law. Giorgio Agamben advances a similar argument when he proposes that the distinction between constituting and constituted power, which he identifies respectively with Benjamin's lawmaking and law-preserving violence, is theoretically understandable as the relation between potentiality and actuality. A constituting act is sovereign, Agamben writes, only insofar as, in crossing over from potentiality to actuality, it does not destroy but merely suspends, while retaining, its "potential not to be." Sovereignty, then, is a "zone of indistinction," a limit at which "pure potentiality and pure actuality are indistinguishable" (1998, 40–47).

In the same manner, the decision of the police to impose certain laws, and in so doing to cross over from potentiality to actuality, preserves its capacity not to impose those very same laws on other occasions. The police, then, is subject neither to the Law as a literal code, nor to the precedents set by its own acts, but rather remains that "zone of indistinction" between potentiality and actuality, lawmaking and law-preserving violence. Selective enforcement is, of course, far from unique to the German context in general or to the penal governance of right-wing extremism in particular. Two prominent and rather well-known examples include racial profiling in the United States as part of the "war on drugs" and as part of the practices of highway patrols. As Bernard Harcourt has demonstrated, similar discriminatory norms shape penal policy at virtually all levels in today's United States, and generally enjoy popular support (2007). Harcourt links such discriminatory practices to the dominant place in contemporary penal policies of actuarial methods, which claim to be cost-effective (though he shows them not to be so). In our case, however, it is difficult to see how actuarial logics could explain selective law enforcement at the Bretterbude. Far from following mathematical, economizing considerations of crime prevention (misguided or hypocritically racist as these may be), it would appear rather to approximate the sorts of sensory, perceptive logics of police work in Giuliani's New York that the anthropologist Allen Feldman has documented (2001), in which the very corporeal appearance of particular people (in that case, of the homeless) comes to embody an act of violence.

One particularly conspicuous way in which the police made use of this power at the Bretterbude and, when it deemed necessary, farther afield in the vicinity of the train station, was the invocation of a legal prohibition on consuming alcoholic beverages outdoors. Now Berlin is a city where alcohol, and more specifically beer, is openly and widely enjoyed on the streets, in public transportation, and at parks just as much as in restaurants, cafés, and bars. At certain times, and on certain train lines or at certain plazas, it often appears as if only a handful of people are *not* carrying a beer bottle in their hand. Indeed, it is telling that virtually none of my other acquaintances in Berlin—those who did not spend their afternoons at the Grünau train station—found my story about a state law prohibiting the consumption of alcohol in public space plausible. And yet that very same law seemed to have been resurrected from the dead at the Bretterbude, where police officers sporadically—again, always reserving the potential not to enforce it, not to cross over into actuality—invoked it, disbursing fines to young people when their groups spilled over from the kiosk's small awning onto the adjacent street. The narrow dimensions of the patio made it practically impossible for such a spillover not to take place whenever more than a few people gathered under its roof. Set at ten euros, the fines were modest yet just high enough to place too heavy a burden on the financially strapped youths and to act as effective deterrents against them.

It was this exceedingly unrelenting gaze and heavy hand of the state that played a central role in motivating the gradual migration of many among the young people at the Bretterbude to the newly opened and more discreetly positioned Bangladeshi eatery Khan's across the railway tracks (though their respite there, as we shall see in chapter 6, was short-lived). But the condensed and closely scrutinized surroundings of the Grünau train station, where law enforcement gained a certain ritualized predictability and tangible visibility, did not detract from the spectral quality of the police with which we have been concerned here. The police haunted the quotidian lives of young right-wing extremists in the district everywhere as a presence that, always hovering over them as potentiality, could at any moment or place gain flesh and blood and erupt onto the scene in the form of raids or unannounced visits, whether at their homes or at other leisure spaces and establishments. The past decade has witnessed a sprouting of specialized police squads assigned to watch over and smother the illegal activities of precisely such young right-wing extremist street cliques as theirs throughout Germany. The Politically Motivated Street Criminality unit (Politisch Motivierte Straßenkriminalität, or PMS) and the Youth Violence Operational Group (Operative Gruppe Jugendgewalt, or OGJ) represented this nascent trend in Berlin.[3] Their teams appeared every so often in favorite hangout spots of the local extreme right groups to carry out routine, preventive police work. But they, as well as other police forces, also made less mundane appearances, like the raid on Freddi's apartment with which I opened chapter 4. More frequently, I heard stories about violent police raids at public places such as favorite bars of right-wing extremists or music concerts. Freddi, for example, once recalled a visit to a concert in the district where one of his particularly favored musicians appeared. "One and a half hours [later]," he said, "the police and everything was there . . . then they took half [of the audience] with them to the police station."

Rarely, it seemed, do such raids go without a measure of violence, especially when targeting groups or crowds of people rather than individuals in their apartments. As the stories that young people told me about such raids plainly recognized, the exercise of violence on such occasions is more often than not reciprocal, even if not symmetrical. Now, it has been observed elsewhere that in their hunt after the enemies of the state, the agents of its repressive apparatuses perform a mimetic violence through which they approximate, if not those very enemies, then at least their hyperbolized representations in the media. The point here is not that police become violent because their adversaries, young neo-Nazis, for example, are violent. The point is rather that the violence of the police takes a certain form of affinity to the figure of their enemy. This becoming-other, and the entire range of fabricated images of the occult that it assumes, appears to operate all the more strongly under the sign of specialized, secretive law enforcement units (Aretxaga 1999 and 2000). Such units replicate that which they are

[3] Other, similar police forces included, for example, the Special Commission Right Extremism (Sonderkommission Rechtsextremismus, or SoKo Rex) in Saxony, the Perpetrator-Oriented Policies against Extremist Violence unit (Täterorientierte Maßnahmen gegen extremistische Gewalt, or TOMEG) and Mobile Task Force against Violence and Xenophobia (Mobile Einsatzeinheit gegen Gewalt und Ausländerfeindlichkeit, or MEGA) in Brandenburg, or the Mobile Information Extremism unit (Mobile Aufklärung Extremismus, MAEX) in Mecklenburg–Upper Pomerania, to name but a few.

delegated to suppress, a logic of mimesis for which Freddi, from his standpoint as their target, accounted as follows:

> They're afraid. I mean they first have to wait until enough people are there. Perhaps that's why it takes so long. Two of them can't just go in there. They wouldn't survive. If two of them go in there, then they have no chance. Then they'll just get smacked and that's that. That's why they have to wait there a little bit more. If there are, I don't know, three hundred neo-Nazis there, then they have to be there with at least three hundred policemen or else it makes no sense.

For Freddi, the violence of the police appeared as dictated by a rational calculation and motivated by quite self-evident fears—they could easily "get smacked." But this mimetic replication, of course, proceeds beyond the mere logic of numerical equivalence. As Aretxaga (1999, 63–64) notes, there is always a certain excitement, a certain enjoyment, to the (dis)organized mimesis of the state. The state, in this sense, is not so much the confluence of (bureaucratic) reason and (legitimate) violence, which results in what Michael Taussig (1992, 111) has called the big S, but rather the fetish effect of a constant performance of mimetic violence (Aretxaga 2000, 53).

In Germany, this performance of mimetic violence is evident in news reports about the officers of the OGJ just as much as during political rallies or sometimes simply on the streets of certain city areas, where members of the special police squads that target young right-wing extremists perform a certain bodily comportment that radiates a masculine burliness and a brutal ruthlessness. In so doing, they fabricate an image that mimics the fantasies of violent physicality that surface in common media representations of those whom they are out to get. Their intimacy with the right-wing extremist scene includes personal acquaintance with at least its more prominent and notorious members. Gino remembered a raid they conducted on a bar where he and his friends convened clandestinely, and in which intimate familiarity, in his narrative, seemed to go hand in hand with physical brutality:

> And then came the raid. Ho ho! This tall, broad guy, his name was Bär [bear], immediately walked up to two cops. Right away they gave him some therapy. Ah . . . Me they treated as brutally. They said "Borschert!" [his family name], Bom! [imitating the sound of a smack]. Then immediately I was dragged away with [my friend] on the floor. Ah, that was brutal. Yeah, and then I could still see Bär . . . totally beaten up.

The police, as the spectral presencing of Law and hence as the incarnation of the state, becomes in Gino's narrative much more than a repressive force. It is linked with a certain fascination, an "obscene enjoyment" (Aretxaga 2003), an illicit "tickling at the heels" (Franz Kafka, cited in Taussig 1993). Gino's narration is anything but horrific, anything but self-victimizing. Quite the contrary, with its lively dramatizations and reenactments ("Ho ho!," "Bom!"), with its ironic turn of phrases ("they gave him some therapy"), and with its vivid and animated tone, the story seemed to recall a magnificent adventure, an awesome experience of proximity to the occult, to the magical, to the enchanted. The police, in this sense, like sorcery for the Maka of Cameroon, is "not just something evil . . . [but also] thrill, excitement, and the possibility of access to unknown powers" (Geschiere 1997, 1). The mimetic pleasure flows both ways, as Aretxaga—citing Derrida—puts it, in "'a phantomatic mode of production' (Derrida 1994, 97) . . . that produces both the state and its threatening Other as fetishes of each other" (2003, 402).

MEN OF CONFIDENCE

In Freddi's and Gino's renderings, the mechanisms through which the state seeks to maintain a tight grip and a close watch over their social circles came to life as mimetic performances imbued with excitement. No doubt, the police collected information about them and their peers, familiarized itself with their names, faces, and biographies, and kept track of their activities and hangout spots. No doubt, too, the possibility of the police bursting into their lives as uniformed, badge-bearing, brutal physicality haunted them. But the state's mimetic performances take more menacing, more ghostly forms than the blatantly violent corporality of such special police squads such as the OGJ or the PMS. In its arsenal of technologies of surveillance, we find more occult, more ephemeral instruments than police patrols and ID checks. And these, in Germany, cohere around the shadowy figure of the Office for the Protection of the Constitution (Verfassungsschutz) and its invisible moles, the "contact persons" (V-Männer; sing., V-Mann).[4]

The Verfassungsschutz, Germany's internal intelligence bureau, was founded in the aftermath of the Second World War to protect the newly founded Federal Republic both against remnants of National Socialism and against communist militants. Placed under the authority of the Ministry of the Interior, it is also answerable to the Federal Parliament, which may (and often does) summon its representatives to give account of specific issues. The agency issues annual reports (Verfassungsschutzberichte) in which it informs the general public about developments in the different domains of anticonstitutional activities: political extremism, Islamic extremism, espionage, even scientology (e.g., Bundesamt für Verfassungsschutz 2007). It also publishes various booklets and brochures that aim to disseminate knowledge about particular topics, for example, the symbolism of right-wing extremist groups (Bundesamt für Verfassungsschutz 2004). The federal Verfassungsschutz is complemented—some would say, redundantly

---

[4]The term at times appears as shorthand for Verbindungsmann (contact person), at others for Vertrauensmann (person of confidence).

duplicated—by state-level Verfassungsschutz agencies at each of the Federal Republic's sixteen states.

The narrow jurisdiction of the Verfassungsschutz contrasts not only with ordinary police but also with many other internal security agencies in other countries. Its mandate restricts it solely to gathering information about activities that are perceived to endanger the state or the democratic order. Political extremism, of course, stands at the center of its attention. Limited to surveillance over anticonstitutional organizations and to the dissemination of knowledge about them, it holds absolutely no executive law enforcement powers. In this strict delimitation of its mandate, we find an institutional trace of the paradoxes that have hovered over the Federal Republic in the postwar era and against the historical menace of despotic tyranny. On the one hand, there was the need to fortify the liberal democratic state and its constitutional order against its enemies—not only against the return of National Socialism but also against the contemporaneous threat of communism. On the other hand, the very mechanisms that were put in place to protect this order needed at the same time to be protected from their abuse by the state itself. We see here, then, another reiteration of the same paradoxes that we found in the legal regimes that we examined in chapter 4, and that struggle to reconcile the guarantee of liberal rights (such as the freedom of expression) with the repression of antidemocratic activities, both deemed equally necessary for staving off the possibility of totalitarianism.

This paradox comes to the fore often enough, as some of the agency's techniques trigger criticism that it reproduces, rather than breaks with, the policing and control traditions of authoritarian regimes. To be sure, accusing the Verfassungsschutz of bearing any resemblance whatsoever to National Socialism or the Gestapo appears to remain outside the discursive boundaries of the tolerable and would likely result in legal consequences for those who would voice such a critique. But comparisons to the GDR, and particularly to the Stasi, are frequent. In these debates, the reliance of the Verfassungsschutz upon V-Männer for gathering information has emerged as particularly thorny. The practice has come under extensive juridical scrutiny and into the heat of public controversy over the past decade and a half (Dietzsch and Schobert 2002), in the course of which it has time and again revealed itself to be a rather disorganized form of mimesis (Aretxaga 1999). Its most notably dishonorable moment came with the fiasco that surrounded the ultimately abortive campaign to ban the NPD in the years 2000–2003 (Fischer 2001).

Triggered by a sequence of macabre instances of racist violence, the convoluted and absurd turn of events that sparked off the legal campaign to ban the NPD provides a classical lesson in the irrational—if not hysterical—logic of mediatized politics. Around the year 2000, a series of relatively well-attended NPD rallies hit the country, together with a number of exceptionally brutal racist assaults. A sustained national media hype mounted pressure on politicians to take action. There was wide talk in the media of "nationally liberated zones" (*national befreite Zonen*) that allegedly covered broad swaths of land, especially in the East, where the state putatively lost its capacity to enforce the law and protect its citizens. The center-left Social Democratic Party, recently elected to the government under the leadership of Gerhard Schröder, blamed the center-right Christian Democrats for inciting racism with their anti-immigrant electoral campaign rhetoric and for failing to act decisively against the far right during their sixteen years in power. The Christian Democratic Union in turn responded with a call to ban the NPD, and challenged the Social Democrats to lead the move. Despite extensive skepticism about the advisability of a campaign to ban the party, about its prospects for success, and most of all about its relevance for curbing racist violence, an accelerating momentum, fueled by scandalized media coverage, seemed to detonate an internal dynamic that could no longer be stopped. An arson attack on a synagogue provided the last straw, and the government finally announced its support for the ban (Staud 2005b).

The federal government, and both the upper and lower houses of Parliament,[5] brought the case against the NPD before the Constitutional Court, which, in a blow viewed broadly as humiliating, proceeded to dismiss it already during the preliminary hearings. As the judges deliberated on whether or not to consider the case, it gradually emerged that an alarmingly high proportion of the NPD's national and local leadership—including at least one cofounder of the party—were on the payroll not only of the federal Verfassungsschutz but also of various others of its state-level cognates, which utterly failed to coordinate their surveillance efforts. Although a majority of the judges in session rejected the party's request to halt the procedures, their number was not high enough according to German law, which sets strong protections for political parties. The minority, which accepted the NPD's request to end the trial, determined that the state could not seek to ban the party for alleged counterconstitutional activities in the sponsorship and stimulation of which it had potentially played such a massively decisive role. It condemned the use of incriminating statements taken from party leaders who had long served as informants to support the case against the party. While holding back from deciding on the constitutionality of the use of informants in the leadership of political parties, it harshly condemned the practice. Most important, it accepted the NPD's claim that no possibility existed for due process since the Verfassungsschutz evidently continued to collect information on the party's activities from several prominent informants during the proceedings, information that could have compromised its defense strategy (Bundesverfassungsgericht 2003).

The ignominious debacle of the attempt to ban the NPD patently revealed not only the sheer scope of the Verfassungsschutz's reliance on informants in its

---

[5] The German political system includes two legislative assemblies: the Bundesrat (Federal Council), whose members are unelected state delegates, and the Bundestag (Federal Parliament), with elected MPs. The comparison to a lower and upper house system therefore holds only partially.

surveillance practices but, more crucially, exposed the paradoxical hindrance that this method poses in the way of any legal action against organizations whose counterconstitutional practices it has been used to corroborate. Unsurprisingly, such revelations have escalated contentious debates and have sparked ever more passionate demands for the discontinuation of informant-based surveillance. And yet the persistence of the state's funding of and dependency upon V-Männer, just as much as the questionable value and nature of such methods, have become evident time and again whenever legal charges have been brought against right-wing extremist groups and organizations. One of the more notable instances of such disorganized mimesis subsequent to the failed NPD ban came to public knowledge following a crackdown on a network of skinhead neo-Nazis in the state of Saxony. As it turned out, at least some of them funded their activities—including, for example, the production and distribution of illegal neo-Nazi media—partially with money they received from the Verfassungsschutz. Despite plentiful information about illegal activities in their circles, law enforcement authorities did not intervene (Hartwig 2004; see also Liebers 2004).

More recently, the almost coincidental discovery in 2011 of a three-member-strong neo-Nazi terrorist cell that, over the course of more than a decade, had been responsible for the cold-blooded, execution-style assassination of nine owners of small businesses, all of immigrant background, and of one police officer, as well as for more than a dozen armed bank robberies, betrayed to the public an unprecedented image of just how messy these forms of state mimesis have been. I will come back to the story of the National Socialist Underground (NSU), the unfolding of which over the past few years has revealed ever new and more disturbing details about just how badly the state mishandled the information it received and mismanaged the investigation into the murder cases, eventually forcing the director of the federal Verfassungsschutz and several of his state-level equivalents to resign their posts. I want to note here, however, that already within a few weeks after the exposure of the neo-Nazi trio, it had become evident that the Verfassungsschutz had an informant who knew the members of the NSU and who had provided warnings about their plans. It took only a few more weeks before it was revealed that the state had not one but many informants who knew about the NSU and that the Verfassungsschutz held extensive knowledge about the group's members and their activities (*Der Spiegel* 2011b and 2011c; Förster 2012). Most recently, it emerged that an important figure in the militant and violent neo-Nazi milieu of Saxony who had collaborated as an informant with the Berlin police for about a decade had, before his recruitment, supplied explosives to the members of the terrorist cell, and on multiple occasions had passed on information to the police that could have led to their capture (Gebauer 2012).

This, the attempt to ban the NPD, and many other cases underline far more than merely the technical juridical problems that the figure of the informant generates. All of them point to a certain excess of power, a certain mess that, sure enough, cannot be accounted for as rational governmental conduct, but that mere incompetence or negligence equally fail to explain. The intimate collusion for which the informant stands between the state and its supposed enemies; the bizarre excesses that render these stories at times tragedy, at others farce, and at yet other times both at once; and the apparent addiction of the state to occult forms of seeing, and its boundless intoxication by them, all disclose the mimetic pleasure and voyeuristic fascination at work.

FRIENDS AND TRAITORS

For my informants, the broad public debates about the use of police informants by state agencies, which circulated time and again in national publicity with every new scandal, insinuated a sense of paranoia into the most mundane of their social interactions. On the one hand, the possible presence of police informants in their midst constituted for them a hard social fact and a banal reality that they simply took for granted. But on the other hand, because of its unlocatability, because of the menace that it posed to them, because it skirted the boundary of the concrete and the immaterial, yet most of all because it constituted a certain form of power that established itself upon the logic of seeing without being seen (what Derrida described as the "visor effect" [1994]), this same presence appeared, too, as a haunting incarnation of the surveillance machinery of the state. It shook their confidence in their ability to engage in illegal activities with any measure of discreetness. And it imbued their daily lives with a sense that they were, at least potentially, everywhere being watched. Most significant, however, this evasive, ephemeral presence weaved itself into their narratives of camaraderie and solidarity and threatened to subvert and unravel the very words with which they sought to fabricate their political selves.

Notably, none of them seemed to know of informants who have been unequivocally outed as such. And yet many entertained a range of ideas about the possible collaboration of people in their circles with the state. At times they formulated such suspicions as firm beliefs, while at other times as mere hypotheses. Regardless of how strong their mistrust, it often relied on information that circulated through discursive modalities of rumor. It thus authorized itself by reference to a presumed series of citations whose often vaguely known path purportedly led backward to a reliable witness. Rumors about the identity of possible informants appeared as "a reaction to the actual, diffuse capillary threading of state surveillance and power through the warp of everyday life" (Feldman 1997, 28–29). In pointing at the informant as the incarnation of the police, "they ascribe to the half-hidden state apparatus an authorial center, a visible place from which its aggressive activity emanates" (1997, 28). Always operating under the weight of uncertainty, rumors serve as prognostics of possibilities that open up a method of classification at the limits of facticity (Feldman 1995). At the same time, and precisely because of their vagueness, suspicions about possible colla- borators display an obsessive concern with what Veena Das (2001) has called "sources of validation." They seek to consolidate themselves through the elabo- ration and assessment of particular signs that come to stand for danger and may trigger alarm about presumed friends. Thus Freddi, for example, having just ex- pounded on the values of unfaltering loyalty and true friendship—which saved him from prison and from falling into the hands of hostile groups, and which, he claimed, distinguished his rightist milieu from others (see discussion in chap- ter 2)—subverted his own discourse as he transitioned into an embittered in- dictment of collaborators:

> FREDDI: That's just the way it always is with us. You don't talk about it, it's just the way it is; you stick together and that's that. Except for informants. Informants are a problem. That's the people who screw you over, who didn't end up in jail just because they were taken up by the police. Who said, "Yeah, I'll help you crack a few people."
>
> NATE: Do you know informants?
>
> FREDDI: I know informants.
>
> NATE: Yeah?
>
> FREDDI: Yeah. I've had [a] fight, more or less, with two informants here already. I knew it. I mean, I'm 80, 90 percent sure that they were informants. Of course, they would never say that they are informants. But they were a couple of people who screwed a few people whom only they knew [about], whom only they could know [about]. And that's why it's clear to us that they were [infor- mants]. The others, they were four people . . . who almost went to jail. And the fifth [person], nothing happened to him. And, only those five people could know about it . . . And then, it was remarkable that he didn't live in Berlin anymore . . . They act just like the Stasi, exactly the same shit . . . and actually, it's our friends. Actually, these are good friends you know, who were already friends earlier, before they became informants. And they betray us . . . And only to avoid half a year in prison they bring four other people into prison or something like that, people whom they actually like.
>
> NATE: Well, actually they receive money for it, no?
>
> FREDDI: No, no, they don't go to jail. You know most of them personally. And that's why we're always careful if someone almost, if someone says, "Yeah I almost ended up in jail." That's when we're always very careful, when something like that is said. Why didn't he go to jail? If he says that [it was] grave physical injury, almost attempted murder, he would have gone to jail. But he didn't even get probation . . . and then you do have to be careful about what you say and all that.

The deep sense of suspicion that hovered over Freddi's reflections subverted his own claims. Despite his attempts at its domestication, an uncertainty saturated his words. Was he 90 percent sure? Or only 80? Was the friend who got away without even so much as probation lucky or treacherous? In this way, the figure of the informant entrenched the menacing gaze of the state deeply within Freddi's most intimate forms of sociability. Its diffuse form would seem to pollute everything and everyone. The uncertainty that surrounded it projected itself toward, and incarnated itself in, presumed friends. It orchestrated a certain mapping of possible dangers and warning signs and demanded the calibration of speech and behavior ("you have to be careful about what you say," Freddi told me) to practices of telling that labor to reveal who is and who is not trustworthy. In their desperate search for sources of validation, rumors about possible police informants "[seem] to cultivate [their] own special perceptual array that weaves new sensibilities between personhood and the state" (Feldman 1997, 49). They become a sort of somatic sensitivity. Thus Freddi, in order to confront the ghostly threat of the police informant, expounded an ultimately futile strategy of domestication and survival that hinged upon the elaboration of a matrix of indexical signs and its subjugation to a series of exegetical operations. To do so, he relied on assessments of the distribution and circulation of illicit knowledge about particular people or events. Who knew, or could have known, about *it* or about *them*? Similarly, he scrutinized the legal dispensation of punishment, looking for the proportionality—or, perhaps more accurately, for the lack of correspondence—between the crimes committed and the sentences received.

Furthermore, while always precarious, such signals of validation may at times prove utterly unavailable, and in their absence mistrust runs wild. Gino once related to me how he and his coconspirator friends decided to form a Kameradschaft and assembled for their second or third meeting—he couldn't quite remember—which, to their dismay, proved to be their last. A police raid terminated their short-lived attempt: "Well, they uncovered us of course. [My friends] said someone betrayed us and so on. And amongst ourselves, so to speak, no one trusted [each other] anymore. And then the Kameradschaft was off. Informants and all of that." Moreover, presumed friends who revealed themselves as informants and disclosed discreet information to police authorities posited only one paranoiac form in which the state's surveillance mechanisms infringed upon the clandestine communicative sphere, based on personal acquaintanceships and mutual trust, that provided the logistical basis for organizing and partaking in illicit activities. Freddi, for example, insisted as well that his telephone line was being tapped: "You hear it once in a while . . . When it crackles or it rustles, or when the line breaks. Then you hear the cracking noise. You notice it, you realize that it's tapped."

But what menaced Freddi's enunciations went beyond the here and now of his quotidian interactions with acquaintances, of the probabilistic mapping of possible dangers and the corresponding calibration of behaviors and speech. It enfolded as well a certain temporal tension that exceeded the present and disrupted far more radically the distinction he so desperately struggled to carve between friends and traitors, and with it, too, the idiom of solidarity for which this distinction was so crucial. Recall that, before they turned in their comrades, the police informants were once "good friends." To be sure, certain signs may suggest, with varying degrees of likelihood, that a particular person *is* an untrustworthy collaborator, that an acquaintance has *already* collaborated with the police. However, the temporal structure of Freddi's narrative implies that the crucial yet truly impenetrable question was a different one, namely, who among one's "good friends" could be trusted not to *become* an informant in the future. All said and done, who would refuse—and who would accept—the burden of sacrifice demanded by the ethic of friendship? Who would incriminate his friends to save himself from prison? Freddi's narrative, which structures a temporal movement between a past of good friendship and a present of treason, turns out to enfold and project backward a certain future anterior into what, borrowing liberally on Reinhart Koselleck's phrase (1985), we might term a future past.

"Friendship," writes Derrida, "is never a given in the present; it belongs to the experience of waiting, of promise or of engagement. Its discourse is that of prayer, and at stake there is what responsibility opens to the future" (1993, 368). Friendship is thus not an established relationship; it is never something that has already arrived, nor something at which one has already arrived. The friend, in that sense, is never really present as such. Instead, friendship designates a temporal experience, and it is the structure of that experience that became displaced into the past in Freddi's story. The friend points to a certain orientation toward the future, which, for Freddi and his peers, was suffused with unnerving possibilities. As such, to borrow yet again on Koselleck, the figure of the friend-as-futurity forms a horizon of expectation, a future informed and at least to a certain extent grounded in experience yet never reducible to it. Thus, as I already described in chapter 1, Freddi and Gino may have—as in fact they did—held in high esteem the loyalty of their most trusted friends. Those were friends who have given them no cause for suspicion. Indeed, some of those friends have even corroborated their trustworthiness in the past through acts of sacrifice and solidarity when the opportunity presented itself, for example, by covering up for their complicity in illegal activities. And yet, however firm they would like to imagine these relationships to be, their own enunciations about the temporality of treason exposed how the present, as Derrida insists, is overrun "by the undeniable future anterior which would be the very movement and time of friendship" (1993, 377). Their friendships, then, were always already inscribed in that future anterior tense of promise and expectation.

Freddi told me that "they act just like the Stasi, exactly the same shit . . . and actually, it's our friends." It is interesting how the figure of what, to him, appeared as a repressive state backgrounded a certain temporal instability in his words. "Actually, these are good friends you know," he continued, "who were already friends earlier, before they became informants. And they betray us." Freddi, recall, was narrating the past event of his encounter with a couple of acquaintances whom he believed to be informants. At some point prior to that encounter, the people in his story allegedly betrayed their friends and became collaborators. At some still earlier time, they became good friends with those whom they would later turn in. And yet Freddi also insisted, in the present tense, that "these *are* good friends" (emphasis mine). I read this last statement as at once reflecting the temporal indeterminacy of his particular narrative about the two suspected police informants and expressing a more impersonal truth about the figure of the friend/informant in general. In Freddy's or any other similar, particular case, a person—specific, known—has become a good friend before turning into a police informant. More generally, however, a person—whoever, as yet unknown—will become a good friend before turning into a police informant. Police informants are, always, good friends who betray you. Freddi's story therefore oscillated between the singularity of a past event that has already happened and the more menacing and abstract potentiality of an unknown future that one must inevitably confront with each and every friendship consolidated. The present tense here, then, reconstitutes and grounds anew in the here and now the temporal figuration of the future anterior, which in Freddi's particular story has been projected backward into the past. This temporal vortex unravels Freddi's discourse of friendship. If a person will have become a good friend before turning into a traitor, then, almost by definition, by the very fact of becoming a good friend, the good friend is always also a possible traitor.

COPS AND THIEVES

The state and its informants thus do far more than merely collect information covertly about young right-wing extremists. If it is in the police that we find the paradigmatic collapse of lawmaking and law-preserving, if it is the police that most palpably performs the (dis)organized mimetic violence of law enforcement, for Freddi and his peers the right-wing extremist police informant represented an ambiguous slippage between the state, as a repressive apparatus, and the nation, as the promise of a community-to-come, of a future fullness. We examined the intricate legal regime that enables these forms of policing in chapter 4, and we saw how they seek to negotiate the paradoxical impositions of Germany's history through a series of indeterminacies and illegibilities. We have also noted how, for the young people at the center of this study, the police and its practices of (dis)organized mimesis rendered Law a self-authorizing force. And yet, there are immeasurably subtler modalities of organized mimesis through which the state keeps track of them. After all, if the informant is unknown in the sense that it remains a haunting potentiality that breeds suspicion but that rarely if ever turns unequivocally locatable as a concrete identity, it is also at the same time hyperknown, inasmuch as its figure frequently hits the limelight of national publicity and that its reality, while evasive, is taken for granted. But the state follows young right-wing extremists with technologies of surveillance that are far more innocuous and intricate and that, despite their seemingly banal nature (or perhaps, like Poe's purloined letter, precisely because of it), appear far less transparently as such.

In chapter 6, I examine how young right-wing extremists experience these mechanisms of governance, which, in stark contrast with the police, they do not identify as aligned with the repressive state (or, indeed, with the state at all). But before I do so, I must touch briefly upon one more aspect of the mimetic violence between the state and its enemies. So far, I have focused on the destabilizing effects to which the ghostly presence of the state gives rise in the quotidian spaces and intimate relationships of young right-wing extremists. And yet, if we are truly to attend to the reciprocal contamination of state and nation, to the anxieties it triggers, and to the labor of separation that it sets in motion, our discussion would remain incomplete if we fail to note the ways in which illicit nationalism also insinuates itself into the mechanisms of governance and policing. Now there is no doubt a myriad of sites and moments in which an unappetizing nationalism bares its face within the apparatuses and discourses of the state. Here, and in-line with the focus of this chapter, I want to consider how young right-wing extremists appear to contaminate the police and the Verfassungsschutz from within.

I have already mentioned in chapter 4 the case of a police officer who exposed an iconic tattoo on his back of a German WWII infantry soldier (Landser) that is highly popular among German right-wing extremists and who successfully appealed against his dismissal from service (Oberverwaltungsgericht Berlin-Brandenburg 2009). My interest was in the semiotic logic that the court employed to construe indexical relations between the Landser tattoo as a sign and the culpability (or, as it turned out, innocence) of the officer. Here, I want to note the importance that the court granted to the possible harm that would be done to the image of the police force by the mere notion that its officers could include right-wing extremists. The Berlin Constitutional Court expressed similar concerns in a ruling, which I mentioned only in passing in chapter 4, in which it considered the appeal of a police officer, charged with voicing counter-constitutional statements, against his dismissal. The officer allegedly not only expressed sympathy to dictatorial regimes but also denied the Holocaust and doubted the right of Poland and Israel to exist, all highly problematic if not outright illegal statements in Germany. The ruling, which found the officer guilty as charged but sweetened the verdict from dismissal to suspension, expressed horror about the contamination of the German state by right-wing extremist elements: "he who attempts to justify or absolve the previous tyranny, undermines at the same time the foundations of our democratic political order." And further, "the playing down and glorification of National Socialist tyranny by a law enforcement officer stains the image of the police greatly" (Verfassungs-gericht Berlin 2007).

The courts have shown similar concerns about expressions of illicit political sympathies not only among law enforcement officers but equally in other apparatuses of the state, such as schools, government ministries, or the armed forces (see, e.g., Oberverwaltungsgericht Berlin-Brandenburg 2007; Bundesver-fassungsgericht 2008; *Die Zeit* 2012a). In some cases, they have not shied away from upholding the dismissal of officials in public service. Nevertheless, as far as the hypervisibility of such cases among the public at large is concerned, the possible presence of presumed right-wing extremists in the police has consistently garnered far more intensive media coverage (e.g., *Berliner Morgenpost* 2011; Lier 2011; *Der Spiegel* 2012b; *Die Zeit* 2012b). And, at least in recent years, this public anxiety has been nowhere as strong as in the already mentioned affair of the NSU. Several of the state's security apparatuses penetrated the intimate social circles of the terrorist cell but failed to track down and arrest its members for the late 1990s explosion that sent them to a clandestine existence. More severely, state agencies failed to link the NSU to a series of suspiciously similar murder cases that kept adding up. According to several critical voices, far from the result of mere incompetence, these failures expose a systematic anti-immigrant bias in the work of police authorities. In the face of much evidence to the contrary, the investigation set out from the assumption that the assassinations could be traced to what was officially termed "milieu-related organized structures" (*milieubezogene organisierte Strukturen*) or, less euphemistically phrased, to criminal immigrants. The entire course of the investigation, then, criminalized the victims together with their families and friends, with concrete and often harsh consequences for lives and livelihoods. According to critics, the bias of the investigation exposed, too, the predominance of a nationalist, racist worldview within the state's law enforcement and security organs.

While all this may very well hold true, the NSU affair brought to light not only the possibly racist worldview of many law enforcement officers but also concrete suspicions about actual collusion and cover-ups. The special parliamentary commission that was created to investigate the affair instructed all security organs at both federal and state levels to send in any relevant documents in their possession. About a year and a half into its work, the committee discovered that within a couple of weeks following the exposure of the cell, the federal Verfassungsschutz shredded a number of files that included information about surveillance on the social milieu of the NSU. Members of the commission raised an outcry and the media followed in their footsteps with frequent and disparaging headlines on the latest twists in the affair. The Verfassungsschutz at first denied any link between the shredded documents, the intelligence value of which it played down, and the investigation into the terrorist cell. But the official position changed quickly, and a few weeks later the authorities confirmed the link between the destroyed files and the NSU investigation. It likewise

emerged that the Verfassungsschutz had been carrying out disciplinary procedures against several of its employees who were involved in the shredding. The
new revelations only increased the already prevalent insinuations in the media
and in political discourse of the possibility of illicit motives and cover-ups (*Der
Spiegel* 2012a; Höll and Schultz 2012; Schultz 2012a, 2012b, and 2012c).

As if all this were not enough, the investigation into the affair unearthed suspicions about several police officers who, in separate cases, allegedly colluded
with right-wing extremist groups. The nature of this presumed collusion varied from the passing on of confidential information to neo-Nazis (for example,
about upcoming police raids), to participation in activities of the scene (such
as pub evenings), or even membership in right-wing extremist organizations
(*Die Zeit* 2012c; Jansen 2012; Jüttner 2012a and 2012b). My point here is not to
consider whether the allegations were true or not (though authorities seemed
to have taken them seriously enough) but rather to underline the public anxiety
about, and discomfort with, the menace of illicit nationalism within the apparatus of the state, and particularly within its law enforcement institutions. If the
figure of the police informant stands for a certain leakage between the state and
the nation, between law enforcement and right-wing extremist criminality, if it
represents a certain unstable mimesis that leaves one always uncertain about
its authentic commitments, the police informant nevertheless finds its tangible
place of activity and belonging among Freddi and his friends and is, literally
speaking, not a policeman. But it finds its mirror image in the figure of the secretly nationalist cop, a policeman indeed, but one who equally signals toward
the mutual contamination of seemingly distinct—if not opposed—categories.

||||||||||||||||||| 6 |||||||||||||||||||

Knowing Intimately

THE FIGURE OF THE POLICE INFORMANT and that of its doppelgänger, the neo-Nazi policeman, form a curious pair in several respects. Most evidently, the question they pose is first and foremost one of locatability. One wants to know who they are. But, of course, by their very nature they can only exist as long as they remain unknown: the police informant can no longer operate as such once exposed, and the cop will be dismissed or disciplined as soon as any right-wing extremist allegiance has been solidly corroborated. Their work therefore takes place in a clandestine space: the informant partakes in or gets word of illegal activities on the one hand and secretly passes on information to the police on the other; the neo-Nazi policeman conceals his illicit right-wing extremist engagements from his colleagues while politically contaminating the police corps and occasionally even sharing details he may acquire about covert law enforcement operations with his nationalist comrades. Their consequently mysterious, ephemeral nature goes hand in hand with their moral ambivalence. They oscillate indeterminately between state and nation so that one can never really pinpoint their authentic location.

In this chapter, however, I examine state agents and technologies of knowing that contrast sharply with the clandestine ambivalence of both the informant and the right-wing extremist cop, but that for all that are no less shrouded in opaqueness. For beyond the repressive apparatuses of the state, beyond covert policing and surveillance, and beyond, too, the legal regimes that regulate political delinquency, we find a whole governmental assemblage of institutions, actors, and practices through which the German state mines for knowledge about the politically illicit and the socially marginalized in order to govern the terrain at which the two meet. Here, we find figures who perform their functions in broad daylight, whose personal identities are well known, and who therefore would seem far more transparent than those we have considered up to this point. And yet, as we shall see, their transparency is only skin-deep. It relies on a series of illegibilities that enables their profound embeddedness in functions of surveillance and governance, indeed—and here the case of the street social workers is particularly illustrative—sometimes even their relation to or affiliation with the state, to pass unnoticed.

The elements of which this assemblage consists are many. They include units within the massive institutional bureaucracies of the social state, from the youth office to the employment office or the welfare office, colossal labyrinths of waiting rooms, bureaus, and service counters where forms are completed, seals stamped, databases maintained, reports produced, and records logged. They also include public venues, such as clubs and cultural or athletic centers where youth workers oversee rehearsal studios, computer labs, libraries, sports activities, self-managed cafés, and gaming rooms, all while mining their young clients for information in casual conversations. Schools, of course, stand as key sites for such surveillance functions, where teachers and counselors pay attention not only to pupils' academic performance, domestic circumstances, or social habits but also to the garments they wear, the music they listen to, or the odd-sounding statements they may utter in history class. But so do, for example, church organizations that target marginalized populations and, often under governmental contracts, provide educational assistance, social work services, or space and resources for cultural events. Justice and law enforcement authorities, beyond their reliance on overt and covert policing, maintain their grip on individuals through conditional sentences and periodic reviews, through parole officers contracted on a case-by-case, overtime basis from among qualified social workers, and through court-mandated alcohol rehab programs and antiviolence seminars. Specialized NGOs commissioned to conduct research on local states of affairs and to provide expert consulting services represent another important node in this assemblage, as do variously organized neighborhood-scale forums—some sponsored by the municipality, others by political parties, residents' associations, or other stakeholders—that keep track of ongoing developments, formulate intervention strategies, and consolidate networks for political mobilizations. Finally, of course, one cannot overstate the significance of social workers, such as the ones I had been accompanying, whose work will stand at the center of my analysis in this chapter. Through all these agents and more, the German state maintains surveillance over, produces information about, and—as we shall see in chapters 7 and 8—engages in both rehabilitative and immunological projects against the menace of National Socialism and its incarnations in the present.

Of course, to each among these varied elements, which we may think of as nodes in a composite configuration of interrelations, there often correspond vastly different jurisdictions and mandates, techniques and professional cultures, and cultural and political stakes: some are staffed with tenured government bureaucrats and others with independent service providers employed under acutely precarious contracts; some administer expansive city areas while others oversee a few modest rooms; some are stationary, highly structured, and bureaucratized institutions and others mobile, flexibly deployable, and readily transmutable modules; and some engage solely with right-wing extremism and racist violence while others address far broader sectors such as youths, criminals, or welfare recipients. To the extent that they come together at all, then, they do so as a rather incongruous and not infrequently discordant assemblage, in which different forms of mediation determine how information circulates, filters, and is inflected in various ways.

At times these relations clearly follow hierarchically structured paths, as when administrative authorities perform periodic evaluations of or receive annual reports from independent associations that they fund, or when political parties summon the social workers as guest experts to a special session on right-wing extremism in the district (always an opportunity for the latter to score points with powerful decision makers). Often, however, they take the shape of laterally organized forums and coalitions that cluster together youth workers, social workers, teachers, municipal bureaucrats, local politicians, church officials, law enforcement representatives, real-estate associations, and so on. Such forums aspire to consolidate networks for the exchange of information, for the coordination of efforts, and for the facilitation of collaboration against right-wing extremism. While I was conducting my fieldwork, for example, two such district-wide networks had been operating in Treptow, as well as a number of smaller-scale, neighborhood-level forums, such as the "Roundtable against Right-Wing Extremism Johannisthal" (Runder Tisch gegen Rechtsextremismus Johannisthal), the "Task Force on Right-Wing Extremism Altglienicke" (Arbeitsgemeinschaft Rechtsextremismus Altglienicke), and the "Task Force on Right-Wing Extremism Grünau" (Arbeitsgemeinschaft Rechtsextremismus Grünau).

My interest in this chapter is to look at the labor of the street social workers in order to interrogate this assemblage and examine how it operates at one level as an intricate machine for the production, circulation, and dissemination of knowledge about my informants, and at another level as an apparatus for marking and policing the political distinction that sets them apart as deviants, as the internal enemies of the German state, in the first place. In turn, I describe how my informants encountered this surveillance interface as a series of seemingly isolated, discrete, and disjointed interactions rather than as interlinked nodes. The special mediating role of the social workers positions them as central to this machinery. Their capacity to produce knowledge about their clients, we shall see, depends on their ability to foster and maintain forms of intimacy between themselves and the nightmarish other of the German state while simultaneously cultivating a series of illegibilities about their work as agents of governance. The conditions that allow them to perform this mimicry and to inhabit the place of this other are the result of neoliberal rescalings of state interventions. The strange and ambivalent position in which they consequently find themselves illustrates how the state comes to all-too-closely resemble the very forces it seeks to repress. This organized mimesis of neoliberal governance, in other words, has as its effect the constant evocation of the National Socialist specter through a disturbing proximity between its agents and its targets.

A CLOSE CALL, OR, THE OCCULT PATHS OF KNOWLEDGE

Under the enduring sunlight of an early evening in June, Helmuth, Andrea, Daniela, and I chitchatted our way absentmindedly toward the recently painted bright pink walls and the red-tiled rooftop of the small, square edifice that housed Khan's restaurant near the Grünau train station. As I noted, during my fieldwork, especially the younger and more right-wing extremist-oriented clientele of the Bretterbude slowly drifted across the train tracks, over the road, and beyond a plaza crowded with the knickknack stalls of an open-air roadside market and the tram rails on its other side to resettle in Khan's, a newly opened Bangladeshi eatery. The door to the modest building opened onto a small dining area in which three rectangular wooden tables were fitted with long wooden benches on each side. A counter exhibiting a selection of beverages and packed food items separated this space from the kitchen, which unfalteringly emitted strong odors of reused frying oil. Outside, some eight similar tables and benches stood in two rows on a concrete landing, topped by the bare skeleton of an awning and the foliage above it. Khan's appeal consisted in unbeatably cheap beer prices, significantly longer opening hours, more diverse—if ethnically inflected—menu choices, and both outdoor and indoor seating. But its allure owed also, and perhaps chiefly, to its inconspicuous location, tucked as it were on the edge of a thickly wooded park and sheathed by a leafy canopy of branches and treetops, which promised a certain refuge from the multitude of forces that converged upon and contested the young people's presence at the Bretterbude.

Soon after the inauguration of his restaurant, Khan recruited as his assistants Robert, the Union fan who raved about the NPD in chapter 3, and his friend Rene, whom we met in chapter 1 when he approached me to promote his idea for a nationalist youth club. Khan left the business entirely in their hands during his frequent and extended absences, which he explained as international travel related to his self-professed involvement in Red Cross humanitarian projects. Thus, in addition to its convenient transportation links, cheap beer, camouflaged location, and ample seating space, with the owner routinely away and under the management of Robert and Rene, the younger regulars gradually made the place in their own image, modifying it to reflect their needs, tastes, and preferences. Opening hours became flexible and, when necessary, extended well into the night to accommodate parties or drinking sessions in the wake of Union soccer matches, and barbecues were now and then organized and publicized by word of mouth.

Like other visits, this one too revealed the ongoing labor of aesthetic enhancement that had within months transformed the initially run-down, bare food joint into a fairly well-furnished and respectable-looking establishment: the naked skeleton of the outdoor awning had been painted a dark brown and fitted with a few scattered flowerpots and a broad white shield that read "Good vibes party at McKhan—Beer Garden" (Wohlfühl-Party bei McKhan—Biergarten), new red trash bins and sunshades featuring the logo of an ice-cream sponsor brand had been placed here and there, a display case exhibiting the restaurant's menu had been hung, a cigarette vending machine was installed on one of the exterior walls, and signs spelling "McKhan Café" (McKhan Imbiss) in red over white decorated the building's entrance and its street-facing side.

Drawing near the clatter of voices that hovered over the modest beer garden area, we first came upon nineteen-year-old Sylvia, whom I introduced briefly in chapter 1, and who was among the steadiest regulars and most faithful followers of Union at Grünau. Short and heavy, with long brown hair, she numbered with the less fortunate characters that congregated in the vicinity of the train station. Her odd face and numerous experiences of bullying at school and on the streets had won her the derogatory nickname "Pit bull." In shaky health, she was hospitalized periodically for liver and kidney problems. According to the social workers, she suffered from acute skin allergies that ruled out physical contact with machines, a severely deficient writing competency that restricted her suitability for office tasks, underdeveloped motor skills that precluded delicate motions and fine digital coordination, and, finally, a disability that barred her from lifting heavy weights. All of these rendered her a particularly challenging case for them, as they tried their best to assist her frustrating search for the practical internships that were required as part of the office personnel vocational training program that they had secured for her. As if this were not enough, she was thrown out of internships and placed on probation at her vocational program for repeated unexcused absences. All the while, her belongings—cell phones, bags, soccer paraphernalia, clothing articles—were stolen or robbed with a regularity that, as Andrea once put it, would surely have raised an insurance agent's eyebrow.[1] Shortly before my arrival in the field, she had finally gathered enough strength to terminate a relationship with an alcoholic thirty-year-old man who time and again abused her physically.

Perhaps precisely because of her rather lowly social standing and her wide gamut of personal afflictions, Sylvia served as an unmatched conduit of meticulously detailed information and wild rumors about pretty much everyone and everything in her social circles, a silent, barely discernible, and yet highly attentive observer from whom no one took the trouble to conceal anything and who had learned to appreciate the social value that the knowledge she could thus accumulate granted her. She first arrived at Grünau—as I mentioned briefly in chapter 1—after municipal budget cuts forced the youth club in her neighborhood, where she used to spend most of her free time in the past, to shut

---

[1] In order to fully understand Andrea's comment, it might be helpful to explain that personal insurance coverage is prevalent in Germany to a far greater extent than, say, the United States. This holds also for more marginalized social sectors. Thus Sylvia could, and did in fact, recuperate the value of her lost items through her family's insurance policy.

down. Soon thereafter, she met and befriended Norman, whom I introduced in chapter 2, as he exchanged neo-Nazi ring-tones with his friend Danny. Norman had already been a regular at Grünau for some time and invited Sylvia to join him and his companions there. Beyond the possibility of sociability, it seemed that first the shanty Bretterbude kiosk and later Khan's restaurant offered her refuge from an overprotective mother with whom she frequently quarreled. It was here that, following her new friends, she cultivated a passion for soccer and before long overtook them all in her fanatic devotion to Union. And it was also from the cliques that gathered here that she had acquired her rudimentary political coordinates, her anti-immigrant hate, and her electoral loyalty to the NPD. This process of her political *Bildung* was very much still under way and evident in the manner in which she would often listen in on exchanges about the criminality and dependency of immigrants or about the treacherousness of political parties, especially in the run-up to the 2005 federal elections.

On most days, then, for the social workers Sylvia was at once a particularly needy client and a prized source of information. That evening, however, she seemed less interested in bringing us up-to-date on the latest developments among her peers and more in lamenting her absence from the season's closing match, which Union had won. We ambled farther toward the doorway amid the long tables, the lonely elderly men who dotted the low benches, and the clutter of assorted adolescent cliques. Inside, an impressively upgraded stereo system blasted sundry selections of techno, heavy metal, and hip-hop music from two massive loudspeakers. By the wall, the flickering colors of a video game danced upon the screen of a personal computer that had not been there before, utterly failing to draw anyone's attention. Khan himself was nowhere to be seen, and his junior deputies operated the kitchen, the concessions counter, and the cash register, together with a few younger-looking subordinates. One got the impression that theirs was a rather leisurely—not to say, indolent—workday. Their chief chore seemed to be maintaining a steady flow of beer bottles from the refrigerator to their friends-cum-customers, one of whom, precariously propped up around the shoulder of a young woman by the doorway, vociferously doubted his own capacity to withstand his kitchen shift later that evening.

Just as Martina, a slim twenty-year-old tomboy, marched in, a panic-stricken roar all of a sudden rumbled across the dining area, disrupting the laid-back monotony of chatter and alcohol: "The cops are here!" In the confused commotion that followed, some of Khan's underage employees shuffled their way to safe haven, while other minors hurriedly divested themselves of their beer bottles. Most of those present, however, gathered at the small windows, hoping to divine what this unexpected intrusion might signify. Following a brief consultation with Helmuth, I moved outside to the beer garden. Behind the tram tracks I could spot an empty police van and next to it a minibus jam-packed with distracted, dozing officers. A few moments later the social workers decided to move on and steer clear of possible trouble rather than linger about to monitor the events, and I went along with them. But as we gave our farewells and commenced our retreat, a tall man saluted Helmuth from the tram stop, and we paused while Helmuth stepped over to greet him.

A long time went by before he returned, and when he did, a morbid expression of anguished despair across his face, he asked us whether we thought the young people at Khan's had taken note of him and the man. Since the two of them stood right across from the beer garden, Andrea and Daniela replied that they probably had been noticed. Helmuth responded with an endless barrage of "shit, shit, shit." He had just brought their entire effort there crashing down, he concluded. That would indeed have been good reason for distress, because for months now they had been toiling to make acquaintances with and win the trust of young people there, and only of late had they sensed that their labors had finally born fruit. Meeting our perplexed gazes, Helmuth clarified that the man with whom he had just spoken was the chair of the local Social Democratic Party (SPD) committee. They had met earlier, during a recent public forum that the Grünau SPD had organized to counter right-wing extremist trends in the vicinity, and to which Helmuth and concerned local residents had been invited. At the event, Helmuth had brought them up-to-date and named Khan's as the new up-and-coming hub for right-wing extremists in their neighborhood. Members of the local SPD assembly had apparently considered that such a disquieting development urgently called for decisive measures and accordingly agreed, as a first step, to hold their regular weekly meeting at Khan's beer garden. Indeed, we could spot a slow but steady trickle of respectably dressed older people gradually building up into a small company around the tram stop. According to Helmuth, they had officially registered their assembly at Khan's with the authorities as a political demonstration—the police troops, then, had arrived to provide them with protection.[2]

A gloomy air settled over the social workers. Fearing that they had irrevocably associated themselves with the SPD intrusion and its police escort in the eyes of Khan's younger customers, they pondered for a brief moment the possibility of alarming the latter about the upcoming assembly and pleading with them to steer clear of any confrontational misconduct. But this, they concluded, would have only implicated them deeper in the affair. Finally, they concurred that they could only hope the evening would proceed peacefully and without escalation. But an acute sense of a looming catastrophe continued to pervade their conversation for the rest of the workday. They expressed resentful anger at their SPD interlocutors, whose conduct they viewed as intolerably reckless: not only did their surprise call jeopardize the social workers' own drawn-out efforts

---

[2]German law requires that demonstrations be officially registered and coordinated with the relevant police authorities in advance. The police must approve the site or itinerary of each demonstration, although any objections or limits it places on proposed plans can be challenged in court. Depending on the type of demonstration, anywhere from a handful to thousands of police officers may be dispatched to secure the event.

at Grünau, but it concomitantly threatened the very sources of information upon which the SPD members themselves depended for their campaign. Surely but a simple warning would have sufficed to keep them away from Khan's on that particular evening and to thereby forestall the entire debacle. Of course, while this seemed downright commonsensical to the social workers, it could have hardly appeared so to the members of the SPD assembly, who could not be assumed to command a refined understanding of the complex relationships between the social workers and the youths they served. Later that night, as we cruised past the train station, the police vehicles remained in their place and the last few Social Democrats were boarding the tram.

As it turned out, the social workers had grossly overestimated the alertness of their clients. A week later, on a grim, drizzly afternoon, we paid a visit to Khan's and found Robert sporting his illegal Thor Steinar shirt and hard at work on a newspaper word-puzzle; Rene chatting with two skinhead friends; Norman, clean-cut and well dressed (as we had never seen him either before or after), rambling about the security guard training program that he had just entered and would soon flunk; and a few others of their friends. They had been pondering with amusement a brief article dedicated to Khan's that appeared in a local news-letter and had been circulating among them, triggering confused laughter. They found the rendering of their favorite restaurant as a neo-Nazi den ludicrous, for it entirely disagreed with their own perception of the place and of their social clique as harmless (recall the discussion in chapter 3 of how, just as the real witch is always the one next door, the real neo-Nazi is always the next one over). But, most of all, they were utterly surprised to learn about the SPD congregation at Khan's the previous week—which they had evidently entirely failed to register—and thus at long last to make sense of the police vehicles that had parked mo-tionless across from them for several hours, the officers aboard them oddly idle. Needless to say, if they noticed Helmuth conversing with the tall stranger at all, the possible significance of that interaction fully escaped them, and its memory had meanwhile faded.

But surely there was more than just miscalculation at play in the social work-ers' excessive concern about the peril they imagined themselves to face, just as there was doubtlessly more than mere inattentiveness about the young people's failure to note that a political action against them had taken place right in front of them. In fact, the entire incident revealed starkly dissonant perceptions of what had actually taken place at Khan's that evening. The SPD members, for one, arriving at the scene escorted by a squadron of police troops to rescue their neighborhood from the sinister hands of dangerous neo-Nazis, apparently imagined their excursion to Khan's as a journey into the heart of darkness or a hostile invasion into enemy territory. Meanwhile, Rene, Robert, and their peers, for whom Khan's constituted neither more nor less than a hospitable hangout spot, and who had hardly imagined themselves as menacing Nazis, could not have possibly made much of the small group of clean-cut people who took their place at one of the outdoor tables and remained there for some time, steeped in conversation.

As for the social workers, the sense of impending doom that had for a while haunted them divulged much more than merely an anxiety about losing their clients at Grünau. If the coincidence of their visit at Khan's with the SPD incursion and its police backup was unfortunate, it was nevertheless far from fortuitous. It hinted at the hidden outlines of intricate conduits through which information about young right-wing extremists flows. In this sense, what Helmuth's exchange with the tall man threatened to devastate was a certain strategically critical illegibility that made possible an elaborate assemblage of surveillance and control mechanisms. The predicament in which the social workers suddenly found themselves spelled a disruptive moment of crisis in a distinction upon which their work vitally hinged. Its collapse would have laid bare perhaps only a fraction, but a fraction nonetheless, of their profound embeddedness as key mediating nodes within the web of a vast and diffuse governmental machine (Deleuze 1992; Rose 2000b; Deleuze and Guattari 2002) through which the German state keeps a close eye on the menace of political delinquency.

THE SURVEILLANCE MACHINE

Mobilizations against the extreme right—and especially the formation of neighborhood scale forums such as the SPD workforce on right-wing extremism in Grünau or others I listed above—come to life enveloped in an idiom of networking (*Vernetzung*). The vocabulary they mobilize echoes ongoing reconfigurations in administrative and governmental structures that proceeded throughout Berlin during my stay in the field, predominantly under the heading "social space orientation" (*Sozialraumorientierung*). Aggressively advanced by municipal and state governments, these reforms have invoked theoretical frameworks dating back to the 1980s that reconceptualized the provision of social services as a praxis focused on flexibly conceived "social spaces" rather than on disadvantaged individuals. They paired those with decentralizing budgetary and structural rescaling aimed to create relatively autonomous, small-scale administrative units in which local needs are identified and addressed, decisions about resource allocations are hammered out, and the entire range of relevant actors comes together to exchange information and coordinate efforts.

In this sense, the conceptual logic evident in both administrative "social space" reforms "from above" and the sprouting of local forums against right-wing extremism "from below" draws liberally on the idiom of "neoliberal networks": presumably self-organizing, bottom-up formations that encourage collaboration, rely upon nonhierarchical relations, benefit from high flexibility, and take on a topological spatiality focused on localities (Leitner and Sheppard 2002). To be sure, such idioms have signaled the emergence of new, neoliberal forms for governing populations not only in Germany but elsewhere as well. Yet what the German case in particular teaches us is how they have become integrated, too, into the manner in which the neoliberal state not only governs its population but also wages a relentless—and desperate—struggle to mark out and to counter its radical others. The footprint of corporatist, free market language is not entirely absent from such discourses, which broadly employ, for example, concepts of efficiency, productivity, results, quality management, and so forth. But their dominant vocabulary appears rather to approximate what Nikolas Rose has termed "ethopolitics": the "activation" of citizens, the empowerment of localities, the enhancement of democratic participation, the binding of individuals to communities, the aesthetics of the facilitating state, the "responsibilization" of subjects, and the generation of self-regulating structures (Rose 2000a; Bezirksamt Treptow-Köpenick 2005).

While Rose certainly captures a crucial mutation in the idioms and ideologies of governance in today's world, two important provisos about the putatively novel character of ethopolitical governance are in order. First, in Germany as in many other European countries, the social workers and other similar actors of the neoliberal state represent an innovative transformation of governance functions, such as the provision of welfare, the redistribution of wealth, and the surveillance over and control of populations only in a relative and limited sense. They do not entirely recast the older architecture of the German welfare state or dismantle it but rather incorporate it—or, more precisely, they become incorporated into it—in a variety of complex articulations in which they come to mediate its already existing provisions. Compared to other European countries, Germany's welfare system has a famously long and innovative history that dates back to the Bismarck era. The laws and regulations that govern the distribution of welfare today, however, owe a great deal to the massive expansion of the welfare state during the late '60s and early '70s. In that period, the ordoliberalism of Christian Democrat chancellor Konrad Adenauer and his economics minister Ludwig Erhard gave way to the neo-Keynesianism of the first postwar period of Social Democrat rule under the leadership of Willy Brandt and later Helmut Schmidt (Schnitzer 1972; Nachtwey 2013). At present, then, the German social state and its mechanisms of governance are importantly shaped by structures put into place during the heyday—and, as it turned out, the twilight—of Fordist, Keynesian capitalism.

Second, one must be wary of taking the catchphrases of contemporary neoliberal governance at their word and confounding them for the actual realities they purport to describe. As with "really existing neoliberal networks" (Leitner and Sheppard 2002) and contrary to their claims, what emerges from under these keywords in the case of campaigns against right-wing extremism in Germany seems often to consist, instead, in uneven topographies of resources and competencies, hierarchical relations between ostensibly equal partners, top-down rather than bottom-up instigation, and continued centralized regulation. Thus, not only hierarchies but also various relations of adversarial competition and antagonistic stakes or, alternatively, of alliances and collusion mediate the information that traverses such meandering conduits. Moreover, these new mechanisms and strategies of power both depend upon and generate novel neoliberal subjectivities—such as, paradigmatically, those of the street social workers—that are burdened with and shaped by a great deal of vulnerability. Working under ever more precarious conditions of employment, these neoliberal agents of the state at the same time come to occupy new mediating positions that entail structurally constitutive tensions and contradictions. It is precisely in this manner that we must understand the angst-ridden impasses that routinely confront the social workers as they perform their mediating function in the surveillance interface through which the state traces right-wing extremists.

Furthermore, the type of knowledge demanded and offered in transactions among nodes in this machine spans a wide spectrum of resolutions, objects, and scales. Sometimes, it is anonymous and relatively general accounts that structure exchanges, as, for example, in the SPD-sponsored meeting in Grünau where Helmuth related, in broad and impersonal terms, Khan's metamorphosis into a favored meeting place for young right-wing extremists, and where a site, rather than particular individuals, emerged as the object of the interaction. On countless other occasions throughout my fieldwork, and in a wide variety of forums, similarly general accounts of burning hotspots or worrying trends were either solicited from or volunteered by the social workers: the condensation of street cliques in parks or train stations, meeting points and consumption establishments popular among their clients, or the general state of various organized groups. In other cases, it was precisely detailed personal information that was at stake. That the social workers, as well versed as anyone in the intricate workings of this governmental machine, were at times themselves astonished by the power that it wielded—its incoherent and discordant articulation notwithstanding—to efficiently produce precise results suggests perhaps just how opaque its operations appear even to its closest intimates.

This remarkable faculty became amply clear, for example, during their struggle to defuse a paranoiac plot that threatened to explode with possibly perilous upshots. At a routine meeting with their superior from the district's municipal administration, they appealed for her assistance in establishing the identity of a certain enigmatic young man they knew only as "Thomas." Thomas's clean-cut and indistinct external appearance betrayed nothing of his ardent ultra-nationalism or the starkly neo-Nazi composition of his social milieu, much less of what the social workers described as his psychopathic delirium. Not the character to risk the dangers of physical violence, his manner of menacing his environment was instead comprised of insidiously cunning manipulations. According to him, as a precocious juvenile delinquent he had spent his early youth at rehabilitation shelters and foster homes before recently returning to live with his parents. Less dubious was that, at the tender age of seventeen, he had already fathered four children, all with different teenage mothers, and a fifth was on its way. For some time now he had been dating Lisa, a short, baby-faced seventeen-year-old who lived with her heavily alcoholic mother, grandmother, and young uncle in Baumschulenweg, on the district's west. Lisa aligned her external appearance—usually dark corduroys or jeans and a black jacket over a shirt featuring the insignia of musical groups or the logos of fashion brands—with her right-wing extremist leanings more patently than Thomas. Before the unremitting police harassment at Grünau had finally discouraged her from frequenting the vicinity of the train station, she had numbered among the regulars at the Bretterbude, where she had consolidated lasting relations with Elsa, Norman, Freddi, and others. For some time, too, Gino was her boyfriend.

As if out of the blue, text messages containing death threats began to show up on Lisa's cell phone, appearing to originate from an unused SIM card she herself owned but could no longer locate. Thomas at first insinuated the collusion of Gino and another of Lisa's ex-boyfriends in a murderous plot against her, then claimed to possess evidence corroborating his allegations (which, however, he never delivered), and later appended the names of a number of Lisa's close friends to his list of would-be coconspirators. What followed were several months of implausible tales, unimaginably intricate intrigues of cellular phones and Internet communications, ominous ultimatums, and mysterious intimidations—with the convoluted unfolding of which I will not bother the reader—that time and again reinforced the social workers' initial skepticism and pointed ever more plainly at Thomas himself as the key culprit in the affair. They eventually confronted him and compelled him to come clean—even while he continued to lay the blame squarely on Lisa—about his calumnious fabrications and deceptive manipulations, a confession that curiously appeared to disrupt his relationship with Lisa only briefly. Meanwhile, however, he had succeeded in severing all of Lisa's independent relations with the outside world. Ostensibly out of concern for her safety, he mediated all communications with her, forbade her from leaving her apartment without his escort, and redesigned her appearance to fit his taste, including an obtrusive Renee hairdo that was more than likely to entice the unfriendly attention of Antifa activists.[3] Equally disconcerting for the social workers were Thomas's stories about his links with the Russian and Turkish mafias and with armed neo-Nazi militants whom he allegedly contracted to handle Gino, not so much because they necessarily accepted such self-aggrandizing claims at face value, but rather because when placed in conjunction with reports from

[3] The "Renee" hairdo is the style conventionally used by skingirls, the equivalent of the shaved head among male skinheads. The Renee's hair is finely clipped, except for fringes at front. Unlike shaved heads among men, which in Germany carry only a weak association with skinhead subcultures, the Renee haircut appears to unambiguously spell a woman's skingirl identification.

other contacts they had amid Lisa's social circles, who recounted that Thomas had asked them to place him in contact with their violent friends, such stories intimated that the saga he had spun could readily spiral out of control. Worse still, wind of his machinations had reached Gino, who, for his part, could also contribute to the unfolding melodrama.

A key hurdle that hampered the social workers from effectively neutralizing Thomas and the scheme he had concocted consisted in his seemingly indeterminable identity. Neither they nor any of his acquaintances appeared to know more about him than his first name; in fact, they could not be certain that Thomas was, indeed, his first name. When asked for personal information, he would unhesitatingly think up and provide a last name, an address, and so on, but these promptly revealed themselves as utter fabrications. Meanwhile, according to Lisa, Thomas claimed he had been recently diagnosed as infertile following an injury, this rendering their use of contraceptives superfluous. The social workers felt compelled to avert her looming conception with what would have been his sixth offspring. From another direction, Lizzie, a twenty-one-year-old who was at that time pregnant with Thomas's fifth child, needed his personal information to secure her child support remittances. All these circumstances further intensified the social workers' sense of urgency.

At the height of these evolving crises, the social workers got together with their direct superior from the municipal youth office for a routine meeting. Such events always placed a certain pressure on them to perform well in front of their employer, partly through the transmission of important—and exclusive—information. The supervisor visiting their office would leave it not only with specific details about particular individuals and groups caught up in their stories but also, and perhaps more significantly, with broader insights into the changing patterns of politically delinquent social milieus in the district, their structures, activities, and meeting points, or with an up-to-the-minute grasp of the problems in specific locations and sites. This time, it was they who pleaded for her assistance with Thomas. They spared her the knotty minutiae and intimate details of the affair and simply pointed out the importance of obtaining precise, identifying information on the young man who was posing such a menace to his social surroundings. Of course, they had little to offer in the way of leads. Indeed, all that they could provide was what they believed to be his first name together with a sketchy physical description. The supervisor promised she would do her best to help them locate Thomas. But, as she thanked them for the briefing and left their office, the social workers hardly seemed reassured. And yet only a couple of days passed before the youth office official called to inform them of Thomas's identity. Although in general knowledge meanders its way upward in such routine meetings and phone conversations between them and their superiors, this same circuitous web of information, once inverted, pinpointed and flung back at the social workers Thomas's precise and verified personal information with an alacrity that left them speechless.

And if, integral as their position was within this web, it could nevertheless so drastically confound them, to the young people they served, its operations appeared all but absolutely illegible.

THE ETHICS AND PRAXIS OF STREET SOCIAL WORK

Buttressing this constant flow of information is an ethical framework of social work that governs and constrains but also renders possible and meaningful distinct transactions in knowledge. This framework addresses first and foremost the relation between the social workers and individual recipients of their services—those to whom they refer as their "clients." Its general outlines were laid out for me already at the very inception of my research with the social workers. As we convened to mull over the possible complications of the embedded ethnography that I proposed to undertake with their team, Helmuth launched our conversation with an emphatic affirmation of the principles and values that guided their professional praxis. In particular, he placed emphasis on honesty, confidentiality, partiality, and respect toward individuals as autonomous agents fully capable of identifying and expressing their needs and desires. These were, he explained, the central pillars of the relationships they sought to nurture with their clients. In this sense, what Helmuth presented to me could describe the general outlines of the professional ethics of social work at large. And yet, for all the reasons already discussed in previous chapters, the social workers' relation with their right-wing extremist clients could not possibly answer to conventional, professional standards alone. No doubt, this relation contrasted sharply with the sorts of relations that other actors in the governmental machinery that revolved around political delinquency sustained with their target populations. To that extent, its distinctness was arguably advantageous, complementing what other, less proximate and perhaps more repressive approaches offered. But, more important, precisely because of the specific nature of their clients and the sort of menace for which they stood in the national imaginary, the social workers' intimacy with the youths they served appeared, for many, as nothing less than downright scandalous.

The social workers thus constantly had to navigate a thin line: while demonstrating their trustworthiness and goodwill to their clients, they at once had to corroborate their antinationalist credentials to various other actors and to reassure their employer—the municipal district—that public funds were not used to sponsor the activities of right-wing extremist groups. Such dilemmas were evident in the case of vertical, hierarchical interactions with superiors, such as the one I discussed above, in which the social workers were acutely aware of the vital importance of securing the prolongation of precarious, annual contracts between the municipality and their organization. But they were present as well in other types of relationships, such as competition for prestige and resources or strategic alliances with colleagues. Keeping influential decision makers happy or assuaging the anxieties of potential allies about their intimacy with the illicit did not always stand in harmony with providing the best assistance to their clients. Their professional ethics offered them a certain transcendent architecture of imperatives that their superiors, just as much as other actors with whom they came into contact, seemed by and large to respect.

Of course, such transcendent ethics could not possibly correspond straightforwardly and unequivocally to the daily completion of duties. Thus, for example, moments after he outlined its principles to me, and in uncomfortable tension with—if not clear breach of—them, Helmuth announced that my name in Treptow-Köpenick would henceforth be Nate and my country of origin the United States. Yet it would be mistaken to view this ethical framework and its principles as mere rhetorical devices or as an ideological mantel that obfuscated some real truth, to which it remained, as it were, external. Instead, the tenets of his professional ethics provided Helmuth with crucial, strategic blueprints to the authority of which appeals could be addressed, according to which behavior could be calibrated, and in terms of which action could be rendered legible. In this sense, while they hardly correspond to it in any simple manner, these ethical principles enabled the always situated and inescapably flexible praxis of social work. Put differently, they outlined generic conventions for the contextualized performance of skilled professionalism (cf. Carr 2009), an enactment that addressed several distinct audiences, myself included.

The social workers understood all too well the calamity that the exposure of my false identity would have spelled for them. The type of threat that such an eventuality presented for their work was not very different from the possible repercussions of Helmuth's inopportune exchange with the tall man across from Khan's. Both exposed a certain structural contradiction that rendered theirs a particularly difficult institutional position to inhabit. On the one hand, the fate of their precarious jobs depended upon their demonstrated ability to fulfill their mission and meet the expectations of their superiors, which included the transmission of precious knowledge about right-wing extremism in their municipality. But on the other hand, securing this knowledge required the cultivation of close relationships that, beyond setting the social workers as easy targets for criticism, also came under threat from the exchanges between the social workers and other governmental actors. I would be very surprised to learn that Helmuth divulged any private details about the young people that gathered at Khan's to the concerned residents and SPD functionaries who took part in the meeting to which he was invited. Yet, while he obviously overestimated the attentiveness of his clients, he was probably correct to assume that, had they discovered his complicity, they would have likely considered it an abuse of trust, confidentiality, and partiality, a dishonest collusion with their adversaries, and an unscrupulous misuse of information he had ultimately obtained through them. But Helmuth and the rest of his team were well aware that the security of their positions depended on the great enthusiasm across the board about their work; in other words, with their value as a highly specialized component of the surveillance machine that converged upon my informants-as-right-wing-extremists. In this acute and ultimately irresolvable conundrum, their tenuous mediating position in a machinery of governance reflected the constitutive antagonism of the state toward their clients-as-right-wing-extremists. And it was within this turbulent terrain that they were forced to navigate their way and relentlessly fend off impending catastrophes.

In practice, then, calibrating their day-to-day performance of responsibilities with their professional ethics demanded of the social workers constant negotiation, positioning, and interpretation in situated contexts. This incessant labor remained by and large implicit, an indefatigable humdrum of taken-for-granted, unarticulated vacillations, decisions, and compromises, with which they delineated through praxis what bits of information should be communicated and which were better kept unsaid, and to whom and in what settings, without either provoking or requiring overt reflection. Only once during my fieldwork did the question of confidentiality emerge into daylight from its implicit obscurity: in the textbook case of Lizzie's baby, Thomas's latest offspring. Twenty-one-year-old Lizzie absconded from her parents' home in a Brandenburgian village as a young teenager and made the Bretterbude her abode. With no school diploma or any interest in vocational training or employment, she had sketched a swastika on her backpack and carried various nationalist-themed pins on her clothes. She had already dated a number of neo-Nazi skinheads since her short fling with Thomas. Despite her denials, there were good reasons to suspect that she had continued with her alcohol and drug abuse throughout her pregnancy. Notwithstanding the advice of the social workers, she thought of childbirth as the promise of material wealth through child-support augmentations to her welfare income. She fantasized—also against the better judgment of the social workers—of motherhood as a talisman against harsh penal sentences that loomed near on several separate charges of violence and political delinquency. There was something deeply unnerving about the mechanical manner in which she held her newborn, as if it were an inanimate object. But more alarmingly, within a few months the unresponsive and physically underdeveloped infant showed clear signs of malnutrition and neglect. Lizzie refused to consult the doctor despite the baby's persistent vomiting. A heated debate ensued among the social workers, torn between their commitment to confidentiality and their concern for the baby's life. Reluctantly, they resolved to anonymously inform the youth office about the situation. They were surprised to discover that the authorities had already been alerted to the problem by some other unknown node within the information machine and were monitoring the case.

The case of Lizzie's baby presented the social workers with a familiar dilemma of their profession: what to do when confronted with fatal risks and at what point to make exceptions to otherwise sacrosanct principles. Lizzie's illicit political leanings and her extroverted manner of asserting them played no significant role in their deliberation, which centered on her dangerously neglectful mothering. The social workers' professional ethics thus already included this exception as part of its framework and provided the instruments for its adjudication. It was precisely for this reason that it emerged as the topic of explicit discussion. And it was also for this reason that its resolution seemed as self-evident to them as the silence around their clients' delinquent activities, about which they regularly harvested a wealth of detailed information. That much was clear. And while, to be sure, even the textbook case of Lizzie's baby entailed some degree of ambiguity (just how bad a mother was she? Just how badly was the baby doing?), it was the sort of ambiguity for the resolution of which their profession provided them with the adequate tools. That this was decidedly less the case when knowledge about extreme right things was at stake had everything to do with the kinds of value that the social workers produced in their labor and with how they produced it. For none of them doubted that the circulation of such precious, exclusive information constituted an essential dimension, if not the centerpiece, of their professional performance within a machine of governance. It formed a critical strategic modality of negotiating and shaping relations that endowed them with a unique, irreplaceable value for the assemblage of forces that hovered over their clients. At the same time, those through whom they obtained such knowledge would have surely viewed its dissemination unfavorably, even if, as was almost always the case, it named no names.

How the menace of illicit nationalism enabled the commerce in occult information and thereby animated the production of such value became patently evident one late October afternoon, on which I arrived at the social workers' modest headquarters to find Daniela at the office typing at the computer and Helmuth seated at the lounge across from Karla and Jens. Application letters for practical training positions and jobs were scattered on the coffee table. Twenty-two-year-old Jens and seventeen-year-old Karla numbered among the small core of committed militants in the local extreme right scene. Their home turf included Johannisthal and Schöneweide, where a park and several pubs served their circles as sites for congregation. Becker, the local cadre, led their troop. He recruited them from various hangout spots around the district, including also Grünau, and at first brought them under the auspices of the NPD. Later they followed him out of the party and formed an independent Kameradschaft by the name BASO (Berliner Alternative Süd-Ost, or Berlin Alternative South-East), which had terrorized the district with diverse political mobilizations and would eventually be banned as an anticonstitutional organization by the Berlin government. By the time I left Berlin, Jens would be in custody and awaiting a long prison sentence for his central role in a series of brutal assaults against alleged child molesters. The extent of their involvement in organized political activities had clearly exceeded the social workers' self-imposed redline. The latter had accordingly discontinued any group undertakings with them and their comrades but still counseled them now and then individually.

Daniela and I chatted at the office while Helmuth concluded his business with Karla and Jens. No sooner were they gone than he rushed in, emulating a convulsion of vomiting. He hurried to the telephone. On the other side of the line was the office of an NGO commissioned by the municipality to consult and coordinate local efforts to counter right-wing extremism in the district. I will elaborate in greater detail about this NGO and its activities in chapter 8. For the time being, let me note that it was no secret that relations between its members and the social workers had been cold, if no longer as openly hostile as they once used to be. No doubt, their antagonism had much to do with their precarious dependency upon the same budgetary basket of constantly dwindling municipal resources. With progressive cuts to social spending, the fact that both organizations fit into the same niche of youth-centered policies against right-wing extremism already set them up as competitors. But their rivalry also pitted against each other contrasting diagnoses of, prognoses for, and remedies against the extreme right. The social workers were enraged by the NGO's zero-tolerance approach and what they perceived as its corollary exclusion and abandonment of young people whom they considered impressionable and hence precisely in dire need of intervention. They found unacceptable what they viewed as a dangerously simplistic reduction of acute and complex social problems to—and their displacement by—purely political formulations. And they resented as well what they felt to be an insufferable know-it-all arrogance on the part of the West German academics who directed the NGO. The latter, for their part, steered clear of any proximity to people or groups who could be suspected of rightist leanings altogether. Instead, they strictly focused on reinforcing civil society structures that would thwart the nationalist menace. Like a number of other local actors in the field, they therefore took exception to what they regarded as the social workers' sponsorship of and hence, according to them, collaboration with right-wing extremist groups and individuals. Enforcing a truce and insisting on collegial relationships, their municipal superiors smoothed out the open conflict that had initially raged between them, yet a manifest air of mutual suspicion remained in place.

That afternoon, however, not a moment had passed after Karla and Jens left his office before Helmuth called in to report the news he had just received: mobilizations for a right-wing extremist demonstration in the district were already under way. This nigh-instantaneous conduction of information from Karla and Jens via Helmuth to the NGO exposed three quite divergent takes on the transfer of such exclusive knowledge. The workers at the NGO held that, in order for them to best fulfill their duties, and in order for the district to stage the most robust resistance against racist nationalism, any piece of news about right-wing extremist activities in the area must come their way. On the other hand, there is little doubt that Karla and Jens would have hardly been pleased to learn that the details they mentioned during their session with Helmuth about ongoing mobilizations for a demonstration traveled to the NGO—a bitter enemy of their grouping—immediately upon their departure. But for the social workers, neither full disclosure nor absolute secrecy appeared strictly binding. There was nothing taken for granted in their rush to share the news they had just received. Yet, from their perspective, neither did doing so disrupt principles of confidentiality or partiality. Instead, the phone call constituted a performance that addressed not only their competitors, but also—and perhaps even primarily—their superiors. It demonstrated at once their compliance with the injunction from above to collegial collaboration and their singularly invaluable role as surveillance probes commanding unique access to occult and precious knowledge.

Lest my discussion here be misread as suggesting bad faith on the part of the social workers, it must be emphatically stated that, quite the contrary, their commitment to the ethical principles of their vocation was both sincere and unyielding, and the lengths to which they went to guard against their infringement were great. Far from casting doubt upon the sense of integrity with which they carried out their work, what I have sought to illuminate are the sorts of necessarily flexible mediations and the situated classifications of information that go hand in hand with this professional ethics. The mining and dissemination of knowledge, from this perspective, are no anathema to the standards of confidentiality and sincerity but rather articulate with them in a range of tentative, interactional deployments.

GOVERNANCE UP CLOSE

Looking at the social workers' production of knowledge about their politically delinquent clientele, then, we see how principles of confidentiality and partiality come together with the demands that an entire assemblage of surveillance and governance places upon them. The result is not a relation of contradiction or incommensurability but rather a productive tension that takes form in a variety of situated engagements and reciprocal dependencies. This constant commerce in information and performance of expertise borrows heavily on a market vocabulary of results-oriented efficiency, quality management, and quantified productivity. Such is the discourse that one finds, for example, in reports the social workers prepare for their superiors on their achievements. But, as I suggested above, it fuses this idiom with the language of ethopolitical governance (Rose 2000a), where emphasis is placed on local expertise, democratic activation, community empowerment, individual responsibilization, and conditional service provision. Such ethopolitical activation was plainly evident, no doubt, in the lengths to which the social workers went to facilitate the compliance of their clients with the requirements of various conditional benefits and in their own participation in diverse horizontal community networks. But it was nowhere more blatant than in the conditional provisioning of their own services upon their clients' political normalization.

To be sure, such idioms of governance shaped norms for the management of information. And yet, most notable for the ethnographer of the neoliberal state was the way in which, far from operating at a distance (as some have suggested the modus operandi that accompanies such neoliberal vocabulary would imply), the flesh-and-blood, concrete figures with which this form of governance at once sensually presented itself to and prodded its objects signaled instead toward emergent modalities of organized mimesis, of intimacy, and of proximity between the state and its proclaimed enemies, forms far less violent and conspicuous, far more subtle and mundane, than those we encountered in chapter 5. Discussing the rise of Third Way politics, Nikolas Rose has suggested that new mutations of government have proceeded along four principle dimensions: its objects, its subjects, its explanatory regimes, and its technologies (2000a). I have already described how municipal governance in Berlin has been shifting its gaze—and its budgetary structure—from the traditional focus on the relation between the individual and the centralized bureaucratic state to a "social space"–oriented strategy that targets the binding of individuals to presumed spatial communities. As a consequence, the social workers were increasingly called upon to prioritize spaces over people as their targets. They were expected to limit the scope of their efforts to relatively small territorial units to which administrative responsibilities were gradually being transferred rather than concentrating their work on assisting individuals throughout the district. This shift in the objects of governance echoed transformations in governance that have been documented elsewhere (Brenner and Theodore 2002). We have also seen how a set of conceptual apparatuses and vocabularies support new explanatory frameworks within which the objects, strategies, and ends of governance gain novel meanings. The stress on community empowerment that accompanies the social-space-orientation reforms goes together with talk of the consolidation of local networks, citizen activation, and democratic participation. As far as the subjects of government and its technologies are concerned, however, the street social workers seemed to collapse any neat distinction between these two dimensions, which Rose considers as separate domains. The social workers, in their function within the apparatus that watched over their clients, stood for both.

This was so not only because they put the administrative and political imperatives of the day into actual practice, facilitating their reach into the nooks and crannies of the social terrain, but also because they embodied the sorts of agents that governance increasingly recruits to fulfill its changing functions. In particular, they illustrated a peculiar form of organized mimesis that the state deploys for persecuting what it construes as its radical internal enemies, and this by means of a twofold proximity. At a first level, they established and mediated an intimacy between the state and its margins inasmuch as they acted upon the quotidian lifeworlds and biographical minutiae of their right-wing extremist clients through remarkably personal relations. In this sense, their work—but not only theirs—suggests a vital proviso on the much-proclaimed advent of "governance at a distance." True enough, new "technologies of freedom" have sought "to govern 'at a distance' through, not in spite of, the autonomous choices of relatively independent entities":

> Hence, as far as organizations are concerned, privatization, marketization, [and] consumerization have been accompanied by the increased use of techniques of accountability such as centrally set but locally managed budgets, and the practices of evaluation and auditing. As far as individuals are concerned, one sees a revitalization of the demand that each person should be obliged to be prudent, responsible for their own destinies, actively calculating about their futures and providing for their own security and that of their families with the assistance of a plurality of independent experts and profit-making businesses. (Rose 2000b, 324)

But at the same time, the neoliberal state appears to have remained as invested as ever in maintaining a firm and hands-on grip on its population, and especially so at the bottom end of growing social polarization (Wacquant 2001; Harcourt 2010; Wacquant 2012). It is arguably also these sectors of the population that, because of their social marginalization and economic precariousness, lend themselves less well to new consumption-based technologies of control. Significantly, it is also largely within these emergent classes that, not only in today's Germany but equally in a range of other European countries (Kalb and Halmai 2011), the specter of an illicit, racist nationalism comes to life.

At a second level, however, we encounter a different sense of proximity that is crucial for the first but not identical with it. It comprises a careful calibration between the sorts of subjects who become recruited as agents of neoliberal governance and those construed as its targets (or, as the case may be, its enemies). For the propinquity that the social workers established with their clients could not be ascribed merely to the trust they cultivated with them, which was a necessary but insufficient condition for ingratiating themselves so robustly into these groups. It also rested, crucially, upon their flawless vernacular fluency and their thorough immersion in colloquial idioms, landscapes, histories, events, and contexts. All three of them, as I described in chapter 1, are East Germans—a category that, as several scholars of post-reunification Germany have noted, has maintained a salient presence in personal identifications, especially in the former East (Bach 2005; Boyer 2006b). In chapter 2, I discussed in particular its resilience and its centrality for young right-wing extremists in East Berlin (see also Shoshan 2008a). But beyond their Ossi identity in general, they were perceived as autochthonous in several more specific ways. Both Andrea and Helmuth are natives of Berlin, while Daniela comes from a small, nearby town. Their native competence in the performance of identities and the interpretation of contexts allowed them to draw upon a wealth of highly localized cultural references so as to navigate the coordinates of their clients' lifeworlds relatively smoothly. They were masters in reading the semiotic subtleties of their dominion, capable of generating sentiments of solidarity and equivalence with various interlocutors and of elaborating refined understandings of the social landscape and of the distinctions that traverse it. They readily conjured a shared past with terms that indexed authentic belonging. For example, they would exchange memories with the older regulars in Grünau of the filthy public men's urinal that once occupied the small house where Khan later opened his restaurant, and in so doing they would at once validate for their younger audience their firm grasp of local lore; they would recall the street clocks that once stood in different public sites and have since vanished; or, finally, they would pepper their discourse with colloquial expressions, jokes, and cultural references. Their sympathy for the local soccer club Union likewise constituted, in this sense, the proper pick, both socially and politically: a loser team, the eternal underdog, the underclass icon of and metaphor for the East, a center of working-class antigovernment sentiment under both the GDR and the FRG. Their view of it contrasted emphatically with its typical, and dominant, western depictions as a neo-Nazi stronghold. It aligned itself, instead, with the commonplace East Berlin perception that reserves this honor for a competing soccer club, BFC Dynamo, which I mentioned in chapter 3. In all of this, they incarnated those novel forms of proximity that neoliberal governance generates through flexibly deployable, privately farmed-out, localized expertise. Viewed differently, in recruiting its agents, the neoliberal state seeks to approximate and mimic the terrain upon which it intervenes.

But perhaps the most important aspect of the social workers' seamless maneuvering of localized identifications had to do with their skillful versatility in vernacular linguistic registers. Virtually all of the young people they served only commanded the Berlinerisch dialect. Historically associated with the industrial working classes of Berlin, nowadays Berlinerisch is spoken throughout the surrounding Brandenburg region. Its unique flavor consists in a number of phonological substitutions, for example, of the sound "s" by the sound "t" at the end of a word (as in *wat* instead of *was*), of the soft "ç" by the hard "k" (*ick* instead of *ich*), of the diphthong "au" by a long "u" (*oof* instead of *auf*), of "g" by "j" at the start of a word (*janz* instead of *ganz*), or of the diphthong "ai" by a long "e" (*alleene* instead of *alleine*), as well as of a number of idiomatic lexical items (for example, *Sonnabend* instead of *Samstag* for "Saturday") specifically associated with East German speakers. The dialect has long been burdened by derogatory stereotypifications of low education and cultural capital.

As dialects are wont to do, Berlinerisch also stands in a hierarchical binary relation with the national standard, Hochdeutsch, and at the same time within a set of lateral—if by no means symmetrical—contrasts with other national dialects. According to common wisdom, Berlinerisch, while nigh extinct in the city's West during the postwar years due to occupation and massive population flows, strongly persevered in the East. While I have heard Berlinerisch spoken by natives of West Berlin, for my subjects, the phonological and lexical markers of their dialect appeared to serve as clear shibboleths for unambiguously deducing easternness or westernness. Indeed, while few among them claimed they could distinguish between Ossis and Wessis based on visual cues alone, most maintained they could effectively tell them apart as soon as they opened their mouths. In post-reunification Berlin, then, the hierarchical dichotomy of national elites fluent in the (superior) national standard and social peripheries limited to (inferior) local dialects (Bourdieu 2001) has become locally transposed onto the hierarchical dichotomy of East and West.[4] The Ossi emerges here, as has already been documented in a variety of other cultural dimensions (see discussion in chapter 2), as a subordinate alterity, now within the national space of linguistic variation.

The Berlinerisch dialect, stereotypified as eastern and vulgar, formed the social workers' native idiom. It was, no doubt, notwithstanding their relatively fine competence in the national standard, the linguistic register of German that they best mastered and within which they felt most at home in language. This vernacular fluency in what has become, at least in Berlin, an Ossi dialect, proved invaluable in supplying them with a colloquial voice that crucially facilitated their access to the people they serviced. But the relation between Berlinerisch and Hochdeutsch—and arguably between dialects and standard languages more generally—that emerged in their interactional linguistic practice extended far beyond the simple logic of a binary opposition. The two registers instead outlined a linguistic space that, for those who, like the social workers, possessed the requisite proficiencies, became an arena for a whole range of deployments, articulations, and tactical positionings. Such linguistic maneuverings consisted not only in register switching between the vernacular and the standard but also in far more refined and elaborate performances that interweaved, accentuated, or tempered Berlinerisch and Hochdeutsch to generate a variety of gradations and permutations.

Let me illustrate this refined linguistic choreography by considering a meeting that took place one early afternoon in May between the social workers and four members of the Berlin Parliament, who arrived at their office to seek enlightenment about the state of right-wing extremism in their city from the horse's mouth. Representatives of the economically right-wing liberal Free Democratic Party (FDP), their elegant business suits and sleek, meticulous hairstyles seemed glaringly out of place in this quarter of the city and drew a sharp contrast with the informal attire of the social workers. Helmuth introduced his team and their work, presented the conceptual apparatus they employed

---

[4] It is important to emphasize that my argument here is not that the Berlinerisch dialect *in fact* distinguishes between easterners and westerners, since, as I mention above, the dialect is common enough in West Berlin, especially among lower socioeconomic sectors. The point, instead, is that my informants *perceived* and *interpreted* competence in and performance of the dialect as clearly indexing an eastern background.

to approach right-wing extremism, paused on their particular strategies for curbing its appeal to young people, provided rough quantitative estimates of its dimensions, delineated the areas in which they worked and the groups with which they maintained contact, and described the architectural, social, and political landscapes of particular neighborhoods in the district. The representatives asked him to elaborate on certain specific points, to explain particular issues involved in social work with right-wing extremists, to identify deficits that they could help tackle, and to recommend policies they should endorse and promote. There was not a trace of vernacular dialect in their voices. As for Helmuth, he deployed flawless Hochdeutsch when seeking to establish authoritativeness and objectivity, when explicating conceptual niceties and theoretical frameworks, or when formulating elaborate arguments and defending his viewpoints. But when discussing concrete episodes, individual characters, or other highly localized topics, he would skillfully weave into his speech a colloquial phrase or enunciate a few scattered words with an exaggeratedly pronounced Berlinerisch accent that far overshot the ordinary phonological structure of the dialect.

As Helmuth addressed the representatives, he navigated a wide and pliable space of phonological contrast between the soft fricatives of the *ich* and *es* of Hochdeutsch and the unnaturally emphasized hardness with which he would selectively pronounce the plosives of the equivalent *icke* and *et* of Berlinerisch. On other occasions, I have witnessed him deploy the overly accentuated *icke* as a diminutive shifter—a first-person pronoun form that indicates the speakers' inferior position with respect to the interlocutor—with which he prefaced severe criticisms of experts and superiors, as in "Icke denke, daß . . ." (I think that . . .). In stark contrast, after the unfortunate encounter in Grünau that I described earlier in this chapter, the social workers concurred that a phone call clarifying their delicate position to the tall SPD man and protesting what they viewed as his irresponsible conduct was in order, and Helmuth performed this task in a superbly polished Hochdeutsch the likes of which I had never witnessed— not naturally spoken, at least—either before or after, employing a plethora of convoluted, conditional, and passive constructions to express at once respectfully and unambiguously his censure of a superior. During the meeting with the FDP representatives, and on many other occasions, he seemed to make tactical, interactional variations in his speech to index a range of relations between him and his interlocutors or between him and the topics of his discourse. In carefully embellishing his by and large Hochdeutsch discourse with unusually highlighted vernacular flavors, he dexterously corroborated an authentic and intimate expertise in and proximity to illicit, local knowledge, all while establishing his professional authority, conceptual erudition, and cultivated personality.

The social workers' proficiency in both Hochdeutsch and Berlinerisch thus allowed them to signal intimacy with young underclass milieus that only master the dialect and perceive the standard as alien, elitist, and "western"; to index a shared identity with adults who may possess some proficiency in the standard register but for whom, too, the local dialect appears "warmer" and easier; or to perform expertise in official meetings with state agents, conversations with local politicians, and interviews in mass publicity. Their linguistic maneuvering contributed crucially to their capacity to appear autochthonous within the landscape in which they operated, to authenticate their value in the eyes of their supervisors, and to construct propinquity with those whom they served— those very haunting figures that the state commissioned them to manage. It therefore helped them navigate the contradictory position in which they found themselves, at once fabricating themselves as intimate natives, as belonging to a collective "us," in the eyes of the young right-wing extremists they targeted, and, as importantly, authenticating their expertise to those very structures through which they became recruited as agents of governance in the first place. It was, put differently, crucial for how the social workers produced value in their work—the value of the highly prized information that they obtained just as much as the value of professional expertise that they performed.

Significantly, these two modes of performing a localized propinquity were not symmetrical. The first, which addressed the social workers' so-called clients, accentuated a monoglot vernacular intimacy and hinged upon the obfuscation of their embeddedness in an entire machinery of governance in which the high standard dominates. The second, with which they addressed, so to speak, this very machinery, interlaced a heteroglossic voice that proclaimed both their belonging to the structures of governance and their privileged access to occult, colloquial realities. In other words, their linguistic performance sustained the constant production of distance between themselves and the "state" on the one hand, and between themselves and their clients on the other. It complemented, then, a whole range of other forms with which they produced and maintained such distinctions. Thus, for example, the social workers dutifully attended the carnivalesque jamborees of colorful protests that inevitably confronted any right-wing extremist rally in the district. And yet, they steered clear of the otherwise all-but-mandatory brandishing of banners and howling of chants. In doing so, they carefully distinguished themselves not only from the marching nationalists but equally from the agitated multitudes of loud protesters against them. Or, to cite another example, they abided by a strict interdiction on physical proximity with the agents of law enforcement. When approaching the locations in which they routinely worked, for example, the mere sight of a police van or of police officers sufficed to keep them away. But on other occasions, more intricate schemes had to be devised to hold them apart. When a neighborhood task force against right-wing extremism was conjured into being at the Ghetto, the social workers found themselves hard-pressed to explain to its members why they could not attend its meetings so long as the latter insisted on inviting, too, representatives of the OGJ police unit (see chapter 5). A compromise arrangement had to be worked out, according to which they and the police would attend alternate meetings.

My point here, of course, is not that the social workers and the police were somehow the same and artificially kept apart by a shroud of misleading dissimilarities. Far from it: the institutional distinctions between them—as well as other agents of governance active in the district—were real enough and remarkably far-reaching. That they could hardly be confused, however, only raises more forcefully the question of why it appeared absolutely vital for the social workers to carve an unequivocal division between them. Their stakes in this ongoing labor of differentiation, then, was not the obfuscation of some presumed equivalence between themselves and the police but rather the maintenance of a certain illegibility about their interrelations, about the murky paths across which knowledge traveled between them, and about the same foundation of their authority. It hid from view not the identity of social workers and cops but rather the fact that information exchanged on alternate meetings of the task force on right-wing extremism at the Ghetto would no doubt circulate across this temporal division. And it was precisely this illegibility that threatened to collapse irredeemably on that June evening at Khan's that I considered above, thereby betraying that the synchronicity of young right-wing extremists, street social workers, SPD members, and a police squadron was far from purely fortuitous. It would have disrupted the vernacular bond that the social workers labored so hard to consolidate with the young people of Grünau, and from which the SPD activists and police officers were excluded.

Thus, if the street social workers embodied some of the much-discussed mutations of governance under neoliberalism—for example, in their relatively precarious employment conditions, in their corporatist as well as their ethopolitical vocabulary, in the reconfigurations of the public and the private that their NGO represented, or in their focus on social space—they illustrated far more than those changes alone. For they pointed as well to a peculiar mimetic logic that the neoliberal German state brings to its project of affective governance and according to which it commissions certain agents to manage hate among those street milieus in which new poor and old ghosts converge. I have always found remarkable the extent to which the groups they served perceived the social workers as intrinsically other than the state, with which they understood themselves to stand on hostile terms and which they associated with various repressive and disciplinary institutions: police, courts of justice, schools, perplexing labyrinths of bureaucratic offices. The contrast between the sentiments of resentment and alienation that they expressed toward the latter, and the general approval with which they embraced the social workers ("they're okay," many would say), could not be sharper. Indeed, more than a few of the social workers' young clients expressed outright admiration for them as role models, and several have told me they would like to become street social workers themselves one day, an entirely implausible ambition given their educational backgrounds.

This ambivalence of the social workers—who oscillated daily between the local vernacular and the national standard, between confidentiality and surveillance, between their illicit right-wing extremist clients and their municipal superiors—was not, as we have seen, a burden they sought to free themselves from but rather a condition they labored to cultivate. It was a strategically necessary ambivalence, to be sure, inasmuch as it underwrote an entire apparatus of affective governance through which the state sought to manage forms of hatred and violence. This is why, above and beyond the work of patching fissures in the social fabric of communities that ordinarily befalls their profession, the social workers constituted such a key element in state surveillance. It is why politicians, administrators, journalists, and youth and social workers solicited their advice on a regular basis, viewing them as the most authoritative and up-to-date resource on social crises areas and extreme right activities alike. But their ambivalence was also, at the same time, an inevitable one, the progeny—or, better yet, the symptom—of a certain instability rooted in deep-seated cultural aporias and political anxieties. In this sense, it referenced the dread that the figures of young, unemployed, nationalist men trigger in Germany; the determined, if often hesitant, and always potentially explosive project of national reimagining in the post-reunification era; but, perhaps most of all, the fascination with the occult and the excitement of proximity to the forbidden. At the intersection of emergent deproletarianized social margins and indefatigable past ghosts, then, we witness how a whole affective field, saturated with meanings, stakes, and projects, animates an entire machine of neoliberal governance.

On the one hand, then, the state now increasingly deploys flexible, locally agile agents to pursue not only the biopolitical governance of its population but also the affective management of that population's unsavory underside. This is no doubt a form of organized mimesis that could not contrast more sharply with the mimetic violence of state-sponsored kidnappings, assassinations, and clandestine operations (Aretxaga 1999), or of special squads and brutal police raids, where it is precisely the emulation of those menacing aspects of the other that is at stake. Here, to the contrary, we witness no blood fantasies. Instead, we see the neoliberal state spawn appendages that replicate not hypermediated representations of violence but rather the implicit, lifeworld contours of those menacing, internal others it seeks to control, their banal routines and quotidian chitchat. On the other hand, the very mimetic desire to become the other, especially the forbidden other, always entails a sharp, excitable tension between pornographic fascination and profound anxiety: the haunting allure of the right-wing extremist other, the irresistible attraction of its occult, illicit mysteries, finds its inverse image in existential angst about contamination and proximity. In their enactment of this nonviolent organized mimesis, the social workers exposed, benefited from, but also bore the brunt of this irresolvable tension. While a plethora of publics supplicated for their rare knowledge to fulfill its voyeuristic cravings, some, too, have accused them of sponsoring and advocating for neo-Nazis instead of persecuting and marginalizing them. Such inexorable ambivalences, as I hope this chapter has amply demonstrated, betray the constitutive dilemmas that haunt the entire field of the management of hate in Germany and that render the social workers' task ridden with contradictions. These same dilemmas, however, also motivate and conjure this whole modality of governance in the first place. How efforts in this field remain utterly under the spell of these contamination anxieties, of these spectral menaces, is the theme to which I turn in chapter 7.

IIIIIIIIIIIIIIIIIIII 7 IIIIIIIIIIIIIIIIIII

Advances in the Sciences of Exorcism

THE ELABORATE LEGAL AND PENAL REGIMES of the governance of hate in Germany, its modes of policing and law enforcement, and its instruments of surveillance and knowledge production at the same time appear as the repressive face of an even broader set of discourses, institutions, and techniques that include, as well, efforts to reform and rehabilitate young right-wing extremists. In this chapter I analyze some of these therapeutic projects in order to reflect upon their sometimes desperate, sometimes bizarre struggles to exorcize the right-wing extremist malaise from bodies, minds, and souls. The excesses that so palpably present themselves in such efforts bear witness to the troubled place reserved for right-wing extremism in contemporary Germany, somewhere between the aporias of German nationhood on the one hand and the contradictions of late capitalism on the other. I begin on a cold January afternoon on which I arrived at the Friedrichstraße train station in the company of Gino, whom we have already encountered in the preceding chapters. We had come from Treptow for a secretive encounter with a representative of the nongovernmental organization EXIT, which aims to assist young right-wing extremists who wish to leave the "scene."

Gino, recall, was a slim twenty-year-old of medium height and trimmed dark hair known throughout Treptow as SS-Gino owing to the HASS (hate) tattoo that decorated the fingers of his right hand, its final two letters styled after the illegal symbol of the SS. On his arms, back, and chest he boasted various other illicit tattoos, including renderings of the Iron Cross, of a *leitwolf*,[1] and of a flag with the inscription "Deutsche Widerstand" (German Resistance). Silver hoop earrings and a thick gilded chain complemented the tattoos. Gino came of age in the Ghetto, the district's poorest neighborhood, with his alcoholic mother

---

[1] The *leitwolf*, or leader of the pack, is a favorite iconic image among many young right-wing extremists of a wolf usually against the background of a snow-clad landscape.

and a number of different male partners she had taken in over the years, most of whom he remembered as violent and abusive. He never completed high school and subsisted on various forms of state support.

Gino's involvement in organized political activities had been minimal and erratic. In contrast, by the time I had first met him, his extensive criminal record already presented an impressive assortment of offenses for his young age, including shoplifting, vandalism, damage to property, physical assault, agitation of the people (*Volksverhetzung*; see chapter 4), and possession of banned symbols and illegal weapons. Our visit to the train station took place shortly after he completed his latest period of incarceration, the last of seven separate sentences he had already served at detention centers, juvenile delinquent reformatories, and prisons, each lasting from a few days to a month. This was no mean feat, for Germany's youth law, under which he had so far been tried as a minor, prescribes relatively lenient punishments and only reluctantly incarcerates offenders.

When out of prison, he had spent the better part of the past few years completing various lesser penal impositions and struggling to comply with the court-mandated stipulations of legal probation periods. With a critical hearing some six months away, he strained—but then again, never too vigorously—to meet the terms set by the court for his current legal probation, the satisfaction of which would in turn serve as criteria for assessing his normative progress. With his parole officer and the street social workers at his side, his efforts benefited from constant and ample professional counseling and practical assistance. The terms set by the court included four primary impositions: divesting himself of his weapons, finding a job, moving into his own apartment, and entering alcohol rehab therapy. Parting from his collection of weapons proved easiest, as well as most profitable: he sold them to his friends. Shortly thereafter he succeeded in securing an apartment for himself, though for months to come it would maintain an appearance of uninhabited desolation. To the dismay of the social workers, he dragged his feet unenthusiastically for quite some time on the employment front, eventually resigning himself grudgingly to a government-funded welfare-for-work position at a bicycle repair shop, which, however, he abandoned almost instantaneously after the aforementioned court hearing. Finally, while he attended his hour-long weekly alcohol therapy appointment not altogether erratically, this seemed to exercise little impact upon his immoderate consumption habits.

Gino found himself at that peculiar intersection of two distinct logics that I have described in previous chapters as political delinquency. His repeated internments and his conditional liberty placed him—as others in his social milieu—under the disciplinary and biopolitical power of modern penology, which posited him as a docile subject receptive to reformative procedures along the same lines as other social deviants in the modern state (Foucault 1995), and from which he emerged as that amalgamation of pathological predispositions and antisocial habits conventionally known as the delinquent. This penal regime, then, subjected him and many among his peers to long-standing technologies of normalization in order to reform them and allow their full reintegration into society: temperamental excesses must be inhibited, immoderate desires reined in, and abnormal demeanors checked. Overindulgence in alcohol and unruly violent propensities invite corrective interventions that draw on therapeutic models to assuage insidious or disgraceful drives. But, as we have seen, in Germany, this disciplinary regime links up with a web of legal codes, juridical norms, and law enforcement procedures that together make up that expansive terrain of praxis and knowledge that I have termed the governance of hate.

Such disciplinary procedures today are already inscribed within neoliberal modes of governance invested in "the 'responsibilization' of subjects who are increasingly 'empowered' to discipline themselves" (Ferguson and Gupta 2002, 989), or, as Foucault (2008, 226) famously put it, in forging out of each subject a consumptive-productive, autonomous "entrepreneur of himself, being for himself his own capital, being for himself his own producer, being for himself the source of [his] earnings" (see also Rose 2000b; Foucault 2007). Their logic is therefore economistic in nature. It exposes itself in the prevention, treatment, and rehabilitation procedures that come to bear upon young right-wing extremists and that seek to instill the sorts of affective dispositions, normative investments, and modes of reasoning that would create self-controlling individuals, rather than costly lifetime targets of penal and welfare regimes. As part of such political rectification, authorities seek to bind political delinquents to the mores of upright citizens by inculcating presumably heretofore absent social virtues and normative habits. These include, for example, a principled labor routine that would repair a faulty work ethic according to conventional standards of productive diligence or dwelling practices that would fortify traditional distinctions between public and private and bolster acceptable notions of property and propriety. As we have seen in chapter 6 (and as we shall see, too, in chapter 8), the specifically neoliberal form of this governmental logic is evident as well in the state-like, state-sponsored, and state-activated organizations that it calls into existence and in the sorts of highly localized agents that such organizations in turn recruit to perform governance functions.

From therapeutic technologies through probationary stipulations to incarceration, then, the mechanisms of neoliberal penality transform the menace of a quasi-fascist criminal class into a particular species of delinquency, a peculiar political deviance for which a special place is reserved within the German penal apparatus. Gino's career in this penal regime of delinquency, like that of many in his group, commenced with rather minor transgressions; his first consisted in unlicensed fishing, while others among his peers cited shoplifting, trivial fights, or similar misdemeanors. With his multiple convictions, incarcerations, and legal probation periods, Gino himself had long surpassed the preliminary, hesitant nudges with which the German youth justice system responds to such pubescent misconduct. During my fieldwork, however, I observed several among my informants as they progressively climbed up the scale of delinquent criminality and penal consequences, initially through mere court warnings; then, often, through so many hours of social service, commonly completed assisting youth and social workers (or, on one occasion, granting an interview to a Chicagoan anthropologist); subsequently, and if violent offenses had been committed, came the dreaded "antiviolence seminar," a weekly group therapy session a long evening commute away in the despised center of the city. Uta, who in chapter 3 complained about the scarcity of kebab stands near her home, described it as follows:

> You had this totally crazy game there. They had cards lying about, and we sat in a huge circle. There were some other people sitting there for similar things but not for such misdemeanors like we had, rather for much worse [things]. For example, on one of the cards that one of the guys there had it asked what he would like to do if he knew he would die soon . . . He sits then next to me and says he would like to skin people from top to bottom sometime so he could see how the blood spurts. I immediately took my chair and moved to the side and thought to myself, "Where have I landed?" It was my first charge! I was really destroyed. I was only about fifteen or sixteen then. It seemed to me like a bad film.

When I asked her for detail, Uta described the would-be butcher as a "Turk." For her, for Gino, and for others who attended its sessions, the antiviolence seminar, as much as other locations within the penal trajectory of political delinquency, stood first and foremost for disagreeable proximity to intimidating ethnic others, not unlike other sites and contexts—schools, shopping malls, workplaces, public transportation—where, as we have seen in chapter 3, the physical presence of ethnically marked alterity provoked discomfort and anxiety. Gino, for example, would frequently tell stories of the physical brutality of Russian, Turkish, Vietnamese, or Arab inmates in the prisons where he served his sentences. In *The Souls of Black Folk*, W.E.B. DuBois argues that the types of encounters between blacks and whites to which racially segregated residential patterns give rise operate to reproduce and reinforce rather than to question racial stereotypes (1997). In a similar manner, for Uta and others like her, these encounters with ethnic delinquents within the institutions of penal governance appear to entail the unintended effect of fortifying already existing xenophobic views.

At the same time, however, and at a second level, the allegedly rationalistic paradigms within which these neoliberally inflected penal regimes take shape cannot but answer, as well, to a very distinct logic in which the right-wing extremist delinquent comes into focus as the contemporary incarnation of the National Socialist specter. We have witnessed this second logic at work in previous chapters, for instance, within the juridical sphere or in the work of the police. Yet some of the most astonishing excesses to which it gives rise find their place in the field of therapeutic praxis, where right-wing extremists emerge as sites and targets for specialized rehabilitative interventions that render theirs a uniquely perverse affliction. It should be clear, at this point in the book, that such excesses betray not so much the follies of governance but rather, and more significantly, the inscription of its discourses and technologies within cultural and historical projects—for example, the national question and its aporias in present-day Germany—that belie biopolitical rationalities. Thus, on the one hand, the multiple procedures of the governance of hate that converge upon Gino and others like him labor to reveal the location of the right-wing extremist Thing, to signify it the better to control it. But, on the other hand, the sense of frustration that this relentless quest generates suggests that the political delinquent sustains a certain externality with respect to the legal and penal order, that something in it defies its localization. This unlocatability and the frustration that it triggers has often reminded me of E. E. Evans-Pritchard's (1937, 1–3) exasperated search for the precise corporal site and physical substance in which, according to the Zande, witchcraft resides. Much like Evans-Pritchard, the techniques of governance I explore in this chapter hunt for the right-wing extremist Thing upon the bodies, minds, and souls of Gino and his peers without ever quite laying their hands on it.

In this chapter, I consider three interventionist modalities that aim to reform political delinquents, of which each locates the right-wing extremist Thing in a different site: states of resentment within the affective self, cognitive incoherencies within the rational individual, and corporeal deviance within the physical body. In my research, the affective subject, the rational subject, and the corporeal subject emerged as particularly salient domains for managing hate. Put differently, serving as a composite laboratory for the germination, testing, and honing of various remedial technologies and theoretical models, the political delinquent appears interchangeably as a reservoir of frustrated desires, as the rational consciousness of communicative action, and, finally, as an anatomical corporeality of bodily comportment. In each of these sites, the painstaking procedures of its management outline the right-wing extremist Thing not only as a special species of modern delinquency created by the German penal state but simultaneously as the effect of those cultural and political antinomies that have bedeviled postwar Germany in general and that have come to the fore with particular vigor since reunification. And it is this indelible surplus that time and again kindles exploratory journeys into the therapeutic sciences of affective management.

ETIOLOGIES

In chapter 1, I discussed the general outlines of conventional scholarly definitions of right-wing extremism that commonly center on a cluster of distinct characteristics (authoritarianism, racism, etc.), and I paused, too, on the analytical and political inadequacies of the concept itself. Despite their short-comings, such renderings of right-wing extremism serve many in the field—including not only legislatures, courts, or police but also the social workers with whom I collaborated—as working definitions that guide their labor, for example, for identifying right-wing extremist individuals and penalizing them accordingly. But to the extent that the management of hate oscillates toward thera-peutic intervention rather than, say, surveillance and repression, such working definitions of its target become insufficient. Here, it must necessarily refer as well to theoretical frameworks that purport to provide understandings of the etiology and pathogenesis of the evil in order to design a cure for it. Such inter-ventionist procedures therefore draw on a range of available scholarly perspec-tives that populate a contested terrain of explanatory frameworks, each with its own intellectual and political genealogy, that are expounded and brought to bear upon young political delinquents in today's Germany. For each perspective—indeed often for each of their many variants—there corresponds an assortment of techniques, strategies, and experts, from individual psychological therapy to the generation of group solidarity, the promotion of participatory experi-ences, or democratic experiments at school (see, e.g., Schubarth 2001). Taken together, they provide a set of orientations for professional practitioners in the field.

At the risk of simplifying an admittedly far more complex theoretical land-scape, we could describe these approaches as falling under a general fourfold classification. First, personality structure theories, strongly influenced by Ador-no's theory of the authoritarian personality (Adorno et al. 1950), typically locate the pathology in the psychological individual, understood as the outcome of family relations, childhood experiences, and other details of biographical his-tories. A second group of approaches, more prevalent among political scientists than among psychologists or other providers of individual therapy, includes political culture theories that stress the key importance of societal norms and cultural conventions in defining the responses of distinct social environments to expressions of racism, xenophobia, or violence. Political culture perspectives often identify "democratic deficits" in particular contexts, from the highly lo-calized realities of neighborhoods or small towns to the broader scale of regions (say, the East) or the discursive, institutional, and legal norms of entire nation-states (Funke 1999; Jaschke 2001; Carlsson 2006; Dacombe and Sallah 2006; Davolio et al. 2006). Third, from quite a different direction and influenced by the practical experience of youth and social work, research on youth has often understood right-wing extremism as a youth phenomenon, a form of belong-ing that answers the local logics of consumption, fashion, and subcultural mi-lieus and in which properly political convictions and formalized institutions count less than everyday dynamics (Hafeneger and Jansen 2001; Schröder 2001; Kohlstruck 2002; Erb 2003; Grubben 2006). Last, a range of sociological ex-planations has emphasized the impact of recent large-scale political-economic processes on the appeal of extreme right worldviews. Whether they formulate their critique of the present in terms of the individualization and disorientation typical of risk societies, the brutal competitiveness and social Darwinist currents ushered in with neoliberal capitalism, the relation between accelerating social change and social anomie, or relative deprivation and perceived loss of social status, such sociological models grant center stage to globally operative societal and economic transformations in their explanations of today's extreme right (Heitmeyer 1992; Steinmetz 1994; Butterwegge and Meier 2002).

Of course, such theories rarely appear as monocausal accounts in the literature. More frequently, they provide a set of empirical and theoretical orientations that are not mutually exclusive, and that enter into a variety of reciprocal articulations. Thus, personality structure theories have often been linked with sociological arguments about the decline of the welfare state, processes of individualization under neoliberal capitalism, or decline in socioeconomic status and plausible expectations for broad populations in today's Europe. Youth culture theories have been matched with political culture theories—the less society aggressively cracks down on racism and violence, and the less forcefully it stakes a commitment to democratic values, the more opportunities exist for right-wing extremist youth subcultures to flourish, and the more difficult it becomes for alternative youth subcultures to oppose them (Kleinert and De Rijke 2001). In turn, studies that have set out to explain the putatively disproportionate levels of right-wing extremism, and particularly of racist and political violence in the former GDR territories, alternately trace such trends back to socialist child-rearing practices (personality structure theories); the lack of a democratic culture, civil society, and cultural norms of tolerance (political culture theories); the relatively harsher socioeconomic realities and the perceived loss of status that came with reunification (sociological, relative deprivation theories); or, finally, to particular subcultural youth scenes that have gained ground there in the aftermath of the dissolution of socialism (youth phenomenon theories) (Watts 1996; Argumente 2002).

At the same time, to each of these theoretical frameworks there correspond an assortment of treatment techniques, countermeasures, preventive strategies, expert communities, and specialist idioms. Personality structure theories, for instance, point toward individual psychological therapy as an appropriate instrument for confronting and alleviating personal pathologies. Individualization and modernization theories, in contrast, place value on strategies that generate positive experiences of solidarity, group integration, and collective participation. Approaches that emphasize political culture, meanwhile, promote democratic educational interventions, often through the school system, and the cultivation of civil society structures (Schubarth 2001). Some frameworks, then, posit right-wing extremists themselves as the apposite sites for interventions, while others invest instead in those who would fight against them: antifascist groups, multicultural centers, antiracist NGOs, or "alternative" subcultural youth milieus.

Others still would rather focus on those who should, but in fact do not, oppose right-wing extremism: the broad and faceless publics of apathetic citizens who ignore the danger and flout the call to arms. The practical investments of these varied approaches would seem to oscillate between two distinct if ultimately inseparable poles: first, the management and domestication of the menace of illicit nationalism, which entails not so much its annihilation as the rendering of its manifestations meaningful and knowable, and second, ensuring the safe fabrication of a rejuvenated national project in the present. The latter efforts stand at the center of chapters 8 and 9. Here, my aim is to explore those rehabilitative regimes and therapeutic techniques that aim at the bodies and souls of right-wing extremists.

FACING THE FACTS

At the time of my research, sociological models seemed particularly salient among theoretical perspectives about right-wing extremism. Their dominance appeared to reflect on the one hand a pervasive sense of an interminable economic stagnation and on the other the implementation of a set of major welfare reforms broadly framed as neoliberal in nature. For scholars, sociological approaches have offered a useful way of evading the prevalent labeling of the East as hospitable to National Socialist ideologies. In referring to the particularly harsh economic realities of East Germany and in grounding these realities within globally documented shifts with parallel effects in other world regions, they have allowed the elaboration of alternative accounts.

For many practitioners, however, critical-theoretical engagements with neoliberal capitalism and with global shifts in the political economy of nation-states address the concrete needs of their clients tangentially at best. Instead, when translated into practice (for example, in the daily grind of street social work), these discourses would appear to suggest two plausible—and not mutually exclusive—paths: on the one hand, alleviating social marginalization by facilitating access to welfare services and mediating processes of workforce integration, and on the other, taming unrealistic expectations and aspirations. Implicit in these translations of theory into praxis is a view of racist violence, xenophobic politics, antidemocratic authoritarianism, and other symptoms of the right-wing extremist malaise as grounded in frustration, resentment, and helplessness. It is the embittered confrontation with an exasperating present and a grim future—and, most important, the allegedly obsolete aspirations that collide calamitously with such realities—that spawn the right-wing extremist Thing. The National Socialist specter, in this account, exposes its sinister face in the crevices of a disintegrating social fabric, and it is here that the battle against it would have to be waged. From this standpoint, then, attempts to unwind this nightmarish threat must seek to collapse the chasm between aspirations and reality in which insidious frustrations simmer. Such attempts become a reality check of sorts, an imperative to face the facts of life as they really are, a call that addresses a historical moment in which twentieth-century European working-class aspirations must be brought in-line with twenty-first-century economic relations. They evoke a historical juncture at which European states struggle to clean up the politically inflammable debris left behind by Fordist-Keynesian social democracy—lingering fragments of crumbled dreams about egalitarian societies and universal prosperity—and to prepare the new precariat classes to embrace their putatively inevitable destiny. The burgeoning ranks of economically supernumerary populations across the Continent appear in this rendering to herald the social fate of the descendants of Europe's postwar industrialization. Not only in Germany but throughout the world people today seem to mourn in a variety of forms the perceived loss of a certain sense of futurity, of certain expectations and aspirations that are imagined to have once been plausible. This generalized, pervasive, yet not always discursively available zeitgeist, which, together with Andrea Muehlebach and following Lauren Berlant I have elsewhere described as post-Fordist affect (Berlant 2007; Muehlebach and Shoshan 2012; Shoshan 2012), often appears to leave its mark on attempts to reform political delinquents.

Yet rehabilitative efforts structured by the logic of post-Fordist affect end up inciting those very same affective forms they presume to target. To see how, let us return to that frosty afternoon at the Friedrichstraße train station. Gino and I descended from the upper platform level into the thick afternoon rush hour crowds that swarmed across the ground floor, drifting and bouncing our way confusedly against the traffic of purposeful commuters, distracted shoppers, and forlorn tourists as we searched for our designated rendezvous. Herr Tomasky had said he would be waiting for us by the local transit ticket machines. He represented the Berlin-based initiative "EXIT Deutschland," a secretive project modeled after its Scandinavian namesake to facilitate a way out of the right-wing extremist scene for those weary with its lifestyle or disillusioned with its politics. Founded in 2000 by former officers of the East Berlin police who specialized in youth violence and criminality, EXIT has relied on funding from diverse sources over the years, including federal programs, EU initiatives, civil society foundations, corporate philanthropy, and private donations. Its representatives talk to school classes and participate in media campaigns, but assisting repentant right-wing extremists has remained the core of its activities. EXIT operates on the not entirely unfounded assumption that its business is better kept concealed to protect its clients from possible retributions by their peers.

The meticulous terms of Gino's legal probation included no explicit stipulation on contacting EXIT. Nevertheless, his appeal to the organization, about which he learned from his parole officer, no doubt reflected his desire to score points with the justice system in the run-up to his looming court hearing, which threatened to cost him a lengthy prison sentence. Following a number of telephone conversations, and in preparation for this first face-to-face meeting, EXIT had supplied him with the standard introductory reading material. This autobiographical book by the reformed neo-Nazi who had founded EXIT Sweden (Lindhal 2001), however, had collected dust on a cabinet in his bedroom during the month or so that had since passed. Now he was summoned for a clandestine encounter in the city's center, an alien terrain for Gino, who seldom journeyed beyond his southeastern city quarter. The social workers requested that I accompany him, and so I found myself at his side on this rare voyage as guide, guardian, and confidant.

At long last we found the spot, whereupon a portly man in his midfifties dressed in a worn-out gray suit approached us and introduced himself as Herr Tomasky. He led us to a small table outside a nearby espresso bar where we took our seats amid the noisy commotion of passersby. With Gino nervously scanning the multitude, clearly concerned that some acquaintance might inopportunely walk past, Herr Tomasky led the conversation. He inquired about Gino's ascent into the extreme right scene, the crimes he had committed, and the dangers he could potentially face as a deserter. Gino recounted his early days as a neo-Nazi, when he and his close childhood friend would drink alcohol together and listen to the violent lyrics of banned CDs. Participation in organized political activities started later, after he had made the acquaintance of some older "Nazis" and of their wider social milieu. He would spend evenings at pubs with his comrades discussing politics over beer. He and his friends would beat people up. "Who would you beat up?" asked Tomasky. "Mostly foreigners," he replied. "What does 'mostly' mean?" Tomasky pressed on. "Also 'normals,' that is, leftists," Gino answered. Tomasky wondered how Gino's old comrades viewed his present conversion, and what threats they may pose to his well-being. "They think I'm a traitor," Gino explained. Tomasky inquired why, at this point in his life, Gino sought to leave behind and turn his back on the milieu of which he had been such an integral part. "Ick bin Icke" (roughly, "I am my own person"), Gino insisted a number of times. He had lost interest, he continued, and no longer saw anything good in his old ways. He wanted to put his life in order.

Tomasky's barrage of terse questions, his dismissive offhand remarks, his bossy tone of voice, and his incredulous facial expressions could be taken to suggest, perhaps, a certain jaded and streetwise attitude of someone who has seen it all. But their stubborn persistence left on me a distinct and rather different impression, namely, that he was mechanically and disinterestedly executing a well-rehearsed script that left little room for—and showed little interest in—the personal narrative that Gino presented to him. When his interrogation failed to produce a response that would satisfy his script, as was only too often the case, he would interrupt Gino's speech, scoff at his reply, repeat the question, demand that Gino think up an alternative answer, and, when necessary, provide the proper formulation himself. Gino's particular life history, personal experiences, and biographical narrative only seemed to matter insofar as they confirmed Tomasky's preconceived agenda. His was not the attentive ear of the therapist but rather a sermonizing discourse that time and again pontificated about how poorly executed and morally reprehensible Gino's entire life had been. For his part, Gino's mostly monosyllabic retorts rendered the exchange all the more frustrating.

Tomasky steered Gino to reflect upon the reasons that motivated his incorporation into the extreme right scene. Gino struggled to produce an explanation. He was "just having fun" with his friends without thinking too much about what he was doing, he said; which, he hurried to add, was what you do when you are young. But Tomasky judged his account to be inadequate and urged him to consider other possible reasons that may have pushed him in this direction. As if he recalled the fact inadvertently, Gino mentioned that he had experienced domestic violence from some of his mother's boyfriends as a child. "I externalized the violence I had internalized at home," he explained. Tomasky remained visibly unsatisfied, and clarified that such an answer remained inadequate inasmuch as many people experience domestic violence yet never become violent right-wing extremists. It would be difficult, therefore, to account for the *political* nature of Gino's violence on these grounds. This went on for some time, until Gino appeared drained of ideas. Perplexed and beleaguered, he seemed unable to meet Tomasky's expectations. Tomasky eventually came to his aid, inquiring whether his right-wing extremist political sympathies and racist violence could not have emerged from frustration and despair, from a feeling of hopelessness and the outlook of a life without prospects, from a sense that he was not in control of his future. Gino nodded indistinctly, neither confirming nor refuting—nor for that matter even indicating he had quite grasped—Tomasky's hypothesis. This was neither here nor there: with the scripted formula now uttered, the interactional performance could resume its course.

For a while thereafter, Tomasky interrogated Gino on his criminal record, on the charges pending against him, and on the whereabouts of his police files. Before long, however, he resuscitated the themes of hopelessness and frustration as he asked Gino about his educational record, employment situation, and professional aspirations. Gino bemoaned the dearth of decent job and vocational training opportunities and clarified that he had never finished school, held no diploma, and had always been unemployed. Tomasky's chastising, patronizing gaze transmuted into a ridiculing grin when Gino professed his desire to someday become an electrician. This clear attempt at modest pragmatism on the part of Gino, who often reported far more inflated life goals—from movie stardom to military glory—nevertheless appeared patently absurd in the eyes of Tomasky. As if following the cue for his final act, Tomasky commenced on a disparaging tirade against delusional hopes and an austere sermon on the indispensability of facing the facts, of seeing life as it really is (*das Leben sehen, wie es ist*).

His diatribe interlaced a vindictive appraisal of Gino with a bleak vision of the present to advocate an ethics that could best be described as hovering somewhere between despair and resignation. The combined impact of Gino's dismal educational record and appalling criminal history would already set him for an abysmally disadvantaged start, Tomasky proclaimed. But even if their repercussions could be attenuated—say, if Gino conjured the willpower to resume his schooling, or if EXIT vouchsafed his repentance to potential employers—they only exacerbated the already disheartening realities of the contemporary labor market, which were likely to continue and deteriorate further in the future. Pickiness, he warned, was a luxury Gino couldn't afford. Given this dire state of affairs, his personal background ruled out any ambitions as illusory fantasies and permitted only the lowliest of expectations. This obliged him, Tomasky said, to gratefully accept whatever offers the employment office could make him. Indeed, Tomasky added, Gino should consider himself extraordinarily fortunate if any opportunities at all came his way.

Tomasky concluded the meeting with an unexpected turn. Apparently seeking to strike a personal note with Gino, he framed his own personal situation as parallel to that of his young interlocutor. Given that his employer, EXIT, was potentially facing major budget cuts, he could not count with any degree of certainty on whether, and for how long, he might be able to keep his post. At the age of fifty-five, he continued, he could very well find himself unemployed and with virtually no prospects of returning to the labor market or otherwise improving his situation. He and Gino, he reasoned, therefore found themselves in the same boat, and neither of them could afford to pick and choose. EXIT, he stated, as he brought the meeting to a close, could not simply manufacture a job for Gino. Possibly, though he could make no promises, the organization might be able to arrange for farming work, which would require Gino to relocate from Berlin to the countryside. Gino sulked.

On the train back to Treptow, Gino brooded glumly over the meeting. No, he said, he found nothing particularly demoralizing in Tomasky's harsh pronouncements. He had heard it all many times before. The precarious despondency of his current standing and future prospects, and the exigency of facing reality without delusions, had already been impressed upon him on countless occasions by social workers, parole officers, government bureaucrats, or judges. What brought him down was instead precisely the fact that, as far as he could see, Tomasky had nothing new to convey, much less to offer. Whatever fantasies Gino had entertained about his appointment with EXIT aside, there was more than a grain of truth in the way in which he voiced his disillusionment. Tomasky's textbook performance invoked a particular diagnosis of the affliction of right-wing extremism as rooted in a space of resentment that extends over the gap between implausible expectations and rough realities, and it prescribed, too, the appropriate cure.

Recall that Tomasky offhandedly rejected Gino's accounts of what it was that set him off on his ignominious trajectory. Gino initially delineated his ingratiation into the "scene" as motivated by social happenstance, by close friends, and by juvenile notions of fun. Tomasky's dismissal of this narrative at the same time repudiated scholarly understandings of right-wing extremism as essentially a youth phenomenon defined by the logic of adolescent subcultural milieus, shifting fashions, and transient social cliques. Gino's subsequent comments expressed a more thoughtful contemplation about the domestic violence that marked his upbringing, and which, having absorbed, he later came to externalize. He voiced this response in a language I had not heard from him before and that smacked of therapeutic contexts like his antiviolence seminar. This interpretation, in turn, tallied with authoritarian personality structure theories, which identify the locus for the emergence of right-wing extremist traits in violent, tyrannical domestic circumstances. But Tomasky's allegiance lay elsewhere. It was the sociological, losers-of-modernization account of the extreme right that he more or less coerced Gino into accepting. And this account, in turn, construed Gino as the contemporary progeny of the long German tradition of the strong, caring state whose genealogy encompasses the socialism of the GDR as much as it does the ordoliberalism and later neo-Keynesianism of the FRG and, indeed, the prewar years. Accordingly, it was that understanding of Gino's racist violence as a symptom of a particular sort of post-Fordist resentment that structured Tomasky's method and that rendered his therapeutic strategy in the form of "facing the facts of life as they really are." Such a reality check entails a flattening of temporality: any imagined future must remain beholden to the outlines of an unsavory present, so that collective investment in a politics oriented toward change becomes meaningless, futile (cf. Jameson 2004). It is precisely in this sense that all Tomasky could offer Gino was an ethics of resignation.

In this hailing of Gino as the locus of resentment and frustration, we see the interpellation of individuals less as the entrepreneurial citizens and autonomous agents that conventionally populate neoliberal imaginaries and more as passive, docile subjects bereft of expectations and resigned to unsavory futures. More important, however, through tiresome repetition ("I have heard it all before"), a certain mode of governance appears invested in inculcating forms of post-Fordist affect and in actively fabricating a particular figuration of lack. In doing so, it incites precisely the sorts of frustrated attachments that, according to Tomasky's own pronouncements, allegedly stand behind xenophobic violence and the extreme right in the first place. Within the management of hate, then, a discursive incitement of resentment appears to emerge, tautologically, as explanation, in the process reaffirming its own claim to truth. The very attempt to exorcise Gino of his specters reveals itself as the moment of their summoning.

THE RATIONAL KERNEL

Tomasky's propositions rang so dreary to Gino's ears, however, not only because of their discomforting implications for his biographical future but also because in the few years that had transpired since he embarked upon his rapid ascent to infamy, Gino had become a walking depository—and battleground—for competing theoretical frameworks and rehabilitation techniques. In this sense, the propagation of the right-wing extremist Thing as an affective form of post-Fordist resentment is neither alone in the field of reforming political delinquents nor the only manner in which such efforts would seem to undermine their own tenets. By way of contrast, I now consider approaches that posit political delinquency not within the affective self but rather as anchored in what is taken to be the cognitive, (ir)rational subject—the subject capable of comprehending logical arguments, of assessing the validity and coherence of predicative statements, and of formulating such arguments on her own. Particularly (though not exclusively) popular with educators and youth workers, such approaches include, for example, "argumentation training workshops," where guides lead exercises and simulations of actual or possible debates against National Socialist ideologies; expert-led seminars, where specialists arm participants with information that would help them refute right-wing extremist statements; or booklets with extensive lists of right-wing extremist arguments, each complemented with an appropriate rebuttal. Ordinarily provided free of charge by municipalities, political parties, NGOs, or government bureaus, such efforts at rational enlightenment target not only wayward adolescents but also—and perhaps more often—certain at-risk practitioners (teachers, youth workers, local politicians), parents of young nationalists, and the general public. Their proponents show particular investment in transforming the pedagogical cultures of educational institutions where, so they claim, exclusion, silencing, or disregard rather than earnest debate commonly characterize responses to expressions of right-wing extremist sympathies. Those who practice or preach these methods consider critical-rational debate (*Auseinandersetzung*) with National Socialist and other racist, right-wing extremist ideologies vital for preventive work with politically rightist youths. Only the careful pedagogical dismantling of susceptibilities to elements of such nationalist ideological frameworks can make extricating young, vulnerable people from their politically delinquent social milieus possible, so they claim. Hence, they insist on the importance of taking the political stances with which these young people identify seriously and literally, as referential predicates about the world, and of deploying "the power of the question" in order to confront them with the contradictions of their beliefs.

Under the auspices of a foundation associated with the Social Democratic Party and supported by both the federal and the Berlin governments, Helmuth and I were invited as presumed specialists in the field to share our praxis-honed opinion on a prototype of one of these methods, called "subversive destabilizing pedagogy" (*subversive Verunsicherungspädagogik*).[2] A professor of law and social work and his assistant had prepared a draft version of a documentary, produced to serve as a pedagogical weapon against right-wing extremism. The film was conceived as the first in a series of documentaries that would engage and question distinct aspects of National Socialist and contemporary extreme right ideology, and that together would provide a handy toolbox for educators. They hoped to eventually show these documentaries in schools and other appropriate locations. The screening took place in a spacious room in a building in central Berlin that belonged to the foundation. Seated with us in a half circle in front of a large television screen were the professor and his assistant, the director of a street social work NGO, the director of a youth work NGO and his assistant, the manager of a youth sports club that specialized in offerings for young right-wing extremists, and a representative of the foundation that hosted the meeting and her intern. It was, hence, an assembly not only of experts but also of the professional target audience for the film.

The professor and his assistant asked for our input on their first documentary in the series, titled Globalization and Xenophobia (*Globalisierung und Fremdenfeindlichkeit*). They introduced the film itself and the theoretical concepts behind it before proceeding to screen it. Divided into five sections, their documentary looked at the World Trade Organization (WTO), international trade and global markets, trade wars and protectionism, the globalization of the extreme right itself, and the historical relation between foreigners and labor. It wove together the damning pronouncements of Gordon Reinholz, a prominent, young, and charismatic figure in the scene of extraparliamentary, organized extreme right militancy, and the rather lackluster explanations of an elderly economics professor. While Reinholz delivered the usual antiglobalization sound bites, the professor, in contrast, clarified in a meticulous yet monotonous way the structure, functions, and powers of the WTO and defended its importance for world trade. Backgrounded by period footage of military parades and National Socialist mass spectacles, the documentary illustrated the different ways in which, propagandistic rhetoric aside, the Third Reich's economy and military were in fact always heavily dependent on trade relations with the United States and on the importation of American technology and supplies. In turn, it showed how Germany's spectacular postwar economic recovery could not have come about without the availability of a globalized labor market (to wit, South European and later Turkish labor migration). It presented historical examples of economic crises and recessions that emerged in the shadow of trade wars and economic isolationism. It used interviews with scholarly experts and industry leaders to reaffirm the historical narrative and to explain the contemporary conjuncture in which, so they asserted, German companies must relocate

---

[2] *Verunsicherung* literally means the making of someone or something insecure, and can be translated as upsetting, disrupting, unsettling, and so on.

portions of their production abroad in order to remain internationally competitive and to maintain workplaces at home. The film displayed images of extreme right Internet websites, their URLs hidden but their illicit symbolism clearly visible, to corroborate growing international links among right-wing extremists. Footage of neo-Nazi marches, demonstrations, rock concerts, and other events from across the world further drove home the point that the extreme right has become a global phenomenon. The place of far right representatives in the political structures of the EU also came under scrutiny.

Each section of the film provoked a range of skeptical responses from the small chorus of invited critics. Some questioned the desirability of placing so much emphasis, in the second section of the movie, on the intimate relations between the Nazis and the Americans, and on the latter's support of the Third Reich's economy, industry, and war machine. Others complained about the superficiality of the film and its failure to treat in a serious and more comprehensive manner the topic of globalization. Before long a manifest sense prevailed that, while well intentioned, the film was glaringly misguided, albeit without consensus on why precisely this was so.

With a look of indignation, the sports club manager insisted that the problem of right-wing extremism hardly lay with opposition to globalization as such but instead with racism and xenophobia in and of themselves. He accordingly reproached the nearly absolute focus of the film on the former and its rather cursory and inadequate attention to the latter. He took issue with the construal of rationality as the discursive prerogative of market-friendly specialists and attacked the message implicit in the film, namely, that any struggle against the dictates of global capitalism could only signal irrational political extremism. According to his critique, in its substitution of an opaque rule of experts for political debate, the film betrayed its alleged democratic aims. In censuring the construal as extremist, populist, or otherwise irrational of any opposition to the global hegemony of neoliberal capitalism, the sports club manager condemned the depoliticization of the economy and the concomitant economization of the political that some scholars have described as the death of politics (see Žižek 1997; Comaroff and Comaroff 2001).

In this sense, the message communicated in the documentary echoed but also contrasted in important ways with the "end of history" narrative that Tomasky delivered to Gino. It equally construed global capitalism as an inescapable reality. However, it represented resistance to this presumably inevitable state of affairs not so much—or not only—as futile but more significantly as irrational. It demanded not a passive acquiescence to a perhaps regrettable yet utterly unavoidable bleak future spelled by the unstoppable encroachment of neoliberal economics but rather a political conversion that would yield the active embrace of this futurity, the firm faith in its promises, the recognition of its allegedly indisputable advantages. Like Tomasky's ethics of resignation, it signaled what Jameson (2003; see also Lomnitz 2003) has described as the contemporary reduction of existential time to a present that no longer qualifies as such because the future and the past that it requires in the first place have already been effaced. Jameson notes that few periods have proved as incapable of framing immediate alternatives for themselves as ours, a condition that he attributes to the contemporary waning of utopia and with it of a critical, substantive relation to the present (Jameson 2004; see also Muehlebach and Shoshan 2012). And yet, to the extent that his observation is correct, this deficit of political imagination and alternative futurities would seem to reflect as well a certain moral incitement to convert, a certain censuring of political difference. The contemporary disenchantment with politics and evacuation of the near future appear to come accompanied today with a condemnation of alternative aspirations as at once heretic and irrational (cf. Rose 2000a; Guyer 2007).

From a different perspective, the directors of the youth work and social work organizations expressed alarm about what they considered the film's imprudent use of images. The sequences that attended to the dependency of the armed forces of the Third Reich on foreign trade especially included mesmerizing footage from period propaganda movies. The images showed the full glory of National Socialist military might and the fascist aesthetics of the mass spectacle: armored divisions, fighter jets, thousands of soldiers marching in formation. In addition, those parts of the movie that attended to the contemporary globalization of right-wing extremism included depictions of large neo-Nazi gatherings, thriving far right movements, white power heavy metal concerts, massive marches and political events, and lively and elegantly designed Internet discussion forums and websites, as well as charismatic leaders of right-wing extremist parties in Europe and beyond it. Through a peculiar exchange of mimetic projections, the directors of the NGOs sought time and again to place themselves in the shoes of potential young right-wing extremist audiences and to imagine how the latter would understand and react to such imagery. "If I were a Nazi," the director of the social work organization said, "I would surely find such images thoroughly inspirational."[3]

Their apprehensive outcry against the documentary's use of footage rested on an implicit binary distinction between a rational, predicative authority of linguistic communication on the one hand and an irrational, affective force of the image on the other. It is the very same separation that Horkheimer and Adorno once linked with the history of the Enlightenment: the irreversible divorce between sign and image, knowing and being, science and poetry (2002 [1944], 17–18). In the words of their contemporary Bertolt Brecht, the film let "decoration distract from the statement" (1996, 231). It was flawed in this view

---

[3] It is difficult not to be reminded here of the witch doctors who, as Peter Geschiere explains, must first master the art of witchcraft, indeed, must first become themselves witches (even if only symbolically, say, by sacrificing a goat as a substitute for killing a man), in order to subsequently wage battle against the evil forces of sorcery (2008).

insofar as it disrupted its own supposedly rational discourse with the sensuous immediacy of its images, or, put differently, inasmuch as it failed to fully subjugate the force of the latter to the rationality of the former. In his interpretation of Mozart's *Le nozze di Figaro*, Slavoj Žižek identifies what he calls a Hegelian moment in which, as he desperately searches for Susanna, the voice of Count Almaviva enunciates his jealous anger to the very same melody in which the reconciled couple—Figaro and Susanna—already celebrate their love (1989, 188). The documentary seemed to entail a similar tension between content and form. Here, this contradiction appeared to hold not between melody and meaning but instead between visual form and verbal content, the latter condemning what the former simultaneously glorifies. At issue, then, was something beyond—though certainly also—the film's failure to recognize what Bourdieu (1998, 21) termed the "reality effect" of images, or what Allen Feldman described as "the evidentiary, typified, and mimetic dimension" that establishes their "privileged claim on truth, facticity, and intelligibility" (1997, 26). More significantly, the disjuncture between image and narration unwittingly replicated the opposition between "picture thinking" and reason. In so doing, it invoked the entire set of binary contrasts—between mimesis and autonomy, infancy and adulthood—that, as William Mazzarella (2010) notes, has shaped modern fears of the susceptible crowd. By heedlessly neglecting the irrational compulsion of images, according to this critique, the film overestimated and thus undermined the pedagogical sway of its own discursive rationality.

The strong version of this critique, its philosophical reductio ad absurdum, can be found in Adorno's insistence, in *Negative Dialectics*, that the object can only be grasped in the absence of its image (1997, 207). A weaker and more historically sensitive understanding of this *Bilderverbot* (ban on images) would note instead the traces of a long-standing cultural prohibition in postwar Germany on public representations of National Socialist imagery and of the Holocaust (Huyssen 2003c and 2010). This taboo has not ceased to exercise its force, if now in the form of careful regulation and palpable discomfort rather than blanket censorship. In this regard, the similarity between the reactions to *Globalization and Xenophobia* and the public scandal that followed the release, in 1993, of the documentary *Beruf Neonazi* (*Occupation Neonazi*) (Bonengel 1993) is telling. An intimate view into the life of a young East Berlin cadre, that film came under harsh critique—resulting in legal charges against its director—for serving as propaganda precisely because of its uncommented and allegedly seductive visual form (Bathrick 1996).

But the dissatisfaction with the film took yet an additional form. At my side, Helmuth squirmed and frowned as the screening progressed. "It's one to zero for the Nazis," he would sigh time and again. On the one hand, he began, once his turn finally came to share his thoughts, there was Gordon Reinholz: youthful, fashionable, and charismatic, passionately weaving nationalism and anti-globalization idioms, and speaking the language of his young public. On the other hand, there was the economics professor, aged and heavy, with his old-fashioned moustache and his bald top, his dull suit answering the grayness of his office, monotonously explicating the nature and importance of the WTO. Utterly irrespective of the actual content of their enunciations, said Helmuth, for the young people whom he served, a figure such as Reinholz would unquestionably command a far more compelling authority. The professor and his assistant responded that their aim had been to expose the contradictions of right-wing extremist demagogy by juxtaposing it with the voices of expert "authorities"—economists, historians, business leaders—who would refute its arguments. The possibility that the relation between authority and voice could be constituted differently in different discursive fields and for different audiences seemed not to have crossed their minds. But Helmuth and others in the audience retorted that the pseudodeliberative format of the film in fact had the effect not of undermining Reinholz's rhetoric but, quite the contrary, of elevating him to the same level of expertise as that ordinarily attributed to a respectable economics professor, in other words, of fortifying rather than dismantling his claim to authority.

Helmuth's critical comments exposed how the assumption of predicative discursive rationality, as the fundamental premise underpinning the entire conceptual edifice of the method of subversive destabilizing pedagogy, in fact rested on an irrational groundwork, and this in three ways. First, he called attention to the rhetorical conventions and stylistics of performance—the poetics of the everyday, just as much as of pedagogical, political, or ritual speech (Sebeok 1964; Caton 1990)—that, beyond their denotational meaning, endow certain enunciations (e.g., those of a charismatic, young, right-wing extremist leader) with efficacy. Second, he pointed at how the attributed force of certain voices and utterances (e.g., those of an economics professor or of a business executive) do not rest on their internal coherence or their truth-value but rather on the institutionalized power differentials that authorize them and do not authorize other speakers (Bourdieu 2001). Finally, in describing the radically distinct modes in which young right-wing extremists would likely interpret the film, Helmuth questioned the assumption of a uniform discursive universe. Instead, he proclaimed the incongruence and unevenness of discourse, its constitutive indeterminacy and openness to heterogeneous meanings, and the potential variation across it of both the norms of rhetorical stylistics and the structures of institutional authorization (see Bakhtin 1998a). In sum, his comments laid bare and unraveled what some linguistic anthropologists have called the language ideology (Schieffelin, Woolard, and Kroskrity 1998; Kroskrity 2000) within which, for its authors, the film appeared at once legible and efficacious. This language ideology—a set of presuppositions about the way that language works—adhered to a notion of rational deliberation within the framework of pure communicative action. It took for granted an ideal speech situation operative within the uniform discursive universe of a homogeneous public sphere.

"Subversive destabilizing pedagogy" thus posited the right-wing extremist as the not-quite-yet fully mature Kantian subject of rational deliberation (Kant 1991). It followed a Habermasian concept of public discourse and communicative action (Habermas 1989) within which the cognitive mistakes of this immature subject could be put right. This framework would have been the ground from which right-wing extremism could appear as sheer cognitive error, the effect of misapprehension and obfuscation, a lacking or distorted knowledge that required rectification.[4] But it turned out to be no ground at all.

All three critiques voiced unease with the way in which the film performed its rationalizing mission of demystification, even if none of them explicitly pursued the implications of their pronouncements to their radical conclusions. The first more or less accepted the film's assumption of an irrational kernel at the heart of the right-wing extremist Thing. What it questioned was not the existence of such irrationality but rather its identification with antiglobalization political idioms. Instead, it demanded that the film recalibrate the enlightening beam of its deliberative rationalism to target racist hatred. The second critique proclaimed a certain tension between the predicative rationality of text and the affective irrationality of images as inherent to audiovisual media. It warned about the alleged predominance of image over discourse, and hence of affect over rationality, in the current version of the film. It demanded, then, that the film safeguard reason from unreason and subjugate image to text more forcefully. The third critique, however, suggested an irrationality inherent to discourse as such. It thereby irreparably shattered the premises of the method of rational deliberation. Taken together, all three critiques left no doubt that, in the eyes of the participants, through its uncritical embrace of free-market idioms, the force of its images, and its misguided appeal to discursive authority, subversive destabilizing pedagogy undermined its own foundations in a manner that was all but certain to invigorate, rather than enfeeble, right-wing extremist ideological commitments.

IF IT WALKS LIKE A NAZI

The interventionist, therapeutic procedures of the governance of hate, whether they orient themselves toward an affective self or a rational cogito, seem to undo their own logics, inciting resentment by interpellating individuals as post-Fordist subjects, or provoking the putatively irrational with their monopolistic claims to discursive rationality. Within each of these domains—the affective soul and the rational mind—a certain self-defeating, tautological thrust marks projects of governance. At an altogether different level, however, the excesses

---

[4]In this sense, it corresponded to a certain notion of ideology as referencing a mystified relation to reality that can and must be dismantled (Woolard 1998).

and apparent irrationalities that haunt the management of hate in Germany make themselves evident in the very proliferation of its varied domains, in the fabrication of ever more specialized and peculiar methods and targets. In order to illustrate this point, I shift now from the relatively conventional frameworks of rational debate and "facing the facts" pragmatism that I described above to a more outlandish instance of therapeutic intervention that targets the corporeal subject.

In late November, a few weeks before my departure from the field, the social workers were invited to partake in a meeting with a group that labored on developing a method for treating right-wing extremists through what its members called "body language therapy." The group appealed to the social workers' expertise in the field of right-wing extremism.[5] Body language therapy, according to its proponents, sought to treat political delinquents by targeting their corporeal habitus. Specifically, it aimed to identify extreme-right-typical bodily styles and to train young right-wing extremists to move differently. Before they attended the session, the social workers seemed perplexed with the notion of reforming their clients in this manner and with the interest in their own specialized knowledge. But they returned amused with what they had witnessed. The session opened with a demonstration video that, to their disbelief, starred none other than Gino himself as its main protagonist. At first, a guide instructed him to act naturally and pace around the room as he normally would while the camera followed his posture and movements. Gino was then asked to describe how he felt, and he responded with "tired" and "stressed." Next, a member of the group coached him in how to adjust his pose, gestures, and gait so that they would become more "relaxed." The camera followed him for some time as he moved about in this newly learned, "relaxed" demeanor. Finally, after he had had the opportunity to try out this novel fashion of bodily motility, he was asked whether he now felt better, to which he replied with a mumbled "yes."

In the discussion that followed the screening, members of the group explained their therapeutic strategy. Gino, they reported, had been delivered to them through his parole officer and had meanwhile proved himself a truly reliable guinea pig, punctually and consistently showing up to all his scheduled appointments. The social workers were particularly surprised, so they said, to learn of Gino's commitment and reliability, which contrasted with their quite different experience of him. Later, when they asked Gino's parole officer—with whom they were closely acquainted—about Gino's involvement in the experiment, he "laughed his lungs out" (as they put it to me) and elucidated that Gino had been receiving a hefty remuneration for each session he attended in

---

[5] Unfortunately, I could not attend the meeting. My attempts to contact the body language therapy group came to naught, and in the short time I still had in the field, I was unable to locate Gino, who by then had all but vanished from the social workers' purview. My reflections here are therefore informed by interviews with the social workers.

a timely manner. Gino's investment in the lucrative business of body language therapy could thus be accounted for relatively straightforwardly in financial terms. There was, to be sure, nothing unprecedented about the way in which this therapy allowed Gino to capitalize on his political delinquency and translate it into profitable transactions. On other occasions, I observed him reap direct financial benefits from the attention of journalists and, less directly, from the heightened investment in his case by state institutions. However, the remuneration he received from those advocating the body language therapy method for leasing himself as a guinea pig signaled a particular (and, arguably, particularly disturbing) valorization of the capital that his racist violence had won him. In transacting himself in this way as an experimentation subject, Gino simultaneously enabled the flourishing of a specific therapeutic science. This scientific agenda included the elaboration of theoretical frameworks and research hypotheses, experimental procedures and specialized technologies, typological classifications and evaluative measurements, variables and models of causality, and modes of representation and dissemination, all of which revolved around his bodily presence.

The science of identifying right-wing extremist-typical bodily composures might evoke the biological-anatomical determinism of early positivist criminology. In criminological phrenology, for example, "a set of distinguishing physical features were stigmas of criminality" (Laclau 2005, 37), and social deviance therefore appeared as inscribed upon and readable from the body. Yet, in matter of fact, body language therapy drastically contrasted with late-nineteenth- and early-twentieth-century positivist criminology inasmuch as its object consisted not in inherited anatomical compositions but rather in acquired locomotive habits that, most important, could be reformed. From another direction, its investment in the micromanagement of corporeal movements could also suggest a correspondence with the normalizing regime of disciplinary power and docile bodies that Foucault famously described (1995). But its peculiar logic articulated deviance and its rectification less with the strict discipline of prisons and standing armies and more with an embodied aesthetics of laxity. It rendered the menace of an illicit nationalism into a pliable corporeal habitus, a locomotive aesthetics of posture and comportment that can be purged of its rough contours and substituted with more refined—or, perhaps better, more "relaxed"—physical mannerisms.

Viewed in this light, body language therapy raises an interesting question. Namely, in what ways, at the outset of the twenty-first century, does a science of the body become the cipher for accessing and engaging with politically deviant subjectivities? Answering this question seems to point neither in the direction of deterministic physiology nor of disciplinary praxis but rather toward style. We are called upon to ask, then, how this positing of style as the locus of politics bespeaks a historical juncture in which, as Jean Comaroff and John Comaroff put it, "as neoliberal conditions render ever more obscure the rooting of inequality in structures of production, as work gives way to the mechanical solidarities of 'identity' in constructing selfhood and social being, class comes to be understood, in both popular and scholarly discourse, as yet another personal trait or lifestyle choice" (2001). In Europe, Douglas Holmes (2000) has argued, not only the politics of class but also and inseparably that of nationalism has recently witnessed its aestheticization into the individualized expressionism of fashion, taste, and style. Of course, it is highly questionable whether politics has ever been entirely separate from aesthetic style, and vice versa.[6] And yet, if there is some truth to the claim that, at the start of the present century, we find politics increasingly collapsed into style, it should come as no surprise that style too appears ever more as the key to the substance of politics.

Body language therapy in this sense did more than merely tweak with surface appearances. Consider, by way of contrast, the appointment that the social workers had arranged for Gino only a few months earlier with a certain tattoo artist who now and then provided her services free of charge for the benefit of people who wished to relieve themselves of their right-wing extremist tattoos. Perhaps because he could expect no financial compensation, Gino missed a couple of appointments before he finally had the letters of the HASS tattoo that decorated the fingers of his right hand—whose illegal rendering of the SS symbol he had increasingly come to view as a liability—skillfully transformed into innocuous playing cards.

While this surgical intervention equally dabbled with his corporeal physicality, and while it certainly entailed a corrective drive, it could hardly be described as therapeutic. The erasure of the tattoo, or more precisely its creative transfiguration, appeared here as a philanthropic act that sought to assist right-wing extremists who looked to remove illicit signs from their bodies, whether because they had disowned their former political identifications, become wary of legal and other consequences that such signs could spell, or for whatever other reason. It posited the skin as surface, as appearance, as canvas, without postulating some other essence beyond, beneath, or within it as its real target. Insofar as the essence it sought to transmute consisted in nothing more nor less than appearance, it genuinely collapsed appearance and essence. Its substance, its Truth, was epidermal, superficial. As such, it corresponded to a form of knowledge

---

[6] Especially in the first decades of the twentieth century, as visual mass media gained ground in the public sphere, critics have noted with concern what Walter Benjamin (1986b) has termed the aestheticization of politics, particularly with a view to the political rise and consolidation of fascist regimes and ideologies. The aestheticization of politics in that sense designated a specific mode in which fascism operated ideologically to guarantee its political success. In sharp contrast, starting in the 1970s especially, British scholars associated with the emergent field of cultural studies looked to the domains of style and aesthetics as sites for the elaboration and performance of social critique and political resistance (Hall and Jefferson 1976; Hebdige 1979).

in which appearance does not conceal the Thing that one imagines to stand behind or beneath it but in fact reveals itself as the only essential Truth (cf. Žižek 1989, 185–97).

Body language therapy, in contrast, conceived of bodily appearance and physical style as the telltale symptoms of a deeper pathological deviance and as the secrets for its undoing. Put differently, it understood style not simply as style but rather as the depository of political substance. In a Kantian manner, it sought to get to the bottom of this substance, of the right-wing extremist Thing, not directly but rather through its phenomenal effects. Fredric Jameson has called such forms of knowledge "depth models" (1991, 12), that is, ways of knowing that cut a clear distinction between the arbitrary and the necessary, the outside and the inside, the profound and the superficial. Beyond its disturbing financial valorization of political delinquency as profitable business, it is as such a depth model that body language therapy ended up reducing political delinquency to a matter of style.

THE NATIONALIST THING

To be sure, something felt admittedly innovative yet awkwardly amiss—if not, as the street social workers would have it, ludicrously farcical—about this therapeutic approach to right-wing extremism. But perhaps it was precisely in its apparent absurdity that body language therapy most patently revealed the untamable excesses to which the right-wing extremist specter gives rise, its perseverance as an occult force and its refusal to wholly give in to the various attempts at its domestication, all of which characterized as well—if somewhat less conspicuously—the two other rehabilitative methods I have examined in this chapter. Whether written off as the whimsical unruliness of adolescents, traced back to the authoritarian formation of a pathological ego, located in a space of resentment between implausible aspirations and immutable realities, or collapsed into bodily style, the right-wing extremist Thing obstinately defies its varied circumscriptions and significations. It is difficult not to be reminded here once more of the opening pages of Evans-Pritchard's classical analysis of witchcraft among the Azande. There, Evans-Pritchard sets the stage for the entire study to follow by describing—and the text conveys more than a hint of frustration—the impossibility of determining the physical substance in which, as his Zande informants nevertheless insist, witchcraft resides (1937, 1–3). A similar sense of frustration makes itself felt in Germany as the unrelenting search for the right-wing extremist Thing passes through the minds, bodies, and souls of people like Gino.

From a different direction, this unlocatable surplus that at once incites and resists its own circumscription suggests certain parallels with what James Siegel has called the truth of sorcery (2003). Siegel notes how, in Levi-Strauss's famous analysis of the sorcerer and his magic, the truth of sorcery appears as its unique capacity to transform inchoate feelings into articulated speech. The confessions of a Zuni boy who stands accused of witchcraft reveal nothing that was not already known before. Yet neither do they lead to the administration of justice. Instead, they serve to elaborate on that which was already assumed to hold true. In the process, sorcery emerges as a site of signification and as an instrument of symbolic articulation. However, the excess that marks its emergence prevents it from functioning, as some anthropologists would have it, only as an ordering, structuring principle in social life. Instead, this excess introduces into sorcery a violent, disruptive force. The application of curing magic to the victim of witchcraft or the naming (and, sometimes, brutal lynching) of a witch fail to bring resolution or closure—there will always be another curse, another witch, another witch hunt (Siegel 2006). If, as Siegel argues, sorcery is supposed to conceal the failure of the social, if naming the witch at once also announces the innocence of society, then the management of hate presents an analogous interest in evacuating the social from traces of the National Socialist specter. The range of theoretical models, preventive strategies, and rehabilitative techniques that came to bear upon my young informants appeared invested in articulating the truth of right-wing extremism, in revealing its location within or upon the surface of the subject, in signifying it the better to control it. And yet, a residual surplus that cannot be subsumed into the social order seems always to be summoned anew in these efforts. This surplus eludes its representation and announces its presence only through unarticulated—and unarticulatable—affects. It is this ineffaceable residue that repeatedly ignites speculative quests into the occult sciences of exorcism, some no doubt more comical than others.

Their claims to scientific rationality notwithstanding, the operations of affective governance that labor to pin down the right-wing extremist Thing reveal themselves as haunted by cultural anxieties and historical apprehensions to a far greater extent than either scholars or practitioners would care to acknowledge. They mediate and enable the articulation of such anxieties as intelligible models and offer themselves as sites for their signification, all while falling short of providing them with a viable and sustainable resolution. They variously describe the right-wing extremist as something on the order of a rebel without a cause, a forlorn casualty of neoliberal capitalism; as a reservoir of drives and desires, the target for therapeutic techniques; as the subject of rational deliberation and a cognitive receptacle of knowledge; as a docile body, the site for the disciplinary performances of modern power; and finally, too, as bodily habitus and locomotive style, a physical appearance responsive to aesthetic refinement. Each of these diagnoses could also be understood as a distinct, contemporary rendering of politics. In diagnosing and treating a "political" malady, these rehabilitative efforts effectively collapse politics itself into an ethics of resignation and affective states of resentment, into the scientific discourses of institutionally authorized expertise, or into aesthetic style.[7]

Perhaps, then, the key to understanding the divergent modes of therapeutic knowledge that operate within the governance of hate is to be found less in the different answers they provide and more in the similar questions they pose: What precisely is the right-wing extremist Thing about the right-wing extremist subject? Where is the locus of this malady? What is its etiology? Such questions are of obvious concern to a project of governance that seeks to manage hate. They sustain a compulsive drive to locate and root out the right-wing extremist Thing within the political delinquent, giving rise to ever more innovative attempts to capture and contain it. At the same time, the ways in which these modes of therapeutic knowledge subvert their own efforts just as much as their relentless proliferation bespeak an excess that defies any reassuring significations: the right-wing extremist political delinquent is never merely a socially disaffected youth, a hardened corporeality, an irrational mind. In their keenness to subjugate the specter of an illicit and genocidal nationalism, these therapeutic sciences cannot bring historical closure or restore the social order. Instead, by reaffirming the truth of the right-wing extremist Thing and implanting it within the operations of governance, they reinscribe it in the very heart of the nascent German national project.

The enchantments that unsettle these efforts to crack open the political delinquent suggest more than a secular project of governance. They indicate a deep concern with understanding how good might turn into evil—for example, how working-class protest might express itself as bigoted, violent resentment, or how domestic violence could turn an innocent child into a brutal neo-Nazi. The governance of hate appears as an arena for making the National Socialist specter, which still haunts Germany today as the sign of pure evil, legible and hence manageable. It provides a space for articulating within concrete discourses, practices, and institutions the need for domestication itself; in other words, the need for domesticating the very possibility that domestication is impossible. The vigorous and constantly expanding spectrum of reformative sciences that flourish today around the political delinquent amounts to a project of signifying, elaborating, and circumscribing this urgent need within a corpus of therapeutic procedures and disciplinary techniques. As we have seen in this

---

[7]Such renderings strongly echo a range of contemporary obituaries to politics: the end of history and the flattening of temporality (Jameson 2003; Lomnitz 2003; Guyer 2007); the seemingly inescapable reign of neoliberal capitalism and the frustrating impossibility of imagining alternative futurities (Jameson 2004; Žižek 2008; Muehlebach and Shoshan 2012); the reduction of social and economic antagonisms to lifestyle choices, consumer identities, and fashions (Comaroff and Comaroff 2001; Shoshan 2012); the delegitimization of political struggle as protest populism and the criminalization of the underclass (Wacquant 2001; Harcourt 2010); and the displacement of substantive political processes by bureaucratic proceduralism, administrative rationalism, and the rule of experts (Žižek 1997; Rose 2000a).

and previous chapters, however, this arena is also precisely the place in which this evil inexorably re-erupts as unmanageable or as not-yet-manageable. The sciences of managing hate time and again resuscitate that which they would tame. Balancing on the edge of domestication, they flirt with their own futility.

This imperative to tame Evil through its signification is not new to Germany, of course. Its urgency has imposed itself upon various intellectuals at least since the Second World War (though arguably already in the aftermath of the First).[8] And yet this project of signification responds not simply to the shadow of National Socialist evil but rather seeks to negotiate the myriad ways in which this sinister past hovers over the very contemporary dilemmas of German nationhood, and particularly its troubled relation to immigration and cultural difference (Shoshan 2008b). In this sense, the management of hate only partially—and perhaps not primarily—addresses the right-wing extremist. If its concern reveals itself to revolve around the working through of a present national aporia, its addressee comprises far wider, national publics. And it is to these publics that I turn my attention in chapters 8 and 9.

---

[8] Some of the canonical reflections on this question include Sigmund Freud's interwar writings, from *Group Psychology and the Analysis of the Ego* (1975b) or *Civilization and Its Discontents* (2005) to *Beyond the Pleasure Principle* (1975a); Hannah Arendt's *The Origins of Totalitarianism* (1973) and *Eichmann in Jerusalem* (1994); Adorno's theory of the authoritarian personality (1950); and, more recently, Klaus Theweleit's *Male Fantasies* (1987).

Part III
||||||||||||||||

Inoculating the National Public

THE GERMAN EXPRESSION "LOVE GOES THROUGH THE STOMACH" (Liebe geht durch den Magen) is roughly equivalent to the English phrase "the way to a man's heart is through his stomach," if less explicitly gender-marked. It would seem to permit greater latitude than its English counterpart for creative variations. According to the heading of a brochure widely distributed throughout Treptow-Köpenick in the summer of 2005, "Tolerance," too, "goes through the stomach." The subheading of the glossy foldout leaflet promised "international gastronomy 'from Döner [kebab] to Dinner' in Berlin Treptow/Köpenick." Its colorful front opened to list some fifteen "foreign" food establishments in the district: several Turkish bistros, a Thai restaurant, a pizza delivery service, a handful of Italian ice-cream parlors and restaurants, and three McDonald's locations. On its backside, a brief text outlined the rationale behind the brochure as follows:

> Many people in the district of Treptow-Köpenick have long worked together with politicians and administrators for a democratic and tolerant collective life for all citizens. Yet time and again the public has also confronted rightist and racist propaganda and violence.
>
> The "Coalition for Democracy and Tolerance, against Xenophobia and Racism," which brings together many associations, initiatives, and political parties, calls to address this development in creative ways.
>
> [This brochure] shows (by no means exhaustively) how colorful and diverse the gastronomy in our district is. Numerous foreign restauranteurs enrich the available [culinary] spectrum, and the citizens of and visitors to Treptow-Köpenick benefit from the wide international variety, "from Döner to Dinner."
>
> Not only love, but also tolerance goes through the stomach. Foreign cuisine is a culinary and cultural enrichment of our everyday life.
>
> For this reason, with this flyer the participants [in the Coalition] promote tolerance and solidarity, while simultaneously drawing attention to the culinary pleasures of our district.

Given the gravity of the issue at hand, the brochure's tone might seem remarkable, perhaps even outlandish. The two puns on its front—"tolerance goes through the stomach" and "from Döner to Dinner"—endow it with a playful, humorous tone. It seeks, in this sense, to present a clever, self-assured textual take on the rather sinister relation between the kebab and the sausage that I described in chapter 3. And yet, in its performance of gastronomical exorcism against the specter of right-wing extremism, armed as it came with McDonald's restaurants and gelato joints, it betrayed at the same time a certain nervousness, a certain hesitation, a certain self-doubt. My informants, as we saw in chapter 3, would view none but the Turkish and Thai establishments as foreign, and few of them would avoid even these. Like the rehabilitative projects examined in chapter 7, here, too, we encounter an uncontrollable reflex of sorts, a stab at taming a phantasmagoric presence that remains as unbearable as it is intractable.

But the curious little brochure also tells a different story, if only we pause to consider the social processes and historical context from which it emerged as a finished product. To begin with, it came to life as a joint initiative of the business association of the district, its tourism association, and its "Coalition for Democracy and Tolerance," an alliance of local civil society organizations and municipal service providers that the mayor of the district called into life and that he has perseveringly supported. In that sense, the brochure no doubt shows how seamlessly the political struggle against racism and xenophobia could be welded with commercial interests in general, and with the business interests of the local gastronomy and tourism sectors in particular. But more important, and at a more general level, the brochure provides a useful illustration of how, through that very struggle, local interests (in this case, commercial) coalesce with a diverse host of other forces operative at multiple scales in today's Germany, including with those at work in other local contexts, to produce a project of national proportions. Groups and associations in Treptow-Köpenick come together with innumerable other civil society actors, municipal initiatives, state programs, and federal projects that perform similar actions, and that replicate and borrow from one another both across scales and within them.

In this view, the little brochure stands as a local token or synecdoche of a far broader, national project. In chapter 1, I described how the national question, already on the horizon throughout the 1980s, made a particularly forceful return with the upheaval of 1989. In the wake of reunification, the national crusade against right-wing extremism, in the arsenal of which we may surely count the leaflet, has supplied one key answer to this question. This crusade has elaborated and made available an entire symbolic vocabulary for reimagining a national collectivity precisely in its very opposition to the nationalist specter. The post-reunification resignification of the national community has proceeded under the slogans of tolerance, democracy, open-mindedness (*Weltöffentlichkeit*), and civil society, which have been brandished as the banners of the war against the right-wing extremist peril.

In serving as a lexicon of metaphors that structure the embryonic project of German nationhood, such catchphrases operate as what Ernesto Laclau termed "empty signifiers" (1996c). They articulate—to the extent that they operate effectively, at least—a heterogeneous array of political stakes and disparate cultural projects into a collectivity, in this case of the national form, that through them gains a relative coherence. How well they do so depends, of course, on the degree to which they have succeeded in becoming hegemonic representations of the community that they seek to call into existence. That they exist today as one salient ideological project of interpellating German nationhood by no means implies that they have in fact attained a hegemonic grip on such representation. They are but contenders, if weighty ones, to be sure, over the project of nation, and their triumphs must always remain incomplete and socially uneven. Thus, for example, multicultural, tolerant Germany must continue to accommodate world export-power Germany, ecologically responsible Germany, and so forth. Significantly, the political function of such representations of the national community as empty signifiers should not distract us from their actual semiotic, historical, and cultural fullness, that is, from the entire spectrum of values with which they are burdened through their genealogical histories, through the sorts of political forces with which they have been associated, by virtue of their social positionality, and as a result of their institutional modes of production (cf. Bakhtin 1998a).[1]

The brochure—and innumerable other artifacts like it—therefore not only expose the sorts of anxieties that violent nationalism provokes and the multiple efforts at its domestication but also signaled how that same anxiety and the varied projects, discourses, and practices that it calls into being serve today to mobilize and fuse together a heterogeneous ensemble of forces. The management of hate here appears, then, less as a set of repressive mechanisms that come to bear on politically deviant attitudes and more as productive precisely of the national Thing. The "Döner to Dinner" brochure and others like it partake in, mimic, and ventriloquize the ideological idioms that government programs elaborate and disseminate, and to that extent they operate as instruments of state apparatuses. They receive their coherence from flagship EU or federal programs such as Civitas, about which I will say more shortly, and which provide the centripetal discursive forces that keep them sufficiently uniform, even if they receive no direct funds from these programs or share no immediate institutional relations with them. Their fields of action overlap, and they borrow their concepts, key phrases, and strategic models from such centralized government programs.

[1] Thus, democracy, for example, has long formed a central pillar of West Germany's construction of difference with respect to its National Socialist past as well as its socialist contemporary, and its political charge today therefore bears strong traces of this history. Yet, bound as it has become with tolerance of cultural difference, its value has also significantly shifted over the past few decades.

At the same time, the ideological project of nationhood of which the brochure partakes links up in interesting ways with the legal and penal regimes and mechanisms of surveillance that I described in chapters 4 through 7. At first sight, a number of contrasts appear to hold them apart. Institutionally, we find on one side juridical authorities, law enforcement agencies, and corrective offices, while on the other we encounter a medley of associations that exhibit far less uniformity and hierarchical structure. The actors seem quite different as well: formally trained practitioners dedicated to the task of repressing or rehabilitating right-wing extremists in one case, and social workers, youth workers, clergy, businesspeople, local politicians, teachers, or concerned citizens who, for a variety of reasons, do their best to support the cause of tolerance and multicultural diversity in the second. Accordingly, too, the methods they employ vary greatly in the extent to which they are formalized, codified, and hierarchically configured. But their strongest point of contrast no doubt concerns their targets: on the one hand, the rather limited if hypervisible population of political delinquents and other aberrant nationalists, and on the other the far wider publics of so-called ordinary citizens, seen as potentially vulnerable to—but not yet under—the spell of racist nationalism, as possibly active allies in the struggle but as still too complacently passive to join it, or as those who could but at present do not sufficiently appreciate the benefits of cosmopolitan openness to cultural diversity.

On closer view, these two fields of affective governance reveal themselves as more intimately intertwined than one might initially suppose. For a start, we find significant crossover between the organizations and groups that carry them through. Local associations that promote cultural diversity sometimes also keep watch over and document extreme right activities or incidents of racist and political violence. An organization dedicated to reforming active neo-Nazis such as EXIT, which we encountered in chapter 7, at the same time sends out its exemplary success cases to speak at schools as a manner of reducing the vulnerability of students to xenophobic ideology and curbing its appeal. Moreover, often the control and reform of right-wing extremists on the one hand and the gospel of multicultural tolerance on the other, even when different organizations stand behind them, and notwithstanding that they purport to address different populations, nevertheless target the very same situations. Consider how Gangway, with its surveillance and governance functions sharply honed on local rightist youths, intervenes upon a scene—the district of Treptow and, more specifically, neighborhoods such as Altglienicke or Johannisthal—that is perceived as particularly problematic, alongside a range of other organizations that, as we shall see, promote intercultural exchange and democratic participation among local residents at large. At a more profound level, the entire effort of orchestrating affective relations to difference—whether by managing violence and xenophobia at the political margins or by positively valorizing diversity at the presumed center—defines itself in relation to similar referents, weaves together parallel narratives, and rests on analogous ideological frameworks. Both modalities of affective governance appeal to the same empty master signifiers, the same building blocks of the new nation, and calibrate their efforts with respect to them.

In the remainder of this chapter, I examine this rather hodgepodge mix of actors and stakes that gain a measure of ideological coherence, if always emergent, around the node of right-wing extremism, and that perform the labor of fomenting, among relatively broad publics, both active opposition to it and a certain passive resilience against it. I begin by considering how the state stimulates this activity as a mode of managing hate, looking particularly at the flagship governmental program Civitas as an illustrative case. I then review some of the varied agents and stakes that merge together in this collective effort by examining several instances taken from my field site. Finally, I interrogate how these disparate forces mobilize into action by looking at one instance of a protest against a right-wing extremist march through Treptow-Köpenick. I focus less on the dramaturgical, ritualized, or spectacular dimensions of this event, which ethnographies often emphasize, and more on its political sociology and its painstaking production in order to reflect upon the labor that it requires, the labor it performs, and the labor performed in it.

My aim is not only to describe how this campaign works but also, more important, to understand the ways in which affective forms traverse and define it; put differently, how the governance of affect is itself affectively saturated. Governance as the mediation of nationalist affect, as its signification, as the management and policing of its taboos and its proscriptions, is perhaps a particularly interesting instance with which to think about this question. As this book argues, the management of hate has been crucial for the project of a German national collectivity in the post-reunification era. The fight against nationalism, in this sense, has become part of the nation-building process itself. It is, of course, precisely those heightened anxieties about nationalist sentiment and politics in the postwar period that today render the fight against the far right especially apposite—if not indispensable—for fabricating a seemingly innocuous German nationalism. The figure of the right-wing extremist, as I explained in chapter 2 (and see Shoshan 2008a), has in post-reunification Germany been invested with East German associations. It therefore incarnates not only the specter of National Socialism but also the trauma of communism. Through it, today's national project therefore comes to terms with both pasts. However, the anxieties evident in the materials I consider in this chapter about the "Nazi within" implant this figure at the heart of a national project that strives, in vain, to claim for itself the status of normalcy.

To be sure, to a certain extent the fight against right-wing extremism provides some sort of alibi that permits ugly nationalism to proceed unheeded elsewhere. This is perhaps particularly the case when it appears as rhetorical gesture or in the form of financial support. However, government-funded projects to counter neo-Nazi movements are certainly not—or not only—cynical public relations ploys to distract attention from nationalism, even as they create valuable capital for political contenders. Yet my point here is different. I am interested in understanding how, in the past two decades, the fabrication and rebranding of German nationalism has increasingly advanced as broad mobilization against right-wing extremism. In other words, I am less interested in asking whether or not this mobilization against illicit nationalism has distracted public attention from the prospering of nationalism elsewhere and more in examining how it has itself provided an important site for advancing a nationalist project. In this view, the national project in contemporary Germany has held a fundamental stake in the management of hate from the start.

A CIVILIZING MISSION

In the year 2000, Chancellor Gerhard Schröder addressed the German public with a call for an *Aufstand der Anständigen*, a phrase perhaps best translated as a "revolt of the righteous."[2] The call for a revolt by the chancellor himself—commanding a comfortable margin in Parliament and already two years into his tenure—cannot but seem deeply ironic. The immediate background for it was an arson attack on a synagogue. With his call, the chancellor urged Germans to stop tolerating anti-Semitism and to show greater civil courage. In Germany, the word *Zivilcourage* carries strong and painful associations with the history of National Socialism. It evokes that which ordinary Germans by and large lacked during the Third Reich. It suggests the question of whether one would have had the courage to take a stand for the Jews and other victims of its atrocities. To be sure, often such questions remain as implicit compulsions that traverse uses of the word *Zivilcourage* and that grant it its ideological charge (cf. AG Netzwerke gegen Rechtsextremismus; Bakhtin 1998a). As frequently, however, these questions are explicitly and vividly discussed in intimate conversations. The national interpellation for *Zivilcourage* is, in this sense, also the promise of self-redemption.

Before long, however, Schröder's call for the revolt of the righteous came to reference much more than standing up for Jews and synagogues alone. It increasingly described civil engagement against racism and xenophobia at large, appearing in association with various efforts in the fight against right-wing extremism or different campaigns for tolerance and diversity. The attack on the synagogue was only the latest in a number of disturbingly brutal incidents of violent nationalism that Germany had witnessed in the late nineties, and Schröder's exhortation was therefore from the start in some sense a desperate and

---

[2] The phrase is difficult to do justice to in English. The word *Aufstand* designates a revolt or an uprising, while *anständig* means respectable, decent, civil.

indiscriminate call of "enough." One of its principal concrete results consisted in the initiative "Youth for Tolerance and Democracy against Right-Wing Extremism, Xenophobia, and Anti-Semitism," which served as an umbrella for several different programs through which the federal government funneled money into the campaign against the extreme right. The resources it made available were key to the mushrooming of projects against right-wing extremism throughout Germany, even as they disproportionately focused their efforts on the East. Funding often came from the European Social Fund, sometimes complemented by state or municipal budgets. When the Christian Democrats under Merkel returned to power in 2005, they hurried to scrap the Social Democrat and Green initiative, but only to replace it with a federal program of their own. While the CDU plan differed in certain respects,[3] it preserved not only much of the federal investment that the previous government had consolidated but also many of the general outlines and operative principles of the earlier initiative. By that time, too, some local projects had become self-sustaining, while others had successfully secured state and municipal support.

My discussion here is of the initiative as it stood between 2001 and 2006, at the time of my fieldwork, when it rested principally on three programs: Civitas, Entimon, and Xenos. "Civitas—Initiative against Right-Wing Extremism in the New Federal States" focused exclusively on the former East German territories and embodied what I described in chapter 7 as a "political culture" approach to the problem of racism and xenophobia. The explicit aim of Civitas was to establish and reinforce, in the presumably empty terrain of the East, civil society structures that would counter the gains of extreme right movements and the pervasiveness of racism and antidemocratic currents by promoting a political culture of democracy and tolerance. It was illustrative of the way in which, as I explained in chapter 1, post-reunification West Germany reenacted the drama of postwar American-driven democratization, this time standing as the protagonist who intervenes to teach democracy and thereby claiming itself as already transformed, as already prepared to play that part (Borneman 1993).

Civitas was initially not projected to continue indefinitely. Instead, it was expected to provide the groundwork for autonomous, self-sustaining civil society structures that would progressively turn resilient enough to persevere without it. The program prioritized three areas: victims' organizations (*Opferberatungsstelle*), so-called network posts (*Netzwerkstelle*), and mobile teams. As members of one victims' organization active in Berlin told me, they engaged in a variety of activities that had victims of right-wing extremist violence and abuse as their principal concern: providing them with psychological and legal counseling, to be sure, but also lobbying for them with the authorities, running public campaigns on their behalf, and compiling chronicles of violent and

---

[3] For example, the CDU plan placed more emphasis on the fight against extremism in general rather than right-wing extremism in particular.

racist incidents. Network posts were expected to coordinate disparate efforts, build coalitions between actors, provide professional know-how, assist with identifying and securing financial resources, organize events, and keep track of developments in regional extreme right scenes. In network post offices in Berlin, one could find innumerable leaflets and brochures of projects past and present. Last, mobile consulting teams were supposed to deploy temporarily to intervene in particular crisis situations, in response to invitations from local authorities, pertinent institutions (schools, for example), or affected groups. The MBR (acronym for Mobile Consulting against Right-Wing Extremism), about which I will say more below, was one such team. It was with this combination of victims-oriented work, networking, and deployable teams that Civitas, it was hoped, would kick-start a critical mass of civil society actors vigorous enough to transform the allegedly defunct political culture of the East.

Two other programs besides Civitas formed part of the initiative, though their immediate presence in the areas where I worked was less pronounced. "Entimon—Together against Violence and Right-Wing Extremism" distinguished itself from Civitas in that it was designed not to sow the seeds for a future civil society but rather to supply presumably already existing structures with resources for projects and events. Accordingly, it operated in both East and West. Last, "Xenos—Living and Working in Diversity" was funded by the EU and targeted the labor market. It promoted initiatives for improving the employment prospects of the unemployed or facilitating their return to work, with particular attention to multicultural tolerance and discrimination or racism at the workplace or in vocational training. In this effort, it targeted and mobilized businesses, professional associations, unions, localities, vocational training institutions, and schools. It was therefore a rather peculiar articulation of the management of hate with the governance of labor and of the unemployed.

While the Federal Ministry for Family, Seniors, Women, and Youth (BMFSFJ) and the Federal Ministry for Economy and Labor (BMWA) administered the programs, the better part of their budget came from the EU Social Fund. The disbursement of funds to individual projects, in turn, often prioritized participatory schemes, leveraging EU and federal contributions with state and municipal ones. In this manner, it was hoped, centralized funding would activate a great range of other resources and forces, from local governments or church organizations to political parties, foundations, labor unions, private sector initiatives, multicultural and immigrant NGOs, sports associations, youth movements, or schools, all of which it motivated to develop and implement appropriate projects. Both the funding structure and the administrative organization of these programs therefore traversed a variety of scales, institutional boundaries, social spheres, and political affiliations. The initiative breathed life into an alliance that brought together distinct scales of the state and disparate groups and stakes in a mode that borrowed heavily on contemporary discourses of neoliberal governance

(Brenner and Theodore 2002; Sharma 2006), which, as I noted in chapter 6, emphasize horizontality, networks, and adaptability. Consider, for example, the very notions of network posts and mobile consulting teams, both central to the strategy of Civitas, and both indicating a specifically neoliberal imagination of what governance should look like.

No doubt, youth movements, immigrant organizations, certain political parties, church groups, and many other forces that this governmental effort targets and mobilizes have long engaged against right-wing extremism and racist violence with steady commitment and independently of state-led campaigns. It would therefore be a gross exaggeration, if not an outright fabrication, to grant the federal programs I have discussed much of the credit for the numerous efforts in this field. Still, at several levels, they have served a key function in binding these heterogeneous forces in particular ways, in molding them into a seemingly cohesive agglomeration of actors, and in endowing them with a certain coherence of content. In installing a network post at a given locality, for example, Civitas facilitated the aggregation and coordination of various local resources and actors. It also boosted their articulation with translocal institutions, knowledge, and funding opportunities. At least to the extent that it operated effectively, it created possibilities for institutional contact and collaboration both within and between scales. The leveraged funding structure no doubt also aimed to integrate different scales of governance by creating local investments in the initiative. Budgetary regulations and the terms of standard evaluation procedures promoted cooperation between distinct instances of governance and/or other stakeholders, stimulating the emergence of coalitions and campaigns with a broad range of participants.

But they also performed work that was as important, indeed, that was indispensable for the management of hate at a symbolic and ideological level. They have provided the management of hate with a stable vocabulary of empty signifiers, which were at once quite ideologically full in the sense I discussed above.[4] Consider, for example, the phrase *bunt statt braun* (colorful instead of brown),[4] which appeared on one occasion as the heading for a flyer urging residents to show up for a protest against a neo-Nazi march through Schöneweide, on another as the slogan of an initiative against racism and intolerance by teachers, students, and parents at a small-town high school, and on yet another as the name of a youth association active against right-wing extremism. Or take, as another example, the term *weltoffen* (open-minded),[5] which may appear as *weltoffenes Deutschland* in the name of a national NGO, as the *weltoffenes und tolerantes Sachsen* (open-minded and tolerant Saxony) state program against

---

[4] The color brown, in Germany's color-coded political system, stands for National Socialism.

[5] More precisely, *weltoffen* means a certain openness to the world, hence, a sort of cosmopolitan open-mindedness.

right-wing extremism in Saxony, or in the name of a local coalition such as the Netzwerk für Toleranz und Weltoffenheit Bernau (Bernau Network for Tolerance and Open-Mindedness). Or, finally, take the expression *Gesicht zeigen* (to show [one's] face),[6] which may serve as the name of a local mobilization against an upcoming extreme right demonstration or appear in countless news reports in the form of *Gesicht zeigen statt wegschauen* (show one's face instead of looking the other way), referring to that which upstanding citizens must do, and sometimes have done, in the face of the nationalist threat.

All these phrases, and a number of others, too, outline a moral space for the nascent nation and set out some of its key ethical principles. It is to be a nation that places value on its own diversity; condemns monochromatic national imaginaries; respects, accepts, and shows interest in the larger world around it; eagerly fulfills its moral obligations to civility; and stands up to evil. Its national subjects, then, would not only subscribe to cosmopolitan and multicultural values but would also be expected to demonstrate the proper character, to show, in other words, the decency, courage, and commitment to defend those values. Defending those values, each of which—including the very courage to fight for them—clearly references and marks a contrast with the National Socialist past (and, to a lesser extent, the communist one), implies here making both Germany and the world at large safe from German nationalism itself. One wants to ask, then, what is precisely the face that the Germans are urged to show? Do the campaigns against right-wing extremism assume, and imply, that fellow nationals are, in fact, largely tolerant of cultural difference, cosmopolitan in their worldview, and democratic in their political orientations, and that they need only make public their convictions and act upon them? Do they call up a silent majority that holds the correct values but remains passively invisible? Or do they seek to interpellate as this new national subject a public that is not only indifferent but that also, by implication, holds unsavory affective and ideological commitments? And further, beyond the question of what face is to be shown, and whose, we may also ask to and for whom. No doubt, one must show one's face to the young neo-Nazis marching through town, and in this way stand up to them, shame them publicly, and hold up to them their political perversion, their rejection by their society, and the intolerability of their intolerance. Yet the crowds of nationalists are not only antagonists who must be made to encounter the disapproving face of their fellow citizens but also a stage set that allows Germans today to show their true face to one another and, perhaps most important, to the world at large. Their presence in that sense creates sites and moments for performing Germany, and for performing it well, in-line with the national project to which these empty signifiers I have discussed give form.

---

[6] *Gesicht zeigen* implies showing up and putting up active resistance, as opposed to passive indifference.

BUILDING COALITIONS

The multicultural dining brochure with which I opened this chapter was not itself directly affiliated with any of the federal programs. It was the product, as I explained, of a joint initiative between local business advocacy associations and the district's Coalition for Democracy and Tolerance (henceforth, the Coalition). The latter, in turn, was called into existence by Treptow- Köpenick's mayor at the time, and, relying on municipal sponsorship, comprised numerous actors: youth clubs, real estate associations, schools, NGOs, municipal officials, and more. The mayor's call to join forces in the Coalition literally hailed these actors as the local protagonists in the struggle against the extreme right in the district. Those who had long held stakes in that struggle—for example, youth clubs whose staff encountered difficulties with right-wing extremist visitors— were no exception. They often found their efforts reframed as they became collaborators within the umbrella initiative.

It is therefore difficult to trace any clear frontiers separating civil society from the state here. The effort to incorporate isolated, relatively independent forces into a centralized front does not seem to suggest an increase in the autonomy of the former from the latter. In one evident sense, the state interpellates the Coalition as civil society in the first place. The result is a relatively wide spectrum of actors with varying degrees of commitment and different stakes, from commercial interests or community and immigrant groups to governmental and paragovernmental agents of governance or NGOs specializing in the management of hate. The Coalition in Treptow-Köpenick included, for example, a school in the district affected by right-wing extremism; a youth club, one of several, where right-wing extremist visitors repeatedly presented challenges; and the Civitas-propelled mobile team MBR, which was called in to intervene in a crisis situation and subsequently established itself more or less permanently in the district. From the publications of federal programs or the offices of the Berlin Commissioner (*Beauftragter*) for Migration and Integration to the documents of mobile intervention teams or the announcement board in the local youth club lounge, members of the Coalition and others with identical commitments enunciate a similar discourse about diversity, tolerance, and open-mindedness. They advance a certain narrative about the nation while often remaining critical of that narrative as well. At the same time, such broad collaborations, despite their numerous members, often remain relatively local and frequently show a strong concern for the image-management of particular places, hoping to re-brand them as safe and tolerant.

On one occasion, for example, the Coalition participated in the organization of an "Intercultural Festival for Democracy and Tolerance" at the vicinity of the Schöneweide train station, an area ill-reputed for high levels of extreme right activities. Under the slogan "Schöneweide lives/loves diversity" (Schöneweide l[i]ebt bunt), the festival symbolically occupied the open area in front of the

train station and the adjacent mall. Its stated purpose was to raise public awareness of, and to counteract, the area's disrepute as a "fear zone" for potential victims of right-wing extremist violence, as well as to protest against the prevalence
of extreme right strongholds in its vicinity. The festival included two stages, one
at each end, which hosted multicultural performances and music concerts. Stands
throughout the area offered their literature—on human rights, local right-wing
extremist activities, and projects for tolerance and diversity—or served delica-
cies from assorted international cuisines. The day saw book readings and public discussions, as well as a street theater performance and an art installation.
Graffiti workshops kept some of the younger visitors busy in one corner. Here,
too, the list of supporters and participants was long and included municipal authorities, church groups, private sponsors, political parties, several local forums
and coalitions, and antiracist, anti-right-wing extremist, and immigrant NGOs.

Preparations for the event had been under way for several months and could
be witnessed, for example, in the rehearsal rooms of youth clubs in the district.
The actual audience at the festival did not number more than a couple of hundred at any given point. Mostly, it consisted of two distinct groups. The first
included the different organizations that participated in producing the festival,
their staff, their members, and people who in one way or another were directly
related to them. The second was comprised of young antifascist militants who
arrived by train from throughout Berlin to take over the notorious Schöneweide station. Virtually all who were present could be assigned to one of these
two groups, a fact that, to some of my informants, indicated failure to mobilize
so-called ordinary citizens. A couple of blocks away, Karl, the eighteen-year-
old militant whose distinction between immigrants of different ethnic groups
I examined in chapter 3, helped out, together with some of his peers, in a soup
kitchen street stall organized by the NPD in response to the festival and held
on the curb across from a restaurant infamous as a popular meeting place for
right-wing extremists. A thick line of police troops blocked raucous crowds of
antifascist activists from reaching Karl and his friends.

The democracy festival exhibited certain unmistakable similarities to the
SPD assembly at Khan's, which I described in detail in chapter 6, and which almost brought the social workers' activities there to an abrupt end. For one, both
construed the right-wing extremist Thing as a quality of place. They operated
on the assumption that, to paraphrase Keith Basso (1996), right-wing extremism "sits in places," and, furthermore, that it should be banished from them.
Second, both involved something of the adventurous thrill of journeying deep
into the heart of darkness. This thrill, to be sure, contained its own measure of
anxiety, evident in the attentive concern with security arrangements at both
events. Finally, they shared the strategic notion of a transitory occupation of
hostile territory as a path to its recuperation. A single intervention, or at best
a periodic one, could, according to this logic, exercise a lasting impact upon a
local, quotidian landscape.

The efforts of mobilization, the range of actors, and the height of effervescence all peak during the periodic extravaganzas of demonstrations and counterdemonstrations. There, the entire spectrum of actors that I have already described, strengthened by many more who join from across the city and beyond it, come together publicly and massively in a moment of nation-making. Taken as events, marches and demonstrations are no doubt spectacular moments blessed with their own ritual poetics. But taken as a process, the demonstration itself appears as the result of painstaking preparations, on all sides, in the weeks and months that precede it. Below, I look at one such demonstration to reflect on its process of production, in which the tolerant nation is imagined, rehearsed, and performed. I show how the very different actors that the event invokes come to march together behind the same national banners.

The demonstration takes us back to Becker, the NPD cadre who, as I mentioned in chapter 3, recruited young activists among the social circles of my informants. Becker's efforts were particularly successful with a clique of dropouts who were kicked out of high school and banned from youth clubs for their nationalism, and who passed their time at the park in Johannisthal. After leaving the NPD and grounding the BASO Kameradschaft with the support of his young followers, in the fall of 2003 Becker staged a demonstration for the future of German youth in general and for a local youth club for nationalists barred from entering existing venues in particular (see chapter 1). In chapter 6, I discussed how Helmuth called an NGO to warn of the advent of a demonstration in the district. The organization he called was the MBR. This phone call took place in the fall of 2004, and Helmuth was reporting news of the planning of a second march, the first alarming sign that the BASO demonstration would, as in fact it did, become an annual ritual. Worse still, on this occasion Becker and his BASO troops were joined by several leading national figures—including Gordon Reinholz, who starred in the documentary film *Globalization and Xenophobia*, which I analyzed in chapter 7—and their followers. This novel development sparked fears that what had begun as a very parochial campaign for a local youth center could crown Treptow as the site for massive annual demonstrations with nationwide mobilizations.

In fact, most of my right-wing extremist acquaintances in Treptow showed little interest in the demonstration. Some were entirely ignorant of it, others indifferent, while still others were concerned about the high risk that attending such a potentially explosive event could entail for them. I found greater awareness of the upcoming march and more sympathy with its organizers among my informants from the social circles of the BASO Kameradschaft, like Karl, Elsa, Jens, Lisa, Karla, and their friends. They reported secret meetings, which they claimed to have attended at a local pub popular with right-wing extremists, not far from the Schöneweide train station, where Becker and the BASO members discussed logistics and tactics. Becker had long established a short message service (SMS) distribution list with which he kept his sympathizers up-to-date on various issues of interest to them: Kameradschaft meetings, political actions, music concerts, TV programs, or demonstrations in Berlin and its vicinity. More than a handful of my informants had been receiving sporadic messages from Becker about the upcoming event and the ongoing preparations. Beyond the restricted circulation of clandestine gatherings and SMS distribution lists, information about the event also took center stage on the websites of several extreme right groups. Internet exposure no doubt provided far broader visibility than SMS lists or pub conversations. Yet these websites too still addressed the initiated: mostly right-wing extremist publics but also Antifa activists and state authorities watching over their activities. They were not aimed for, and did not reach, the general public.

Thus, extreme right publicity for the march aimed at an audience of insiders, many of whom were linked through personal acquaintance. The broad and less discriminate publicity of the event was left to the Antifa, the press, and various civil society associations and coalitions that called for wide mobilizations against it. On the streets of the district, where Antifa posters calling to halt the "Nazis" were hanging everywhere, announcements about the demonstration from those "Nazis" themselves were nowhere to be seen. Working according to a well-rehearsed routine and utilizing established circuits of communication, the forces that sought to oppose the march amplified its echo far beyond intimate or local circles. Militant calls for countermobilization quickly appeared throughout Antifa websites. As the date grew near, Antifa posters urging residents to "Get out on the streets!" and "Whip BASO's ass!" suffused the district's sidewalks. In a less belligerent tone, the local press informed the wider public about the demonstration and the planned protests against it. Newspapers published petitions signed by politicians, intellectuals, celebrities, and other public figures to ban the march. Reporters covered the deliberations on possible countermeasures against it within the district's Coalition. They detailed the expected turnout of demonstrators, counterdemonstrators, and police troops, and mapped the projected route of the march. And they listed the various associations engaged in sponsoring and organizing the protests, which included the entire spectrum of forums and coalitions that I already mentioned (*Berliner Morgenpost* 2004a and 2004b; RBB 2004b).

The MBR played a crucial role in securing broad media exposure. Its members granted interviews and appeared in public forums to inform citizens about the BASO Kameradschaft, its campaign for a nationalist youth club, and the planned protests against it. The website of the organization offered detailed information on these issues as well, and continually provided updates on new developments. It included an annotated map, on which color-coded lines and dots marked the predicted route of the march, the sites of counterdemonstrations and protest events, and the likely locations of police barriers. The MBR found itself in a difficult, ambivalent position. On the one hand, it held a clear stake in maximizing the public visibility of the protests, first so as to augment recruitment and mobilization and second as part of its public relations management. This required the intensive circulation of knowledge, as widely as possible, not only about the event itself but also about its background, and particularly about extreme right activities in the Schöneweide area. The strategic need to mobilize otherwise indifferent people into political action permitted little nuance, requiring instead doomsday renderings of the district. On the other hand, the MBR's work often came under criticism for stigmatizing neighborhoods. Following one protest that the organization led against extreme right trends in Schöneweide, for example, one display of graffiti ironically thanked the leader of the MBR for labeling the entire area a neo-Nazi hotspot. The very work of rebranding place as tolerant and democratic entailed as well its prior stigmatization as racist and violent.

In the weeks prior to the demonstration, at youth clubs throughout the district, youth workers and teenagers were hard at work printing posters, painting banners, rehearsing musical shows, and putting together "multicultural" parties. The social workers kept a safe distance from all this animated labor, visible involvement in which could risk their standing with their clients. But they had their own preparations to attend to. Now that they were slated to become an annual routine, the demonstrations offered the social workers a periodic litmus test. They granted them a rare opportunity to assess the level of concrete involvement of their clients in organized political action. As I mentioned in chapter 6, the social workers have drawn a putatively clear redline that precluded them from offering their services to organized right-wing extremists. The problem, of course, was that too often that line appeared anything but clear, and determining who could be classified as organized and who couldn't presented a daunting task that confronted the social workers with highly ambiguous imputations. While joining a march, as they well knew, held no necessary relation to sustained organized activism, the demonstrations nevertheless had the advantage of providing an unequivocal, definite criterion for evaluating the political commitment of youths in the district: either you were there, or you weren't. They therefore facilitated for the social workers the weeding out of those who were too extremist for their taste, and too zealous, in their view, to be helped. But rather than waiting passively for the demonstration to betray to them the true nature of their clients, the social workers took preventive action and made it a point to discuss the march with youths they considered at-risk of participating in it, urging them, instead, to abstain from attending it. The weeks that preceded the demonstration thus witnessed the social workers busily debating the intentions of particular youths, comparing what they had heard from different people, and conjecturing as to which of them might in fact march with the right-wing extremists in the end.

The entire array of forces that had participated in the buildup to the demonstration, each holding its own stakes and carrying its own flags, were all present and expectant as the day of the showdown arrived. The unfolding of the encounter between them, and the way in which its events would be retrospectively understood and narrated, gained critical importance. The respective turnouts that each of them could mobilize would be noted. The different obstacles that they would place in each other's schemes, and particularly the fate of attempts to halt the march, would come under analysis. The media would report, no doubt, about the decibel levels of their altercations. And people present at the demonstration, as much as those who would learn of it from newspapers, radio, or television, would compare the size and number of banners, as well as their aesthetic qualities and their wittiness. All of these suggested that the significance of the events of the day would extend far beyond the demonstration itself, that the latter was perceived and staged as but a metonymic sign of something altogether different. The crowds, noise, paraphernalia, and street confrontations that would inevitably take place all indicated something of vital importance about Treptow-Köpenick in particular and Germany more generally. They would disclose the state of extreme right nationalism, reveal the resilience of antifascist traditions and the esprit de corps of their troops, expose the vitality and commitment of civil society, and say something, too, about the general condition of democratic culture in the country. In short, they would render in visual, spatial form nothing less than the state of the German nation in the neighborhood and, by extension, across the city and beyond it. In what follows, then, I look more closely at the demonstration, not in order to analyze its theatrical spectacles but rather in order to reflect on the publics and projects that converge upon it, and on how, together, if sometimes unwittingly, they perform the labor of nation-building.

WHOSE DEMONSTRATION?

It was a frosty morning in early December and the ordinarily quiet and sparse residential neighborhood of Adlershof, from which the march would set sail, had already metamorphosed into a busy mixture of characters, costumes, noises, and signs. In a small open square across from the train station, dozens of young people who arrived to march in solidarity with German youth gathered. Riot police troops spread around and among them. They huddled close together, flags carrying the shields of various German states and localities or other sundry banners in their hands. Taken as a group, they looked nothing like the conventional images of neo-Nazi demonstrators, and this in two ways. First, the authorities placed strict conditions on the demonstration that precluded the participants from sporting many of their favorite garments or wearing uniforms (understood as any coordinated dress code) and banned any items displaying the black-white-red color combination. Most oppressive, perhaps, the rules prohibited alcohol and cigarettes, both of which were integral to the social life of virtually all my young informants. Their absence in the long hours to come detrimentally slashed the measure of enjoyment to be had at the event. Every so often, the police would plunge into the midst of the young right-wing extremist crowd to circle a transgressor. Some of those who violated the restrictions would face the choice of returning home or braving through the slow and chilly hours that awaited them shirtless or with only socks on their feet. The second notable aspect of their appearance had to do with the sort of young, militant, and extraparliamentary groups that this march in particular mobilized (recall my discussion of shifts in extreme right consumer identities in chapter 1). More than a few people on the small square displayed fashions traditionally associated with radical leftism: Che Guevara shirts, Palestinian scarves, workers' movement red flags, banners hailing international solidarity, and "anarchist" outfits. Meanwhile, the leaders and their helpers were busy with preparations nearby, fitting a vehicle with loudspeakers, while a film crew hovered around them.

In some sense, of course, this was *their* demonstration. After all, their leaders had registered it with the authorities in the first place. But the event, as it unfolded, was decidedly not only—and perhaps, in important ways, not even primarily—theirs. The one-hundred-fifty-odd enthusiasts that they mustered composed but a miniscule fraction of the multitudes that converged upon the district on that day. One notable group on the streets included older antifascist activists, members of Antifa associations that have their roots in the immediate aftermath of the war. Their loyalists paced up and down the sidewalks and displayed their affiliations with buttons, armbands, or banners. A significant number of them bore, in some form or another, the initials of Germany's largest and oldest Antifa organization, VVN-BdA (Vereinigung der Verfolgten des Naziregimes—Bund der Antifaschistinnen und Antifaschisten [Association of the Persecutees of the Nazi Regime—Federation of Antifascists]). While for much of its history the VVN-BdA was banned in the GDR, which set up its own parallel organizations, the association has always kept a communist profile. For many in Treptow who had been active in antifascist associations in the former East, the affinity with the organization, once it returned after reunification, seemed natural. Sympathizers with the VVN-BdA, which survivors of Nazi concentration camps founded within months of the war's end, thus tended to include a relatively older population, with many in their seventies and eighties. The two other important references whose symbolic vocabulary members of this group brandished included the East German peace movement, which gained pace in the 1970s, and the Party of Democratic Socialism (PDS). A small crowd of this group lingered at the gates of a community cultural center that faced the main avenue of the neighborhood, where the march would soon advance. Choral music played through the open windows of the second floor. A wide banner that hung from the roof hailed the antifascist legacy of Stefan Heym, the communist Jewish literature Nobel laureate who narrowly escaped the Nazis only to return from his exile in the United States after the war to the GDR, where he made Treptow-Köpenick his home. The VVN-BdA office was located one train stop away, and its forces were strongly anchored in local life.

Another group that stood out from the rather disorderly multitude of antifascist protesters was the radical and militant anarchist wing of the Antifa, the Autonome. Their young activists sported the standard outfits of sneakers, dark pants and sweatshirts, caps, and sunglasses. For many of my young informants, their figures harbored a secretive aura of fascination and fear. They provided the material from which rumors and myths were woven and circulated. Often, they called up fantasies of merciless brutality (recall Gino's story in chapter 2), sinister sophistication, and menacing omnipresence. Some of my informants told me about identity theft and credit card fraud, with which Autonome activists have financially ruined extreme right activists. I could never verify these stories, but there is no doubt that Autonome activists regularly hack right-wing extremist websites and online shops and subsequently publish the credit card information of their users. One example of less high-tech Antifa tactics was how masked militants intercepted Axel, the former right hand of Becker, whom we met in chapter 3, outside his parents' apartment house. The Antifas clarified that they would leave his parents' place in ruins unless he discontinued his political activism (he obliged). Gino, whose portrait and name dominated Antifa webpages for a while, once recounted to me how three masked Autonome ambushed and punched him. Several of my informants expressed apprehension about participating in the demonstration for fear of possible retaliation by the Autonome.

A splinter within the Autonome scene, the Antideutschen (anti-Germans) were also conspicuous on the streets of Adlershof that morning. Their group matches an uncompromising, fervent hatred of all things German with a zealous, unquestioning support of Israel and of Zionism. It is the latter point especially that marks the tension between the Antideutschen and many other Antifa groups. Some of its followers held Israeli flags that they would later wave, as they always do, at their nationalist enemies (incidentally, their Israeli flag gesture finds its response in the increasing ubiquity of Palestinian flags among right-wing extremist demonstrators in recent years). It is as if they were driving away evil spirits with a crucifix. But their ardent Zionism aside, they shared much with other Autonome Antifa groups, including not only their dress code but also their antagonism to German nationalism, their view of the government as authoritarian, and their critical perspective on capitalism. They were predominantly young, and many arrived from other parts of the city.

Last, another sizable group that found its natural home within the Antifa crowd included punks. In chapter 1, I described how the extreme right in recent years has diversified its styles and incorporated a wide and constantly expanding spectrum of subcultural niches and consumer identities into its circles. Yet the punk has remained among the few characters that still seem to resist such an appropriation. Extreme right nationalists, including almost all of my informants in Treptow, perceive the punk as the most palpable incarnation of the left and of all that is wrong with it: disorder, dirt, indiscipline. In fact, however, the life-style of the punk corresponds in important ways to that of many among my informants, and often involves extended lingering in open spaces such as streets, parks, or train stations. Precisely for that reason, for their similarities rather than their differences, conflicts between the two groups are relatively frequent. Statistically, punks are among the prime targets of extreme right violence.

Several attributes distinguish the Antifa forces from other civil society and governmental actors that partake in the management of hate, many of whom counted with at least some representation in Adlershof that morning. Particularities of fashion and style include several specifically antifascist dress codes, especially for its younger members. More important, the overwhelming incidence of young members, in their teens and early twenties, and of older people, many retired pensioners, makes for a peculiar and atypical age demographics. The long historical genealogy of many Antifa organizations also contrasts with the relatively later appearance of the government agencies or civil society associations that turned out for the protest. Most significant, the different Antifa publics stand apart from other activists against racism and nationalism in their peculiar position within the political landscape. The very use of the term "fascism"—in contradistinction to "right-wing extremism"—already indicates, now perhaps more emphatically than in the past, a strong leftist affiliation, and the Antifa has indeed been home to the socialists, communists, and anarchists who, after all, set it up in the first place. Given its location on the leftist margins of Germany's political map, various voices, including the official Verfassungsschutz reports, have frequently accused several of its groups of antidemocratic political extremism. In all of this, the Antifa remains somewhat heterogeneous to the broad amalgamation of "legitimate" political parties, national labor unions, engaged local politicians, midlevel municipal officials, NGO staff, and various publicly funded initiatives against right-wing extremism, which together converged into a nebulous sphere of civil society in Adlershof.

These last groups flooded the streets with color and noise. Only a stone's throw away from where the crowd of indignant nationalists assembled, the SPD set up a stand. Its activists distributed brochures, flyers, stickers, and colorful balloons to passersby. The loud musical sound track they blasted from speakers spilled relentlessly into the scene like a sonic weapon of spirit exorcism, with selections clearly handpicked to inflict maximal displeasure upon the right-wing extremist ear. The SPD governed Treptow and together with the PDS dominated its political landscape. Its mayor breathed life into the Coalition, just as the party's chancellor at the time, Schröder, put Civitas together. Its local party functionaries (recall here the group whose meeting at Khan's I discussed in chapter 6) took the far right in their neighborhoods seriously and worked diligently to combat it. Many among them shared a commitment to the tradition of antifascist struggle.

The streets around them, and along the projected route of the march, were inundated with identical posters that, under the heading "Berlin against Nazis," showed a crossed-over Hitler Playmobil figure. It was the Coalition that conceived this iconic rendering of Evil in the image of a harmless toy and crowned it as the mascot for the protest. In the run-up to the event, it seemed like all around us we could witness the busy preparations that filled up the schedules of organizations and venues throughout the district. The results of the sustained efforts of the Coalition were everywhere visible. Its members distributed hundreds of small flags and buttons with the Playmobil Hitler logo to passersby. At two small openings along the central avenue, youth clubs had set up stages and sound equipment. At one of these spots, bands took turns blasting at high volume the music they had rehearsed for so long to a young audience that, whether for the rhythm or to avoid hypothermia, danced along. At another stage local DJs filled the air with the sounds of hip-hop, techno, reggae, "ethnic" world music, and other cosmopolitan flavors as an antidote to German nationalism. It was as if they and the throngs of young people who moved to the beat were asserting, at top decibel levels, that there was significantly more fun to be had on the democratic side of things.

Pacing to and fro was virtually the entire lineup of youth workers in the district. For them, as for a number of other municipal service providers who were present, the day saw the culmination of a protracted and arduous buildup that, whether out of their own enthusiastic volition or because they were evidently expected to comply, for a while took priority over other projects and activities at their establishments. Making our way through the crowd, the social workers and I would greet each one of them and stop to chat. Most of them were expectant as to what the day would bring. Most, too, reported fatigue and were pleased that work could soon return to its normal routine. Their different contributions to the protest constituted performances not only in the sense of manifesting publicly their undoubtedly sincere commitment to tolerance and democracy but also to the extent that the fruits of their efforts would come under the scrutiny of a municipal administration that expected them to cooperate and deliver, and that could cut their funding at relatively short notice.

The same double logic held as well for the MBR, whose members shuttled hurriedly and busily between different sites along the route, mobile phones to their ears. Theirs was a particularly frantic morning. They managed much of the press relations for the event, and granted numerous interviews to journalists. They also served as key contacts for municipal officials and local politicians, who would chitchat with them about the protest. Additionally, they carried through much of the coordination and negotiations between the protesters and the massive police forces. They were in charge of the smooth distribution and circulation of the propaganda materials of the Coalition, of which they handed out wholesale quantities to their collaborators. Last, they were the driving force behind the production of the protest as a coherent, organized composition out of scores of individual efforts, a role they fulfilled both in strategic planning and careful preparations during the run-up to the demonstration, and, feverishly, throughout the entire event.

In fact, the Civitas-sponsored MBR played a vital role not only in sparking off and giving outline to counterdemonstrations or to the democracy festival at Schöneweide but also in breathing life into a number of the forces that converged upon the district in the first place. It did so, on the one hand, by mediating between distinct actors and institutions to stimulate the formation of neighborhood-scale associations and district-wide coalitions. But on the other hand, as I have suggested above, it also secured local investment in its cause by ensuring continuous bad press for the district. The image problem that it thereby fomented for the district may have infuriated—as in fact it did—residents and local actors, who resented its conventional portrayal of the city quarter as a sort of National Socialist territory. Yet it also guaranteed the steady commitment of at least certain forces within the district to the struggle.

The different distinctions I describe here are, of course, always ambiguous and oftentimes hardly legible. Though certain tendencies mark them unevenly, no definite ideological, social, or generational boundaries separate the Antifa and so-called democratic civil society, for example. This became uncannily clear at one moment during that morning. As Helmuth and I navigated the multitude, observing and commenting on all the familiar faces, a young person whom I had met only a couple of months earlier crossed our path. I had seen him at a public panel discussion on "New Tendencies of the Extreme Right in Berlin" in a leftist cultural center in another district. There, some ten people sat sparsely on rows of chairs, many of which remained empty. They faced a panel of two speakers, a representative of the MBR and a PDS expert, and a moderator, a former East German economics professor who had been active in the PDS. The young man made several smart and clearly well-informed contributions that triggered my curiosity. After the event had ended, I found him outside with the MBR representative, whom I had already met before, and introduced myself to him. I told him briefly about my research—I had only commenced my fieldwork shortly before—and inquired about his own experience with and knowledge of right-wing extremism. He exchanged uncomfortable looks with the MBR representative and said, eventually, that he did Internet research for the MBR as a volunteer. I expressed interest and asked for his contact information, and he scribbled his e-mail address for me on a note before leaving with his companion. "He is also with the MBR," I informed Helmuth as I pointed at him, discreetly I thought. Helmuth became furious and yelled at me to keep my hand down, and especially not to point it at the Treptow Antifa. The young man had been one of the key activists of the local militant Autonome group. The social workers and their clients had encountered him and his peers on more than one unpleasant occasion. Clearly, the Treptow Autonome shared not only political postures or strategic priorities but also its very members with the MBR, and through it, with the Coalition.

Curiously, one group of actors virtually absent on the streets included the residents of Adlershof, and of other neighborhoods where the march would pass. Above our heads, from the tribunes of small balconies and open windows, the gazes of curious spectators surveyed the turbulence below. Banners and posters, accompanied with a letter from the mayor that urged them to come out in numbers and join the protest against the demonstration, had been distributed to all mailboxes along the route of the march. The municipality and the Coalition had hoped that should the neighbors decide to stay at home after all, they could at least manifest their political sympathies from the safety of their terraces with the printed material that they included with the letters. But, beyond a voyeuristic interest, the balconies and windows along the avenue disclosed no investment in what was happening on the street below.

At stake in mobilizing the neighborhood's residents and in corroborating, with their presence, their broad support for the counterdemonstration was the establishment of local authenticity. How far such authenticity could be validated would inform the verdict that would be passed on Treptow-Köpenick following the event, and hence was crucial for bettering the image of the district. The ritualized spectacle of extreme right demonstrations and democratic or antifascist protests transpires in the Federal Republic routinely. Mass publicity representations of such events place as much—if not more—emphasis on the response of affected localities as they do on the right-wing extremists themselves. Has countermobilization been effective in sabotaging the demonstration? Has it been massive enough to overwhelm the marchers? Was it loud enough? Was it colorful enough? How broad was the public support it enjoyed? Did it successfully bring "ordinary citizens" out to the street?

The answers to such questions form a grid that allows media, and its publics, to morally assess localities unfortunate enough to host a right-wing extremist march. Such assessments usually come in the form of a limited number of highly scripted idiomatic verdicts. Thus, a newspaper might report sympathetically that Treptow-Köpenick "defends itself against Nazis" (*wehrt sich*), that it "shows itself to be colorful" (*zeigt sich bunt*) or "democratic," "sets an example" (*setzt ein Beispiel*), "sends a sign" (*setzt ein Zeichen*), "its citizens fight for it" (*kämpfen für ihre Stadt*), and so on. Or, should the verdict be a negative one, the newspaper could fault the district for being "helpless" (*hilflos*), "remaining silent" (*schweigen*), "looking the other way" (*wegschauen*), or permitting "Nazis [to] march undisturbed" (*ungestört*) (see, e.g., Barthelme 2005; *Berliner Morgenpost* 2005a; *Berliner Zeitung* 2007). Such phrases carry with them mighty historical associations. To remain silent or look the other way is presumably what too many Germans did back then, as the expression "wer schweigt, stimmt zu" (he who remains silent, agrees) also illustrates. In contrast, defending themselves, fighting for their cities, or setting an example represents what they had failed to do. In this manner, the entire project of interpellating into existence a new national collectivity as tolerant, diverse, and democratic takes its bearings from the traumatic historical failure of Germany, and Germans, to stand for such values. Given its location in Berlin, a city that not only struggles to brand itself as tolerant and cosmopolitan but is also blessed with numerous strong antifascist forces, nothing but a full endorsement of the district's response to the Nazi threat would have cut it. And indeed, largely as a result of the efforts of the groups I listed above, the media coverage of the district's performance was by and large laudatory.

The progress of the march followed a familiar choreographic script, performances of which unsettle little towns or sleepy neighborhoods on most weekends in Germany. The Antifa and the right-wing extremists maintained surveillance upon each other, deploying clandestine agents armed with cameras and cell phones. The demonstrators advanced slowly and intermittently, delayed by sit-ins, blockades, and street skirmishes between protestors and squadrons of riot-geared troops, convoys of armored vehicles and water-cannon trucks, and teams of conflict de-escalation policemen. Some one hundred fifty to two hundred marchers passed by, we estimated, though they were visible for but a fleeting moment before the police troops closed in.

CRAFTING RESILIENCE

Around this thin, ephemeral march, however, an entire universe of actors, investments, and forces came together in a coherent configuration, not only on the day of the demonstration but, as we have seen, already during the protracted weeks and months that preceded it. Beyond the performance of opposition to the far right marchers, the entire labor of coordinating different activities with police and municipal authorities, opening and maintaining communication lines between the different participants, recruiting activists and mobilizing sympathizers, managing publicity and handling the media, and conceiving, producing, and rehearsing direct actions and stage acts—all of these painstaking preparatory procedures and practices provided the sites and the moments for the articulation of these diverse forces. The activities around demonstrations, it is important to note, constitute but a drop in an ocean of projects and initiatives. In the municipal district of Treptow-Köpenick alone, during my research I documented an "Educational Market: 'Learning Democracy'" that showcased a variety of pedagogical organizations, programs, and possibilities in the municipal city hall; expert-led town-hall discussion forums about right-wing extremism in the district; "intercultural gardens" that sought to smooth immigrant integration and cross-cultural understanding; multicultural youth centers; workshops for training in argumentation against racism; Internet portals with information about the local extreme right scene; poster competitions on democracy or diversity; billboard campaigns against intolerance and racism; printed news-letters with updates on recent developments; and support groups for parents of young right-wing extremists.

In cutting across such distinct investments and forces, this articulation aggre-gates them into a collective, national project. Consider, again, the intervention of the Grünau SPD committee at Khan's beer garden, and the sort of vernacu-lar familiarity that put it in motion, which similarly characterizes, for example, the Johannisthal task force on right-wing extremism or an Asian-themed mul-ticultural evening at a neighborhood youth club. At the scale of the district, the Treptow-Köpenick SPD also stages events against right-wing extremism, and numerous organizations, forums, and municipal programs target racist violence and intolerance. At the level of the city, the Berlin State Senate routinely holds sessions on the extreme right in the capital, and its representatives occasionally drop by to seek enlightenment from the social workers, while the government funds and promotes a variety of policies and initiatives. In turn, as we have seen, federal programs that benefit from EU funding intervene in shaping the gen-eral outlines of the struggle throughout the country, and, as I witnessed during my fieldwork on several opportunities, Bundestag committees organize discus-sion panels in which members of NGOs, concerned citizens, and affected immi-grants testify and debate with legislators, government officials, and experts on how best to combat the menace.

This mediation of scales follows the familiar patterns of neoliberal gover-nance that I reviewed in chapter 6, and is vulnerable, as well, to the critiques that have been raised against such discourses of governance (see Brenner and Theodore 2002). Nevertheless, the struggle against right-wing extremism ap-pears to more or less effectively bring together the forces and investments that we surveyed in this chapter. It binds them in its modes of action, in the sort of praxis that I discussed above, but it also hails them collectively through its ideological banners of tolerance, diversity, and democracy, the empty signi-fiers (Laclau 1996a) of this national project that are, in fact, semantically over-determined and bursting with values. Drawing on Laclau, we could say that these signifiers stake a claim to the ideological outlines of an emergent national project, setting in motion a chain of equivalences that extends over—and ties together—otherwise disparate forces.

The local march of the BASO Kameradschaft and its supporters through Treptow-Köpenick revealed particularly well how this ideological formation could recruit and incorporate even unlikely actors. Significant movements within the German Antifa, for example, proclaim an absolute opposition to what they describe as an authoritarian and undemocratic state, condemn both state and civil society for their presumed hypocrisy and indifference to the fight against fascism, decry their collusion in institutionalized and everyday racism, and protest against what they consider the criminalization of antifascist en-gagement. Such voices express repulsion at anything that smacks of nation, particularly, of course, of German nation. And yet, in their sheer presence on the streets, just as much as in backstage collaboration, they converge with the state/civil society formation that spearheads the national crusade against racism and xenophobia.

Such presumably oppositional forces ultimately operate under the very same orchestrated performance of a responsible, friendly nation, to which they have become indispensable in at least four significant ways. First, they increase the street body count for the allied democratic forces, an important public index, as I have explained, of the state of the nation in general, and of local democratic commitment in particular. Second, they create spectacular images of flames and projectiles that capture well in TV and print media, corroborating a militant opposition to the extreme right menace. Third, they enact a certain form of street censorship as a sort of informal moral policing that stands apart, but remains inseparable from, the formal legal regime that regulates the liberties of congregation and speech (see Mazzarella 2013). Ordinarily, the police may violently disperse their blockades, and yet when considerations of public visibility and political stakes demand it, they can be useful for calling off demonstrations ostensibly in the name of public order and despite their legal approval. In that sense, fourth, they allow at once the public staging of a vibrant popular opposition to nationalism and the fabrication of the state as a liberal sovereign committed to defending its citizens' rights. In William Mazzarella's terms, the Antifa inhabits the same performative dispensation (2013) as the right-wingers—the same space of publicity afforded but also controlled by the state as both patron and police.

But if this dispensation marks the performative space within which a national project is staged, to whom does it address its enactments? Whom does it seek to recruit or to activate? In front of whom does it corroborate its ideological commitments? There are five principal types of addressees to which this nascent national project directs its performances, and their roles as concrete audiences, abstract publics, or performers themselves vary greatly. The first cluster of addressees includes the *participants* in these performances, those very same social agents that the management of hate mobilizes into action as both leading cast and key audience. The youth workers preparing for a counterdemonstration or producing a multicultural evening, the adolescents rehearsing for a gig at a festival for democracy or putting together antiracist newsletters or websites, or the representatives of public institutions, law enforcement units, or private businesses who deliberate and promote strategies and initiatives, all heed the call and recalibrate their idioms, investments, and practices accordingly. Far from sharing some prior political investment in which their particular interests are already coherently articulated, it is precisely the signifying force of this campaign, the project it delineates, and the spaces it creates that bring this heterogeneous array into an "equivalential chain": a collectivity that emerges from a hegemonic ideological interpellation.

The second group includes the actual *spectators* that gather as tangible audiences for concrete performances: the crowds that attend concerts at democracy festivals, the residents who congregate at discussion panels on right-wing extremism in neighborhood cultural centers, those who arrive to experience an evening of international dance and cuisine at a local youth club, and so on. These groups, too, are in a sense both audiences and participants: while they arrive to witness these performances, hailed by the ideological force of the management of hate, their very physical presence enables the successful completion of ritualized enactments and sets them as part of the cast.

The crucial role of the spectators emerges patently with respect to the third audience: the *national public*. This group, an abstract collectivity constituted by the circulation and consumption of images and discourses in mass publicity, remains absent from the battlefield yet observant of the skirmishes of the ongoing war. It stands at once for the principal target of the campaign and for its ultimate failure. Its members turn their backs on it, neither participating in its performances nor honoring them with their physical presence as spectators. They form an anonymous multitude, a frustratingly unlocatable entity whose nature nonetheless appears crucial to decipher both in order to design strategies for intervening upon it and in order to assess the dimensions of the nationalist problem in the first place. Accordingly, the national public is subjected regularly to surveys and studies that measure and document its political opinions, authoritarian inclinations, xenophobic prejudices, and nationalist self-understanding. Results are generally perceived as alarming. The national public is thus constituted reflexively in a double (or, rather, circular) movement. It is the very collectivity in which certain discourses, having first constructed it as such, seek to read the state of the nation. But it is also a public that reads the unfolding of the struggle against bad nationalism through incessant media coverage that, in turn, refers to representations of that very same national public. This absent audience therefore learns time and again from socially authorized voices that a particular neighborhood, a given city, a state, the entire Federal Republic, a soccer league, a labor union, or a political party is in fact—or else is not and ought to become—diverse (*bunt*), tolerant, or open-minded (*weltoffen*).

A fourth audience consists of the international public toward which many performances of benevolent German nationalism also orient themselves. Its significance becomes evident less in neighborhood settings, such as the Treptow march, and more in events that entail different stakes and scales of exposure, and on which I will elaborate in chapter 9. For now, let me note, first, that international publicity regularly reports on racist violence and extreme right developments in Germany and, second, that German media, politicians, legislators, and judges frequently consider and debate how to manage their country's international image.

Finally, those very right-wing extremists against whose figure the democratic camp rallies its forces are also addressed by its performances. Of course, they provide, in a sense, the very condition of possibility of its mobilizations. But they also participate in more significant ways in the communicative actions that emerge around their presence. At times they appear as the addressee of demands, threats, and denunciations, while at others as the third person in debates and proclamations about them. In different roles, then, they are already included as more or less active participants in a range of communicative transactions. In their rhetoric, many efforts within the management of hate preach not the rehabilitation of political delinquents but rather their absolute exclusion. But even the barring of nationalist teenagers from their neighborhood's youth club constitutes a communicative action that addresses the very groups that it excludes. Similarly, the convening of the SPD neighborhood committee's weekly assembly at Khan's formed a performance that intended to address the restaurant's young clientele as its audience, even if, as we saw, it fell flat. In this sense, the police troops at Khan's signaled concern that the audience could turn into an (adversarial) interlocutor. Often, it is this very inclusive exclusion that renders political actions against right-wing extremists meaningful in the first place.

One could usefully think of the sorts of efforts that have stood at the center of this chapter (from multicultural cuisine to street protests) as inoculatory operations concerned with preventive care, in contrast, for example, to the rehabilitative interventions I described in chapter 7, where remedial therapy was at stake. The metaphor of inoculation seems appropriate insofar as the performance of an officially endorsed national collectivity introduces a neutralized, benign version of the very entity it sets out to vanquish. The fabrication and safeguarding of a healthy, normal nation proceeds in and through its inoculation against a sick, deviant one. Taken as a set of strategies, discourses, policies, institutions, and performances, the suppression of the national specter hence enables the safe return of the nation in two crucial senses. First, it mollifies anxieties and misgivings about the menace of latent nationalist undercurrents by parading as a guarantee against their resurgence and as a pledge of sustained investment in their suppression. But, second, it generates a collective idiom, an institutional architecture, and a set of practices around which a different figure of the national collectivity comes into focus.

The aptness of the management of hate for these tasks reveals itself in its effective incorporation not only of Antifa militants but also of other sectors of German society (and perhaps especially among its intellectual elites) that are or had been profoundly apprehensive about the notion of a national German collectivity. It leaves them little choice in the matter. The oligarchs of Germany's leftist intellectual elite (the likes of Jürgen Habermas, Günter Grass, or, in the GDR, Stefan Heym) at the time published copiously against reunification and warned of the nationalist Phoenix that it could reawaken (Grass 1990 and 1991; Habermas 1991; Heym 1991). Habermas in particular insisted on reading as artificially produced the national sentiment that in political rhetoric appeared to frame reunification as a foregone conclusion. He warned against viewing this putative national sentiment as authentically grounded in a broad base of popular support, and called for integrating the GDR as an independent nation-state into the European Community. Grass, meanwhile, preached the vision of a cultural (rather than political) nation. Their obdurate hostility to the prospects of a Berlin Republic was mercilessly criticized by writers on the conservative right (Bohrer 1991), just as much as on the liberal left (Huyssen 1992), as arrogantly self-righteous, politically out of touch, and transparently self-serving. Habermas has continued to decry the discursive collapsing of National Socialism and communism into totalitarianism in the unified Berlin Republic (1997c), carrying on a row that dates back to the Historikerstreit of the mid-1980s (see chapter 1, footnote 15) and in which, despite having been crowned as victors, he and his allies appear increasingly on the defense. Grass, in a recent novel (2002a), issued a clear challenge to the hegemonic taboos of Germany's dominant historical narrative and political memory. Like the radical fringes of the anarchist Antifa camp, however, neither they nor others who share their convictions can conceivably turn their backs on a nation-crafting project that has increasingly defined itself as a campaign against insidious nationalism itself.

National Visions

STARS OVER BERLIN

On the morning of October 14, 2005, a passerby spotted a large, white Star of David sprayed on a statue of Bertolt Brecht, a seated bronze rendering of the author that oversees a small, tranquil park and behind it the Spree River, not far from the central Friedrichstraße train station.[1] As the day progressed, reports accumulated of Stars of David scrawled over a Jewish memorial facing Grosse Hamburger Straße, at the heart of Berlin's top tourist area; on a window of the Anne Frank Center, in front of a broad, busy avenue;[2] and on the graves of Brecht, the communist writer and politician Johannes R. Becher, and the leftist author Heinrich Mann, all three of which are located in the Dorotheenstadt cemetery, a stone's throw away from the Friedrichstraße shopping corridor. The distribution of the signs charted an itinerary through the northern streets of the Mitte district, once home to much of the city's Jewish community and today prime real estate, an entirely revamped, cream-colored, upscale area.[3] For weeks thereafter nearly every daybreak saw new imprints of the Jewish symbol someplace in the city.

Initially, new Stars of David appeared in white and on special sites near or within the perimeter of Mitte's tourist and shopping areas: Berlin's City Hall at Alexanderplatz, the statues of Marx and Engels a few steps away, or a tall sculpture of the letter "E" that announced the current "Einstein Year" on Hausvogteiplatz,

---

[1] In narrating this incident, I have complemented my own firsthand research with some of the innumerable newspaper articles that reported on it (see, e.g., *Berliner Zeitung* 2005a, 2005b, and 2005c; *Der Tagesspiegel* 2005c; *Die Tageszeitung* 2005a; Hasselmann 2005; Kopietz and Strohmaier 2005; Schulz 2005).

[2] The Anne Frank Center has since moved to a different location.

[3] The area known as the Scheunenviertel was the Jewish ghetto of Berlin. It is splendidly represented in Alfred Döblin's majestic *Berlin Alexanderplatz* (1996).

in a business and upmarket consumption area. Their geographical spread suggested that the perpetrators aimed for hypervisibility by hitting at the city's business, consumption, and tourism center, and that they targeted in particular sites of shame and sites of commemoration, Jewish places and communist places, the memory of the victims and that of the resistance. As time went by, however, the Stars of David began to appear not only in different colors but also, increasingly, on seemingly indiscriminate targets and across more extensive areas of the city: from the Socialist Memorial Cemetery near the Lichtenberg train station and the vast, isolated Soviet War Monument in Treptow to a commemorative plaque for Alfred Döblin that hung on a residential building on West Berlin's Kaiserdamm Avenue or a range of structures, memorials, cemeteries, museums, and, indeed, the walls of buildings along various streets and avenues. All of these fell victim to invisible, nocturnal raids that always left the same uncaptioned and unsigned mark. About a month later, the police had already tallied dozens of incidents of the mysterious symbols but still confessed that it had come no closer to uncovering the identity of the shadowy perpetrators.

The enigmatic saga of the Stars of David that inundated Berlin in the fall of 2005 opens up a host of questions about the nature of the symbols, or, more precisely, about the nature of the political contestations within which they were deployed. Crucial in this respect, of course, were not only the indexical relations of physical proximity between the inscriptions and their sites of occurrence (to which I shall return below), but equally the interpretative frameworks that guided the readings of these relations. What was it, precisely, that they rendered visible in the urban landscape? Was it, as some experts suggested, that they were employed—as they were with the Nazis—to visibilize the alleged enemies of the German nation? Or did they make the presence of ultranationalist undercurrents in today's Germany tangibly perceptible? How did the sites where they appeared inflect their meanings? What horizons did they evoke? And what sort of anxieties did they provoke?

As we will see in this chapter, at the crux of this astral splatter that suffused Berlin's streets with uncanny icons, we find a certain politics of visibility, a certain contestation over the visual representation of the new Germany through the visual management of its past. This contested politics of visibility binds together distinct domains, from monumental architecture or spectacular public performances to small-scale tactical interventions or quotidian fashion habits. At stake in it is what, following Allen Feldman, I will call "regimes of visibility": discourses and practices that govern the politics of visualization. Writing on violence and vision in Northern Ireland, Feldman describes visibility regimes as follows:

> By scopic regime I mean the agendas and techniques of political visualization:[4] the regimens that prescribe modes of seeing and object visibility and that proscribe

---

[4]Feldman appears to use "scopic regime" and "regime of visibility" interchangeably.

or render tenable other modes and objects of perception. A scopic regime is an ensemble of practices and discourses that establish the truth claims, typicality, and credibility of visual acts and objects and politically correct modes of seeing. (1997, 30)

In-line with this definition, here I use the term "visibility operations" to designate practices that address themselves, as it were, to given visibility regimes, whether in order to consolidate, fortify, or contest them.

The national vision, in turn, refers to how the national narrative is visualized, to the policing of its frontiers and the engagement with transgressions against it just as much as to the forms that these very transgressions take. The governance of the national vision can only be understood in relation to the legal regimes that criminalize multiple visibility operations and operators and that define what can be displayed and seen in Germany, and precisely how. As I discussed in chapter 4, much of the legal governance of right-wing extremism and illicit nationalism concerns itself with establishing the legal status of different forms of visualization. Prohibition begets the elaboration of secret registers and cryptic codes that elide legal consequences and address themselves, as it were, to a limited public of intimates, effectively creating a differentiation of audiences. On the one hand, then, many actors—including the state—invest great efforts in rendering the illicit visible, in documenting and publishing information about the extreme right and its activities.[5] On the other hand, in the national vision the state enacts a form of what William Mazzarella (2013, 41), as I mentioned in chapter 8, has called a performative dispensation: "an order of things" handed down "from a transcendent authority and overseen in its earthly enactment by a sovereign person/power who is ambiguously at once patron and police, whose banner staff is at once the umbrella under which the performance may take place and the weapon that crushes those who challenge its integrity." A dispensation, according to Mazzarella, "combines two kinds of claims to sovereign authority: the sovereignty that opens and maintains a protected space in which a form of life can be performed" and that which "decides on the exception, on what falls outside the symbolic order of the law." In a similar way, the German state carefully delineates the terms of national visibility, toiling to incite and enable visual performances of a new and officially endorsed German nationalism while struggling to maintain a tight grip on the forms that such performances take.

This chapter is concerned with the governance of national visibility as a performative dispensation. It opens with a discussion of the ways in which the Stars of David, despite their initial illegibility, rapidly came to be read and interpreted along certain lines and in relation to the only piece of evidence apparently available about them—their locations. The significance of the sites on which they were spotted will lead us to examine the geography of special places (heterotopias

---

[5] No doubt, researchers, including me, are actively complicit in this visibilization.

[Foucault 1986]) in Berlin's cityscape, its intensive production over the past few decades, and its concern with policing visibility regimes; put differently, the national vision, or the ways in which the hegemonic project of a post-reunification German nationhood has sought to present and represent itself and its past through the built environment of its new capital. Next, I will consider the rather varied catalog of tactical operations—some of which we have already encountered in passing in chapter 5—on which young right-wing extremists draw to manage their own visibility and to confront dominant visibility regimes. I will pay particular attention to how these operations often orient themselves toward the heterotopic landscape of Berlin. I will then describe how they contest dominant visual idioms of commemoration and mourning, and particularly how they stake claims to narratives of remembrance in cemeteries. The chapter concludes with a detailed review of the sixtieth anniversary of the Reich's surrender to the Allies, an event that well illustrated not only the paradoxical logic of visualization that marks the governance of the national vision but also the dimensions of the panic that attempts to challenge it trigger.

READING THE STARS

The mysterious nature of the Stars of David affair, and its obstinate refusal to die out, inspired much debate about how to properly interpret and respond to it. Early press coverage showed a mixture of bafflement, indignation, and frustration, for there was little here, so it seemed, that could be taken for granted. Not only the identities of the nimble sprayers but even their political leanings and possible motivations were difficult to extrapolate from the results of their actions, at least initially. Its context ambiguous and its audience unspecified, the message to be read in their anonymous, uncommented, and reiterative acts of writing appeared inscrutable (cf. Derrida 1982). Thus, shortly after the sightings had begun, the newspaper *Berliner Zeitung* could report:

> For days now the police have been hunting after mysterious paint-vandals. The anonymous persons have been spraying in Berlin's Mitte district not some graffiti, "tags," or even swastikas, which the police routinely comes across. The perpetrators have been using white paint for spraying Stars of David, a Jewish symbol. *Nevertheless, the police does not rule out that the acts could have an anti-Semitic background.* (*Berliner Zeitung* 2005d; emphasis mine)

In other words, immediate reactions saw anti-Semitic motives as one among a number of possible understandings of the sign, and not necessarily the most likely of them. Indeed, in my experience, graffiti of the Star of David most frequently appeared in tandem with philo-Semitic slogans—for instance, "Solidarity with Israel," "Fight anti-Semitism," "Never again, Germany—defend Israel," or "Long live Israel"—that fairly plainly signaled pro-Zionist factions within militant Antifa groups as their authors. Such compositions displayed not the stigma with which National Socialism marked the Jews but rather the coat of arms of the state of Israel. Only rarely did I witness juxtapositions of the Star of David with clearly anti-Semitic signs—the phrase "Juden raus," swastikas, or other right-wing extremist symbols—that endowed it with different, sinister meanings.[6] But standing in utter isolation of captions and commentary, its signification in the case at hand remained exasperatingly opaque. In technical language, we might say that, in the absence of any syntagmatic relations with other signs in their vicinity, the Stars of David found themselves bereft of any paradigmatic relations as well. In other words, without a broader text within which to situate them, their value was difficult to determine. What could serve as their synonym? Were they substitutable by a swastika? A pro-Zionist catchphrase? Perhaps a pro-Palestinian slogan? Bewildered extrapolations repeated across newspapers in Berlin. In the first few days following the discovery of the first graffiti, the police concluded that the sprayers probably lived in Mitte or its vicinity but reported no progress besides.

Yet the Stars of David did not in fact appear in isolation. They came into view scribbled on sites, buildings, and monuments that held special meanings and gestured toward particular historical and political horizons, and for a while at least they plagued only a very specific perimeter in the city's geography. Before a week had passed, the police had become convinced that, while "there is no concrete evidence as to the perpetrators, we believe they come out of the rightist scene" (*Die Tageszeitung* 2005b). A police specialist, for example, commented that a right-wing hand was evidently behind the graffiti, considering that "it's not only about Jewish memorials, but also about 'people like Brecht, who resisted during the Third Reich'" (*Der Tagesspiegel* 2005c). The reiterative juxtapositions of the Stars of David with special locations emerged in public discourse as inconsistent with a philo-Semitic, pro-Zionist interpretation, but neither did they seem to support the hypothesis that Muslim anti-Semites were behind the graffiti. After all, if it appeared unlikely that Zionist antifascists would repeatedly vandalize memorials for communists or for Jewish victims of National Socialism, nor was there any apparent explanation for why anti-Semitic Muslims might desecrate the graves of three non-Jewish German leftists such as Brecht, Mann, and Becher.

Some specialists concluded that the spatial distribution of the Stars of David strongly suggested the involvement of "East Berlin fraternities (*Ostberliner Kameradschaften*)" (*Die Tageszeitung* 2005a). One professor at the Center for Research on anti-Semitism at the Technical University of Berlin argued that "with the Star of David one seeks to render the enemy visible, in the same way that anti-globalization activists mark capitalists with the dollar sign." According to

---

[6] Even in such cases, the Star of David often seemed to cross out, in a different color, a right-wing extremist sign rather than to belong with it or to somehow complement it.

professor Rainer Erb, neo-Nazis increasingly employed the Jewish symbol, one of whose greatest relative advantages as compared with, say, the swastika, was its legality (Kopietz and Strohmaier 2005). One expert went as far as to declare that the sprayers could well belong to the banned Kameradschaft BASO, on which I elaborated in chapter 8. "Treptow is their home district," he affirmed (Schulz 2005).

Therefore, to the extent that the graffiti constituted tactical operations in contestations over the politics of visibility (and the visualization of politics) with which the nation displays itself to itself as well as to others, their efficacy owed to the singular cityscape of Germany's capital. Their capacity to weave legible significations into the urban landscape and to indicate the copresence in the city of violent potentialities hinged on their spatial articulation with a topography of special sites, the sheer density of which, just as much as its peculiar meanings, are unique to Berlin. The Stars of David rendered these potentialities tangibly evident through their graphic inscription on the built environment, conjuring at once, for many in the city, the historical memory of genocidal nationalism and, inseparably, its doppelgänger, the lingering, latent potentialities of an illicit and violent nationalism in the present. It was the careful and repetitive emplacement of the symbols in the cityscape that facilitated the fusion of these two temporal horizons in a form both visible and, given some time for the pattern to sink in, legible.

The sites that allowed this fusion between past and present to become meaningfully visible offered far more than their mere concrete physicality, the way that, say, a nondescript wall might stand as a canvas for graffiti art or that a blank sheet of paper might provide surface for writing. Instead, they formed part of a semiotic composition within which the symbols came to reference certain significations and to secure, gradually, a degree of textual coherence. In other words, the particular configuration of these sites allowed the graffiti to become increasingly meaningful. Such progressive consolidation of meaning and coherence proceeded to the extent that every new incident made the proximity between the symbols and special kinds of sites appear less as the possibly arbitrary attribute of a singular event and more as a rule governing conventionalized regularity. In a sense, it was these sites that constituted the Stars of David as signs by making their interpretation possible and by imbuing them with specific values. In the public discourse of the media and in the opinion of many of my acquaintances in Berlin, these values pointed unambiguously eastward and rightward.

HETEROTOPIC LANDSCAPES

The sites on which the graffiti appeared operated not only as grounds for signification but also as points of amplification, as transmitters of sorts that bequeathed upon the Stars of David heightened intensities and magnified exposure. It is useful to think of them as heterotopic places in the sense suggested by Foucault

(1986). For Foucault, heterotopias designate places that command peculiar qualities and social functions and that, in contradistinction with utopias, are real and tangible. Three attributes that Foucault's rather elaborate and peculiar notion of heterotopias includes seem to me particularly helpful for the present discussion. First, heterotopias point elsewhere. They function as loci for the representation, negotiation, and contestation of other socially important real or imagined places, whose significations they condense. Second, their experience corresponds to that of the mirror. They reflect other places and become overdetermined by them. Their mirrorlike quality includes both their own heterotopic material presence and the utopian material absence of those other places that they represent but that are not actually there. Finally, they are linked with special temporalities that entail a radical break with normal, everyday senses of time.[7] In employing this term I seek to draw the reader's attention to the ways in which, in any given social context, certain special places gesture toward, gather, and represent distinct spatiotemporal horizons of meaning and memory, and how they serve to territorialize these horizons in tangible locations. In doing so, they gain the capacity to represent society to itself. Thus, they prove crucial for the fabrication and stabilization of dominant national narratives, at the same time that they become key strategic targets for efforts to unsettle these same narratives.

There is a certain sense in which Berlin in its entirety could be conceived as a heterotopic place. As the recuperated capital of the Federal Republic, it forever points elsewhere, standing iconically for the nation, presenting and representing a collective memory and a shared imagined future, even fractally reproducing the historical division of national territory (and the lingering rift in national identity) between East and West. In all this, its political and cultural resonance echoes that of many other national capitals. Indeed, it may well be that the capitals of modern nation-states have typically taken on heterotopic qualities—in the sense I indicated above—everywhere. And yet, Berlin appears to present in some respects a unique case of this more general rule. On the one hand, as a city, its heterotopic qualities gesture not only to the national scale, not only those other places and times that belong, so to speak, to the German nation; nor does it reflect them only to German audiences. Rather, it speaks to some of the most salient ideological visions, human calamities, and historical horizons that have both shaped and frustrated ideas about European modernity and Western civilization. As Andreas Huyssen once commented about the then upcoming erection of the Holocaust Memorial,

---

[7] Specifically, Foucault argues that such temporalities, which he terms heterochronies, fall into two types. First, there are those places that present an indefinite accumulation of time, for example, museums or, in our case, monuments and cemeteries. Second, there are heterotopias that express time in its most fleeting, transitory aspects, as in the carnival or, I would submit, the demonstration.

Thus in the very center of the new Berlin, there will be a national memorial to German crimes against humanity, that ultimate rupture of Western civilization which has come to be seen by some as emblematic of the twentieth century as a whole, a curse on the house of modernity that we now inhabit with enormous trepidation. (2003a, 81)

On the other hand, Berlin's own cityscape itself hosts a great multitude of special sites that conjure the city's utopias and dystopias, that hint to its dreams and its catastrophes, that juxtapose with its present-day rejuvenated image those other times and places: from the imposing height of the TV tower at Alexanderplatz, once a metaphor of state power, to the innumerable gray cement slabs of the Holocaust memorial; from the vast Soviet War Memorial, the resting place of thousands of anonymous Russian soldiers, to the monumentality of the Olympia stadium, built by the Nazis for the 1936 Olympic games; or from the field of rubble that rises over the partly exposed dungeons of the Gestapo's demolished headquarters to the few remaining watchtowers from where East German border guards would once open fire at those who attempted to flee across the wall. Such places enfold into the city a multiplicity of temporal and spatial significations.

This abundant yet relatively decentralized (Saunders 2009) geography invests certain locations, indeed at times entire city areas, with a profusion of sinister, heroic, or melancholic values—as places of shame, of commemoration, or of pride. The condensation of times and places in these heterotopic sites and the seepage of their special meanings into the surrounding city together define a certain urban geography of political values. And this geography in turn forms a strategic map for the visualization of contested national narratives in the urban landscape. This spatial logic explains how the Stars of David initially appeared only upon central sites, from which they garnered both semiotic significations and hypervisibility. It helps us understand as well why, only subsequently, having, so to speak, already harnessed within them those special values through repetitive association with them, the symbols poured out into the cityscape at large. This geography of special sites makes available a spatiopolitical lexicon of legible, visual interventions, from mammoth construction projects and other material representations of hegemonic power to small-scale visual alterations of specific sites or from starting points, routes, and destinations for marches and rallies to places for silencing or for rendering that which has been silenced visible.

In post-reunification Berlin, the outlines of such territorializations and with them the general terms of struggles over visibility in the city have been shaped by massive projects dominated by a hegemonic articulation of state, market, and civil society. The incipient project of German nationalism has encompassed not only the restructuring of historical narratives or the production of new master signifiers but equally and inseparably the remaking of architectural landscapes. The spectral presence of illicit pasts has not only defined this national project as a fight against violent nationalism but has equally guided vast interventions into the built environment.

Numerous scholars have written about the transformations that Berlin has witnessed in recent decades, analyzing the symbolic, political, architectural, urban, aesthetic, and social dimensions of monumental changes in the new capital's cityscape (De Soto 1996; Huyssen 1997; Ladd 1997; Verheyen 1997; Binder 2000; Glaeser 2000; Binder 2001; Strom 2001; Huyssen 2003a; Saunders 2009). Street renaming, for example, has been shown to perform a politics of Western domination (De Soto 1996; see also Verheyen 1997).[8] Throughout this ongoing process, material transformations have been closely linked with symbolic ones, with the inscription of certain narratives into the urban landscape and its purging from others (Binder 2001). If, as Lefebvre has argued (1991), a new hegemony cannot but produce new spaces, then the Berlin Republic has done so with exceptional vigor. And for good reason. Political hegemony is inherently a relation of representation that at once delineates the collective and produces it.[9] It demands not only the more or less effective management and policing of narrative forms, discursive circulations, and semantic values but, as important, the development of methods for defining the terms of an economy of visibility. The capacity to erase or render visible particular forms in the built environment, tangible traces of certain social processes, or signs of competing political orders and historical narratives is key for hegemonic domination.

In post-reunification Berlin, on the one hand, capitalism has reshaped expansive landscapes—especially in the East—through the commodification of urban space and the consolidation of new geographies of production. But, on the other hand, the new political sovereign has inscribed its power in the built environment through erasure, resignification, and hypervisibilization. Nowhere have the debates surrounding this process been as controversial, and received as much international exposure (see, e.g., Harding 2005a; PBS 2006), as with the question of the fate of the Palast der Republik (Palace of the Republic). A Soviet modernist work eclipsing the Museuminsel, where Berlin's cathedral and several of its top museums follow late-nineteenth-century architectural styles, the Palast faced off the city's best-known monument, the Brandenburg Gate, at the opposite end of the historical Unter den Linden Avenue. Surrounded by stylishly renovated old buildings, postmodern architectural experimentations, contemporary consumption spaces, and an emerging topography of sightsee-

---

[8] Street renaming has been documented as central to the resignification of places in the context of political transition in a variety of cases in Eastern Europe and elsewhere. See, for example, Robinson, Engelstoft, and Pobric (2001); Light (2004); Palonen (2008).

[9] Hegemony is a relation of representation in both senses of the word: first, as delegation, entailing the emergence of a particular term as the incarnation of the political collective (Laclau 1996b and 2005); and, second, as a power-laden and large-scale social process of semiotic signification and mediation.

ing landmarks, its mammoth cubic form presented a singular reference to the memory of state socialism. The immense building that once hosted the GDR's Parliament, as well as a range of leisure and cultural public offerings, was now perceived as incompatible with newly hegemonic forms of representation. The seemingly broad agreement on the inevitability of its demolition in fact expressed the all but unconditional triumph of a West German historical narrative and of western modes of representing power in the built environment, not least by excluding from the debate—at least in the public sphere—other perspectives, more popular among the city's eastern residents.[10]

In Berlin, the national vision has come to terms with haunting pasts and menacing presents in quite particular ways. For example, rather than demolished, the former Stasi headquarters have been converted into a museum and documentation center for the sins of its previous masters. The most secretive of GDR spaces was thereby transformed into a beacon of enlightenment. As illustrative is the transparent new dome of the Reichstag, from which the public enjoys at once a panoramic view of the landscape of central Berlin, dotted with government edifices and tourist attractions, and, gazing downward, a glimpse into the main assembly hall of the Federal Parliament. The glass walls of the adjacent building of the Bundestag, meanwhile, expose the legislature at work. The production of a new visibility regime has entailed the erection of material representations of the new power, most notably the grandiose quarters of the Federal Parliament and the chancellor, but also the comprehensive face-lifts given to museums and landmarks such as the Brandenburg Gate and Unter den Linden Avenue, and the exuberant consumption and leisure complexes around Potsdamer Platz and Alexanderplatz. All of these, and many more, aimed to visualize in material form a collective image of the new Germany as democratic, liberal, transparent, tolerant, and friendly, yet also historically responsible. At stake was the generation of distance between the nascent Germany and its ghosts. Hence, while changes to the built environment in the wake of reunification patently gestured to the city's history and incorporated it into contemporary architectural idioms, they did so highly selectively, invoking the nostalgic memory of the Weimar Republic but carefully dodging allusions to Nazism and communism (Binder 2000 and 2001).

Such visibility operations, of course, always answered also to another master—the commodity form. The recreation of Berlin's center, if it has sought to symbolically represent the new nation, at the same time has aimed to repackage the city as an attractive commodity. The decision to replace the Palast with a pastiche structure featuring a facade that emulates the Prussian royal castle that once stood nearby reveals the intimate articulation between the political and the economic. With the castle reinstated, the transfiguration of Berlin's center

---

[10] I have heard many fond recollections of the Palast from my East German friends. Helmuth, for example, met his wife at a disco there.

into a tourist-friendly theme park competitive with the nostalgic harmonies of many other European capitals will have been completed.

TACTICS OF VISIBILITY

This seemingly unstoppable proliferation, reconfiguration, and resignification of special sites in the city—castles, memorials, museums, commemorative plaques, statues, squares, exhibitions—weaves together a geography of values and meanings that, as I have suggested, provides a map for tactical interventions that would seek to unsettle it. Paradoxically, it is precisely the persistent investment in the production of such places that has made available a particularly rich bank of targets for those who, like the anonymous sprayers of the Stars of David, might wish to contest it. It is no coincidence that their actions set in motion debates about the terms and norms of visibility in the city. The rapidly cohering consensus about the significance of the symbols as the work of German nationalists provided a measure of comfort insofar as it rendered them legible. But the failure to pinpoint the elusive sprayers who continued to strike relentlessly at the same time generated ever more acute distress. The Jewish Community of Berlin demanded the installation of surveillance cameras throughout "sites particularly at risk." "It is time," said the head of the Jewish community, "that we finally use modern instruments for surveillance" (Kopietz and Strohmaier 2005). Berlin's minister of the interior, ordinarily mindful of the concerns of the city's Jewish community, nevertheless rejected the call as impractical, arguing that the number of sites and buildings potentially at risk was simply too high. Instead of video surveillance, he implored citizens to "[increase] alertness in order to detain the culprits" (*Der Tagesspiegel* 2005b). The CDU opposition, in turn, criticized the city's government and blamed the embarrassingly fruitless hunt for the perpetrators on cuts to the police force. Police representatives for their part warned that the hypermediatized reporting on each new inscription counterproductively inspired the anonymous culprits to continue with their misdeeds.

Meanwhile, debates on the Stars of David were not absent from extreme right forums. There, however, expressions of enthusiasm were few and far between. One commentator in a popular online portal protested against the hasty attribution of the graffiti to German nationalists and the consensus that the perpetrators could not be Jewish:

> What can you say. Anything of this sort and they immediately blame the rightists. Of course there are no evil J[ews] . . . I can only say that I would have used other symbols. Very gladly. But I don't vandalize walls! (Rocknord 2005)

Others commented more ironically on the idea that German right-wing extremists could have sprayed Stars of David: "Here on the Donauinsel there was once a swastika with the inscription 'Final victory is near' on a public toilet.

Could these have been J[ews]?" asked one commentator, tongue in cheek. Some took a far more severe tone:

> I find this simply brainless and stupid!!!
> People like that have nothing to look for in our movement,
> In case these were at all young rightists.
> What do these vandalistic graffiti bring?
> Absolutely nothing! (Rocknord 2005)

With a handful of laudatory exceptions, commentators generally expressed resentment at what they described as the automatic impugnation of right-wing extremists. Some suggested that Muslims were to blame. Many condemned the acts as senseless and unhelpful vandalism unbecoming of the "movement" and especially deplored the desecration of graves (Altermedia Deutschland 2005; Rocknord 2005). As visibility operators, the Stars of David were broadly judged to be counterproductive, unbecoming, or inadequate. By late November, about one and a half months after the first symbols had been observed, the story had all but vanished from the public eye. A chronology of anti-Semitic incidents published in early 2007 by an antifascist research center cited a total of 126 incidents, the last two of them in January and February 2006 (Apabiz 2007). The sprayers have never been identified.

Its uneven appraisals and varied interpretations aside, the Stars of David episode reminds us of two crucial points. First, it effectively generated hypervisibility and with it not a small measure of panic and speculation; this, with low-tech instruments, high precision, and impunity. Second, it exposed how the national vision in turn forms a terrain, a target, and an adversary for those who would frustrate its efforts. Dominant visibility regimes open up spaces for a range of local visibility games that introduce into the material fabric of the city intimations of present pasts and that haunt the project of a tolerant, liberal democratic nationhood. Because they touch upon profound cultural taboos, such interventions constantly entail the transgression of both social norms and legal codes.

For many, violence forms a salient dimension as much of the historical horizon that such signs evoke as of the contemporary discontents to which they gesture. But violence designates quite different things, and differentially so for different people. There is a world of difference between displays—and perceptions—of potential threat and those moments of its all-too-tangible actuality, or between the collective commemoration of a brutal past and the here and now of a racist everyday. Talk of nationalist violence ordinarily refers to premeditated executions by terrorist cells, brutal raids on immigrant businesses, or physical aggression between rival cliques of inebriated youths, but less to the production of fear in the visual realm. Often, however, visibility practices are about the material territorialization of potentialities and intimations, not of physical brutality as such. In Berlin as elsewhere (Pred 2000; Comaroff and Comaroff

2006), geographies of fear correspond only partially to the spatial distribution of physical assaults.[11] Right-wing extremists more commonly make their presence felt in the urban space in visual forms that for some audiences, they well know, evoke threatening possibilities.[12] Tactically maneuvering the frontier between the visible and the invisible, the explicitly stated and the implicitly intimated, they provoke visual conspicuousness, public attention, and, for many, menacing anxieties.

Even as it baffled the authorities and startled residents, then, the story of the Stars of David was not in fact a unique or unprecedented incident. Instead, it numbered among a range of visibility operations that right-wing extremists perform routinely. Such tactics of visibility contrast sharply in scale with the kinds of monumental politics of visibility that we examined thus far. They include both the actions of militant political groups and the routine fashion habits of particular individuals, such as Gino or Freddi. Their instruments are varied and range from fashion items, paint and brushes, or graffiti spray cans to stickers and posters or banners and slogans. They comprise the rudimentary calibration of bodily appearances just as much as intricate clandestine interventions in the cityscape. In short, they constitute a wide spectrum of distinct communicative practices that address themselves to quite different audiences, from the residents of a neighborhood to international publics. As communicative acts, they participate in a number of different conversations that proceed at different social scales. They therefore come in very different shades.

The physical appearance of right-wing extremist bodies plays a crucial role in their visual performance of self and, for those who have good reason to worry about their presence, it territorializes terrorizing potentialities. The body offers itself as a site for a broad range of visibility operations. Three qualities make it particularly adaptable and effective: its mobility, or its capacity to navigate the cityscape using a variety of methods; its singularity, or the way in which its physical being-there grants it concreteness and facticity; and its manipulability, or the multiple and flexible operations that, as we shall see presently, it can combine in seemingly innumerable permutations.

In order to render their politics in visual form upon their bodies and under the watchful eye and iron fist of the state, right-wing extremists employ a lexicon of conventional symbols, cryptic codes, and graphic styles—for example,

---

[11] For example, a study of the spatial distribution of right-wing extremist violence, its perpetrators, and its victims, published by the Verfassungsschutz Berlin, indicated some of the higher incidence rates of assaults in neighborhoods such as Friedrichshain and Prenzlauer-Berg, broadly considered the heart of the city's multicultural, hip, and gay-friendly areas (Verfassungsschutz Berlin 2004).

[12] Of course, actual physical violence remains vital as a signifying horizon, even in its absence, enabling multiple violence-based operations of visibility (I thank Michael Silverstein for the phrase). The prolific mass publicity of physical brutality allows right-wing extremists to conjure menacing potentialities and project them metonymically onto material objects.

Gothic fonts, iconic renderings of Nordic mythological figures, or numerical ciphers for banned letter combinations (such as 18 for A[dolf] H[itler] or 88 for H[eil] H[itler]). Consider again the case of Gino's HASS tattoo, with its last two letters fashioned after the legally banned, lightning-like SS symbol. Tattooed across four fingers of his hand, its letters, as I suggested in chapter 5, allowed for several tactical operations. Fully exposing its illegal characters ran the risk of legal consequences and required at least the perception of safety from the law, say in the privacy of apartments or in places viewed as sufficiently intimate. Under less favorable circumstances, rings permitted the selective concealment of the tattoo's discrete elements and the differential addressing of distinct audiences. Slipping a ring over one of the two letters that composed the illegal symbol cast a protective cloak vis-à-vis the law, which—let us recall the discussion in chapter 4—prohibits not the symbol per se but its display in public. Yet such partial erasure at the same time glaringly announced the existence of the tattoo to other audiences, including Antifa activists or fellow comrades. It would ordinarily occur in more extensive contexts—in certain neighborhoods, public parks, or train stations—as an assertion of power, as an expression of solidarity, and as calculated provocation. A third possibility is the complete concealment of the tattoo. Where relations of power appeared clearly disadvantageous, covering the entire HASS inscription removed it as a significant visual marker of political identity. Last, one might opt to exit this visibility game altogether, as Gino did when he had the characters of his tattoo transformed into playing cards and thereby indicated the conclusive termination of his participation.

The particular powers of the HASS tattoo as a pliable instrument for tactical, visual performances owed to its discrete elements, which lent themselves to precise management.[13] Additional accessories further refine the body's tactical capacities: hairstyles, as with the Renee trim that Thomas imposed on Lisa (see chapter 6); jewelry pieces, like Freddi's Odal rune pendant (see chapter 4); and, most prominent, fashion brands (see chapter 2). Outfits, like tattoos, present a cascading grid of provocation and transgression, and permit a differential addressing of distinct audiences. Some brands are illegal and only exposed with caution. Others, though legal enough, unambiguously indicate an extreme right identification, at least to certain eyes, so that, depending on circumstances, they may invite expressions of camaraderie or provoke hostile reactions. Others still only hint, more or less vaguely, at the possibility of right-wing political orientations. Finally, so-called normal or neutral outfits allegedly hold no political values. In fact, more than a few among my informants preferred to avoid any

---

[13] Other popular tattoos among right-wing extremists that similarly visibilize the threat of violence include symbols I reviewed in earlier chapters: depictions of the Nordic god Thor with his legendary hammer, representations of the *leitwolf* (the leader of the pack), commonly as an arctic wolf in a snow-clad landscape, or drawings of the Iron Cross or of the black eight billiard ball, which stands for "H," the eighth letter in the alphabet, and thus for Hitler.

possibility of provocation altogether. As Sylvia put it, while attempting to explain to me the difference, in her view, between left and right, "left is punk," while

[n]eutral is neither rightist, or neither skinhead nor punk, and rightist, I mean I'm slightly rightist myself . . . but it's not so extreme that I somehow run around with boots . . . I have my opinion, but I just don't show it publicly . . . I can't imagine myself running around with those shoes because it would be a provocation, and then I can't complain if someone harasses me or if a cop approaches me.

Of course, what Sylvia considered neutral others could well perceive as ultranationalist. Context and audience are thus key to performance, and the calibration of right-wing extremist visibility always already orients itself to them. For example, not all will recognize the Thor Steinar garments (see chapter 4) as legally banned or, where legally condoned, as clearly indicating neo-Nazi leanings. Many in Berlin perceive certain clothing brands, like Lonsdale, as strongly indicating extreme right sympathies and proclivity to racist violence, even though they are widely popular among other subcultural milieus (for example, anarchists and leftist skinheads in the case of Lonsdale). The significance of that which becomes visualized in such performances depends therefore upon the uneven erudition of distinct publics. Acts of interpretation become responses to acts of performance in the Goffmanian sense (1976): it is not so much, or not only, that performances always already orient themselves toward their interpretations, but rather that the latter define the former as performative acts in the first place.

Different material domains articulate with each other and with shifting contexts to allow a range of combinations and interpretations. In demonstrations, for example, the arms of more than a few marchers often display what would otherwise appear as an inconspicuous Band-Aid. In such events, however, attached exactly at the height of the shirt's sleeve, the Band-Aid becomes a plain signal of the presence of an illegal tattoo beneath it, even as it masks the precise nature of the symbol and refrains from transgressing the law. Whether the alleged tattoo that the Band-Aid at once conceals and so glaringly reveals in the very act of concealment actually exists or not is utterly irrelevant—the very operation of erasure visibilizes that which it purportedly hides from view. Erasure, in other words, may well enhance visibility.

In chapter 4, I described how some of my informants wore jackets over their Lonsdale shirts in a way that left only the letters NSDA in plain sight, in reference to the illegal acronym of the National Socialist Party (NSDAP). I explained how they thereby evaded the legal prohibition on the public display of the symbol. But this operation of partial erasure did more than that. Consider now how zipping the jacket entirely could effectively eliminate any traces of political significations. The wide-open jacket, on the other hand, would expose the entire Lonsdale logo. Depending on context and audience, this latter

Figure 4. A Junge Nationaldemokraten (the NPD's youth wing) march demanding
more resources for "German youth" in Pankow, Berlin. A Band-Aid on the arm suggests the presence of an illegal tattoo.

possibility could suggest, to a greater or lesser degree, a right-wing extremist
association (specialists and intimates would tend to make this assumption less
than laypeople in my experience). Many may not even register the careful manipulation of the jacket and the display of the NSDA letters that the first of these
three possibilities entails. Anyone with as much as a novice acquaintance of the
field, however, would not fail to interpret it—correctly—as a provocatively unequivocal performance of a committed right-wing extremist persona. A discrete
operation of partial erasure produces here, for those sufficiently literate to read
it, the effect of hypervisibilization.[14]

[14]The need for secrecy and coded communication under strict legal limits and heavy-handed
penal regimes is in turn productive in a number of ways. Perhaps most important, the circulation
and exchange of arcane, insider knowledge is generative of senses of belonging and of group solidarity. Some right-wing extremist manipulations of visual signs, however, appear less in the register
of secrecy or encryption and more in that of mockery in the face of the state, though always safely,
as it were. Gino's manipulation of his tattoo, which elided the law but kept the fact of the tattoo—if
not all its letters—patently visible, is less reminiscent of a coded argot than it is of taboo defor-
mation, which turns the visualization of the taboo harmless (think of French Connection "fcuk"
branding as another example). I thank Michael Silverstein for this last observation.

The body's tactical assets as an instrument of visibility—its *mobility, versatility*, and *singularity*—render it inadequate for purposes that require a degree of durable *fixedness*, the possibility of exact *iterability*, or a *multiplicity* of simultaneous interventions in different locations. Various propaganda elements— stickers, leaflets, posters, graffiti—open up a different arsenal of visual tactics, allowing the stabilization of meanings, their duplication, and their territorial expansion. For those who can perceive and interpret them, they operate not through proximity, as with the body, but instead as representations of something other, of the abstract possibility that physical violence could erupt concretely onto the scene. In divorcing the sign from the body, they minimize the measure of individual risk (recall that the sprayers of the Stars of David were never identified) while allowing a higher visual density than what bodies alone would permit. Such tactical assets are particularly significant because of the penal regime that governs the national vision, and under which, as we have seen in chapter 4, the linking of a sign and a body can carry serious legal consequences for individuals. They allow visual interventions in wide regions: neighborhoods, municipal districts, or the city.

Reiteration has the advantage of boosting the visibility of particular terms: recurring patterns become incorporated into a habitus of perception so that, when encountered, they are consciously registered without the labor otherwise entailed in visual scrutiny. Formulaic designs, standard typesets, and conventional color combinations—for instance, Gothic-style renderings of runic script or the black-white-red colors of the German Reich—come to constitute, at least for some perceptive sensibilities, visual genres that operate, as it were, automatically. For the habituated viewer, they become visible and perfectly legible not through the gaze but through a fleeting glimpse out of the corner of one's eye. In one telling case, in the fall of 2004 Andrea and Helmuth expressed premonitions that a restaurant still under construction near their office would soon turn into the up-and-coming rendezvous point for right-wing extremist groups in the district. They based their suspicions solely on the restaurant's signboard, which had already been installed weeks before its doors opened: a red background on which the restaurant's name, Spreehexe (the Spree witch), was imprinted in white Gothic characters with a black outline, and beneath it, also in white, were the words "German cuisine" (*deutsche Küche*). Some six months later, in the spring of 2005, Helmuth and I paid the establishment a visit. It was a typical German *Kneipe*, with simple wood furniture, most clients seated at the long bar, and a few scattered tables. Union and Hertha soccer fans (the latter a clear minority) were exchanging jokes over beers. Helmuth recapitulated to me, with more detail than I had so far commanded, the story of the police raid on the Spreehexe on the night preceding its scheduled inauguration. The raid interrupted a loud party whose crowd included some sixty prominent right-wing extremists. According to Helmuth, the mother of a key figure in the local militant group, who had long worked as a waitress at another nearby pub popular with the extreme right scene, had just been fired at the time.

Figure 5. The Spreehexe restaurant. To the social workers, the font and the red-black-white color combination on the signboard raised suspicions already months before the restaurant opened.

The party at the Spreehexe took place on her first day at her new workplace. The restaurant remained closed for months thereafter. It was on the curb in front of the restaurant, too, that Karl and his peers assisted at the NPD-organized soup kitchen that coincided with the democracy festival in nearby Schöneweide (see chapter 8).

Of course, the successful gloss of the restaurant as an incipient favorite owed not only to its suspicious signboard but, crucially, also to its location in Schöneweide, a neighborhood infamous—not entirely without reason—for its range of extreme right offerings. The very same sign could call up other significations elsewhere, or to other eyes. In fact, many of my informants associated the black-white-red combination at least as strongly with the colors of their favorite soccer club, Union. Simply by virtue of Union fandom and the paraphernalia that went with it, this color combination dominated their wardrobes. Far from viewing it as a problem, many, too, appreciated the chromatic agreement between Union and National Socialism. During matches, it was often difficult to determine whether certain items—buttons, tattoos, shirts—referred to this or that horizon of meaning. It is crucial, therefore, to remember that the manners in which different people read signs in context bespeak multiple ways of telling and a broad range of aesthetic sensibilities. These, in turn, translate into differential perceptions of places and signs—and of the relations between them—in the cityscape (see Shoshan 2008b). The following two extracts from my field notes are meant to give a sense of my own particular way of reading right-wing extremist places, shaped, no doubt, in part by an outsider's blissful ignorance, which led me repeatedly to places most Germans would strictly avoid, but in part also by a progressively habituated gaze:

> Crossing Sophienstraße, the renovated apartment houses, florists, toy shops, ethnic groceries, and anarchist graffiti metamorphose into derelict buildings, shutdown garages, stickers and flyers carrying slogans like "Deutschland erwache!" (Germany awake!) or "Rote Banden zerschlagen!" (Smash the red mobs!), and encoded inscriptions—"88" (for "Heil Hitler"), "KSG" (for "Kameradschaft Germania"), "134 DVZ" (for a WWII Waffen-SS division), or others that escape my powers of decryption. A heavily tattooed, broad-shouldered skinhead sporting a black leather jacket, high boots, and metal chains walks his husky dog through the deserted park and past the bench on which I paused to scribble down my impressions. (Berlin-Lichtenberg, July 19, 2003)

> Four muscular men—in their early thirties, I would guess—board the U5 train car in which I sit, heading back from Hellersdorf. Their heads shaved and their arms tattooed, their attire comprises CONSDAPLE and LONSDALE shirts—whose brand logos flaunt the illegal NSDA and NSDAP acronyms—as well as jeans and black boots. They take a position at the aisle's center, eyeing the passengers, many of whom exhibit visible signs of anxiety and transfer to adjacent cars at the next stop. (Berlin, July 27, 2003)

Such places presented me with a concentrated constellation of legible signs, both corporeal and noncorporeal. The indexical relations—the relations of physical proximity—between these places and the visual signs on display allowed the territorialization in the city of violence as potentiality. For me, but also for all those wise or experienced enough to avoid abandoned gardens in Lichtenberg or to move to the next train car, they summoned both the specter of a violent past and the latent violence of the present. Their spectrality lies in this doubling that they performed: the fusion in concrete sites of the violent nation and of nationalist violence.

One particularly effective manner of achieving visibility and legibility, as we have seen in this chapter, consists in the juxtaposition of special signs with special sites. For the Spreehexe restaurant, it was its spatial location in an area broadly perceived as friendly to right-wing extremists and in the proximity of other, similar establishments that inflected how it was perceived—an ecological determination, one might say. But for the Stars of David, it was their inscription upon monuments, gravestones, statues, and other heterotopic places that motivated their interpretation. Cemeteries in particular seem to feature prominently in the politics of visibility of the extreme right. Highly heterotopic places anywhere (according to Foucault), cemeteries in Germany are particularly profuse with exceptional values because they juxtapose not only life and death but also historical perpetrators and historical victims, cultural ideals and cultural taboos, and the honoring of the dead with the dead who must not be honored. The policing of Germany's taboos therefore frequently passes through its cemeteries, as do nationalist activists.

In Berlin, small "heroes' commemoration" rallies to honor German war fatalities have taken place at several cemeteries in recent years, each drawing a couple of hundred-strong crowds of right-wing extremists and Antifa protesters. In one instance, a group of activists challenged what its members described as the silencing of the memory of "German" (read, belonging to the German nation, as opposed to citizens of the German state) war victims. The group clandestinely transformed a commemorative plaque to the victims of National Socialism at the entrance to a cemetery in the central district of Friedrichshain. The original inscription, "At this cemetery victims of war and tyranny found their final rest in 315 graves," referred to the number of casualties of National Socialist atrocities or the war who were buried there. While not explicitly distinguishing between different kinds of victims, the mention of "tyranny" clearly referred to National Socialism as the main perpetrator, indeed, as single-handedly responsible for the war and all its deaths, while mentioning no other possible culprits. The activists replaced the dedication with an inscription that read "To the victims of the Anglo-American bombing terror against Germany's civilian population." Rendering the hundreds of thousands of casualties from the Allied forces' carpet bombings of civilian areas visible, and thereby reconfiguring the balance of historical responsibility,[15] went hand in hand with contesting the

---

[15] The phrases "bombing terror" (*Bombenterror*) or "bombing Holocaust" are, of course, far from neutral and are used strictly on the very far political right in Germany. Far beyond redressing a certain historical silencing that ordinarily avoids mention of the Allies' part in the deaths, and that takes caution not to attribute any responsibility to them, such terms set up the Allies as

memory not only of the victims of National Socialism but also of all victims of the war *as* victims of National Socialism, regardless of the circumstances of their deaths.

The replacement of the commemorative inscription challenged the terms with which a dominant regime of visibility polices the national vision. But it equally intervened in the representation of Germany's contemporary extreme right. The activists documented their action (as well as the cleanup they subsequently granted the cemetery) photographically and published the images in a Berlin-based nationalist website. As photographs, the very resignification of the cemetery and its aesthetic face-lift became signs that made themselves available for further recursion. Recall how the initial matching of the Stars of David with carefully selected, special sites charged them with certain meanings and associations that subsequently allowed their legible reiteration in far less discriminate locations. Here, too, the cemetery enabled successive visual operations, recursive acts of signification and interpretation.

Andreas Huyssen notes the salience of visibility and invisibility in architectural debates about the reconstruction of Berlin as the new national capital, where they articulated with remembering and forgetting (2003a). Right-wing extremist visibility tactics, however, are not strictly speaking about conjuring the National Socialist past into memory. After all, Berlin's landscape teems with visual invocations of that violence and its calendar full with ritualized representations of its history. Penciling a swastika on one of the gray slabs of the Holocaust Memorial—not a rare incident—is not about visibilizing a silenced past, for the 2,711 cement stelae that comprise the memorial surely achieve as much, and far more extravagantly. At stake in extreme right tactics is therefore not visualization per se but rather visibility regimes—the terms under which things are rendered visible and are seen.[16] Visual representation constitutes a fundamental dimension of memory cultures, and visibility regimes crucially shape modes of remembering and forgetting (cf. Huyssen 2003d, 9, 15). Dominant visibility regimes in contemporary Berlin incorporate the National Socialist past into the tangible cityscape along strictly regulated and austerely monumentalized outlines. The traumatic past is evacuated from the present. Or rather, in the present, it must appear only *as* historical memory and *as* practices of commemoration. The Holocaust Memorial presents an extreme case in this regard: its ascetically abstract, nonrepresentational monumentality evokes

---

terrorist and genocidal forces, bracketing National Socialist atrocities, the war itself, and German responsibility for it.

[16]Therein, too, lies a crucial difference between the two traumatic historical horizons of Germany—National Socialism and communism. As much as the two have recently been collapsed together as totalitarian pasts (see my discussion in chapter 1), the visual rendering of GDR symbols remains not only thoroughly legal but also socially condoned and even perceived as nostalgic kitsch. Such displays do not seem to provoke the kind of anxieties that are linked with the Nazi past.

the past purely as *Erfahrung*, as past experience whose presence in the present takes the form of an object for reflection, as acquired wisdom and accumulated knowledge, not as *Erlebnis*, as lived, phenomenological experience.[17]

The violent past is therefore plentifully visible, but always remotely, as it were, as a receding horizon of historical difference, as a radical other against which to imagine the here and now. Its varied appearances in the city carefully confine violence to the past. They visualize it precisely as memory, as memorial. But, as Robert Musil reminds us, "there is nothing as invisible as a monument" (cited in Huyssen 2003b, 32). Paradoxically, then, the visibilization of the National Socialist past in the present through its confinement to special sites of collective commemoration purifies the present of that past. The trouble with extreme right visibility practices has everything to do, then, with their manner of disrupting such dominant chronotopes of temporal rupture and spatial confinement—cemeteries, memorial plaques, monuments—by collapsing the temporal divide, by intruding upon it and disputing its spatial boundedness, by signaling their own presence not only *in* the present but as *of* the present. In the chronotopic articulations to which their manner of invoking this violent past in the cityscape give rise, the historical horizon of National Socialism fuses with contemporary forms of ultranationalist racism and violence. The past contaminates the present with its ghosts.

JUST MOURNING

Throughout this book, I have argued that in today's Germany, the management of hate opens up a terrain for enacting the national project of a reunified German polity, and that young right-wing extremists have been indispensable for elaborating this project and for performing this enactment. At the same time, right-wing extremists unsettle the national project. They territorialize uncanny visual remainders that disclose its incompleteness. They obstruct those regimes of visibility through which it would domesticate its specters. On most days, they do so in their quotidian habits, through a gamut of fashion, tattoos, jewelry, and other operators the spatial density of which marks certain places, like Schöneweide,

---

[17] This is not to say, of course, that the Holocaust Memorial does not present a very unique kind of *Erlebnis*. Quite the contrary, its design is conceived to create a sense of disorientation. Yet the relation between the *Erlebnis* it generates and its referent, the historical events it commemorates, is abstract and conceptual, not representational or mimetic. In this sense the memorial follows Horkheimer and Adorno's discussion of *Bilderverbot* (interdiction on representation) and mimesis in *The Dialectic of Enlightenment* and Adorno's later interdiction on representations of the Holocaust (Horkheimer and Adorno 2002 [1944]; see also Huyssen 2003c). A small, four-room space called the "Place of Information" with an exhibition about the Holocaust and its victims has been added to the original design of the memorial precisely because of its opaque abstractness. Tucked underground, however, it remains visually and experientially apart from the memorial itself.

as right-wing extremist. Occasionally, as with the Stars of David and the commemorative plaque at the cemetery, their interventions appear as sudden disruptions, as sharp incisions into the urban everyday. But every so often, the profound anxieties that they trigger and the colossal exertions that they set in motion crystallize into spectacular moments of ritualized performances. In such moments the charged, antagonistic encounter between incongruent—though inseparable—nations plays itself out.

Just how massive, frenzied, and hypervisible they become depends, of course, on the places where they occur and on the pasts that they conjure. Several such massive rites of collective effervescence stood out at the time of my fieldwork: the Rudolf Hess march in Wunsiedel, the Bavarian resting place of the former vice-führer, whom sympathizers acclaim as a peace-seeking role model betrayed by the Allies, imprisoned unjustly for life, and finally assassinated in his cell; the "heroes' commemoration" (*Heldengedenken*) at Germany's largest WWII military cemetery in Brandenburgian Halbe, where scores of thousands of SS and Wehrmacht soldiers, Home Guard (Volkssturm) recruits, National Socialist functionaries, known war criminals, and unfortunate civilians—all mostly casualties of the hopeless and gruesome last battles against the advancing Red Army—had been buried next to executed deserters and Soviet forced laborers; and the annual commemoration march for the bombing of Dresden, where right-wing extremists regularly unsettle the claims that masses of respectable citizens stake for a peaceful, socially sanctioned performance of mourning. Every year all three events bring together thousands of demonstrators, protesters, and police troops, as well as prominent politicians and a host of national and international media crews.[18] Hence, while one often finds significant crossover not only of people but also of slogans, outfits, and banners between such massive and mass-mediated mobilizations and smaller, local political rallies (such as the annual BASO demonstration in Treptow that I examined in chapter 8), the former clearly distinguish themselves from the latter by their scale, their stakes, and the sorts of political conversations in which they partake.

In such collective performances, the commemoration of "German" suffering and victimhood would seem to frustrate the national vision, to threaten its privileged position, and to contradict its pronouncements. At the war cemetery

[18] Also, with annual regularity, these events stand at the center of protracted legal contestations, the results of which remain unpredictable and varied. A legislative amendment hastily passed in 2005, on which I elaborate at greater length below, drastically changed the terms of these disputes, allowing the state of Brandenburg to place a permanent ban on demonstrations near the Halbe war cemetery. Recent "heroes' commemoration" rallies have proceeded through the town of Halbe but could not approach the actual burying place of the "heroes." The implications of the legal amendment to the Hess march initially appeared less clear-cut. Attempts by the town of Wunsiedel to employ it as a legal instrument for banning the annual march meandered through different juridical instances for years before winning the approval of the Federal Constitutional Court.

in Halbe, for example, the officially endorsed heroes are the executed deserters, not those who obeyed (or worse, issued) orders to kill. In a similar vein,
by any conventional account, Hess was a devout Nazi and a top war criminal,
not a peace-seeking hero. And while no doubt all acknowledge—and many
deeply mourn—Dresden's near evisceration by the Allies, its tragedy is generally understood to result from German warmongering. Socially approved ways
of talking about and remembering the German past therefore see themselves
violated by right-wing extremist memory discourses,[19] and not gratuitously, for
the right-wing extremists I knew did in fact attack hegemonic narratives of the
national past. Often running up against legal limits, their acts aimed to provoke,
indeed to scandalize, the outer frontiers of historical memory in Germany.

But their significance in such events and their role in mass publicity turn out
to be far more ambivalent. In chapter 3, we saw how no neat distinction could
be drawn between the so-called extreme and the mainstream. The words of
my informants resonated uncannily even with certain mass-publicized political discourse, not to mention neighborhood pub talk. And yet, this discursive
porosity notwithstanding, my informants performed crucial work in national
mass publicity as markers of radical difference and forbidden terrain. For example, politicians who express strongly racist positions are often called out and
shamed for the similarity between their enunciations and those of right-wing
extremists. The latter are therefore constituted politically in a curious dialectic.
On the one hand, they take form as they tactically maneuver the repressive
state. On the other hand, however, they mark and define what counts in the first
place as illicit ways of remembering German suffering, of narrating its experiences, or of sequencing its histories. This forbidden terrain, put differently, is in
significant part understood to consist of that which right-wing extremists actually say and do. And it is this very dialectic of reciprocal constitution that allows, too, the fabrication of distance with respect to it.

One might be tempted to say that my informants and others like them have
facilitated the work of official and dominant discourses of historical memory
by allowing the production of radical difference from bad nationalism. But
they stand, in fact, as a far more disquieting rem(a)inder. Their talk of German suffering and their performances of remembrance are widely perceived as
metonymic signs of concealed—because tabooed—Nazi sympathies; in other
words, as dishonest, as really being about something else. But the line that separates honest from dishonest mourning is porous and shifting. It has not always
stood where it stands today. Without claiming to pinpoint the precise historical
moment in which it shifted (but see Habermas 1997b), one could safely say

---

[19] As we have seen throughout the book, and especially in chapter 4, the principal concern in the
policing of these boundaries—by legal or cultural interdictions—consists in those disruptions of
dominant narratives that aim toward publicity, and less in the regulation of discourse and behavior
in intimate spheres.

that well into the 1980s the public recollection of "German" victimhood and suffering had been strongly tabooed. The ways in which official and socially dominant discourses today engage these once-prohibited questions would have won them, not long ago, the reputation of nationalist revisionists.[20] Public memory of German suffering—in literature, art, political discourse, intellectual debates, or mass events—is still uncertain and hesitant, still unsure of its legitimacy.[21] Nevertheless, that such a shift has occurred is evident in a range of recent cultural productions.[22] If extreme right memory practices seem to pose a threat so menacing to the national project in Germany, this is also because they are correctly perceived to stand not so far (temporally) from today's awakening attention in mass publicity to German suffering and victimization. What they provoke, then, are fears that today's newly legitimized commemorations of German suffering could unleash the same imputations of Nazi sympathies as in the near past.

CATASTROPHE AT THE GATE

In order to give the reader a more concrete sense of the panic that surrounds such visual transgressions against cultural frontiers, I conclude with a detailed look at one especially extravagant contestation of this sort. Among all the different sites that Berlin has to offer for nationalist marchers, the capital's best-known monument, the Brandenburg Gate, has been a particularly prized

[20] However, in a critique of W. G. Sebald's thesis in his *Luftkrieg und Literatur* about the silencing of German suffering, and particularly of the horrors of mass bombardment of civil areas late in the war, Andreas Huyssen shows that, quite to the contrary, several German authors have taken up the topic (Sebald 1999; Huyssen 2003e).

[21] See, for example, my discussion in chapter 1 of Günter Grass's treatment of German suffering in his novel *Im Krebsgang* (*Crabwalk*), and of how its convoluted structure and chronotopic transpositions reveal an anxiety about the legitimacy of the text itself.

[22] Transformations in mass publicity memory cultures have been evident in a number of recent literary and critical works, including W. G. Sebald's *Luftkrieg und Literatur* (translated as *On the Natural History of Destruction* [1999]) or Günter Grass's *Im Krebsgang* (*Crabwalk* [1992]) and *Unkenrufe* (*The Call of the Toad* [2002a]). Besides a general growing interest of the German film industry in the National Socialist period and in the war over the past couple of decades, which has produced multiple new titles, several recent movies have represented German history in ways previously unthinkable or at least controversial, including, for example, *The Downfall*, which not only paints a picture of Hitler that for some is too complex for comfort but also portrays some members of his inner circle in a positive, almost humane light; *Sophie Scholl: The Final Days* and *The Edelweiss Pirates*, which present stories of German resistance and martyrdom; and, more recently, *The Book Thief*, which depicts German victimhood (particularly, political persecution) under the Nazis and solidarity with refugees (Glasow 2004; Hirschbiegel 2004; Rothemund 2005; Percival 2013). The drastic resignification of the rather long tradition of marking the anniversary of Dresden's bombing—for decades sponsored by the GDR state, later associated with the Church and the opposition, and now, in the Federal Republic, a matter of civil society—reveals a similar reconfiguration of national taboos.

location, no doubt at least in part because the desire to parade past it has been repeatedly frustrated. The investment in marching under the monument surely owes something as well to its invocation of more than one German Reich. But at least as significant is the monument's strategic value for visibility and publicity. As the newly crowned icon of the old Federal Republic, as the trademark (see Huyssen 2003d, 48) and the logo for rebranding a unified, confident, yet neighborly Germany, the Brandenburg Gate forms a key emblem for representing the German nation not only to itself but also to the world at large. To its east the historic Unter den Linden Avenue, overflowing with embassies, government and parliamentary offices, national memorials, opera houses, museums, and other prime attractions, to its north the renovated Reichstag, southward the new Holocaust Memorial, and to the west the Victory Column, the Gate marks the center of gravity—in both senses of the word—of both Berlin and the Berlin Republic. It signals, too, the center of Berlin's sightseeing and diplomatic ambit. Unlike remote quarters of the city like Treptow, where marching neo-Nazis would be accompanied by junior reporters for the local press, at the Brandenburg Gate they would no doubt come under the cameras of countless international media crews and under the bewildered gazes of many foreign tourists. The state's investment in foreclosing precisely such an eventuality no doubt reveals the palpable effect of this international dimension.[23]

All the more so when the NPD duly registered a march from Alexanderplatz, down Unter den Linden, under the Gate, and past the Holocaust Memorial for May 8, 2005, the sixtieth anniversary of the Third Reich's capitulation to the Allies. This was by any standard an occasion of international proportions. The event would have no doubt been marked by several ceremonies, some with representatives of the Allied forces, as well as historical journalism, political speeches, and television documentaries. But the public panic into which it gradually spiraled effectively charged the Gate with fetish-like qualities.

The NPD registered the event under the heading "60 Years of the Liberation Lie—Enough with the Guilt Cult!" (60 Jahre Befreiungslüge—Schluss mit dem Schuldkult!). Instead of "day of liberation," they advocated the terms "day of defeat" and "day of capitulation." They could hardly have chosen a more incendiary vocabulary for their demonstration, at least without dangerously transgressing legal boundaries. But in fact, that the NPD could launch such a lexical assault on the notion of liberation in the first place, and, more significantly, that such an assault would be broadly taken as metonymic of National Socialist sympathies, signaled just how far the tideline of collective memory and historical narrative has recently shifted. The rather celebratory notion of liberation (*Befreiung*) as a designation for that which is to be commemorated on May 8 took root in national public discourse only in the 1980s. Its rise displaced earlier terms

---

[23] As I have noted, the international gaze upon Germany is taken seriously and discussed explicitly in court decisions, journalism, political discourse, and in informal chat.

that many employed until then—the "day of the defeat" (*Niederlage*) and the "day of the capitulation" (*Kapitulation*), the very phrases promoted today by the NPD.

Especially on the political left, many still express profound unease about this discursive substitution (see, e.g., Habermas 1997a). They, too, sense a fundamental deception in the idiom of liberation, namely, its underlying implication that the Allies had somehow emancipated the German *Volk* from the yoke of National Socialism in the same manner that, for example, the French had been liberated from its occupation. In such a narrative, National Socialism remains, as it were, external to Germany, which is cleared of historical responsibility. Simply put, if Germans were liberated from National Socialism, then they could not have been Nazis. If Germans were indeed Nazis, and hence bear historical responsibility for actions they accept as "theirs," then they could only have been defeated.[24] And yet, by 2005 the discourse of liberation had become commonplace enough that it could serve as the rallying cry for an attack from the right. We see here again, then, just how near right-wing extremist political idioms stand to what are usually understood to be mainstream, legitimate discourses.

At the same time, regardless of the catchphrases they used, the mere imagery of thousands of NPD supporters advancing past Unter den Linden, the Gate, the Holocaust Memorial, and multiple diplomatic missions, brandishing nationalist banners and chanting nationalist slogans, and this on the sixtieth anniversary of German surrender, would in itself have been sufficient to constitute a national scandal. The struggle over the Gate opened up a peculiar political space in which right and left came together, where all traces of a frontier between state and civil society vanished, and where the presumed system of liberal democratic checks and balances was suspended as government, administration, courts, police authorities, legislators, and militant protestors colluded—sometimes quite transparently, sometimes less so—to avert a national catastrophe.[25]

When news of the NPD's plans broke in mid-November 2004, politicians from across the board vowed that the march would not come to pass, certainly not in its proposed route. The conservative CDU Party, then in opposition, had long pressed for legislation that would restrict the constitutionally guaranteed freedom of assembly. This time, too, it found itself isolated against a broad parliamentary coalition that rejected any talk of further limitations on basic civil rights. The existing laws, so the emerging consensus insisted at the time, should

[24] Some embrace the term critically, as appropriately indicative not of the liberation of National Socialist Germany from itself but rather of the liberation of occupied Europe from Germany, a rather questionable twist considering that by May 8, 1945, most of Europe had already been liberated.

[25] I rely here on numerous newspaper articles from my press archive (see, e.g., Averesch 2005; *Berliner Morgenpost* 2005b; *Der Spiegel* 2005; Emmerich 2005; *Netzeitung* 2005; Rogalla 2005).

suffice for banning the demonstration. One way or another, no one seemed to doubt, the looming calamity would have to be forestalled. But by mid-February, composed tranquillity had turned into outright panic. At about that time, the sixtieth anniversary of Dresden's bombing had witnessed thousands-strong crowds of right-wing extremists gathering to mark the occasion (together with thousands of "respectable" mourners, Antifa militants, and riot police troops) under the limelight of international media (see, e.g., Harding 2005b). There was hardly any question that a similar event in Berlin on May 8 would present an even more embarrassing image of the new Germany to the world. Even worse, it slowly emerged that existing legislation would likely fail to obviate this eventuality. The tables had turned and now all but the small, liberal FDP—including long-standing opponents to curbs on demonstration rights—enthusiastically advocated swift and decisive legislative action to meet the impending challenge. But in the deliberations, statements, and objections about how precisely to act that marked the following month, eagerness seemed to be matched by confusion and discord.

By mid-March an agreement between different political parties about proposed legislation nevertheless seemed to surface. Specifically, the legal reform, advanced by a clear parliamentary majority, included two key amendments. The first, applied to the Federal Assembly Right Law, allowed the prohibition of demonstrations at memorial sites "of historically outstanding, supra-regional importance" dedicated to the memory of the victims of National Socialism,[26] especially if circumstances suggested that the demonstrations would detract from the dignity of the deceased. It declared the Holocaust Memorial explicitly as one such site and authorized state legislatures to name others (Bundesministerium der Justiz 2005). The second amendment applied to the criminal law (specifically to section 130, "incitement"; see chapter 4), which had previously criminalized only the approval, denial, or underplaying of National Socialist *atrocities*, but was now fitted with an additional clause that banned the approval, glorification, or justification of *any aspect* of National Socialism in general (ibid. 2008). By eliminating the distinction between National Socialist crimes and other dimensions of National Socialist history and ideology (though maintaining that very distinction, of course, in the form of two separate clauses), this last change aimed directly at the commemoration of the alleged peace mission of Rudolf Hess, the former vice-führer—or, for that matter, of any recollection of him in positive light—and therefore provided an effective legal weapon against the annual Hess march.

But by the time such agreement cohered, juridical experts had already clarified that the proposed legislation, while protecting sites of commemoration

---

[26]Note the weight given by this formulation to the question of publicity and its scale. The phrase "outstanding, supra-regional importance" refers to places that, put differently, would attract international attention.

such as the Holocaust Memorial or the military cemetery at Halbe, and while salvaging the town of Wunsiedel from hordes of neo-Nazi pilgrims, would nevertheless leave the Brandenburg Gate—alas, neither a site of remembrance nor one of shame—utterly exposed and defenseless against the imminent catastrophe. Their prayers for a legal deus ex machina shattered, authorities now turned to ordinary residents and civil society groups for salvation. A handful of civil associations had already registered small commemorative events along Unter den Linden and in the vicinity of the Brandenburg Gate well before the NPD had made its plans public. Following in their footsteps, Berlin's mayor and other city dignitaries issued urgent calls for interested parties to organize additional events along the projected route of the march and to mobilize en masse for the designated day in order to obstruct the NPD and defend democracy. Many organizations heeded the call. Within a few weeks, the Berlin Senate announced its plan to fight off the NPD threat by organizing a "Day for Democracy" festival at the Brandenburg Gate. With strong backing from the federal government and from the national leadership of most parliamentary parties, the democracy festival was intended to serve as an umbrella for numerous particular initiatives that would bring together a broad and colorful coalition of forces.

As the month of April drew to a close, all eyes were set on the Assembly Authority (Versammlungsbehörde) of the Berlin police, which seemed to hold the fate of Germany in its hands. Charged with overseeing all public assemblies in the state, it held ultimate power of adjudication between competing events and could approve, reject, or modify their designs. The Assembly Authority, it was repeatedly made clear, saw itself under no obligation—and, indeed, found itself under no legal requirement—to abide by a first-come, first-served principle. Its principal concern consisted in maintaining public order, and other considerations could well weigh heavier in its final decision. Of course, the degree of disorder that the march could be anticipated to unleash had everything to do with just how serious, massive, and effective the mobilizations against it seemed to have been. Given the soaring momentum of the Day for Democracy and of multiple other, related gatherings, there was little surprise when the Assembly Authority ruled that the NPD march would only be permitted to advance about halfway down Unter den Linden before terminating at the Friedrichstraße train station, far from the Gate. Nor were any eyebrows raised when Berlin's High Court of Justice and later the Federal Constitutional Court upheld the decision against the NPD's appeals. In fact, most experts and politicians insisted with striking confidence that, given the public stakes involved, the march was highly unlikely to ever leave its initial gathering place at Alexanderplatz, much less to arrive at its newly assigned, truncated destination at the Friedrichstraße train station. I heard similar pronouncements from many of my young informants in Treptow.

The overcast morning of Sunday, May 8, saw Berlin's center transformed into a strange chronotope, at once carnival and battleground. In the multitude,

Figure 6. Pariser Platz. A panoramic rendering of the Brandenburg Gate and its surroundings as they appeared in the wake of World War II, installed to mark the sixtieth anniversary of the Third Reich's capitulation to the Allies.

numbering many thousands, law enforcement troops, militant antifascists, engaged middle-class citizens, top politicians, curious passersby, and unfortunate, mystified tourists bounced against each other. Food and beer stands encircled a large outdoor performance stage by the Gate. June Seventeenth Street, the broad avenue leading from the Gate into the Tiergarten park, had been crammed with the pavilions of political parties and government agencies, the Bundestag and Berlin's House of Representatives, the EU Commission and the EU Parliament, church societies and labor unions, foundations and pedagogical institutions, immigrant advocacy groups and Antifa associations, social work and youth work organizations, antiracism and refugee advocacy NGOs, newspapers and professional associations, and coalitions for democracy and tolerance or against racism and right-wing extremism, as well as a multicultural assortment of ethnic food stalls. Crossing the Gate eastward to Pariser Platz, an art exhibit displayed a gargantuan, panoramic, photo-realist rendering of the area in ashes after the war. Farther east, various other commemorative happenings spotted Unter den Linden.

It was, then, through and around the Brandenburg Gate—that singular logo of the newly branded Berlin Republic—that Germany had been rendered visible to itself and to the world as a nation of democracy, tolerance, and diversity. For many who showed up for the festivities, however, the real action took place at the other end of Unter den Linden. Arriving at the Alexanderplatz train station that morning, I stood at the platform and watched the NPD supporters as they disembarked from incoming trains. The German friends with whom I arrived there quickly abandoned me—they could not bear the physical proximity to so many neo-Nazis, they explained. The NPD crowds slowly made their way down from the platform level to the ground floor of the station, where a cacophonous commotion of protests welcomed them. Riot police directed them to long queues that crawled slowly into long tents from which, after passing security checks, they emerged into a fenced area and ambled toward their assembly spot near the Rote Rathaus (City Hall). This was the last that I—or for that matter virtually anyone else—would see of them that day. Around them, the police had cordoned off a vast area, stretching from Alexanderplatz almost 700 meters (about 765 yards) to the bank of the Spree River. The fences kept onlookers too far from the NPD demonstrators to spot anything but the thick layer of police that surrounded them, and even that only barely and from select spots. It was as if the threat of contamination was perceived to be so high that nothing but total visual enclosure could safeguard society from it.

At the circumference of this (de)militarized zone, thousands of loud demonstrators marched under the flags of the Soviet Union, the United States, Great Britain, France, and Israel, holding banners with antifascist slogans and signs that thanked the Allies for defeating the Third Reich. On the bridges leading over the Spree, multitudes of animated protestors keen on blockading the march with their bodies faced battalions of water cannons, armored vehicles, and storm trooper–like phalanxes. In other, seemingly similar occasions (recall the BASO march through Treptow), police and protesters had clashed violently. Ordinarily, only on isolated occasions have the forces of law failed to prevail and protect the constitutional right of assembly and allow the right-wing marchers to proceed.[27] But on that day there would be no ritualized skirmishes between antifascists and law enforcement troops at the heart of the German capital. Having securely invisibilized the menace, the authorities prevented the NPD crowds from advancing even toward their revised and police-sanctioned itinerary, citing the massive multitudes of protesters and the risk of violent escalation. It later emerged that the police had rejected the organizers' proposal for an alternative route that would have either skirted or kept to a minimum clashes with counterdemonstrators. And so, following a strangely peaceful—and rainy—six-hour standoff, the police announced that it was forced to call off the march. Few seemed surprised by the decision, and the crowds gradually

---

[27] I should note that the present balance of power between violent Antifa protesters and the police, unfavorable as it is toward the former, has only been established recently. The German far left had in the past been extraordinarily successful in sabotaging by force the plans of its political antagonists. Yet the German police force has been as effective in devising methods for countering such protests. Most notably, its ban on any face masks during demonstrations irreparably curtailed black block tactics.

dispersed more with a sense of having dutifully fulfilled their role in a well-choreographed performance than of having valiantly defied an authoritarian state that some of them, at least, routinely accuse of colluding with neo-Nazis.

"The police didn't want to meet its duties for political reasons, because pictures of thousands of 'neo-Nazis' demonstrating in the middle of Berlin against the liberation festivities simply didn't suit the political mafia of this decayed system," so ran one of the many vindictive commentaries that appeared on extreme right online forums immediately thereafter. Indeed, the only reports on the event that attempted convolutedly to portray it as anything but outright defeat could be found on the NPD's official website. And yet most commentators voiced little indignation, much less surprise, about how the demonstration unfolded. There had never been any doubt, so ran the general tone of the discussion, that, somehow or other, the state would hinder the marchers from reaching the Gate (Berliner Infoportal 2005a and 2005b; Freier Widerstand 2005; NPD 2005).

Mainstream national media, on the other hand, warmly applauded the routing of the NPD as unequivocal corroboration of the ironclad commitment of Germany's citizens to the values of democracy and tolerance, to the respectful memory of the victims of the Third Reich, and to the unrelenting fight against racist nationalism (see, e.g., Der Tagesspiegel 2005a; Fahrun 2005; Schmale 2005). Reports cited tens of thousands of participants in the Day for Democracy festival, in various commemoration events, and in the protests, as against the three-thousand-odd-strong NPD crowd. A range of public personalities described the unfolding of May 8 as signaling the country's abhorrence of its past, its democratic steadfastness, and its peaceful nature. Similarly, congratulatory accounts appeared in international media as well (see, e.g., Bernstein 2005; Haaretz 2005; Harding 2005c).

For the participants and spectators who gathered in Berlin's center that day, for the national public that learned of it via mass publicity, and for international audiences that chanced upon laudatory reports on Germany's sixtieth liberation anniversary, the NPD and its followers were for all purposes disappeared, staved off from any meaningful sites and carefully kept away from the eyes, cameras, and microphones of countless media crews that swarmed the city. The latter, instead, basked in the conviviality of a resolutely democratic Germany, historically both guilty and grateful on that day of remembrance, the sounds and sights of which overwhelmed the entire area, condensing with particular intensity around its multiple monuments and memorials. The NPD appeared as a black hole, a rupture in the space-time of the cityscape that remained invisible but at once defined the center of gravity around which the visible world revolved. Pushed out of sight, it worked as an abstract, occult force perceptible solely through its spectacularly hypervisible effects.[28] Had I not rushed to the

---

[28] On the relation between the occult and the abstract, and between the two terms and violence, see Comaroff and Comaroff (1999).

train station that morning to witness the busy influx of NPD demonstrators, I could have well wondered whether they had even been there, and—much like the tattoo putatively under the Band-Aid of a marching nationalist—whether that would have made any difference. It was as invisible specters, as a present absence, and not as concrete adversaries, that they enabled the visualization of a different German nationhood. Looked at differently, in its frenzied prance around its mortal nemesis, the democratic German nation gained shape and form against its ghosts, and in so doing incorporated these ghosts as an indispensable yet unsettling rem(a)inder of its own lingering incompleteness.

Afterword
IIIIIIIIIIIIIIIIIIIIIIIII

IN RECENT YEARS, as tensions between Athens and Berlin over the former's debt crisis have deepened, Germany's past was staged not only on the streets of Greece, where portraits of Chancellor Merkel and Finance Minister Schäuble, rendered as Nazis, decorated demonstration posters. Under the shadow of sour negotiations, the Greek government announced it would seek 162 billion euros in damages from Germany over unpaid WWII reparations and a forced wartime loan. Later, citing a figure of 341 billion euros, Justice Minister Paraskevopoulos raised the possibility of property seizures should Germany fail to respect its alleged obligations. Prime Minister Tsipras and other prominent politicians spoke of "an open wound" and a "moral issue." For the most part, Berlin and German media hit back with anger and denial, some complaining about "moral blackmail." Germany's debts and reparations have been legally, politically, and definitively resolved during its reunification, Merkel insisted; 1989, we see once more, continued to re-sequence history and signal a new "Stunde Null" and a new national project.

However, the issue was in fact far from resolved, and not only throughout Europe but also at home. The left-wing Linke Party has called to acknowledge and repay part of the claims, and to resolve others legally. Key Greens and SPD politicians—the latter, members of Merkel's ruling coalition—followed suit and broke ranks, insisting that the question of Germany's historical responsibility must remain open and that the claims be given due consideration. While Merkel and Tsipras bickered in public on the merits of the Greek claims during the latter's visit to Berlin in March 2015, the international press reported on a German tourist couple who, in order to make up for their governments' attitude, calculated and donated their share of the national debt, at 875 euros per German, at the city hall of the Greek town of Napflio. But already before the reparations claims appeared, some accused Germany—in the words of one historian, "the biggest debt transgressor of the twentieth century" (*Der Spiegel* 2011a)—of historical amnesia and hypocrisy for its uncompromising position. Critics now urged Germany to emulate once more the example of the American occupiers, and specifically their generous and vital postwar debt forgiveness (Ritschl 2011).[1]

---

[1] In chapter 2, I explained how the narrative of the United States as the strong, democratic, liberal, and triumphant power that rebuilds a devastated economy and disseminates a culture of democracy in a post-totalitarian society became transposed to the relation between West and East

With anger over German policy toward Greece still fuming and uncanny historical comparisons in the air, during the second half of 2015, the so-called refugee crisis painted Chancellor Merkel in a drastically different, almost diametrically opposed light. Whereas numerous EU-member states pressed for strict asylum policies and tightened border controls, the German government has advocated for European solidarity with and responsibility for the refugees. This call has found an echo in broad voluntary civil mobilizations across the country in support of asylum seekers, even as incidents of xenophobic violence have also climbed steeply, particularly against the background of political indifference, rhetorical fearmongering, and historical amnesia across the Continent. Germany now seems to have emerged as the torchbearer of European moral values, political solidarity, and historical responsibility. This celebratory image, too, has been read with reference to the country's National Socialist and communist pasts. As one observer put it, "Raised in East Germany, [Merkel] owes her freedom to European unity. It is a personal matter. The last time Europe was awash in millions of refugees was in 1945 as the Third Reich collapsed. It is a historical matter. Germany could not turn its back" (Cohen, 2015). Whether favorably or not, then, Germany today continues to confront its history on the European and international scene.

While first the Greek debt crisis and later the refugee crisis brought Germany's historical and moral responsibility back into focus, the national project at home has remained fragile and contested, regularly beset by flashes of ugly nationalism. In 2010, SPD politician Thilo Sarrazin's best seller *Deutschland schafft sich ab* (*Germany Is Doing Away with Itself* [2012]) denounced Germany's immigration policy, proclaimed the failure of integration, and argued, among other inflammatory Islamophobic claims, that the intelligence of Muslims in Germany is lower than that of the country's non-Muslim citizens. Sarrazin is no fringe figure. He had served for seven years as Berlin's minister of finance before joining the executive board of the Deutsche Bundesbank (Germany's central bank), a position from which he later resigned under heavy political pressure. Notwithstanding his defiant defense of his hugely popular book, the Social Democratic Party ruled against revoking his membership (see, e.g., *Der Spiegel* 2010).

Before the dust has settled, the Alternative für Deutschland (Alternative for Germany, or AfD) Party made its debut on the far right of the political field. The AfD, whose electoral gains have alarmed the traditional right, has stood for

---

Germany in the aftermath of reunification (cf. Borneman 1993; Glaeser 2000). In the current demand of Germany to follow the example of the Americans' generous debt politics, we encounter yet another possibility for performing the German nation in the figure of the liberators, but it is a call that Germany has dismissed. For English press coverage of the debates about the claims and the tensions in Greek German relations over them, see, for example, the following the *Guardian* articles: Ritschl (2011); Dearden (2013); Inman (2013); Agence France (2015); Connolly and Smith (2015); Reuters (2015); Smith (2015); Traynor (2015).

cultural conservatism and economic liberalism. While its leaders have repeatedly rejected accusations of anti-immigrant stances as defamatory, some of the most prominent among them have publicly supported the PEGIDA (Patriotische Europäer gegen die Islamisierung des Abendlandes, or Patriotic Europeans against the Islamization of the West) movement. In late 2014 and early 2015 PEGIDA mobilized thousands weekly under an openly Islamophobic agenda.[2]

Some three months after the rallies had begun, and faced with embarrassing international press coverage, Merkel unequivocally condemned the PEGIDA movement (as she also earlier did Sarrazin) in an interview in a major national newspaper. Like other prominent politicians, she emphasized her sympathy with PEGIDA followers and their preoccupations. But she warned them against their political manipulation by the leaders, whom she strongly denounced:

> I understand many problems that worry many people, such as the indisputable questions raised by immigration, which in other ways is a gain for our land and besides indispensable, or the criminality in the big cities or in certain border areas . . . Among those who organize these demonstrations, prejudices, bitterness, even hate too often play a role . . . I must understand the concerns, but I need not have understanding (*Verständnis*) for all forms of demonstration. (*Der Spiegel* 2015; my translation)

Merkel's assignation of responsibility distinguishes between innocent, legitimately preoccupied, vulnerable, but misguided citizens (*besorgte Bürger*, or "concerned citizens") and their irresponsible, hateful, but few leaders. To be sure, in exculpating and humanizing the marching masses while singling out the culprits, Merkel's words struggle to isolate and control the menace of bad nationalism. But this book allows us, I think, to hear a different voice as well. Merkel's distribution of sympathy and censure between naive followers and manipulative leaders at the same time acknowledges and embraces the formers' (Islamophobic) feelings, concerns, and demands. It only insists that official taboos be respected in the expression of such sentiments. Far from condemning hateful affects per se, Merkel's exhortation to Islamophobic respectability aims to orchestrate their political expression, to regulate their public performance, to manage them.

Throughout this book, we have encountered an entire universe of forces and interests that perform the everyday labor of managing hate. In Treptow, since I concluded my fieldwork, the social workers are still afoot, marches have repeatedly rolled through the district, racist and political violence has not abated,

---

[2]PEGIDA's founder, Lutz Bachmann, described himself as "foreigner-friendly" and expressed support for asylum seekers. The language of both speakers and attendants at the demonstrations he organized, however, was often blatantly anti-refugee and anti-immigrant. According to press reports, leaked correspondence from internal online forums included vitriolic xenophobic nationalism. The movement, which originated in Dresden, gave rise to local imitations in a number of other German cities, including, for example, Berlin, Cologne, and Leipzig.

and varied organizations have continued to struggle against the extreme right. Farther afield, another eastern district to the north of Treptow has in recent years become the center of right-wing extremist mobilizations and activities in protest against the planned erection of a refugee shelter. While it has regularly hosted nationalists from across Berlin and nearby Brandenburg, as well as a range of forces that have arrived to demonstrate against them, my visits there in recent field trips have confirmed that the campaign had also won significant local support. Speakers at demonstrations or town-hall meetings aired grievances about their neighborhood and anxieties about its future. Meanwhile, a whole response mechanism—local NGOs, public figures, cultural centers, city offices, party chapters, police forces—was activated and deployed to contain them, to govern their hate.

What I have called the management of hate in this book appears today, if anything, even more enduring than a decade ago, when I commenced my fieldwork. Its robust anchoring and performance in constitutional and penal codes, law enforcement and state surveillance, welfare and social services, expert discourses and media apparatuses, or schools and soccer club regulations will likely grant it a certain longevity. In this book, I have understood the management of hate as an immense project of affective governance. This, in turn, implies thinking of affect as publicly mediated and hence as a potential object—and locus—of projects of intervention, regulation, and control. It equally suggests that such projects themselves—the very strategies, structures, and operations of the management of hate—are pregnant with affective stakes.

At the same time, this book is also a study of how the management of hate emerges from, articulates, and responds to the fundamental contradictions of post-wall German nationalism. Young right-wing extremists operate as reminders of Germany's illicit pasts and tabooed traditions, which they bind to the present (no doubt, Sarrazin or PEGIDA have had similar effects, albeit in different ways). Their exclusion as political deviants and their expulsion to an extremist elsewhere, we have seen, are simultaneously inclusionary gestures. First, while young right-wing extremists stand for radical otherness, theirs is an internal form of otherness nonetheless. It is an allochronic otherness that—in contrast with the figure of the immigrant other, for example—sits squarely within "our" history, "our" past. Second, insofar as the national project has turned into a campaign against bad nationalism, the management of hate has secured the latter's fundamental place in Germany's future nation-building process. The governance of what I have called "the national vision" forms a vital part of this nation-making enterprise. It is, recall, around the NPD as a black hole that a democratic, liberal, tolerant, cosmopolitan nation is performed.

Thus understood, hate becomes, on the one hand, the site and object of interventions and regulations, of proscriptions and prescriptions, of institutions and discourses, of scientific experiments and preventive public health measures.

On the other hand, it becomes the spectral sign that incarnates the past in the present, that threatens constantly to subvert the brave new world discourse of historical closure and new beginnings (recall Merkel on war reparations). Put differently, the right-wing extremist Thing and other contemporary rem(a)inders of the national past enable an entire politics of affective management that is at once, too, a politics of memory and a nation-building project. And yet, they also escape and frustrate this endeavor, producing excesses and illegibilities that both invite and stubbornly defy domestication, interpretation, and control.

The management of hate in Germany operates where the shadows of the past join the exigencies of the present. This is a different way of describing it as the place where social and political-historical peripheries come together, or, as I described it in chapter 1, where new poor and old ghosts meet. Since the end of my fieldwork, the previous European miracle economies of the real estate bubble busted in sequence and the common currency has faced its most difficult crisis by far yet. Germany's economic outlook, by contrast, has turned substantially more optimistic than it did a decade ago. Unemployment has fallen and positive—if low—growth has stabilized.[3] Branded the sick man of Europe only a decade ago, today Germany parades itself as the Eurozone's success story and role model. But, as one observer sardonically put it, this is a Eurozone that has performed "worse than Japan during its lost decade in the 1990s, worse even than Europe in the 1930s" (Legrain 2015). As important, it is an increasingly polarized Europe in which Germany compares less favorably with the Continent's other rich countries. Domestically, inequality and poverty shot up at the start of the new millennium and have since remained high.[4] Immigrants and their descendants, East Germans, and the young have continued to fare worse. In Treptow, groups of young working-class right-wing extremists maintain an active and visible presence on the streets. For the foreseeable future, they will continue to fuse together illicit histories and unsavory presents.

As significant, the crawling economic recovery of the past few years shows no signs of success in rehabilitating the viability of economic patriotism organized around the mass utopia of collective prosperity. In recent visits to Germany, I have encountered not so much a recuperated sense of economic patriotism as deep anxieties about the crises at the doorstep, whose devastating impact many considered inevitable. Any fresh economic crisis, it is assumed, will offer a sure gain for the extreme right.

At a broader level, this book is conceived as a contribution to the study of governance. In anthropology, research on governance has increasingly attended to

---

[3] From more than 11 percent in 2005 to less than 6 percent in 2011 according to OECD figures.

[4] The Gini coefficient went from 0.259 in 1999 to 0.297 in 2005, and the poverty rate from 6.4 to 9.1.

the politics of affect as constitutive to its analytical object. More and more, governance is understood as a political operation that addresses, draws on, and answers to a series of affective stakes (see, e.g., Muehlebach 2012; Navaro-Yashin 2012; Schwenkel 2013; Shoshan 2014). The analyses I offer in this book reveal affective dimensions of legal codes, norms and methods of law enforcement, the surveillance functions of the neoliberal social state, therapeutic efforts of rehabilitation, inoculative interventions that target the national public, and the management of the national vision. Beyond highlighting the multiplicity of sites and stakeholders, my aim has been to reveal their reciprocal porosity, proximity and intimacy, mutual slippage, and inseparability. *The Management of Hate* in that sense offers a methodological framework for exploring the governance of affect, a no doubt tentative and inconclusive map of its principal sites, ethnographically observable processes, and relevant context.

Potentially, a framework of this kind could serve—selectively, of course—to explore a range of projects of affective governance. But hate in particular has strangely suffered from insufficient ethnographic attention.[5] In *The Management of Hate*, my interest has been to understand hate as an object, a dimension, and a field of governance, but also as mediated by the urgent political battles of the day. More ethnographic work that would approach hate less as an individual emotion and more as publicly transacted, socially managed, and politically governed would enrich an underexplored field and is certain to produce valuable insights.

It is difficult to imagine that such an anthropology of hate would suffer from scarcity of research topics. But it may arguably prove especially propitious for studying the centrality of xenophobic affects in the political life of European countries today. More or less robust and successful movements and political parties with unapologetically anti-immigrant agendas have become a staple across the Continent. Most countries have also witnessed racial and political violence. Under such conditions, hate becomes precisely that which is in dispute, that which must be effectively managed, controlled, defined, and exorcised. In Germany, all this proceeds under the shadows of a particular past. Elsewhere in Europe, of course, the politics of hate may follow quite distinct paths. In the near future, however, hate and its governance promise to remain salient to public life throughout the Continent. They promise, too, to remain near where xenophobic nationalism and economic anxieties run into each other. No doubt, economic concerns have increasingly come to the fore in European politics over the

---

[5] In the preface, I discuss a number of reasons why anthropology has been reluctant to study the far right. Among the few sustained ethnographic explorations of European far right nationalism is Don Kalb and Gábor Halmai's edited volume *Headlines of Nation, Subtexts of Class* (2011), which describes how hate often figures as a symptom—as the effect of deeper processes and particularly in today's Europe as the expression of experiences of dispossession. Outside anthropology, Wendy Brown's *Regulating Aversion* (2009) has explored tolerance as a political strategy of governance.

past several years. But their rise to prominence has hardly come at the cost of nationalism and racist hatred, from which they have been symbiotically inseparable.

The words with which Germany rethinks and reconfigures its national Thing—democracy, tolerance, cosmopolitanism—point, finally, to the disintegration of ideological regimes dominant throughout much of the short twentieth century. Against the waning of prosperity and of the German state's ability to sustain the material promises that had become its raison d'être, a democratic, tolerant civil society is called upon to suture a shattered social terrain. But, as Jean and John Comaroff have suggested, the appeal to civil society is a desperate plea for an empty signifier to recompose the social in a moment of acute historical confusion (2001, 44). With the nationalizing narrative of economic prosperity no longer (or not yet) plausible, it is through the management of hate that Germany (re)thinks its national imagination in the wake of the opulent welfare state, and it is through civil society that it toils to outline its new contours.

The anthropologist John Borneman (2002) once described the centrality of the opposition between *Multikulti* and *Schweinerei* (obscenity, vulgarity) to national identity and cultural debates in Germany at the turn of the millennium. For Borneman, in the aftermath of reunification this opposition has defined the critical confrontation (*Auseinandersetzung*) of German society with its problematic relation to other culture(s). And we have seen this opposition between Multikulti and Schweinerei replicated throughout this book in the pairs of democracy and right-wing extremism, tolerance and racism, or cosmopolitanism and xenophobia. But the social and political projects that it enables, and that in turn define it, signal beyond the present need of a united Germany to confront the impasses of its relation to "different" cultures. Side by side with the synchronic oscillation between Multikulti and Schweinerei, they outline a temporal shift from Wohlstand Deutschland (prosperity Germany) to Multikulti Deutschland. The first served as a national designator under the golden age of skyrocketing economic growth. The second, as the reverse image of the nationalist specter, announces the precarious project of renaming and thus recuperating a rapidly fading national imaginary.

Bibliography
||||||||||||||||||||||||||||||

Adorno, T. W. (1997). *Negative Dialectics.* New York: Continuum.

Adorno, T. W., E. Frenkel-Brunswik, D. Levinson, and N. Sanford. (1950). *The Authoritarian Personality.* New York: Harper & Row.

Agamben, G. (1998). *Homo Sacer: Sovereign Power and Bare Life.* Stanford, CA: Stanford University Press.

Agence France. (2015). "German couple pay Greece £630 'war reparations.'" *Guardian.*

AG Netzwerke gegen Rechtsextremismus. (2003). "Grundbegriffe." Originally accessed on June 20, 2003, from http://www.respectabel.de/infos_rechtsextremismus/grund begriffe.htm, but the link is no longer available.

Alonso, A. M. (1994). "The politics of space, time, and substance: State formation, nationalism, and ethnicity." *Annual Review of Anthropology* 23:379–405.

Altermedia Deutschland. (2005). "Dunkel -Tapsiges - Von Berliner Stolpersteinen und Davidsternen." Originally accessed on October 26, 2005, from http://de.altermedia .info/general/dunkel-tapsiges-von-berliner-stolpersteinen-und-davidsternen-261005 _3930.html, but the link is no longer available.

Althusser, L. (2001). "Ideology and Ideological State Apparatuses." In *Lenin and Philosophy, and Other Essays,* 127–88. New York: Monthly Review Press.

Amtsgericht Rathenow. (2006). 2 Ds 496 Js 37539/05 (301/05).

Apabiz. (2007). "Chronologie antisemitischer Vorfälle 2006." Berlin, Apabiz: 18.

Appadurai, A. (1998). "Dead certainty: Ethnic violence in the age of globalization." *Public Culture* 10 (2): 225–47.

Arendt, H. (1973). *The Origins of Totalitarianism.* New York: Harcourt Brace Jovanovich.

———. (1994). *Eichmann in Jerusalem: A Report on the Banality of Evil.* New York: Penguin Books.

Aretxaga, B. (1999). "A Fictional Reality: Paramilitary Death Squads and the Construction of State Terror in Spain." In *Death Squad: The Anthropology of State Terror,* ed. J. A. Sluka, 47–69. Philadelphia: University of Pennsylvania Press.

———. (2000). "Playing terrorist: Ghastly plots and the ghostly state." *Journal of Spanish Cultural Studies* 1 (1): 43–58.

———. (2003). "Maddening states." *Annual Review of Anthropology* 32:393–410.

Argumente. (2002). . . . *in der Mitte angekommen: Rechtsextremismus und gesellschaftliche Gegenaktivitäten in Mecklenburg-Vorpommern.* Berlin: Argumente.netzwerk antirassistischer bildung.

Asad, T. (2003a). *Formations of the Secular: Christianity, Islam, Modernity.* Stanford, CA: Stanford University Press.

———. (2003b). "Muslims as a 'Religious Minority' in Europe." In *Formations of the Secular: Christianity, Islam, Modernity,* 159–80. Stanford, CA: Stanford University Press.

Austin, J. L. (1975). *How to Do Things with Words.* Cambridge, MA: Harvard University Press.

Averesch, S. (2005). "Das Brandenburger Tor ist keine Gedenkstätte." http://www
.berliner-zeitung.de/archiv/auch-mit-dem-neu-geregelten-versammlungsrecht-koennen
-nicht-an-allen-zentralen-orten-rechte-aufmaersche-untersagt-werden-das-branden
burger-tor-ist-keine-gedenkstaette,10810590,10266184.html.

Bach, J. (2005). "Vanishing Acts and Virtual Reconstruction: Technologies of Memory
and the Afterlife of the GDR." In *Memory Traces: 1989 and the Question of German
Cultural Identity*, ed. S. Arnold-de Simine. Oxford: Peter Lang.

Bakhtin, M. M. (1998a). "Discourse in the Novel." In *The Dialogic Imagination: Four
Essays*, ed. M. Holquist, 259–422. Austin: University of Texas Press.

———. (1998b). "Forms of Time and of the Chronotope in the Novel." In *The Dialogic
Imagination: Four Essays*, ed. M. Holquist, 84–258. Austin: University of Texas Press.

Balibar, É. (2002). "What Is a Border?" In *Politics and the Other Scene*, ed. E. Laclau and
C. Mouffe, 75–86. New York: Verso.

———. (2004a). "At the Borders of Europe." In *We, the People of Europe? Reflections on
Transnational Citizenship*, 1–10. Princeton: Princeton University Press.

———. (2004b). "Outline of a Topography of Cruelty: Citizenship and Civility in the
Era of Global Violence." In *We, the People of Europe? Reflections on Transnational
Citizenship*, 115–32. Princeton: Princeton University Press.

Banks, M. (2006). "Performing 'Neo-nationalism': Some Methodological Notes." In
Neo-Nationalism in Europe and Beyond: Perspectives from Social Anthropology, ed.
A. Gingrich and M. Banks, 50–65. New York: Berghahn Books.

Banks, M., and A. Gingrich. (2006). "Introduction: Neo-nationalism in Europe and Beyond." In *Neo-Nationalism in Europe and Beyond: Perspectives from Social Anthropology*, ed. A. Gingrich and M. Banks, 1–26. New York: Berghahn Books.

Barthelme, C. (2005). "50 Wunsiedler kämpfen für ihre Stadt." *Frankenpost Online*.

Barthes, R. (1972). *Mythologies*. New York: Hill and Wang.

Basso, K. H. (1996). *Wisdom Sits in Places: Landscape and Language among the Western
Apache*. Albuquerque: University of New Mexico Press.

Bathrick, D. (1996). "Anti-neonazism as cinematic practice: Bonengel's *Beruf Neonazi*."
New German Critique 67 (Winter 1996): 133–46.

Benjamin, W. (1986a). "Critique of Violence." In *Reflections: Essays, Aphorisms, Autobiographical Writing*, ed. P. Demetz, 277–301. New York: Schocken Books.

———. (1986b). "The Work of Art in the Age of Mechanical Reproduction." In *Illumi-
nations*, 217–52. New York: Schocken Books.

Berdahl, D. (1999). "'(N)Ostalgie' for the present: Memory, longing, and East German
things." *Ethnos* 64 (2): 192–211.

Berlant, L. (2007). "Nearly utopian, nearly normal: Post-Fordist affect in *La Promesse*
and *Rosetta*." *Public Culture* 19 (2): 273–301.

———. (2011). *Cruel Optimism*. Durham, NC: Duke University Press.

Berliner Infoportal. (2005a). "Der 8. Mai bleibt eine Schande!" Originally accessed on
May 9, 2005, from http://www.berliner-infoportal.org/modules.php?name=News&fi
le=article&sid=31, but the link is no longer available.

———. (2005b). "Ein kurzer Erlebnisbericht vom 'Tag der Demokratie.'" Originally
accessed on May 17, 2005, from http://www.berliner-infoportal.org/modules.php?na
me=News&file=article&sid=37, but the link is no longer available.

Berliner Morgenpost. (2004a). "Neonazi-Demo: Anwohner beantragen Verbot."

———. (2004b). "Protest gegen Demo-Pläne von Neonazis."

———. (2005a). "Dresden setzt ein Zeichen gegen Rechtsextremismus."

———. (2005b). "NPD darf nicht ans Brandenburger Tor." http://www.berliner
-zeitung.de/archiv/route-zum-8--mai-verboten-npd-darf-nicht-ans-brandenburger
-tor,10810590,10279466.html.

———. (2011). "Berliner Polizist wegen Neonazi-Kontakte entlassen."

Berliner Zeitung. (2005a). "Jeden Tag mehrere neue Sterne." http://www.berliner-zei
tung.de/archiv/warum-vermutlich-rechtsextreme-an-vielen-stellen-in-berlin-das
-juedische-symbol-aufspruehen-der-stern-als-stigma,10810590,10330694.html.

———. (2005b). "Polizei entdeckt weitere Schmierereien." Originally accessed on October 18, 2005, from http://www.berlinonline.de/berliner-zeitung/berlin/492659.html,
but the link is no longer available.

———. (2005c). "Polizei jagt die Sprayer der Davidsterne." http://www.berliner-zei
tung.de/archiv/taeter-verunstalteten-denkmaeler-und-rathaus-polizei-jagt-die
-sprayer-der-davidsterne,10810590,10329078.html.

———. (2005d). "Schönbohm empört den Osten." http://www.berliner-zeitung.de
/archiv/nach-kindstoetung-streiten-politiker-ueber-ursachen---brandenburgs
-innenminister--ddr-verantwortlich---thierse-warnt-vor-schuldzuweisungen
-schoenbohm-empoert-den-osten,10810590,10307582.html.

———. (2007). "Hilfloses Schweigen." http://www.berliner-zeitung.de/archiv/hilfloses
-schweigen,10810590,9634300.html.

Bernstein, R. (2005). "German war commemoration ceremonies stress responsibility for
Europe's 'mass graveyard.'" *New York Times* online, http://www.nytimes.com/2005/05
/09/world/europe/german-war-commemoration-ceremonies-stress-responsibility-for
-europes-mass-graveyard.html?_r=0.

Bezirksamt Treptow-Köpenick. (2005). *Weiterentwicklung der Sozialraumorientierung
im Bezirk Treptow-Köpenick.* Berlin: Bezirksamt Treptow-Köpenick von Berlin.

Biebricher, T. (2011). "The biopolitics of ordoliberalism." *Foucault Studies* (12): 171–
91.

Binder, B. (2000). "Political Stage-Setting: The Symbolic Transformation of Berlin." In
*Myth and Memory in the Construction of Community: Historical Patterns in Europe
and Beyond*, ed. B. Strath, 137–55. New York: P.I.E.-Peter Lang.

———. (2001). "Capital under construction: History and the production of locality in
contemporary Berlin." *Ethnologia Europaea* 31 (2): 19–40.

Blommaert, J., and J. Verschueren. (1998). "The Role of Language in European Nationalist Ideologies." In *Language Ideologies: Practice and Theory*, ed. B. B. Schieffelin, K. A.
Woolard, and P. V. Kroskrity, 189–210. New York: Oxford University Press.

BMFSFJ. (2002). *Protection of Young Persons Act.* Berlin: Bundesministerium für Fami-
lie, Senioren, Frauen und Jugend.

Bohrer, K. H. (1991). "Why we are not a nation, and why we should become one." *New
German Critique* 52:72–83.

Bonefeld, W. (2012). "Freedom and the strong state: On German ordoliberalism." *New
Political Economy* 17 (5): 633–56.

Bonengel, W., dir. (1993). *Beruf Neonazi.* Documentary. Produced by Ost-Film.

Borneman, J. (1992). *Belonging in the Two Berlins: Kin, State, Nation.* New York: Cambridge University Press.

———. (1993). "Uniting the German nation: Law, narrative, and historicity." *American
Ethnologist* 20 (2): 288–311.

———. (1997). "State, Territory, and National Identity Formation in the Two Berlins, 1945–1995." In *Culture, Power, Place: Explorations in Critical Anthropology*, ed. A. Gupta and J. Ferguson. Durham, NC: Duke University Press.

———. (2002). "Multikulti or Schweinerei in the year 2000." *German Politics and Society* 20 (2): 93–114.

Botsch, G., and C. Kopke. (2013). "National Solidarity—No to Globalization! The Economic and Sociopolitical Platform of the National Democratic Party of Germany (NPD)." In *Right-Wing Radicalism Today: Perspectives from Europe and the US*, ed. S. v. Mering and T. W. McCarty, 37–59. New York: Routledge.

Bourdieu, P. (1998). *On Television*. New York: New Press.

———. (2001). *Language and Symbolic Power*. Cambridge, MA: Harvard University Press.

Boyer, D. C. (2000). "On the sedimentation and accreditation of social knowledges of differences: Mass media, journalism, and the reproduction of East/West alterities in unified Germany." *Cultural Anthropology* 15 (4): 459–91.

———. (2001). "Yellow sand of Berlin." *Ethnography* 2 (3): 421–39.

———. (2006a). "Conspiracy, history, and therapy at a Berlin Stammtisch." *American Ethnologist* 33 (3): 327–29.

———. (2006b). "Ostalgie and the politics of the future in Eastern Germany." *Public Culture* 18 (2): 361–81.

Brandenburgisches Oberlandesgericht. (2005). 1 Ss 58/05 vom 12.9.2005.

Brecht, B. (1996). *Brecht on Theatre: The Development of an Aesthetic*. New York: Hill and Wang.

Brenner, N., and N. Theodore. (2002). "Cities and the geographies of 'actually existing neoliberalism.'" *Antipode* 34 (3): 349–79.

Brown, W. (2009). *Regulating Aversion: Tolerance in the Age of Identity and Empire*. Princeton: Princeton University Press.

Brubaker, R. (2009). *Citizenship and Nationhood in France and Germany*. Cambridge, MA: Harvard University Press.

Brubaker, R., and D. D. Laitin. (1998). "Ethnic and nationalist violence." *Annual Review of Sociology* 24:423–52.

Bugiel, B. (2002). *Rechtsextremismus Jugendlicher in der DDR und in den neuen Bundesländern von 1982–1998*. PhD diss., Universität Hamburg.

Bulli, G., and F. Tronconi. (2012). "Regionalism, Right-Wing Extremism, Populism: The Elusive Nature of the Lega Nord." In *Mapping the Extreme Right in Contemporary Europe: From Local to Transnational*, ed. A. Mammone, E. Godin, and B. Jenkins, 78–92. New York: Routledge.

Bundesamt für Verfassungsschutz. (2004). *Symbole und Kennzeichen der Rechtsextremisten*. Berlin: Bundesamt für Verfassungsschutz.

———. (2007). *Verfassungsschutzbericht 2006*. Berlin: Bundesministerium des Innern.

Bundesgerichtshof. (2000a). 3 BJs 47/99 - 4 (22) vom 14 Januar 2000.

———. (2000b). 3 StR 378/00 vom 22 Dezember 2000.

———. (2002a). 3 StR 270/02 vom 15.10.2002.

———. (2002b). 3 StR 446/01 vom 7.2.2002.

———. (2002c). 3 StR 495/01 vom 31.7.2002.

———. (2002d). 5 StR 485/01 vom 10.4.2002.

————. (2005). 3 StR 60/05 vom 28.07.2005.

————. (2007). 3 StR 486/06 vom 15.3.2007.

————. (2008). 3 StR 164/08 vom 1.10.2008.

————. (2009). 3 StR 228/09 vom 13.8.2009.

Bundesministerium der Justiz. (2005). "Gesetz über Versammlungen und Aufzüge (Versammlungsgesetz)." http://www.gesetze-im-internet.de/bundesrecht/versammlg/gesamt .pdf.

————. (2008). "Strafgesetzbuch (StGB)." http://www.gesetze-im-internet.de/bundes recht/stgb/gesamt.pdf.

Bundesverfassungsgericht. (2003). 2 BvB 1/01 vom 18.3.2003, sections 1–154.

————. (2007a). 1 BvB 1584/07 vom 10.9.2007.

————. (2007b). 2 BvR 967/07 vom 4.9.2008.

————. (2008). 2 BvR 1012/08 vom 27.11.2008.

————. (2010). 1 BvR 1106/08 vom 8.12.2010.

Bunzl, M. (2005). "Between anti-Semitism and Islamophobia: Some thoughts on the new Europe." *American Ethnologist* 32 (4): 499–508.

Butterwegge, C., and L. Meier. (2002). *Rechtsextremismus*. Freiburg: Herder.

Bybee, K. J. (2000). "The political significance of legal ambiguity: The case of Affirmative Action." *Law & Society Review* 34 (2): 263–90.

Calhoun, C. (2007). "Nationalism and cultures of democracy." *Public Culture* 19 (1): 151–73.

Carlsson, Y. (2006). "Violent Right-Wing Extremism in Norway: Community Based Prevention and Intervention." In *Prevention of Right-Wing Extremism, Xenophobia and Racism in European Perspective*, ed. P. Rieker, M. Glaser, and S. Schuster, 12–29. Halle: Deutsches Jugendinstitut e.V.

Carr, S. (2009). "Anticipating and inhabiting institutional identities." *American Ethnologist* 36 (2): 317–36.

Casey, E. S. (2007). "Boundary, place, and event in the spatiality of history." *Rethinking History* 11 (4): 507–12.

Caton, S. C. (1990). *"Peaks of Yemen I summon": Poetry as Cultural Practice in a North Yemeni Tribe*. Berkeley: University of California Press.

Chin, R., H. Fehrenbach, G. Eley, and A. Grossmann. (2009). *After the Nazi Racial State: Difference and Democracy in Germany and Europe*. Ann Arbor: University of Michigan Press.

Cohen, R. (2015). "Germany, refugee nation." *New York Times*. http://nyti.ms/1S4b4Yz.

Coliver, S., F. D'Souza, and K. Boyle, eds. (1992). *Striking a Balance: Hate Speech, Freedom of Expression, and Non-Discrimination*. London: International Centre against Censorship, Human Rights Centre, University of Essex.

Comaroff, J. (2005). "The End of History, Again? Pursuing the Past in the Postcolony." In *Postcolonial Studies and Beyond*, ed. A. Loomba, 125–44. Durham, NC: Duke University Press.

Comaroff, J., and J. L. Comaroff. (1999). "Occult economies and the violence of abstraction: Notes from the South African postcolony." *American Ethnologist* 26 (2): 279–303.

————. (2001). "Millennial Capitalism: First Thoughts on a Second Coming." In *Millennial Capitalism and the Culture of Neoliberalism*, ed. J. Comaroff and J. L. Comaroff, 1–56. Durham, NC: Duke University Press.

———. (2006). "Figuring crime: Quantifacts and the production of the un/real." *Public Culture* 18 (1): 209–46.

Connolly, K., and H. Smith. (2015). "German anger over Greek demand for war reparations." *Guardian*.

Crapanzano, V. (2000). *Serving the Word: Literalism in America from the Pulpit to the Bench*. New York: New Press.

Dacombe, R., and M. Sallah. (2006). "Racism and Young People in the United Kingdom." In *Prevention of Right-Wing Extremism, Xenophobia and Racism in European Perspective*, ed. P. Rieker, M. Glaser, and S. Schuster, 79–95. Halle: Deutsches Jugendinstitut e.V.

Das, V. (2001). "Crisis and Representation: Rumor and the Circulation of Hate." In *Disturbing Remains: Memory, History, and Crisis in the Twentieth Century*, ed. M. S. Roth and C. G. Salas, 37–62. Los Angeles: Getty Research Institute.

Davis, M. (1992). *City of Quartz: Excavating the Future in Los Angeles*. New York: Vintage Books.

Davolio, M. E., B. Gerber, M. Eckmann, and M. Drilling. (2006). "The Special Case of Switzerland: Research Findings and Thoughts from a Context-Oriented Perspective." In *Prevention of Right-Wing Extremism, Xenophobia and Racism in European Perspective*, ed. P. Rieker, M. Glaser, and S. Schuster, 30–47. Halle: Deutsches Jugendinstitut e.V.

de Certeau, M. (1984). "Spatial Stories." In *The Practice of Everyday Life*, 115–31. Berkeley: University of California Press.

Dearden, N. (2013). "Greece and Spain helped postwar Germany recover. Spot the difference." *Guardian*.

Deleuze, G. (1992). "Postscript on the societies of control." *October* 59:3–7.

Deleuze, G., and F. Guattari. (2002). *A Thousand Plateaus: Capitalism and Schizophrenia*. Minneapolis: University of Minnesota Press.

Derrida, J. (1982). "Signature, Event, Context." In *Margins of Philosophy*, 309–30. Chicago: University of Chicago Press.

———. (1992). "Force of Law: 'The Mystical Foundation of Authority.'" In *Deconstruction and the Possibility of Justice*, ed. D. G. Carlson, D. Cornell, and M. Rosenfeld, 3–67. New York: Routledge.

———. (1993). "Politics of friendship." *American Imago* 50 (3): 353.

———. (1994). *Specters of Marx: The State of the Debt, the Work of Mourning, and the New International*. New York: Routledge.

Der Spiegel. (2005). "Koalition einigt sich auf geändertes Versammlungsrecht." http://www.spiegel.de/politik/deutschland/0,1518,345292,00.html.

———. (2010). "Sarrazin rechnet mit seinen Gegnern ab." http://www.spiegel.de/politik/deutschland/kritik-an-integrationsthesen-sarrazin-rechnet-mit-seinen-gegnern-ab-a-726264.html.

———. (2011a). "Germany was biggest debt transgressor of 20th century." http://www.spiegel.de/international/germany/economic-historian-germany-was-biggest-debt-transgressor-of-20th-century-a-769703-druck.html.

———. (2011b). "Verfassungsschutz hatte über V-Mann Kontakt zu Zwickauer Zelle." http://www.spiegel.de/panorama/justiz/0,1518,805223,00.html.

———. (2011c). "Verfassungsschutz war detailliert über Zwickauer Zelle informiert." http://www.spiegel.de/panorama/justiz/0,1518,806365,00.html.

———. (2012a). "NSU-Ausschuss fordert sofortigen Aktenvernichtungsstopp." http://
www.spiegel.de/politik/deutschland/nsu-ausschuss-fordert-sofortigenaktenvernich
tungsstopp-a-845295.html.
———. (2012b). "Rechtsextremer Offizier soll für Bundeswehr im Einsatz sein." http://
www.spiegel.de/politik/ausland/rechtsextremer-offizier-soll-fuerdie-bundeswehr-im
-einsatz-sein-a-859288.html.
———. (2015). "Merkel versteht, hat aber kein Verständnis." http://www.spiegel.de
/politik/deutschland/merkel-zu-pegida-ich-verstehe-die-sorgen-a-1013231.html.
Der Tagesspiegel. (2005a). "Die Rechtsradikalen blieben im Regen stehen." http://www
.tagesspiegel.de/berlin/die-rechtsradikalen-blieben-im-regen-stehen/606940.html.
———. (2005b). "In Mitte 27 Davidsterne gesprüht." http://www.tagesspiegel.de/berlin
/in-mitte-27-davidsterne-gesprueht/657240.html.
———. (2005c). "Serie von Denkmal-Schmierereien fortgesetzt."
De Soto, H. G. (1996). "(Re)inventing Berlin: Dialectics of power, symbols and pasts,
1990–1995." City and Society 8 (1): 29–49.
Die Tageszeitung. (2005a). "Eine unverständliche Provokation." http://www.taz.de/pt/2005
/10/20/a0258.nf/text.
———. (2005b). "Rechte sprühen Sterne." http://www.taz.de/pt/2005/10/19/a0267.nf
/text.
Die Zeit. (2012a). "Bundeswehr duldete bekennende Neonazis." http://www.zeit.de
/politik/deutschland/2012-11/nsu-bundeswehr-geheimdienst.
———. (2012b). "Mehrere Polizisten waren Mitglied im Ku Klux Klan." http://www
.zeit.de/gesellschaft/zeitgeschehen/2012-10/polizisten-mitliedschaft-ku-klux-klan.
———. (2012c). "Thüringen prüft Geheimnisverrat an Rechtsextremisten." http://www
.zeit.de/gesellschaft/zeitgeschehen/2012-08/thueringen-polizei-informationen-nsu.
Dietzsch, M., and A. Schobert. (2002). V-Leute bei der NPD: Geführte Führende oder
Führende Geführte? PDS.
Döblin, A. (1996). Berlin Alexanderplatz: Die Geschichte vom Franz Biberkopf. Zürich:
Walter.
Döring, U. (2008). Angstzonen: Rechtsdominierte Orte aus medialer und lokaler Perspek-
tive. Berlin: VS Verlag.
Dornbusch, C., and J. Raabe. (2002). RechtsRock: Bestandsaufnahme und Gegenstrate-
gien. Hamburg: Unrast.
Douglas, M. (2002). Purity and Danger: An Analysis of Concept of Pollution and Taboo.
New York: Routledge.
DuBois, W.E.B. (1997). The Souls of Black Folk. Boston: Bedford Books.
Edelman, L. B. (1992). "Legal ambiguity and symbolic structures: Organizational me-
diation of civil rights law." American Journal of Sociology 97 (6): 1531.
Eidson, J. R. (2005). "Between heritage and countermemory: Varieties of historical rep-
resentation in a West German community." American Ethnologist 32 (4): 556–75.
Emmerich, M. (2005). "Fest der Demokratie am Brandenburger Tor." http://www.ber
liner-zeitung.de/home/10808950,10808950.html.
ENAR. (2005). ENAR Shadow Report 2005: Racism in Germany. Hamburg: European
Network Against Racism.
Erb, R. (2003). "Rechtsextremistische Jugendszene in Brandenburg." Originally ac-
cessed on June 22, 2003, from http://www.aktionsbuendnis.brandenburg.de/sixcms
/detail.php/67576, but the link is no longer available.

Ervin-Tripp, S. (1976). "Is Sybil there? The structure of some American English directives." *Language in Society* 5 (1): 25–66.

Evans-Pritchard, E. E. (1976). *Witchcraft, Oracles, and Magic among the Azande.* Oxford: Clarendon Press.

Fahrun, J. (2005). "Kein Durchkommen für die NPD." http://m.morgenpost.de/print archiv/politik/article104452200/Kein-Durchkommen-fuer-die-NPD.html.

Fanon, F. (1967). *Black Skin, White Masks.* New York: Grove Press.

Feldman, A. (1991). *Formations of Violence: The Narrative of the Body and Political Terror in Northern Ireland.* Chicago: University of Chicago Press.

———. (1995). "Ethnographic States of Emergency." In *Fieldwork under Fire,* ed. C. Nordstrom and A.C.G.M Robben, 224–53. Berkeley: University of California Press.

———. (1997). "Violence and vision: The prosthetics and aesthetics of terror." *Public Culture* 10 (1): 24–60.

———. (2001). "White public space and the political geography of public safety." *Social Text* 19 (3): 57–89.

Ferguson, J., and A. Gupta. (2002). "Spatializing states: Toward an ethnography of neoliberal governmentality." *American Ethnologist* 29 (4): 981–1002.

Fillitz, T. (2006). " 'Being the native's friend does not make you the foreigner's enemy!' Neo-nationalism, the Freedom Party and Jörg Haider in Austria." In *Neo-Nationalism in Europe and Beyond: Perspectives from Social Anthropology,* ed. A. Gingrich and M. Banks, 138–61. New York: Berghahn Books.

Fischer, J. (2001). *Das NPD Verbot.* Berlin: Espresso.

Förster, A. (2012). "Fünf V-Leute bei Terror-Zelle." *Frankfurter Rundschau.* http://www .fr-online.de/neonazi-terror/rechtsextremismus-fuenf-v-leute-bei-terror-zelle ,1477338,11453446.html.

Foucault, M. (1986). "Of other spaces." *Diacritics* 16 (1): 22–27.

———. (1995). *Discipline and Punish: The Birth of the Prison.* New York: Vintage Books.

———. (2007). *Security, Territory, Population: Lectures at the Collège de France, 1977– 78.* New York: Palgrave Macmillan.

———. (2008). *The Birth of Biopolitics: Lectures at the Collège de France, 1978–79.* New York: Palgrave Macmillan.

Foulkes, I. (2007). "Swiss move to ban minarets." BBC News online, http://news.bbc.co .uk/2/hi/europe/6676271.stm.

Freier Widerstand. (2005). "8. Mai, Berlin: Weder feiern, noch Demonstrieren!" http:// www.widerstand.info/meldungen/543.html.

Freud, S. (1975a). *Beyond the Pleasure Principle.* New York: Norton.

———. (1975b). *Group Psychology and the Analysis of the Ego.* New York: Norton.

———. (2005). *Civilization and Its Discontents.* New York: Norton.

Friedman, J. (2003a). "Globalization, Dis-integration, Re-organization: The Transformations of Violence." In *Globalization, the State, and Violence,* ed. J. Friedman, 1–34. Walnut Creek, CA: AltaMira Press.

———, ed. (2003b). *Globalization, the State, and Violence.* Walnut Creek, CA: AltaMira Press.

Funke, H. (1999). "Unsere Gleichgültigkeit ist ihr Triumph: Für eine Renaissance der liberalen und sozialen politischen Kultur." In *Braune Gefahr: DVU, NPD, REP; Geschichte und Zukunft,* ed. J. Mecklenburg, 281–89. Berlin: Elefanten Press.

Gal, S. (2002). "A semiotics of the public/private distinction." *Differences: A Journal of Feminist Cultural Studies* 13 (1): 77.

———. (2007). "Circulation in the "new" economy: Clasps and copies." The 106th Meeting of the American Anthropological Association. Washington, DC.

Gebauer, M. (2012). "NSU-Sprengstofflieferant war V-Mann der Berliner Polizei." *Der Spiegel* online. http://www.spiegel.de/panorama/justiz/nsu-sprengstofflieferant-war -v-mann-derberliner-polizei-a-855719.html.

German Bundestag. (2001). *Basic Law for the Federal Republic of Germany.* Berlin: German Bundestag.

German Law Archive. (1998). "Criminal Code (Strafgesetzbuch, StGB)." http://german lawarchive.iuscomp.org/.

Geschiere, P. (1997). *The Modernity of Witchcraft: Politics and the Occult in Postcolonial Africa.* Charlottesville: University Press of Virginia.

———. (2008). "Witchcraft and the state: Cameroon and South Africa." *Past & Present* 199 (Suppl 3): 313–35.

Geyer, M. (1997). "The place of the Second World War in German memory and history." *New German Critique* 71:5–40.

Gingrich, A. (2006). "Nation, Status and Gender in Trouble? Exploring Some Contexts and Characteristics of Neo-nationalism in Western Europe." In *Neo-Nationalism in Europe and Beyond: Perspectives from Social Anthropology,* ed. A. Gingrich and M. Banks, 29–49. New York: Berghahn Books.

Gingrich, A., and M. Banks, eds. (2006). *Neo-Nationalism in Europe and Beyond: Perspectives from Social Anthropology.* New York: Berghahn Books.

Glaeser, A. (2000). *Divided in Unity: Identity, Germany, and the Berlin Police.* Chicago: University of Chicago Press.

Glasow, N. v., dir. (2004). *Edelweisspiraten.* Germany.

Goffman, E. (1976). "Replies and responses." *Language in Society* 5 (3): 257–313.

———. (1981). "Footing." In *Forms of Talk,* 124–59. Philadelphia: University of Pennsylvania Press.

Goodwin, M. J. (2008). "Backlash in the 'hood: Determinants of support for the British National Party (BNP) at the local level." *Journal of Contemporary European Studies* 16 (3): 347–61.

Gramsci, A. (1997 [1971]). *Selections from the Prison Notebooks.* New York: International.

Grass, G. (1990). *Two States—One Nation? Against the Unthinking Clamor for German Unification.* San Diego: Harcourt Brace Jovanovich.

———. (1991). "What am I talking for? Is anybody still listening?" *New German Critique* 52 (Winter 1991): 66–72.

———. (1992). *Unkenrufe: Eine Erzählung.* Göttingen: Steidl.

———. (2002a). *Im Krebsgang: Eine Novelle.* Göttingen: Steidl.

———. (2002b). *Crabwalk.* Orlando: Harcourt.

Grattet, R., and V. Jenness. (2005). "The reconstitution of law in local settings: Agency discretion, ambiguity, and a surplus of law in the policing of hate crime." *Law & Society Review* 39 (4): 893–942.

Grubben, G. (2006). "Right-Extremist Sympathies among Adolescents in the Netherlands." In *Prevention of Right-Wing Extremism, Xenophobia and Racism in European Perspective,* ed. P. Rieker, M. Glaser, and S. Schuster, 48–66. Halle: Deutsches Jugendinstitut e.V.

Grumke, T., and B. Wagner. (2002). *Handbuch Rechtsradikalismus: Personen, Organisationen, Netzwerke; Vom Neonazismus bis in die Mitte der Gesellschaft.* Opladen: Leske + Budrich.

Gupta, A., and J. Ferguson. (1997). "Beyond 'Culture': Space, Identity, and the Politics of Difference." In *Culture, Power, Place: Explorations in Critical Anthropology,* ed. A. Gupta and J. Ferguson. Durham, NC: Duke University Press.

Guyer, J. I. (2007). "Prophecy and the near future: Thoughts on macroeconomic, evangelical, and punctuated time." *American Ethnologist* 34 (3): 409–21.

Haaretz. (2005). "Thousands of left-wing activists in Berlin confronted thousands of neo-Nazis who marked the day of capitulation." Originally accessed on May 9, 2005, but the link is no longer available.

Habermas, J. (1988). "Concerning the public use of history." *New German Critique* 44:40–50.

———. (1989). *The Theory of Communicative Action.* Vol. 2. Boston: Beacon Press.

———. (1991). "Yet again: German identity; A unified nation of angry DM-Burghers?" *New German Critique* 52:84–101.

———. (1997a). "1989 in the Shadow of 1945: On the Normality of the Future Berlin Republic." In *A Berlin Republic: Writings on Germany,* 161–81. Lincoln: University of Nebraska Press.

———. (1997b). *A Berlin Republic: Writings on Germany.* Lincoln: University of Nebraska Press.

———. (1997c). "What Does 'Working Off the Past' Mean Today?" In *A Berlin Republic: Writings on Germany,* 17–40. Lincoln: University of Nebraska Press.

Hafeneger, B., and M. M. Jansen. (2001). *Rechte Cliquen: Alltag einer neuen Jugendkultur.* Weinheim: Juventa.

Hale, C. R. (2005). "Neoliberal multiculturalism: The remaking of cultural rights and racial dominance in Central America." *Political and Legal Anthropology Review* 28 (1): 10–19.

Halfman, J. (1997). "Immigration and citizenship in Germany: Contemporary dilemma." *Political Studies* 45:260–74.

Hall, S., and T. Jefferson. (1976). *Resistance through Rituals: Youth Subcultures in Post-War Britain.* London: Hutchinson.

Hannemann, C. (2005). *Die Platte: Industrialisierter Wohnungsbau in der DDR.* Berlin: Hans Schiler Verlag.

Hansen, T. B. (2002). *Wages of Violence: Naming and Identity in Postcolonial Bombay.* Princeton: Princeton University Press.

———. (2006). "Performers of sovereignty." *Critique of Anthropology* 26(3): 279–95.

Harcourt, B. E. (2007). *Against Prediction: Profiling, Policing, and Punishing in an Actuarial Age.* Chicago: University of Chicago Press.

———. (2010). "Neoliberal penality." *Theoretical Criminology* 14 (1): 74–92.

Harding, L. (2005a). "Lights go out at Honecker's palace." *Guardian.* http://www.theguardian.com/world/2005/mar/28/germany.lukeharding.

———. (2005b). "Neo-Nazis upstage Dresden memorial." *Guardian.* http://www.theguardian.com/world/2005/feb/14/secondworldwar.germany.

———. (2005c). "Thousands join in rallies to hail wartime heroism." *Guardian.* http://www.guardian.co.uk/uk/2005/may/09/world.secondworldwar.

Harris, O. (1996). *Inside and Outside the Law: Anthropological Studies of Authority and Ambiguity.* New York: Routledge.

Hartwig, T. (2004). "Der Verfassungsschutz und das braune Propagandamaterial." http://www.aktion-Zivilcourage.de/Start_Der_Verfassungsschutz_und_das_braune _Propagandamaterial.42d686s3612/.

Harvey, D. (1989). *The Condition of Postmodernity: An Enquiry into the Origins of Cultural Change.* Cambridge, MA: Blackwell.

———. (2001). *Spaces of Capital: Towards a Critical Geography.* New York: Routledge.

Hassel, A. (2010). "Twenty years after German unification: The restructuring of the German welfare and employment regime." *German Politics & Society* 28:102–15.

Hasselbach, I., and W. Bonengel. (2001). *Die Abrechnung: Ein Neonazi steigt aus.* Berlin: Aufbau Taschenbuch.

Hasselmann, J. (2005). "Hunderte Davidsterne gesprüht—kein Täter gefasst." http:// www.tagesspiegel.de/berlin/hunderte-davidsterne-gesprueht-kein-taeter-gefasst /661342.html.

Hebdige, D. (1979). *Subculture: The Meaning of Style.* London: Methuen.

Heitmeyer, W. (1992). *Die Bielefelder Rechtsextremismus-Studie: Erste Langzeituntersuchung zur politischen Sozialisation männlicher Jugendlicher.* Weinheim: Juventa.

Hell, J. (2006). "Remnants of totalitarianism: Hannah Arendt, Heiner Muller, Slavoj Zizek, and the re-invention of politics." *Telos* 136:76–103.

Hervik, P. (2006). "The Emergence of Neo-Nationalism in Denmark, 1992–2001." In *Neo-Nationalism in Europe and Beyond: Perspectives from Social Anthropology,* ed. A. Gingrich and M. Banks, 92–106. New York: Berghahn Books.

Heym, S. (1991). "Ash Wednesday in the GDR." *New German Critique* 52:31–35.

Hirschbiegel, O., dir. (2004). *Der Untergang.* Germany.

Hobsbawm, E. (1969). *Bandits.* London: Weidenfeld and Nicolson.

———. (1994). *The Age of Extremes: The Short Twentieth Century, 1914–1991.* London: Michael Joseph.

Hofmann, R. (1992). "Incitement to National and Racial Hatred." In *Striking a Balance: Hate Speech, Freedom of Expression, and Non-Discrimination,* ed. S. Coliver, K. Boyle, and F. D'Souza, 159–70. London: University of Essex.

Höll, S., and T. Schultz. (2012). "Verfassungsschutz vernichtete Neonazi-Akten." *Süddeutsche Zeitung.* Munich. http://www.sueddeutsche.de/politik/verfassungsschutz-vernichtete -neonazi-akten-aktion-konfetti-1.1396410.

Holmes, D. R. (2000). *Integral Europe: Fast-Capitalism, Multiculturalism, Neofascism.* Princeton: Princeton University Press.

Horkheimer, M., and T. W. Adorno. (2002 [1944]). *Dialectic of Enlightenment: Philosophical Fragments.* Stanford, CA: Stanford University Press.

Huntington, S. P. (1997). *The Clash of Civilizations and the Remaking of World Order.* New York: Touchstone.

———. (2004). *Who Are We? The Challenges to America's Identity.* New York: Simon & Schuster.

Huyssen, A. (1991). "After the wall: The failure of German intellectuals." *New German Critique* 52:109–43.

———. (1992). "The inevitability of nation: German intellectuals after unification." *October* 61:65–73.

———. (1997). "The voids of Berlin." *Critical Inquiry* 24 (1): 57–81.

———. (2000). "Present pasts: Media, politics, amnesia." *Public Culture* 12 (1): 21–38.

———. (2003a). "After the War: Berlin as Palimpsest." In *Present Pasts: Urban Palimpsests and the Politics of Memory*, 72–84. Stanford, CA: Stanford University Press.

———. (2003b). "Monumental Seduction: Christo in Berlin." In *Present Pasts: Urban Palimpsests and the Politics of Memory*, 30–48. Stanford, CA: Stanford University Press.

———. (2003c). "Of Mice and Mimesis: Reading Spiegelman with Adorno." In *Present Pasts: Urban Palimpsests and the Politics of Memory*, 122–37. Stanford, CA: Stanford University Press.

———. (2003d). *Present Pasts: Urban Palimpsests and the Politics of Memory*. Stanford, CA: Stanford University Press.

———. (2003e). "Rewritings and New Beginnings: W. G. Sebald and the Literature on the Air War." In *Present Pasts: Urban Palimpsests and the Politics of Memory*, 138–57. Stanford, CA: Stanford University Press.

———. (2010). "German painting in the Cold War." *New German Critique* 37, no. 2 (110): 209–27.

Inman, P. (2013). "Greece is right to expose German loans hypocrisy." *Guardian*. http://www.theguardian.com/world/blog/2013/apr/26/greece-expose-german-loans-hypocrisy.

Irvine, J. T., and S. Gal. (2000). "Language Ideology and Linguistic Differentiation." In *Regimes of Language: Ideologies, Polities, and Identities*, ed. P. V. Kroskrity, 35–83. Santa Fe, NM: J. Currey.

Jackson, J. E., and K. B. Warren. (2005). "Indigenous movements in Latin America, 1992–2004: Controversies, ironies, new directions." *Annual Review of Anthropology* 34:549–73.

Jäger, S., M. Jäger, G. Cleve, and I. Ruth, eds. (1998). *Von deutschen Einzeltätern und ausländischen Banden*. Duisburg: DISS.

Jameson, F. (1984). "Postmodernism, or the cultural logic of late capitalism." *New Left Review* (146): 53–92.

———. (1991). *Postmodernism, or, The Cultural Logic of Late Capitalism*. Durham, NC: Duke University Press.

———. (2003). "The end of temporality." *Critical Inquiry* 29 (4): 695–718.

———. (2004). "The politics of utopia." *New Left Review* (25): 35–54.

Jamin, J. (2012). "Extreme-Right Discourse in Belgium: A Comparative Regional Approach." In *Mapping the Extreme Right in Contemporary Europe: From Local to Transnational*, ed. A. Mammone, E. Godin, and B. Jenkins, 62–77. New York: Routledge.

Jansen, F. (2012). "Thüringer Polizistin deckte Neonazis." *Der Spiegel*. http://www.tagesspiegel.de/politik/rechtsextremismus/ermittlungen-zum-nsu-terror-thueringer-polizistin-deckte-neonazis-/7109336.html.

Jarausch, K. H. (2006). "The collapse of communism and the search for master narratives: Interpretative implications of German unification." *Telos* 136:59–75.

Jaschke, H.-G. (2001). "Rechtsstaat und Rechtsextremismus." In *Rechtsextremismus in der Bundesrepublik Deutschland: Eine Bilanz*, ed. W. Schubarth and R. Stöss, 314–32. Opladen: Leske + Budrich.

———. (2013). "Right-Wing Extremism and Populism in Contemporary Germany and Western Europe." In *Right-Wing Radicalism Today: Perspectives from Europe and the US*, ed. S. v. Mering and T. W. McCarty, 22–36. New York: Routledge.

Jaschke, H.-G., B. Rätsch, and Y. Winterberg. (2001). *Nach Hitler: Radikale Rechte rüsten auf.* München: C. Bertelsmann.

Jüttner, J. (2012a). "Polizist streitet Hilfe für Neonazis ab." *Der Spiegel.* http://www .spiegel.de/panorama/justiz/nsu-polizist-sven-t-wehrt-sich-gegen-geheimnisverrat -a-853014.html.

———. (2012b). "Was wusste Spitzel 'Corelli'?" *Der Spiegel.* http://www.spiegel.de /panorama/v-mann-und-nsu-helfer-thomas-r-ist-spitzel-corelli-a-856522.html.

Kafka, F. (1953). *Das Urteil und andere Erzählungen.* Frankfurt am Main: Fischer.

Kalb, D. (2011). "Introduction." In *Headlines of Nation, Subtexts of Class: Working-Class Populism and the Return of the Repressed in Neoliberal Europe,* ed. D. Kalb and G. Halmai, 1–36. New York: Berghahn Books.

Kalb, D., and G. Halmai, eds. (2011). *Headlines of Nation, Subtexts of Class: Working-Class Populism and the Return of the Repressed in Neoliberal Europe.* EASA series. New York: Berghahn Books.

Kant, I. (1991). "An Answer to the Question: 'What Is Enlightenment?'" In *Kant: Political Writings,* 54–60. New York: Cambridge University Press.

Kapphan, A. (2002). *Das arme Berlin: Sozialräumliche Polarisierung, Armutskonzentration und Ausgrenzung in den 1990er Jahren.* Berlin: VS Verlag.

Karapin, R. (1998). "Explaining far-right electoral successes in Germany." *German Politics and Society* 16 (3): 24–61.

Kleffner, H. (2002). "Kampf um die 'Befreite Zone' am Antalya Grill." *tageszeitung.* Berlin. http://www.taz.de/1/archiv/?dig=2002/03/13/a0050.

Kleinert, C., and J. De Rijke. (2001). "Rechtsextreme orientierungen bei Jugendlichen und jungen Erwachsenen." In *Rechtsextremismus in der Bundesrepublik Deutschland: Eine Bilanz,* ed. W. Schubarth and R. Stöss, 167–98. Opladen: Leske + Budrich.

Klumbyte, N. (2010). "The Soviet sausage renaissance." *American Anthropologist* 112 (1): 22–37.

Knecht, M. (1999). *Die andere Seite der Stadt: Armut und Ausgrenzung in Berlin.* Köln: Böhlau.

Kohlstruck, M. (2002). *Rechtsextreme Jugendkultur und Gewalt: Eine Herausforderung für die pädagogische Praxis.* Berlin: Metropol.

Kopietz, A., and B. Strohmaier. (2005). "Der Stern als Stigma." *Berliner-Zeitung.* http:// www.berliner-zeitung.de/archiv/warum-vermutlich-rechtsextreme-an-vielen -stellen-in-berlin-das-juedische-symbol-aufspruehen-der-stern-als-stigma,10810 590,10330694.html.

Koselleck, R. (1985). *Futures Past: On the Semantics of Historical Time.* Cambridge, MA: MIT Press.

Kroskrity, P. V., ed. (2000). *Regimes of Language: Ideologies, Polities, and Identities.* Santa Fe, NM: J. Currey.

Laclau, E. (1996a). *Emancipation(s).* New York: Verso.

———. (1996b). "Power and Representation." In *Emancipation(s),* 84–104. New York: Verso.

———. (1996c). "Why Do Empty Signifiers Matter to Politics?" In *Emancipation(s),* 36–46. New York: Verso.

———. (2005). *On Populist Reason.* New York: Verso.

Ladd, B. (1997). *The Ghosts of Berlin: Confronting German History in the Urban Landscape.* Chicago: University of Chicago Press.

Legrain, P. (2015). "Five minutes with Philippe Legrain: 'The Eurozone has become a glorified debtors' prison.'" London School of Economics and Political Science (LSE). http://blogs.lse.ac.uk/europpblog/2015/03/09/five-minutes-with-philippe-legrain-the-eurozone-has-become-a-glorified-debtors-prison/.

Lefebvre, H. (1991). *The Production of Space*. Cambridge, MA: Blackwell.

Leitner, H., and E. Sheppard. (2002). "'The city is dead, long live the Net': Harnessing European interurban networks for a neoliberal agenda." *Antipode* 34 (3): 495–518.

Liebers, P. (2004). "Erneut V-Mann aufgeflogen. " *Neues Deutschland*. Berlin. https://www .neues-deutschland.de/artikel/54441.erneut-v-mann-aufgeflogen.html.

Lier, A. (2011). "Polizist nimmt an Demo von Rechtsextremen teil." *Berliner Morgenpost*. Berlin. http://www.morgenpost.de/printarchiv/brandenburg/article103004280 /Polizist-nimmt-an-Demo-von-Rechtsextremen-teil.html.

Light, D. (2004). "Street names in Bucharest, 1990–1997: Exploring the modern historical geographies of post-socialist change." *Journal of Historical Geography* 30 (1): 154–72.

Lindhal, K. (2001). *EXIT*. Munich: DTV.

Lomnitz, C. (2003). "Times of crisis: Historicity, sacrifice, and the spectacle of debacle in Mexico City." *Public Culture* 15 (1): 127–48.

Low, S. M. (1996). "The anthropology of cities: Imagining and theorizing the city." *Annual Review of Anthropology* 25:383–409.

Ludwig, C., and B. Dietz. (2008). "'There's not a single book there, no PC, no Internet': Increasing poverty in Germany and a lack of political answers." *Journal of Contemporary European Studies* 16 (1): 25–39.

MacIntyre, A. C. (1984). *After Virtue: A Study in Moral Theory*. Notre Dame, IN: University of Notre Dame Press.

Mammone, A., E. Godin, and B. Jenkins. (2012a). "Introduction: Mapping the 'Right of the Mainstream Right' in Contemporary Europe." In *Mapping the Extreme Right in Contemporary Europe: From Local to Transnational*, ed. A. Mammone, E. Godin, and B. Jenkins, 1–14. New York: Routledge.

———, eds. (2012b). *Mapping the Extreme Right in Contemporary Europe: From Local to Transnational*. New York: Routledge.

———. (2013a). "Introduction." In *Varieties of Right-Wing Extremism in Europe*, ed. A. Mammone, E. Godin, and B. Jenkins, 1–16. New York: Routledge.

———, eds. (2013b). *Varieties of Right-Wing Extremism in Europe*. New York: Routledge.

Markell, P. (2009). *Bound by Recognition*. Princeton: Princeton University Press.

Märkische Allgemeine Zeitung. (2008). "Anzeige aus Norwegen gegen Modemarke 'Thor Steinar.'" Originally accessed on March 29, 2008, from http://www.maerkischeallge meine.de/cms/beitrag/11170177/62249/Anzeige_aus_Norwegen_gegen_Modemarke _Thor_Steinar_Geschaeftsfuehrer.html, but the link is no longer available.

Massumi, B. (1995). "The autonomy of affect." *Cultural Critique* (31): 83–109.

Mayer, K. U., M. Diewald, and H. Solga. (1999). "Transitions to post-communism in East Germany: Worklife mobility of women and men between 1989 and 1993." *Acta Sociologica* 42:35–53.

Mazzarella, W. (2010). "The myth of the multitude, or, who's afraid of the crowd?" *Critical Inquiry* 36 (4): 697–727.

———. (2013). *Censorium: Cinema and the Open Edge of Mass Publicity*. Durham, NC: Duke University Press.

Mentzel, T. (1998). *Rechtsextremistische Gewalttaten von Jugendlichen und Heranwachsenden in den neuen Bundesländern: Eine empirische Untersuchung von Erscheinungsformen und Ursachen am Beispiel des Bundeslandes Sachsen-Anhalt.* München: W. Fink.

Merleau-Ponty, M. (1962). *Phenomenology of Perception.* New York: Routledge.

Miller-Idriss, C. (2006). "Everyday understandings of citizenship in Germany." *Citizenship Studies* 10 (5): 541–70.

Mingione, E., ed. (1996). *Urban Poverty and the Underclass: A Reader.* Studies in Urban and Social Change. Cambridge, MA: Blackwell.

Mitchell, T. (1990). "Everyday metaphors of power." *Theory and Society* 19 (October 1990): 545–77.

———. (1991). "The limits of the state: Beyond statist approaches and their critics." *American Political Science Review* 85 (1): 77–96.

Modood, T., and P. Werbner, eds. (1997). *The Politics of Multiculturalism in the New Europe: Racism, Identity, and Community.* New York: Zed Books.

Mouffe, C. (2000a). "Democracy, Power and the 'Political.'" In *The Democratic Paradox,* 17–35. New York: Verso.

———. (2000b). "For an Agonistic Model of Democracy." In *The Democratic Paradox,* 80–107. New York: Verso.

Muehlebach, A., and N. Shoshan. (2012). "Post-Fordist affect: An introduction." *Anthropological Quarterly* 85 (2): 317–44.

Muehlebach, A. K. (2012). *The Moral Neoliberal: Welfare and Citizenship in Italy.* Chicago: University of Chicago Press.

Müller, J. (1997). "Preparing for the political: German intellectuals confront the 'Berlin Republic.'" *New German Critique* 72 (Fall 1997): 151–76.

Nachtwey, O. (2013). "Market social democracy: The transformation of the SPD up to 2007." *German Politics* 22 (3): 235–52.

Navaro-Yashin, Y. (2012). *The Make-Believe Space: Affective Geography in a Postwar Polity.* Durham, NC: Duke University Press.

Netzeitung. (2005). "CDU gegen Gedenkfeier am Brandenburger Tor." Originally accessed on February 10, 2005, from http://www.netzeitung.de/deutschland/324986 .html, but the link is no longer available.

Niesen, P. (2002). "Anti-extremism, negative republicanism, civic society: Three paradigms for banning political parties." *German Law Journal* 3.

Nolte, E. (1969). *Three Faces of Fascism.* New York: Penguin.

NPD. (2005). "Berlin: Establishment konnte Marsch gegen Befreiungslüge verhindern, aber 4.000 sind trotzdem kein Pappenstiel!" National Democratic Party of Germany. Electronic copy is in my possession.

Oberverwaltungsgericht Berlin-Brandenburg. (2007). OVG 80 D 6.05 vom 19.04.2007.

———. (2009). OVG 6 S 38.08 vom 29.01.2009.

———. (2010). OVG 1 L 71.10 vom 17.09.2010.

OECD. (2014). "OECD.StatExtracts." 2014. http://stats.oecd.org/Index.aspx#.

Olick, J. K. (1998). "What does it mean to normalize the past? Official memory in German politics since 1989." *Social Science History* 22 (4): 547–71.

Palonen, E. (2008). "The city-text in post-communist Budapest: Street names, memorials, and the politics of commemoration." *GeoJournal* 73 (3): 219–30.

Parmentier, R. J. (1994). "Peirce Divested for Nonintimates." In *Signs in Society: Studies in Semiotic Anthropology*, 3–22. Bloomington: Indiana University Press.

Partridge, D. J. (2012). *Hypersexuality and Headscarves: Race, Sex, and Citizenship in the New Germany*. Bloomington: Indiana University Press.

Pätzold, K. (2005). "Die soziale Demagogie der Rechtsextremen." *Junge Welt*. https://www.jungewelt.de/1998/03-26/014.php.

PBS. (2006). "Germany: Heart of Berlin." *Frontline World*. PBS. http://www.pbs.org/frontlineworld/rough/2006/06/germany_heart_o.html.

Peirce, C. S. (1960). *Collected Papers*. Cambridge: Belknap Press of Harvard University Press.

Percival, B., dir. (2013). *The Book Thief*. Germany.

Peter, F. (2007). "Moschee-Streit in Berlin." *Die Welt*. http://www.welt.de/politik/article1021826/Moschee-Streit_in_Berlin.html.

Petrocivi, N. (2011). "Articulating the Right to the City: Working-Class Neo-Nationalism in Postsocialist Cluj, Romania." In *Headlines of Nation, Subtexts of Class: Working-Class Populism and the Return of the Repressed in Neoliberal Europe*, ed. D. Kalb and G. Halmai, 37–56. New York: Berghahn Books.

Pohl, R. (2000). "The macroeconomics of transformation: The case of Eastern Germany." *German Politics and Society* 18:3 (56): 48–93.

Postone, M. (2006). "History and helplessness: Mass mobilization and contemporary forms of anticapitalism." *Public Culture* 18 (1): 93–110.

Povinelli, E. A. (1998). "The state of shame: Australian multiculturalism and the crisis of indigenous citizenship." *Critical Inquiry* 24:575–610.

———. (2000). "Consuming *Geist*: Popontology and the spirit of capital in indigenous Australia." *Public Culture* 12 (2): 501–28.

———. (2001). "Radical worlds: The anthropology of incommensurability and inconceivability." *Annual Review of Anthropology* 30:319–34.

Pred, A. R. (1997). "Somebody else, somewhere else: Racialisms, racialized spaces and the popular geographical imagination in Sweden." *Antipode* 29 (4): 383–416.

———. (2000). *Even in Sweden: Racisms, Racialized Spaces, and the Popular Geographical Imagination*. Berkeley: University of California Press.

Preuß, U. K. (2003). "Citizenship and the German nation." *Citizenship Studies* 7 (1): 37–56.

Rabinbach, A. (2006). "Moments of totalitarianism." *History and Theory* 45:72–100.

Rau, L. M. (2001). *Entwicklung einer rechtsextremen Jugendkultur in Ostdeutschland*. Master's thesis, Humboldt Universität Berlin.

RBB. (2004a). "Landgericht Neuruppin bestätigt Verbot von SS-Symbolen auf Kleidung." Originally accessed on March 4, 2008, from http://www.rbb-online.de/_/nachrichten/politik/beitrag_jsp/key=news1451894.html, but the link is no longer available.

———. (2004b). "NPD macht mobil: Aufmärsche in Köpenick und am Brandenburger Tor geplant." Originally accessed on November 17, 2004, from http://www.rbb-online.de/_/nachrichten/politik/beitrag_jsp/key=news1452585.html, but the link is no longer available.

Recherchegruppe "Investigate Thor Steinar." (2008). Investigate Thor Steinar. Berlin:36.

Reuters. (2015). "German politicians admit Greece has case for wartime reparations." *Guardian*. http://www.theguardian.com/world/2015/mar/17/german-politicians-admit-greece-case-wartime-reparations.

Rieter, H., and M. Schmolz. (1993). "The ideas of German ordoliberalism, 1938–45: Pointing the way to a new economic order." *European Journal of the History of Economic Thought* 1 (1): 87.

Ritschl, A. (2011). "Germany owes Greece a debt." *Guardian*. http://www.theguardian .com/commentisfree/2011/jun/21/germany-greece-greek-debt-crisis.

Robinson, G. M., S. Engelstoft, and A. Pobric. (2001). "Remaking Sarajevo: Bosnian nationalism after the Dayton Accord." *Political Geography* 20 (8): 957–80.

Rocknord. (2005). "Rechter Hintergrund? Hunderte Davidsterne gesprüht—bisher kein Täter gefaßt." Originally accessed on December 2, 2005, from http://www.rocknord .net/viewtopic.php?t=3604, but the link is no longer available.

Rogalla, T. (2005). "Der Senat will die NPD mit einem Fest vertreiben." Originally accessed on March 23, 2005, from http://www.berlinonline.de/berliner-zeitung/berlin /432945.html, but the link is no longer available.

Rohde, H. (2006). "Erster Moscheebau in Ost-Berlin erhitzt die Gemüter." http://www .tagesspiegel.de/berlin/Berlin;art114,1863662.

Rose, N. (2000a). "Community, citizenship, and the Third Way." *American Behavioral Scientist* 43 (9): 1395–1411.

———. (2000b). "Government and control." *British Journal of Criminology* 40:321–39.

Rothemund, M., dir. (2005). *Sophie Scholl: The Final Days*. Germany.

Sarrazin, T. (2012). *Deutschland schafft sich ab: Wie wir unser Land aufs Spiel setzen*. Munich: Deutsche Verlags-Anstalt.

Sassen, S. (1999). *Guests and Aliens*. New York: New Press.

———. (2003). "Economic Globalization and the Redrawing of Citizenship." In *Globalization, the State, and Violence*, ed. J. Friedman, 67–86. Walnut Creek, CA: AltaMira Press.

Saunders, A. (2009). "Remembering Cold War division: Wall remnants and border monuments in Berlin." *Journal of Contemporary European Studies* 17 (1): 9–19.

Schieffelin, B. B., K. A. Woolard, and P. V. Kroskrity, eds. (1998). *Language Ideologies: Practice and Theory*. Oxford Studies in Anthropological Linguistics. New York: Oxford University Press.

Schmale, H. (2005). "Neonazis kapitulieren in Berlin." Originally accessed on May 9, 2005, from http://www.berlinonline.de/berliner-zeitung/politik/446091.html, but the link is no longer available.

Schmitt, C. (1996). *The Concept of the Political*. Chicago: University of Chicago Press.

Schnitzer, M. (1972). "Soziale Marktwirtschaft revisited: West German economic policy, 1967–1971." *Journal of Economic Issues (Association for Evolutionary Economics)* 6 (4): 69.

Schröder, B. (1997). *Im Griff der rechten Szene: Ostdeutsche Städte in Angst*. Reinbek bei Hamburg: Rowohlt Taschenbuch.

———. (2001). *Nazis sind Pop*. Berlin: Espresso.

Schubarth, W. (2001). "Pädagogische Strategien gegen Rechtsextremismus und fremdenfeindliche Gewalt: Möglichkeiten und Grenzen schulischer und außerschulischer Prävention." In *Rechtsextremismus in der Bundesrepublik Deutschland: Eine Bilanz*, ed. W. Schubarth and R. Stöss, 249–70. Opladen: Leske + Budrich.

Schubarth, W., and R. Stöss. (2001). *Rechtsextremismus in der Bundesrepublik Deutschland: Eine Bilanz*. Opladen: Leske + Budrich.

Schultz, T. (2012a). "Gelöschte Akten hatten doch mit NSU zu tun." *Süddeutsche Zeitung.* http://www.sueddeutsche.de/politik/verfassungsschutz-geloeschte-akten-hatten-doch -mit-nsu-zu-tun-1.1418558.

———. (2012b). "Verfassungsschutz ließ wichtige Akten vernichten." *Süddeutsche Zeitung.* http://www.sueddeutsche.de/politik/ermittlungen-zur-neonazi-mordserie -verfassungsschutz-liess-wichtige-akten-vernichten-1.1395481.

———. (2012c). "Verfassungsschutz spielt Wert vernichteter Akten herunter." *Süddeutsche Zeitung.* http://www.sueddeutsche.de/politik/ermittlungen-zur-neonazi -mordserie-verfassungsschutz-spielt-wert-vernichteter-akten-herunter-1.1398718.

Schulz, D. (2005). "Davidsterne als stille Drohung." *Die Tageszeitung.* http://www.taz.de /dx/2005/10/26/a0077.1/text.

Schwenkel, C. (2013). "Post/Socialist affect: Ruination and reconstruction of the nation in urban Vietnam." *Cultural Anthropology* 28 (2): 252–77.

Scott, J. W. (2010). *The Politics of the Veil.* Princeton: Princeton University Press.

Sebald, W. G. (1999). *Luftkrieg und Literatur: Mit einem Essay zu Alfred Andersch.* München: Hanser.

Sebeok, T. A. (1964). "The Structure and Content of Cheremis Charms." In *Language in Culture and Society: A Reader in Linguistics and Anthropology,* ed. D. H. Hymes, xxxv. New York: Harper & Row.

Seils, C. (2007). "Ende einer Posse." *Zeit* online. http://www.zeit.de/online/2007/12 /BGH-Urteil-Hakenkreuz.

Senders, S. (1996). "Laws of belonging: Legal dimensions of national inclusion in Germany." *New German Critique* 67 (Winter 1996): 147–76.

Sharma, A. (2006). "Crossbreeding institutions, breeding struggle: Women's empowerment, neoliberal governmentality, and state (re)formation in India." *Cultural Anthropology* 21 (1): 60–95.

Shoshan, N. (2008a). "From SS to Stasi and Back Again? Ossis, Wessis, and Right-Extremists in Contemporary Germany." In *Ossi/Wessi,* ed. A. Sakalauskaite and D. Backman, 241–66. London: Cambridge Scholars Publishing.

———. (2008b). "Placing the extremes: Cityscape, ethnic 'others,' and young right extremists in East Berlin." *Journal of Contemporary European Studies* 16 (3): 377–91.

———. (2011). "Neoliberal displacements: Political delinquency and the eclipse of the social in Germany." *Carceral Notebooks* 6:33–47.

———. (2012). "Time at a standstill: Loss, accumulation, and the past conditional in an East Berlin neighborhood." *Ethnos* 77 (1): 24–49.

———. (2014). "Managing hate: Political delinquency and affective governance in Germany." *Cultural Anthropology* 29 (1): 150–72.

———. (2016). "'There goes the neighborhood': Narrating the decline of place in East Berlin." In *The Anthropology of Postindustrialism: Ethnographies of Disconnection,* ed. I. Vaccaro, K. Harper, and S. Murray, 166–82. New York: Routledge.

Siegel, J. T. (2003). "The truth of sorcery." *Cultural Anthropology* 18 (2): 135–55.

———. (2006). *Naming the Witch.* Stanford, CA: Stanford University Press.

Sievert, A., and M. Bittner. (2008). "Wenn es Nacht wird, explodiert die Gewalt." *Bild.* http://www.bild.de/politik/2008/angst-nacht-3434986.bild.html.

Silverstein, M. (2003). "The whens and wheres—as well as hows—of ethnolinguistic recognition." *Public Culture* 15 (3).

Silvia, S. J. (2010). "The elusive quest for normalcy: The German economy since unification." *German Politics & Society* 28 (2): 82–101.

Simmel, G. (1964). "The Metropolis and Mental Life." In *The Sociology of Georg Simmel*, ed. K. H. Wolff, 409–24. New York: Free Press.

———. (1971). *On Individuality and Social Forms: Selected Writings [of] Georg Simmel*. Chicago: University of Chicago Press.

Smith, H. (2015). "Greece sours German relations further with demand for war reparations." *Guardian*.

Soja, E. W. (1989). *Postmodern Geographies: The Reassertion of Space in Critical Social Theory*. New York: Verso.

Stacul, J. (2006). "Neo-Nationalism or Neo-Localism? Integralist Political Engagements in Italy at the Turn of the Millenium." In *Neo-Nationalism in Europe and Beyond: Perspectives from Social Anthropology*, ed. A. Gingrich and M. Banks, 162–76. New York: Berghahn Books.

Statistisches Bundesamt. (2014). "DEStatis." https://www.destatis.de/DE/Startseite.html.

Staud, T. (2005a). "Auf den Rummel kannste nicht gehen." *Die Zeit*. http://www.zeit.de /2005/11/Antifa/seite-2.

———. (2005b). *Moderne Nazis: Die neuen Rechten und der Aufstieg der NPD*. Köln: Kiepenheuer & Witsch.

Stegbauer, A. (2007). "The ban of right-wing extremist symbols according to section 86a of the German Criminal Code." *German Law Journal* 8 (2): 173–84.

Stein, E. (1986). "History against free speech: The new German law against the 'Auschwitz' and other 'lies.'" *Michigan Law Review* 85 (2): 277–324.

Steinmetz, G. (1994). "Fordism and the 'immoral economy' of right-wing violence in contemporary Germany." In *Research on Democracy and Society*, 2:277–316. Greenwich, CT: JAI Press.

Sternhell, Z. (1995). *The Birth of Fascist Ideology: From Cultural Rebellion to Political Revolution*. With M. Sznajder and M. Asheri. Trans. D. Maisel. Princeton: Princeton University Press.

———. (1996). *Neither Right nor Left: Fascist Ideology in France*. Princeton: Princeton University Press.

Stevenson, P., and J. Theobald. (2000). *Relocating Germanness: Discursive Disunity in Unified Germany*. New York: St. Martin's Press.

Stöss, R. (2000). *Rechtsextremismus im vereinten Deutschland*. Bonn: Friedrich-Ebert-Stiftung, Abteilung Dialog Ostdeutschland.

Stradella, E. (2008). "Hate speech in the background of the security dilemma." *German Law Journal* 9 (1): 59–88.

Strauss, S. (2006). "CDU-Kreischef äußert sich in rechter Zeitung." *Berlin Online*. Originally accessed on September 11, 2006, from http://www.berlinonline.de/berliner -zeitung/print/berlin/585351.html, but the link is no longer available.

Strom, E. A. (2001). *Building the New Berlin: The Politics of Urban Development in Germany's Capital City*. Lanham, MD: Lexington Books.

Sunier, T., and R. v. Ginkel. (2006). "'At your service!': Reflections on the Rise of Neo-Nationalism in the Netherlands." In *Neo-Nationalism in Europe and Beyond: Perspectives from Social Anthropology*, ed. A. Gingrich and M. Banks, 107–24. New York: Berghahn Books.

Tambiah, S. J. (1996). *Leveling Crowds: Ethnonationalist Conflicts and Collective Violence in South Asia*. Berkeley: University of California Press.

Taussig, M. T. (1992). *The Nervous System*. New York: Routledge.

———. (1993). *Mimesis and Alterity: A Particular History of the Senses*. New York: Routledge.

Taylor, C., and A. Gutmann. (1994). *Multiculturalism: Examining the Politics of Recognition*. Princeton: Princeton University Press.

Theweleit, K. (1987). *Male Fantasies*. Minneapolis: University of Minnesota Press.

Thorer, T., A. Rickmann, and A. Sievert. (2008). "Jeder 5. Schüler wurde schon Opfer von Gewalt." http://www.bild.de/politik/2008/serie-2-3425768.bild.html. *BILD* online.

Torpey, J. (1988). "Introduction: Habermas and the historians." *New German Critique* 44:5–24.

Traynor, I. (2007). "The rise of mosques becomes catalyst for conflict across Europe." *Guardian*. http://www.theguardian.com/world/2007/oct/11/thefarright.religion.

———. (2015). "Tsipras raises Nazi war reparations claim at Berlin press conference with Merkel." *Guardian*. http://www.theguardian.com/business/2015/mar/23/tsipras-raises-nazi-war-reparations-claim-at-berlin-press-conference-with-merkel.

Trouillot, M.-R. (2001). "The anthropology of the state in the age of globalization: Close encounters of the deceptive kind." *Current Anthropology* 42 (1): 125–38.

Van der Veer, P. (2006). "Pim Fortuyn, Theo van Gogh, and the politics of tolerance in the Netherlands." *Public Culture* 18 (1): 111–24.

Verfassungsgericht Berlin. (2007). 80 Dn 43.06 vom 5.4.2007.

Verfassungsschutz Berlin. (2001). *Symbole und Kennzeichen des Rechtsextremismus*. Berlin: Senatsverwaltung für Inneres, Abteilung Verfassungsschutz.

———. (2004). "Rechte Gewalt in Berlin." In *Im Fokus*, 64. Berlin: Senatsverwaltung für Inneres, Abteilung Verfassungsschutz.

Verfassungsschutz Brandenburg. (2001a). *"National befreite Zonen"—Kampfparole und Realität*. Potsdam: Verfassungsschutz Brandenburg.

———. (2001b). *Verbotene Kennzeichen rechtsextremistischer Organisationen*. Potsdam: Verfassungsschutz Brandenburg.

Verfassungsschutz Sachsen. (2001). *Mit Hakenkreuz und Totenkopf—wie sich Rechtsextremisten zu erkennen geben*. Dresden: Verfassungsschutz Sachsen.

Verheyen, D. (1997). "What's in a name? Street name politics and urban identity in Berlin." *German Politics and Society* 15 (3): 44–72.

Veugelers, J. (2012). "After Colonialism: Local Politics and Far-Right Affinities in a City of Southern France." In *Mapping the Extreme Right in Contemporary Europe: From Local to Transnational*, ed. A. Mammone, E. Godin, and B. Jenkins, 33–47. New York: Routledge.

Von Mering, S., and T. W. McCarty. (2013). "Introduction." In *Right-Wing Radicalism Today: Perspectives from Europe and the US*, ed. S. Von Mering and T. W. McCarty, 1–12. New York: Routledge.

Wacquant, L. (2001). "The penalisation of poverty and the rise of neo-liberalism." *European Journal on Criminal Policy and Research* 9 (4): 401–12.

———. (2007). *Urban Outcasts: A Comparative Sociology of Advanced Marginality*. Cambridge, UK: Polity Press.

———. (2012). "Three steps to a historical anthropology of actually existing neoliberalism." *Social Anthropology* 20 (1): 66–79.

Wagner, B. (1998). *Rechtsextremismus und kulturelle Subversion in den neuen Ländern.* Berlin: Zentrum Demokratische Kultur.

———. (2001). "Entwicklungen des Rechtsextremismus in Berlin von den 80ern bis heute." In *Berliner Forum Gewaltprävention*, 23–32. Berlin: Landeskommission Berlin gegen Gewalt.

Walzer, M. (1997). *On Toleration.* New Haven, CT: Yale University Press.

Watts, M. W. (1996). "Political xenophobia in the transition from socialism: Threat, racism and ideology among East German youth." *Political Psychology* 17 (1): 97–126.

Weiss, D. (1994). "Striking a difficult balance: Combatting the threat of neo-Nazism in Germany while preserving individual liberties." *Vanderbilt Journal of Transnational Law* 27:899–940.

Weiss, M. (2003). "Wir sind drinnen, der Staat bleibt draussen." *Monitor.* Issue 8 (January). Berlin: Apabiz.

Whitehead, N. L. (2004). "Introduction: Cultures, Conflicts, and the Poetics of Violent Practice." In *Violence*, ed. N. L. Whitehead, 3–24. Santa Fe, NM: School of American Research Press.

Willis, P. E. (1977). *Learning to Labor: How Working Class Kids Get Working Class Jobs.* New York: Columbia University Press.

Willis, P. E., and P. Corrigan. (1983). "Orders of experience: The differences of working-class cultural forms." *Social Text* 7:85–103.

Woolard, K. A. (1998). "Language Ideology as a Field of Inquiry." In *Language Ideologies: Practice and Theory*, ed. B. B. Schieffelin, K. A. Woolard, and P. V. Kroskrity, 3–47. New York: Oxford University Press.

Zentrum demokratische Kultur. (1998). *Bulletin 1998-1. "National befreite Zonen"—von Strategiebegriff zu Alltagserscheinung.* Berlin: ZDK.

———. (1998). *Bulletin 1998-Sonderausgabe. Rechtsextremismus und kulturelle Subversion in den neuen Ländern, Studie.* Berlin: ZDK.

Žižek, S. (1989). *The Sublime Object of Ideology.* New York: Verso.

———. (1997). "Multiculturalism, or, the cultural logic of multinational capitalism." *New Left Review* 1/225:28–51.

———. (2006). "Against the populist temptation." *Critical Inquiry* 32:552–74.

———. (2008). "Tolerance as an ideological category." *Critical Inquiry* 34 (4): 660–82.

Index
||||||||||||||||||||||||||||||||